Geisha : The Secret History of a Vanishing World.

GEISHA

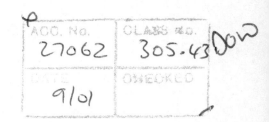
GEISHA

THE SECRET HISTORY OF A VANISHING WORLD

LESLEY DOWNER

HEADLINE

First published in 2000
by HEADLINE BOOK PUBLISHING

10 9 8 7 6 5 4 3 2

British Library Cataloguing in Publication Data

Downer, Lesley
   Geisha : the secret history of a vanishing world
   1.Geishas – Japan 2.Japan – Social life and customs
   I.Title
   305.4'339'0952

Hardback ISBN: 07472 7105 4
Trade paperback ISBN: 07472 7106 2

Typeset by Palimpsest Book Production Limited,
Polmont, Stirlingshire

Printed and bound in Great Britain by
Clays Ltd, St Ives plc

HEADLINE BOOK PUBLISHING
A division of Hodder Headline
338 Euston Road
London NW1 3BH

To the memory of my father and mother
Professor Gordon Downer
and Mrs Lilian Downer

CONTENTS

ACKNOWLEDGEMENTS

First of all I would like to thank the many Japanese women who have, over the years, opened their world to me and with whom I have spent many happy hours enjoying women's pursuits, women's talk and women's life. I should also record my debt to Arthur Golden and his enchanting novel, *Memoirs of a Geisha*. It inspired me to look again at Japan, its women and their history and made me curious to look into the living reality of the geisha today.

In researching the world of the geisha I was immeasurably helped by the work of many great scholars. Like everyone who studies the geisha, my first step was to turn to Liza Dalby's brilliant anthropological analysis *Geisha*, the bible of geisha studies. Ms Dalby generously offered suggestions and encouragement in emails and phone conversations.

One important source in examining the background and rise of the geisha was Cecilia Segawa Seigle's marvellous *Yoshiwara*, a fascinating work of scholarship which provides huge amounts of detail about the Yoshiwara and evokes it very colourfully. Searching out details of the hidden history of the geisha I scoured many other scholarly works, beginning with the classic texts by the grand old men of Japanese studies, Donald Keene and Edward Seidensticker. I was fortunate to have access to the unparalleled collections of the School of Oriental and African Studies' library at the University of London and also the fine collection at International House in Tokyo; both include many rare and wonderful Victorian volumes.

Hiroshi Sugita, author of scholarly works on, among other subjects, Taka-jo the Literary Geisha, was a fount of knowledge. He introduced me to Sadayakko and Taka, loaded me down with books and took me to many tiny historical nooks connected with Taka.

Many western scholars of Japan offered friendship, suggestions, introductions and inspiration. I am particularly grateful to Patricia Fister who shared time and friendship as well as her great scholarship with me, and also to Monica Bethé (thank you for recommending the book on *kabuku*!), Richard Emmert, Drew Gerstle who kindly read through the historical section of the first draft (though all errors, of course, are my own), Peter Grilli, Gaye Rowley and Timon Screech.

In Japan many friends, both new and long-time, were unfailingly kind and also helped to provide introductions.

In Tokyo I should like to record my debt of gratitude to Yutaka and Kazuko Aso and to Lady Boyd who kindly introduced me to them; to Kioichi Tsuzuki, maverick author who provided a mobile phone as well as friendship; Johnnie Walker, Svengali of my Tokyo social life; and Junko Koshino, who kindly introduced me to Toshiki Takahashi of the Wachigaiya. My old friend Seiko Taniguchi of the Japan National Tourist Organisation introduced me to Mr Mochizuki of Ryokan Sadachiyo in Asakusa who in his turn introduced me to Shichiko Sakuragawa (to whom much gratitude for friendship as well as help). Junichi Yano and Kazuko Koizumi-Legendre of the Foreign Press Centre provided sterling back-up. I am also grateful to Takashi Azumaya, Shi Yu Chen, Mr Fukumoto and Mr Kubota of All-Wave Productions, Toshiaki Honda of Tokyo Video Centre, Keisuke Muratsu, Kiyoha, Iwamoto-san, Donald Fontayne (even though we failed to meet) and the geisha of Shimbashi, Asakusa, Akasaka and Mukojima who were very generous with their time and hospitality. Many of these people became my friends and played a huge part in the making of this book. I hope they are pleased with it. Thanks also to Bernard Krisher, my old friends Michihisa Kitashirakawa and Yukiko Shimahara, and Kiharu Nakamura in New York.

I have fond memories of all the people who were kind to me in Kyoto, starting with Mr and Mrs Sawai, whose inn became my home from home, and the master and mistress of Suzuya, where I breakfasted. Many of the geisha, older sisters and house mothers of Miyagawa-cho, Gion, Gion Higashi, and Kamishichiken were exceedingly generous of their time and hospitality and I am very grateful to all of them. I would like to express my thanks to Hara-san of Yukinoya, Haruta-san, Imae-san of Daimonji teahouse in Kamishichiken, Ishihara-sensei of Yamato hairdressing salon, Takae Kaida, Koito, Komae-san of Komaya and many more members of the geisha world who asked me not to name them in order to protect their privacy. I am very grateful to all of them for their friendship and open-heartedness. Thanks also to my old buddy Hal Gold, Malte Jaspersen, Reiko Kato of Shoho-in temple, Alex Kerr, Ritsuko Kishi, Satoshi Kita, Kanji Mori, Yasuyoshi Morimoto, Kojiro Sakai, Satoyu, Seto-san, Mr and Mrs Shimofuri of Kazurasei, Kyoko Sugiura, Toshiki Takahashi, Zenzaburo Yamamori of Kyoto City Tourist Association and to Mr Kimura, my wonderful tea ceremony teacher.

In Osaka, my old friend Narito Sasaki of the New Otani was, as always, bubbling with ideas. In Kanazawa, Mr Keiichiro Yagi and Mr Yoshihisa Kita of Yagi Corporation were my kind hosts. Thanks also to the geisha of Kanazawa, Fukuoka and Atami.

Many thanks to my two helpers, Sarah Roche in Kyoto and Chieko Tsuneoka in Tokyo, who read books fast and furiously and put up patiently with all my demands.

Kyle Crichton applied a critical and expert eye to the first draft, for which I am enduringly grateful. Thanks also to Carolyn Watts who provided many invaluable suggestions as well as being responsible for the author photograph, and to Kishi Yamamoto who calligraphed the character 'gei' for the chapter headings.

I owe a bottomless debt of thanks to my wonderful agent, Bill Hamilton of A.M. Heath, who insisted that I embark on this project and has been a part of it all the way through, offering wise advice and support. Thanks also to Doug Young and everyone at Headline who have been full of support, enthusiasm and patience when required. And thank you to my extremely supportive network of friends, in London, New York and Tokyo, who have continued to be my friends despite my refusal to take phone calls while writing.

Lastly I would like to remember my mother, who was Chinese-Canadian, and my father, also Canadian and Professor of Chinese, first at the School of Oriental and African Studies in London, then at the University of Leeds. Both passed away within a year of each other while I was working on this book. They are sorely missed. This book is dedicated to them.

Note on geisha names

Like sumo wrestlers, geisha have a professional name like a pen-name or an actor's name, and no surname. These names are quite different from Japanese women's names and immediately recognisable as professional names. The name also indicates a geisha's relationship with her 'older sister'.

Usually only one person at a time in a geisha district bears a particular name. In order to preserve the privacy and discretion of women who very kindly spoke with extraordinary openness to me, I have used pseudonyms – ordinary Japanese women's names – for some of them and blurred their identities by, for example, not specifying their district. One Shimbashi geisha told me that if it was known that she had spoken with such openness, she would never be able to work as a geisha again. I have taken precautions not to betray these women's trust.

Note on pronunciation

Japanese names and words are pronounced as they are spelt, with each syllable distinct. Vowels are pure and consonants non-aspirated, rather like Italian. All syllables are equally stressed. Thus 'karaoke' is pronounced 'ka-ra-o-ké' and 'mizuage' 'mi-zu-a-gé'. The word 'geisha' incidentally is pronounced not 'gee-sha' but 'gay-sha'.

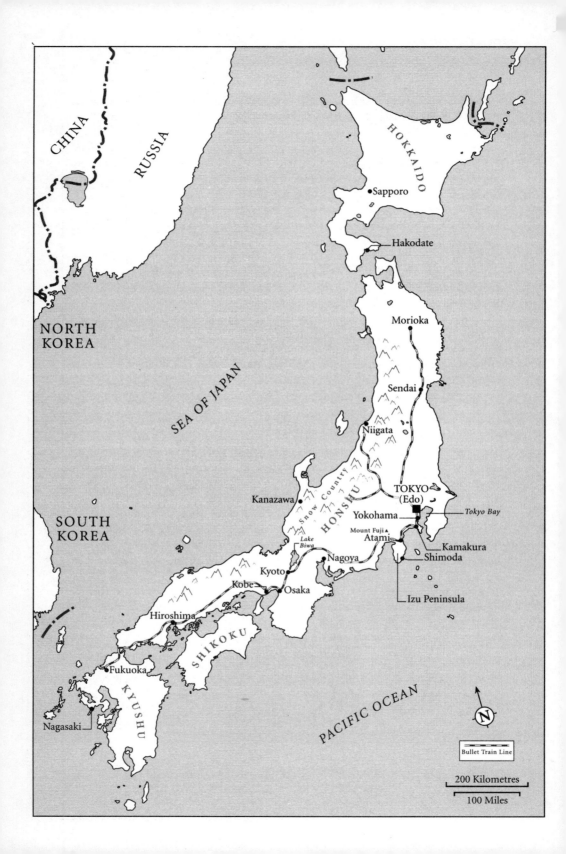

CHINA

RUSSIA

HOKKAIDO

Sapporo

Hakodate

NORTH
KOREA

Morioka

SEA OF JAPAN

Sendai

Niigata

Kanazawa

HONSHU

TOKYO
(Edo)

Snow Country

Yokohama

Tokyo Bay

SOUTH
KOREA

Mount Fuji ▲

Atami

Kamakura

Lake
Biwa

Shimoda

Nagoya

Izu Peninsula

Kyoto

Kobe

Osaka

Hiroshima

SHIKOKU

Fukuoka

KYUSHU

PACIFIC OCEAN

Nagasaki

N

▬▬▬▬
Bullet Train Line

200 Kilometres

100 Miles

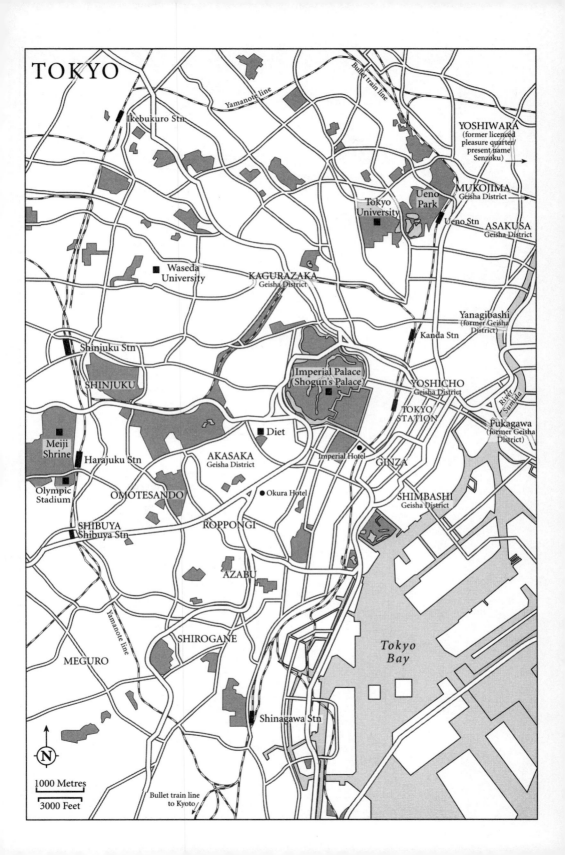

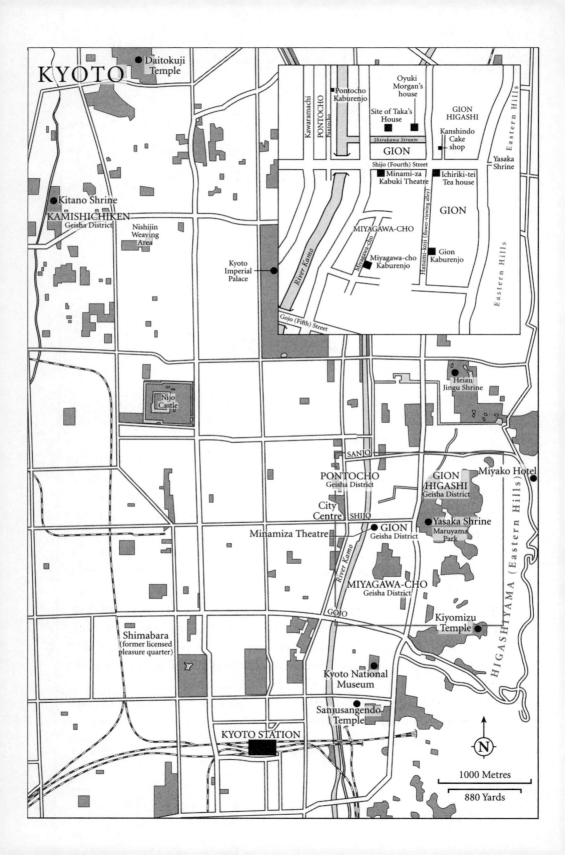

KYOTO

Daitokuji Temple

Kitano Shrine

KAMISHICHIKEN
Geisha District

Nishijin Weaving Area

Kyoto Imperial Palace

Nijo Castle

SANJO

PONTOCHO
Geisha District

City Centre

SHIJO

Minamiza Theatre

GION
Geisha District

GION HIGASHI
Geisha District

Miyako Hotel

Yasaka Shrine

Maruyama Park

Heian Jingu Shrine

MIYAGAWA-CHO
Geisha District

GOJO

Kiyomizu Temple

Shimabara
(former licensed pleasure quarter)

Kyoto National Museum

Sanjusangendo Temple

KYOTO STATION

HIGASHIYAMA (Eastern Hills)

River Kamo

1000 Metres

880 Yards

N

Inset (Gion detail)

Kawaramachi

PONTOCHO

Pontocho

Pontocho Kaburenjo

Oyuki Morgan's house

Site of Taka's House

GION HIGASHI

GION

Kanshindo Cake shop

Yasaka Shrine

Shirakawa Stream

Shijo (Fourth) Street

Minami-za Kabuki Theatre

Ichiriki-tei Tea house

GION

MIYAGAWA-CHO

Miyagawa-cho

Hanami-koji (flower-viewing alley)

Miyagawa-cho Kaburenjo

Gion Kaburenjo

Eastern Hills

River Kamo

Gojo (Fifth) Street

INTRODUCTION

THROUGH THE LOOKING GLASS

I t was nearly sunset when I got to Kyoto on a mild evening in early May. I had to ask the taxi driver to drop me off at the end of the lane where I was to stay; it was too narrow for cars to squeeze through. I lugged my suitcase the last hundred yards to the inn, over the doorstep, through the door, then up a couple of dark, very steep wooden staircases to my room.

It was bright, airy and wide open to the elements. One wall was barely a wall at all but a rickety wooden balcony with flimsy slatted doors which you could slide shut to close off the room when it was hot, cold or rainy. The tatami matting of the floor was moth-eaten. On it sat a dumpy bandy-legged wooden table, a worn flat cushion and a doll's house-sized dressing table perilously supporting a tall thin mirror with a piece of ancient brocade draped over it. In one corner was a wobbly wooden frame with a few hooks for hanging clothes.

Bamboo blinds attached under the eaves created the illusion of a fourth wall, flapping and banging in the slightest breeze. Standing on the balcony I peeped through at the vista of grey tiled rooftops interspersed with telegraph poles and a mad cat's cradle of wires. The road below was lined with little wooden houses very similar to the one I was in. In the house opposite a couple of women were silhouetted behind the blinds. Voices, laughter and the jangling plink-plonk of the shamisen, a banjo-like instrument, hung in the air. Women pattered up and down the street, pausing to bow and greet each other in high-pitched coos.

As darkness fell, round white lanterns began to glow in front of each wooden door. Then I heard the sound of clopping and a faint tinkling of bells. I looked down to see an extraordinary vision, a young woman – swathed in an ornate kimono in shades of blue and rusty gold – teetering by on absurdly high hoof-like clogs, her long sleeves swaying as she walked. Her hair gleamed with oil and glittered with combs and swinging silvery ornaments and her painted face glowed white in the gloom. She was an apparition out of another age.

I had come to the ancient city of Kyoto in search of geisha. The capital of Japan for more than a thousand years, it was still the country's cultural heart, home of temples, palaces, gardens and theatres, and the place where the classical heritage was most fiercely preserved. The picturesque streets of the geisha districts, the old pleasure quarters, looked more than anywhere else like the Japan portrayed in nineteenth-century woodblock prints. Kyoto was also the only place where the strict geisha training continued and the geisha traditions were handed down.

I wanted to meet the real women behind the painted faces, the charming chitchat and the eternal mysterious smile. The geisha, it seemed to me, were purveyors of dreams. Theirs was a misty world of romance created for the enjoyment and entertainment of men, in which the most browbeaten office worker could be king. It was not my intention to spoil the illusion or dispel the mystery. But as a woman, I wondered out of what past the geisha had come. Who were the women who, in modern Japan, had chosen to live this life? For men it was a dream world; but who were the women whose job it was to create this dream? I hoped it might be possible somehow to befriend them and to see their world from the inside.

I had lived, talked, travelled and daydreamed my way through a couple of decades in Japan, filtering my experience of a country which was often shockingly ugly through the prisms of its past. I absorbed myself in the passionate stories of heroes, villains and beautiful temptresses recorded in its spare but evocative poetry, drama and literature – like the tale of the all-time femme fatale, Ono no Komachi, the most beautiful woman in the world; or Narihira, the great lover, who cut a swath through women's hearts; or the Heian courtiers of the tenth century who made love into the essence of life, to be studied, cultivated and perfected as an art form. The geisha were the heirs to this romantic heritage. I hoped I would find that they prospered still, that the past had not faded completely into the realm of imagination and dusty scholarly tomes.

But at the dawn of a new century, was there a place for geisha in the land of Nintendo, Sony, Nissan and Honda? Persistent reports in papers and magazines had suggested that they were an endangered species, if not already extinct. Although I had come across geisha in the small provincial town where I had lived when I first arrived in Japan, for years I had barely had even a glimmering of that world. And if I did succeed in befriending them, would they be 'real' geisha or mere shadows, play-acting at being the real thing?

Nevertheless, by chance, I had ended up staying not just in one of the geisha areas but in a house which had until recently done service as a geisha house. When I finally did meet geisha, I learnt that they lived in bare little rooms as poorly furnished as mine.

Before I had even reached Kyoto I had discovered that there was something strangely unsettling about the very notion of geisha. On the plane, on my way to Japan, I had mentioned to the Japanese man next to me that I was planning to do some research on geisha. Suddenly he changed from the mild-mannered moustachioed academic he had seemed – he had told me he was a specialist in car ergonomics – and poured out a torrent of abuse. 'Fujiyama,' he foamed, spitting out the word which foreigners mistakenly use when speaking of Mount Fuji and a symbol to Japanese of our inability to muster even the faintest understanding of their country. '"Fujiyama", "geisha"! Stereotype, prejudice!' I had said nothing about my attitude or approach to geisha or why I was interested in them. The very idea that a foreigner would dare to even think of writing about them filled him with rage.

At least one foreigner had already done so – Arthur Golden, whose

3

novel, *Memoirs of a Geisha*, took a generation of western readers inside the geisha world of 1920s Gion. The book – at that time – had yet to be translated into Japanese. The west, meanwhile, had been swept by geisha fervour. Inspired by Golden's heroine, Sayuri, the fashion world rediscovered the allure of femininity. The collections of 1999 were full of kimono-like creations which wrapped and concealed the body, hinting at the mysteries beneath rather than revealing them. That summer Madonna appeared at the Grammies in an extraordinary outfit described as a kimono, with long flapping sleeves and a plastic obi. It would be hard to imagine anything further from the traditional garment. Nevertheless it was the talk of Tokyo.

My neighbour on the plane was not just an eccentric. To my amazement, confiding in Japanese men that I was planning to look into geisha and their culture exposed me to my first experiences of rudeness in this country of protocol and courtesy. Enraged, they laid into me for taking an interest in such a trivial, old-fashioned and banal aspect of their culture.

A Japanese woman who, as a teacher of the shamisen, lived her life on the borders of the geisha world, asked me with gentle puzzlement why I wanted to look into the 'dark, bad side of Japan'. And when I went to bookshops I found intriguingly little on the geisha.

There was plenty on the Yoshiwara, the glamorous old pleasure quarter whose languid courtesans were celebrated in exquisite woodblock prints by artists like Utamaro Kitagawa, which, I suspected, was because the Yoshiwara no longer exists. Sanitised by becoming a subject for works of art or academic study, it is no longer threatening; it no longer reflects on contemporary Japan. There was also material on 'comfort women' and sex slaves, on the Japanese women who used to be trafficked to South-East Asia as prostitutes and the South-East Asian women who are to this day forcibly trafficked to Japan for the same purpose. These were matters to which there could be no ambiguous response, which could be tackled with proper twenty-first century outrage. And on geisha? Besides the few excellent works in English there was surprisingly little.

When I mentioned geisha to friends and acquaintances in Tokyo, many said with, it seemed to me, unnecessary forcefulness that no, they did not know any. But some did. They took me aside, sat me down and explained that geisha were dancers, musicians, entertainers and conversationalists who filled a specific niche at the highest levels of Japanese society. They were absolutely not prostitutes, high class or otherwise. That established, they suggested particular geisha that I might care to look up and, most importantly, indicated that I might mention their name.

First Days in Kyoto

On my first morning in Kyoto I was woken by a strange shouting, like the cry of an animal. Sunlight was streaming into the small room where I slept on the floor, sending motes of dust sparkling and spinning. I went to the balcony. Standing motionless in front of a small shrine was a mendicant monk in black robes and leggings, his face hidden under a domed wicker hat, silently holding a begging bowl. After a while he walked slowly away, every now and then uttering his cry. Gradually the street came alive. A woman in a negligée slipped out of a house to dust the shrine and lay flowers and fruit in front of it. A group of girls in *yukata* (simple cotton kimonos), their hair elaborately coifed but their faces clean-scrubbed and bare of make-up, congregated there, then clattered on wooden clogs into a large concrete building nearby, set back from the road.

I went in search of breakfast and found a coffee shop along the street. Inside, mellow jazz emanated from the speakers. The master of the shop, nervy and balding, tapped his fingers on the counter while he brewed up coffee in a glass percolator. The mistress, warm, plump and smiling in a pink-and-white checked apron, prepared industrial-sized slabs of cotton-woolly toast. The shop was full of women sitting over breakfast, flicking through newspapers or chatting.

Later, wandering the neighbourhood, I found myself in a warren of alleys lined with wooden houses pressed so close together that only the occasional shaft of sunlight pierced the gloom. Every now and then a motorbike or scooter skidded past but mainly there was silence. I had never been anywhere in Japan so untouched by the passage of time. It was as if I had stepped back into a pre-industrial era.

There were five geisha areas or *hanamachi* ('flower towns'), of which three clustered together on the eastern side of the River Kamo which rolled, wide and brown, a couple of minutes' walk away from the inn where I was staying. These three — Gion, the most famous and classy, Gion Higashi (East Gion) and Miyagawa-cho — were bordered to north and south by two thoroughfares, Sanjo and Gojo (Third and Fifth) Streets. Cutting through the middle, the nerve centre of the area, was Shijo (Fourth) Street, crammed end to end with shops dealing in all the paraphernalia of the geisha world — hairpins, tortoiseshell combs, dangly hair decorations, fans, clogs, kimono fabric, white face paint, sticks of safflower lipstick, hair wax, camellia oil and small beautifully moulded cakes of sugar, rice and beans. At one end of the street, where it met the river, was the imposing Minami-za Kabuki Theatre, at the other the massive red-painted entrance porch, temple buildings, pagoda and extensive grounds of Yasaka Shrine. Behind that rose the green and impenetrable Eastern Hills, Higashiyama.

The river divided this small alternative universe from the modern city with its snarled traffic, air-conditioned department stores, clashing neon and bustling people. Across the river from Gion was the fourth of the five *hanamachi*, Pontocho, a tiny picturesque alley lined with restaurants which in summer were extended at the back to make platforms lined with reed matting where one could dine, sip saké and enjoy the cool breezes above the rolling waters of the Kamo. It was several days before I visited the fifth, Kamishichiken (literally 'Seven Houses to the North'), in the north-west of the city. To my mind it was the most charming of all, a couple of quiet intimate lanes lined with dark prosperous houses, many with a lantern glowing outside, meandering in a gentle curve up to the stone lanterns and plum trees of Kitano Shrine.

That evening I was to have my first appointment with one of the grande dames of the geisha world. I had mentioned on the phone that I was a friend of a friend, an important and powerful businessman whom I will call Mr Suzuki. Far from seeking publicity, the geisha shun it. Their whole profession depends on their ability to keep secrets. Many have been the friends of the nation's most powerful men, often for a lifetime. Such men choose to entertain at geisha houses because they can trust these women to keep their lips sealed, no matter what they see or hear. But I also knew that in Japan, as elsewhere, the most important thing is who you know.

With the help of introductions from friends I had made over years of living and working in Japan, I was confident that – little by little – I would be able to breach this closed world.

The innkeeper's wife, a kindly soul, offered to show me the way. She got on to her bicycle and led me through the maze of streets, past rows of shadowy wooden houses with lanterns glimmering outside, while I panted along behind. At the end of an alley she stopped and pointed to a closed door, then pedalled away. I paused to pluck up courage, hearing the sounds of voices inside, then tentatively pushed it open.

Faces turned to look as I walked in. 'Irasshai! [welcome!]' shouted the barman.

I was in a small brightly lit room with a bar along one side and some leather sofas arranged to make a couple of alcoves. A small, regal woman in a kimono greeted me, offered me a whiskey, then turned back to banter with a group of noisy elderly men. Rather awkwardly I perched on a stool at the bar and began to chat to the barman. Finally the woman came to perch alongside me.

'So you are here through the introduction of Ken-chan,' she said, using the affectionate, diminutive form. 'I've known him for years, since he was a little boy. I used to bounce him on my knee.'

It was hard to imagine the leathery Tokyo businessman I knew being bounced on anyone's knee. Added to which, if that was the case, I realised with surprise, she had to be in her seventies. She was as tiny and frail as a butterfly, with the kind of looks that become, if anything, more beautiful with time – a fine-boned, delicate face, perfect skin without a trace of lines. Dressed in a modest indigo blue kimono with a subtle pattern woven through it, her hair drawn back into a pristine bun, she sat very upright, poised and gracious.

'So . . . what would you like of me?' She spoke in Kyoto dialect, ineffably polished and stylised, where everything is hinted at and nothing is said directly. Fresh from Tokyo, I found it difficult to pick up every nuance.

Clumsily I launched into an explanation. As she knew, I was a writer. I was hoping to write about the geisha world. Hopefully I could meet geisha, some young, some at the height of their careers, perhaps even spend time in a geisha house living like one of them, seeing life from

7

the inside. I gathered she might be able to help me. I'd be very grateful if she could do so.

I stumbled to a close. She sat in silence, looking straight ahead.

'Mmm,' she said slowly after a long pause, pursing her lips. 'But how can you ever understand our shikitari?'

'Shikitari?' I queried. I prided myself on my spoken Japanese but this was new to me.

'You see?' she smiled, tight-lipped. 'You do not even know the word.'

Many of the customs and practices in the geisha world, I was to learn, have their own terminology, a sort of jargon known only to insiders, incomprehensible to most Japanese. Other words which they regularly use – such as *shikitari* – are rare and sound rather archaic to the Japanese ear. It was only after considerable research that I discovered that *shikitari* meant 'customs, practices, the way of doing things'. It was indeed the *shikitari* which I wanted to learn about, among much else.

'How long are you planning to stay in Kyoto?' she went on.

'Several months,' I replied uncomfortably, adding hastily, 'but I've lived in Japan for many years. I first came more than twenty years ago . . .'

'I have been to London many times,' she snapped. 'I have met all the top people – the aristocracy, musicians, singers . . . But you would still say that I cannot understand England, would you not?'

I had to confess, I murmured as politely as possible, that that was not exactly the way that English people thought. For a start, she said, ignoring my response, geisha were of different sorts and different status. Some, like her, had been born in Gion. She herself was third generation; her mother and grandmother before her had been geisha. Then there were those – here there was the faintest, barely perceptible curl of the lip – who had come in from elsewhere. They, she implied, were a different class altogether. Of the five *hanamachi*, Gion, Pontocho and Kamishichiken had long histories. They had always been geisha districts. But I must bear in mind that East Gion and, worse still, Miyagawa-cho were different, unspeakably low, in fact quite beyond the pale; in the past, prostitutes – she breathed the word with distaste – had lived there.

'I would not like to see Miyagawa-cho written about in the same breath as the others,' she said emphatically.

Even Gion, Pontocho and Kamishichiken were all completely dissimilar, with entirely different histories and *shikitari*. She had met many westerners, she concluded, writers and journalists, who had come to Kyoto on the same quest as mine. They had all failed. They had all given up and so should I.

'No matter how long you are here you will never understand the intricacies of our system.'

Gloomily I took another sip of whiskey. I had never met a Japanese woman so formidable and steely. In the alcoves the men were shouting and laughing. Ties were loosened, faces flushed.

'Mama!' shouted one. With the indulgent smile of a mother for a naughty child, the *mama-san* – my hostess – slipped away to join them, topping up their drinks and admonishing them teasingly. One, rather the worse for wear, came over to try his English skills on me.

At that moment the door opened. With a rustle of silk and brocade, a clatter of wooden clogs and a faint tinkling of bells, a creature like a painted doll appeared.

'Okasan, oki-ni!' she cooed in breathy, high-pitched tones, using the Kyoto word for 'thank you': 'Mother, thank you.' Tottering unsteadily into the room on platforms a good 4 inches high, she stood nodding, smiling and giggling, covering her mouth with her hand.

'She has just become a maiko,' explained the *mama*. 'This is her third day.'

I was dumbstruck, as many people are on first coming face to face with a maiko. (Maiko literally means 'dancing girl' but is usually translated 'trainee geisha' or 'apprentice geisha'.) Later, as the days and months passed, I was able to see the childish faces underneath the thick white paint. But that first time, I could not stop myself staring in amazement and curiosity at this extraordinary confection. I was not the only one. For a moment there was silence before the chatter started up again.

She was wearing a sumptuous black kimono with an intertwined design of bamboo leaves and stems in browns, whites and greens around the hem. The kimono sat flatteringly low on her shoulders, revealing a layer of brilliant red brocade at the throat which I took to be an under-kimono; in fact it was a separate under-collar. Around her waist, wrapping her like a corset from armpit to hip, was a thick cummerbund – the obi – of pale gold embroidered with flowers.

But the most extraordinary thing was her face. It was a pure white oval, with the sides of the nose and the eye sockets shaded in pink, the eyes outlined in black, the eyebrows brushed in feathery brown and the lower lip a startling crimson crescent; the upper lip, disconcertingly, was white. To accentuate the mask-like effect, there was a line of unpainted flesh between face and hairline. The hair – 'Her own hair, not a wig,' said the *mama* – was teased and lacquered into an undulating landscape of hills and valleys, adorned with flowers, dangling silver pins, ribbons and combs which appeared to end in miniature rock gardens.

When she turned she revealed a breathtaking expanse of exquisitely painted white back. I had not realised that the kimono was worn quite so shockingly low. It was like a décolletage in reverse, enormously erotic. At the nape of the neck, which Japanese men find especially sexy, was a titillating three-pronged fork of naked, unpainted flesh.

She was not so much a woman as a walking work of art, a compilation of symbols and markers of eroticism, as far removed from a human being as a bonsai is from a natural tree. Geisha have been described as icons of femininity. If that is the case, it is a very stylised image of femininity, following conventions utterly different from western notions of beauty and sexiness. There was certainly not the slightest pretence that this was a real woman. She was an actress, painted up to play a role; it would be as absurd to confuse the girl with the role as to assume that the star of a soap opera actually was the character she was playing.

The make-up, I imagined, dated from an era when geisha used to flit through the gloom of unlit teahouses, their magical mask-like faces glimpsed only in darkness or by flickering candlelight. Then it transmuted its wearers into shamanesses who could transport men into another world, a world of dreams. Now too it gave the child – who, underneath it all, must have been a shy, gawky teenager – an inexplicable power and allure. She had become a representative of beauty.

Rather unsteadily, with much rustling of fabric, she perched on the edge of one of the sofas; the enormous obi prevented her from sitting any further back. Under the harsh neon lights, the illusion was harder to maintain; close up the thick white paint looked a little lumpy, suggesting either that it had been applied with an unskilful hand or that it concealed a less than perfect adolescent complexion. I glanced at the *mama*, hoping that I might slip over and join the group; but with a barely perceptible pursing of the lips she indicated that I should keep quiet and stay where I was. So I watched and listened, curious to see what this painted creature might have to say.

'When were your parents born?' began the stringy, grey-haired man next to her, basking in her presence.

She smiled, giggled, covered her mouth with her hand.

'Showa 29,' she trilled, using the Japanese calendar (1944 by the western calendar).

The man roared appreciatively as if she had just uttered a scintillating witticism.

'Showa 29, same as my son!' he beamed.

Smiling she picked up one of the bottles of beer which littered the table and offered to fill his glass. One by one she moved from guest to guest, filling their glasses, giggling, repeating 'Oki-ni!' Her job, it seemed, was just to be there. Chatting was an optional extra. Soon the men had reverted to talking among themselves.

Time passed. She rose to her feet. Bustling and clucking like a mother hen, the *mama* tugged, pulled and patted her kimono into place and adjusted the heavy gold obi until the two long ends, which crossed one over the other and hung to her feet, were perfectly symmetrical.

'Oki-ni! Oki-ni! Okasan, oki-ni!' sang the girl. Bowing and giggling, with a clatter of clogs and a tinkle of bells, she backed out of the door and was gone. The room was a little duller, a little gloomier without her.

The *Mama-san*

It seemed an auspicious beginning. But, as the days and weeks passed, I began to fear that I would never get any further than this. I could see the geisha, I lived among them. But I was always an outsider, I could never step through the looking glass. And the more curious I became, the more the geisha world presented me with a blank face.

Every connection I thought would be hopeful turned out to be a dead end. From time to time I was introduced to women who I knew were ex-geisha and the proprietresses of geisha houses.

'Well,' they would say graciously. 'I would love to help you. Let me think now. Who do I know who can introduce you to geisha? My neighbour is an okami-san, a proprietress. She might be willing; she's not from Gion, she's from out of town. But then again, her girls are very busy at the moment.'

'But what about the geisha and maiko in your house,' I would murmur tentatively. 'I wonder if perhaps . . . Might it be possible . . .'

'Much too busy,' they would snap. 'Geisha are busy all day. They go to classes, they appear at parties. They certainly wouldn't have time to talk to you. But call me next week, I'll see what I can do.'

Hardly daring to hope, I would call them the following week. The answer was always the same.

But on the fringes of the geisha world I was making friends. Every day I went to the coffee shop for breakfast. By now the motherly owner and her jazz-loving husband were used to my eccentric foreign ways. Instead of the tiny container of cream substitute which they served to everyone else, they gave me, smiling at the oddness of it, real milk to top up my coffee and indulgently cut me thin slices of toast instead of doorstop-thick slabs. Sometimes I wrote my diary; sometimes I chatted to the owners or the other women.

Then, tape recorder and notebook in bag, I would set off. Sometimes I would drop in to see Mr Ishihara, the hairdresser. Maiko usually came in to have their hair done in the morning. I would sit in a corner and watch. He would start off with a long thick mane of hair and, while the maiko pored over a teenage magazine, he would crimp it with curling irons, comb in gobs of wax, part and knot and tug and tie, slip in a tail of yak's hair and wads of stuffing, then add ribbons and string and pins until the hair had been transformed into an immaculate gleaming coiffure. He was not so much a hairdresser as a sculptor who worked in hair. Between customers he would sit down to chat. He knew everything one could ever want to know about geisha and their hairstyles, the history and the meanings of the different styles, and had written four books on the subject.

Or I would sit at the back of the knick-knack and paper goods shop on Shijo, the main street, and listen to Mr Sakai, a cheerful 75-year-old whose family had had a shop there since 1862. Reminiscing about the days when rickshaws rattled by and girls were still sold into servitude, he would bring out photographs of his favourite geisha over the years and show me the flowery perfumed name cards they had given him.

As much as I could I absorbed the geisha arts. The word *gei-sha* literally means 'arts person'; perhaps it could be translated 'artiste'. Maiko spend five years studying dance and music before they graduate; and fully qualified geisha continue to study for the rest of their lives, honing and perfecting their technique. As I walked the streets I would hear the plangent plink-plonk of shamisen riffs being practised over and over again.

Soon after I arrived the Pontocho geisha gave a series of public dance performances. The small theatre, tucked on one side of the narrow lane which made up the Pontocho district, was packed out with women in dark-toned kimonos who looked much like the owners of geisha houses and their elderly escorts, who might have been husbands, friends or patrons. While the spectators fluttered their fans, the all-female troupe gave an abbreviated performance of *Chushingura* ('The Tale of the Forty-seven Ronin' or lordless samurai), a drama as familiar as a Shakespeare play or a performance of Swan Lake would be to a western audience.

Little by little my ear was becoming attuned to the melodies and rhythms of the music (at first rather dissonant for western taste), while my eye was becoming sharper, better able to perceive the quality and crispness of the movements. One way of stepping inside the geisha world, I thought, might be to sit in on some of the maikos' music and dancing classes. But to do this I needed an introduction. Taking a deep breath, I called the formidable *mama* again, thanked her very much for her kindness and asked if I might come and see her.

'Of course,' she replied, all icy politeness.

Whenever you visit anyone in Japan you take a gift, beautifully wrapped in the shop's brandname paper and presented in the shop's carrier bag. A mere glance at the choice of shop communicates to the recipient your savoir faire and your degree of respect. So it was an urgent priority to find a suitable gift. Should I take cakes or, as a westerner, expensive French wine? Several guidebooks recommended a celebrated cake shop on Shijo with a long pedigree. So I went along, asked what were their most famous cakes of the season and bought a boxful. The cakes were of rice paste filled with red bean jam, beautifully moulded.

Carrying my offering, I arrived at precisely the appointed time. The bar was silent, dark and empty apart from the barman who was leaning on the counter, smoking a cigarette.

'Wait a while,' he said, turning on some lights, and offered me a drink. He had a swarthy, rather flat, melon-seed face and sharp, watchful eyes. He might have been anything between thirty and fifty but had become fixed forever in the ageless role of 'boy'. There were plenty of men around but they were all adjuncts, 'employees' as one ageing geisha put it, servicing the geisha – shopkeepers, barmen, men whose job it was to help the geisha dress, men who worked in the geisha unions.

The barman seemed unnervingly knowledgeable about me and the difficulties I was having.

'The geisha world is not a Yes/No society,' he said, apropos of nothing in particular. 'You offer a maiko a cake and she just says "Oki-ni" ["Thank you"]. She doesn't say, "Yes, please," or "No, thank you."'

I was beginning to understand what he was driving at. If I made a request, no one would ever say, 'No, that's impossible.' Neither would they say, 'Yes, I'll do that, I'll help you.' They would always make encouraging noises and tell me to call them again, any time, and they would see what they could do. But no matter how many times I called, nothing would ever come of it.

The *mama* was a case in point. I had heard from others that she was one of the most powerful geisha in Kyoto. She had been, like her mother before her, a famous beauty. Indeed, she was still extraordinarily lovely. Rumour had it that she had a *danna* (a patron), effectively a husband, who supported her whole enterprise. 'They've been together for decades,' the innkeeper's wife had told me. Yet I wondered where that steely core came from. In my decades in Japan I had met many Japanese women, almost all of them married, who were strong, confident, yet also eager to befriend me, a foreigner. I had never before encountered such suspicion and intransigence. It was as if these women had built a self-sufficient world in which I was just a flea, an irritation. They had no need of me; they wanted to brush me off.

When the *mama* appeared, as exquisite and tight-lipped as ever, she took my carefully chosen cakes with barely a glance and put them aside, then asked me what I wanted to drink.

'Ocha de mo ii desu,' I said. ['Tea will be fine.']

'That's rude!' she snapped, rounding on me fiercely. 'You say, "Ocha o itadakimasu" ["I'll have tea, please"].'

Biting my tongue I apologised profusely and thanked her for being so kind as to correct me. There were no concessions to the fact that I was speaking a foreign language. The geisha were unforgiving of the tiniest error. Trying to communicate deference and humility with my body language, nodding, keeping my head bowed, I waited for an appropriate moment when, with the utmost politeness, I could put my request to her. I thought it would help my research, I explained, using the most formal and polite Japanese I could manage, if I was able to sit in on some classes at the Kaburenjo, the 'Music and Dance Practice Place', housing classrooms, a theatre and the union offices, which formed the nerve centre of the district.

'Let me teach you,' she said, suddenly kind. 'Last time we met, you asked too many things – you wanted to meet geisha, meet maiko, stay in a geisha house, do this, do that. You must learn to be patient. Take it step by step.'

'Step by step,' echoed the barman, who seemed to have more authority than one would have expected.

'When you meet maiko, you do not ask, "Why did you become a maiko? What is your training?" In a gentle way, you say' – putting on a piping little girl voice – '"If you don't mind, could I ask . . . ?" And only one thing at a time. You ask too much!'

Taking out one of her business cards, she pencilled a few neat characters on to it.

'Take this to Mr Kimura at the union offices in the Kaburenjo,' she said. 'We will practise what you will say. I will run through it with you.'

'Well,' I said, 'I guess I'll introduce myself, tell him that I've lived in

15

Japan, show him my books, then say that I want to sit very quietly and watch some classes, maybe meet maiko and talk to them, talk to the teachers . . .'

'No, no,' she said. 'Just say something very modest: "I did these books, there's others too but this is all I have; if possible it would be really wonderful if I could sit in on a dance class . . ." And don't say anything else. Then the next time you make your next request. You see?'

I repeated the words after her in my best high-pitched little girl voice, full of deference and self-deprecation, inserting thanks and apologies after every few words. I was beginning to understand. Within the geisha scheme of things, I was right at the bottom of the pecking order. Here I was, a female, trying to swim along within the geisha community yet ignorant of all their codes. Had I been a man, it would have been natural for me to be an outsider. I would have fitted neatly into the category of customer. The geisha would have indulged me, flirted with me, overwhelmed me with charm and attentiveness. But in this closed, secretive world of women, there was no place for a female who did not know the proper way to behave.

In a word, I was in need of training. Hence the *mama*'s harshness; anyone entering the geisha world at the bottom – as a *shikomi* (a housemaid), the pre-maiko stage – would doubtless experience far worse. This must be at least akin to that. I was undergoing the most basic geisha training, such as would be given to a raw recruit fresh from the countryside.

And – though she probably disagreed with me – I felt I was learning. Living among the geisha, dealing with them on a day-to-day basis, their ways were beginning to rub off on me. I found myself carrying my body differently, walking with dainty steps, bowing, nodding, smiling until my face hurt. Most disconcertingly, when I called Japanese who had nothing to do with geisha or the geisha world, I found myself talking with exaggerated politeness in sweet, high-pitched velvety tones: 'Oh, that would really be too kind, thank you so, so much!'

The next day, full of anticipation, I went along to the large concrete Kaburenjo carrying the precious business card. It was a rather unprepossessing building to house such an august body as the geisha union. My hopes rose when I discovered that Mr Kimura was really quite young, maybe only forty or fifty. He had clipped hair, glasses and an office worker's suit. He took me off to a small side office and asked me brusquely what I wanted. I repeated my speech in my most unctuous tones, being as modest and undemanding as it was possible to be.

'No chance,' he said. It struck me that, for all my efforts, neither the *mama* nor anyone else in authority bothered much with politeness at all.

'I'll ask them upstairs, but I'm sure they'll say "No",' he added, scowling, and showed me the door. 'You can try again next week if you like,' he added, which I now understood to mean, 'Forget it.' Downcast I went back to my small sunny room to lick my wounds and ponder my next step.

The Best Cakes

Whenever I had time, I went to tea ceremony class. I had studied the Urasenke school of tea ceremony years before when I lived in a small provincial Japanese town. I took it up again when I arrived in Kyoto, thinking it might be a way of making contacts and furthering my research. But after the first class I remembered how much I loved it and after that it became my weekly treat.

The class took place at a house round the corner from the inn where I lived. I would slip off my shoes at the entrance and put on white socks; walking around in bare feet on tatami matting is unthinkable and coloured socks would be déclassé. Then I went upstairs, slid open the paper door, bowed on my hands and knees and greeted the teacher and the other students. The teacher, a comely, charismatic young man, had two faces. When he was conducting the class he wore *hakama* (the formal starched and pleated men's kimono) and took on the persona of the *sensei* (teacher), barking orders and correcting the smallest mistake. Off duty he was a hip young man who worked as a stylist for a glossy magazine.

Tea ceremony is a series of precise choreographed movements performed in a spirit of stillness and concentration which also involves the serving and consuming of food and drink. It is somewhere between tai chi and the Roman Catholic mass but on a very small, intimate scale. It is a wonderful way to learn how to function in a Japanese environment: how to walk on tatami matting in a kimono, sliding the feet one in front of the other, toes turned inwards; how to open and close a sliding door with grace; and how to kneel down and rise to one's feet elegantly. Being very rusty, I was at the bottom of the class and had to be coaxed to remember even the most basic things, such as to hold my arms as if there was an egg tucked into each armpit. Fortunately the teacher too was Urasenke so at least I did not have to relearn details like the folding of the silk napkin.

One day, as we nibbled bean jam cake and sipped foaming green tea the colour of spring leaves, the conversation turned to grades and varieties of tea. One of the students was Miss Koyama, whose family had been growing, grinding and selling tea for generations. Despite the fact that she wore faded jeans and two earrings in each ear, she knew exactly how to conduct the many different versions of tea ceremony and had no need to be reminded to keep her elbows out.

'For the name, Ippodo; for the history, Kamibayashi; for the taste, Koyama – that's what we say in Kyoto,' the teacher told us, naming the three most famous tea ceremony shops in the city. Then he listed the four most famous cake shops. To my relief, the shop where I had bought the mama's cakes was among them.

'Do you know Kanshindo?' he added, glancing at me. 'You should go there this season. It's very old, it's where the geisha buy their cakes. It's famous for its mizu yokan [a bland slab of red bean paste jelly eaten in summer]. It's very difficult to find, only Gion people know it. If you take them Kanshindo mizu yokan, the geisha will be very surprised and impressed. Shall I tell you where it is?'

And he drew me a small sketch map.

I needed to report back to the mama and take her a gift to thank her for her kindness in introducing me to Mr Kimura; it was irrelevant that it had not been a success. I called her, made an appointment to visit and went in search of the cake shop. I walked down Shijo Street, looking carefully. There were plenty of alleys off the main road but nothing where the teacher had indicated. Then I noticed a gap between two buildings just wide enough to slip through. It led to a dark, narrow path lined with blank walls and the closed doors of bars. Halfway along was a small stall, not even a shop, with wrapped slabs of dark red aduki bean jelly in a display case. I bought a couple, wrapped in Kanshindo paper, and carried them off in the Kanshindo carrier bag.

That evening I went to see the *mama*. As always, I was precisely on time. As always, she was not there. When she finally appeared, I offered her the cakes, bowing and murmuring in self-deprecating tones, 'This is really nothing at all, but please take it.'

She took the bag and gave me a warm smile.

'The most delicious cakes!' she said. 'You're learning, little by little.'

I had also learnt to ask no more. I thanked her profusely for her very great kindness and for teaching me so much, apologised for my shortcomings, chatted inconsequentially for a while, then left, feeling pleased with myself.

I had never guessed that cakes would make such a difference. After that, whenever I was to visit anyone, I always made a pilgrimage to Kanshindo. I became a regular customer. The two apron-clad women who ran the shop took to asking how I was and I always stopped for a chat. And when I proffered my cakes, the geisha would exclaim with delight or nod approvingly and look at me as if to say, 'Aha, I can see you know what's what.' I had found one of the keys to the door.

Doors Open

There was another key lying around waiting to be found – or maybe it was a door rather than a key.

One day I was walking home when a geisha caught up with me, scurrying along on her silk-covered sandals. She was tall and slender with a dancer's long neck and a striking face, handsome rather than beautiful, with a long chin, high cheekbones, thoughtful eyes and a wide sensuous mouth. She was wearing, as geisha (as opposed to maiko) do, an elegant, understated kimono in shades of pale mauve, with a plain obi, and her hair was swept back. Perhaps it was because she was wearing heavy make-up (though not the white face paint of the maiko, which geisha wear only on formal occasions) that I failed to recognise her, though – to my embarrassment – she seemed to know me well.

'Going home, are you? Or dropping in to the coffee shop?' she asked gaily. Then she mentioned that she was on her way back from Tokyo where she had been performing in an *odorikai*, a convention for professional dancers, and suddenly I realised who she was.

Whenever I had seen her before, I had always taken her for a university student or a secretary. When I went for breakfast she was often there, a quiet, serious girl with large owlish glasses who sat at the far end of the counter reading her paper. She usually wore a dress or a simple blouse and skirt over slim bare legs and had short neat hair and a scrubbed clean face. I had always been rather curious about her. She looked like a bit of a bluestocking, very far removed from a geisha; as if, like me, she was an outsider, not really part of this world at all.

Recently, knowing that I knew Tokyo, she had mentioned that she was going there for a dance convention. Bluestocking or not, everyone, from the innkeeper of my inn to the master and mistress of the coffee shop, lived out their lives entirely within the geisha world, whether or not they were geisha themselves. That was all they talked about – the recent dance performance at Pontocho, the next shamisen and drum concert at the local Kaburenjo, how the maiko were getting along, which ones showed promise, which ones did not. So I guessed that what she wanted to know about was the Tokyo geisha scene. I was pleased that I was able to tell her a little about which districts were flourishing, which struggling, and about a recent performance of geisha dancing that I had seen in the Shimbashi district.

I knew that she was a talented dancer. But plenty of women learnt *Nihon buyo* or *jiutamai*, the forms of traditional Japanese dance practised by geisha, as a hobby. It had never occurred to me that such a serious-looking, intellectual young woman might be a geisha herself.

The following day at breakfast she was not there. By now it was midsummer, approaching the season of the Gion festival. All the geisha had had fans made of handcrafted paper shaped like gingko leaves and inscribed with their professional names in beautifully brushed black characters, which they handed out as souvenirs. The master and mistress of the coffee shop had a whole collection, pinned up in rows across the wall.

'Look,' said the master, reading some of the names to me. 'And see this one? That's our Fumiko. You know her. She's famous, she's one of the top dancers in the district.'

I looked blank.

'She sits just over there. You know, with the big glasses!'

Something was changing in my perception of the coffee shop and its customers and in their perception of me. For weeks I had gone there simply to have breakfast. Sometimes I chatted to people, often I didn't. Sometimes some of the older ladies engaged me in conversation. And as I became a familiar face, the plump, motherly owner would inquire how I was getting on with my research.

Once, thanks to a fortuitous introduction, I spent an afternoon with a frail chirrupy woman who told me she was ninety. She had parchment skin and finely sculpted features, and wore an immaculate, pale pink, silk netting kimono. The next morning, when the owner quizzed me, I mentioned that I had seen her. A buzz rippled through the little shop as the name was batted from person to person.

'Is she still alive?' queried one voice.

'What was she like?' demanded another. 'How was she? Was she genki [full of life]?'

'Yes,' I said. 'She was very genki.'

'She's "main",' they told me in tones of awe, using the English word. 'She's legendary. Before the war there was no one more famous than her. She's the most famous geisha of all.'

I looked at these women I knew so well, with their unmade-up faces, in their slacks and blouses, some still in flimsy night-gowns, with their piled-up helmets of lacquered hair. How could I not have realised? All this time I had been scouring the district, making phone calls, using connections, trotting here and there with cakes, when I was already right inside the geisha world.

In fact it was just as well that I had been so oblivious. For instead of behaving like a journalist and alienating everyone by bombarding them with questions, I had, entirely by accident, done exactly the right thing. I had sat quietly, not being obnoxious, not asking nosy questions, speaking when spoken to, just eating breakfast, day after day. It was a bit like stalking wildlife. They were used to me. I had won their confidence.

I still did nothing. I was well-trained by now. I had plenty of people to meet and places to go. Then, several days later, the owner leaned across the counter and said in confidential tones, 'You wanted to find out about geisha, didn't you? Hara-san says she'd like to talk to you.'

Hara-san was sitting right behind me. I knew her well, a warm rather beautiful woman in her mid-seventies with a pile of snowy-white hair, large luminous eyes and a smile which lit up her face. It turned out that she was the *okami-san* – the owner-mistress – of a teahouse a few doors away from my inn. The word 'teahouse', incidentally, is a literal but rather misleading translation of *ochaya*. Geisha live in a 'geisha house' (*okiya*) and work in a 'teahouse' (*ochaya*), where there is music, dancing, partying, sometimes food and always plenty of alcohol; tea is the last thing you would expect to find there.

I went off to visit Hara-san, taking, of course, Kanshindo cakes. Talking to someone so familiar was an entirely different experience from quizzing a geisha who barely knew me. With a child-like innocence, she poured out her heart, showing me photographs of herself as a beautiful, grave-faced young geisha.

Suddenly doors were flying open. I traipsed in and out of houses with my notebook and tape recorder, listening to stories. Some were uneventful, others extraordinarily moving. I was amazed at the openness with which women would reveal the most harrowing experiences of their youth.

Now, a couple of months later, when I walked down the street, maiko recognised me. They stopped to bow and say 'Ohayo dosu!' (the quaint geisha phrase for 'Good morning'), or 'Oné-san, oki-ni' ('Big sister, thank you!'). The ones I knew would whisk me off on shopping expeditions, clattering along beside me on their clogs, taking my arm to make sure I was not swept off my feet by one of the lethal passing motorbikes, sheltering me with their oiled paper umbrellas when it rained, chattering and giggling sweetly. I felt pampered, protected, charmed and hugely honoured that they had chosen to befriend me. It was easy to see how beguiling such behaviour must be for the wealthy businessmen who were their customers.

As a single woman, I had always been something of an oddity in Japan. People would ask why I was not married and had no children until, as

I passed some unspoken but recognisable age, they became embarrassed even to ask. None of the geisha were remotely interested. After all, they themselves were not married. Some had children, some not. Those who had were single parents. No doubt they assumed that I had the occasional lover, as they did. As I lived among them it began to dawn on me that I – a modern western career woman – was not far removed from a geisha myself; though when I put this theory to the geisha I knew they looked distinctly dubious. Perhaps that was the answer. Perhaps they were the original liberated women and the rest of the world had just caught up with them.

I realised I felt extraordinarily at home. In Japan, outside the geisha community, everyone seemed to get up with the lark. Here, like me, they got up late. One would not dream of dropping in to see a geisha before noon. And unlike the punctual Japanese, they were never on time, as I had discovered when I was paying court to the *mama-san*. It was in many ways the looking glass image of 'real' Japan. All the usual rules were subverted. One should not take the comparison too far. Like Japan, it was a hierarchical, stratified society. But, within the small confines of the geisha communities, it was women, not men, who wielded power; and everyone hoped for girl children, not boys, so that they could carry on the line of geisha. It was a back-to-front world – which was of course the whole point. Men came to the 'flower towns' looking for an escape from drab reality in a world of dreams.

So how had this dream world arisen? This was something I could only understand by looking into the past. Over the following months I sifted through texts to try and understand where the geisha had come from, what their role was in Japanese society and why Japan had developed this parallel universe. I befriended geisha in Tokyo and in some of the hot-spring resorts where Japanese go on holiday. I hung out with different classes and varieties of geisha. And I began to get some clues as to why Japanese men (some, anyway) might be angry at the very notion of my writing a book on geisha.

Geisha Past and Present

The first section of this book deals with the history of the geisha, their changing face and role through the centuries, and the many romantic tales (both fact and fiction) which have grown up around them. It is a secret history. In the standard histories of Japan, geisha are never mentioned; yet when I probed a little deeper, I found them there, playing a part in the great events of their day and consorting with the most powerful men of the country as friends, confidantes, mistresses and sometimes wives. But they are always in the shadows, the women behind the decision-makers.

Today they seem respectable enough; in fact there is a powerful geisha PR lobby driving home the point that geisha are not prostitutes with such insistence that even the most out-of-touch westerner must have got the message by now. But in Victorian times and before, when geisha were in their heyday, they were the pinnacle of an outrageous alternative society. Like rock and roll stars today, they were the queens of a popular culture created by, with and for the people; so subversive that the shogunate (the government of the day) spent much of its time hopelessly attempting to repress it, or at least to keep it within controllable bounds. Many of the writers who celebrated this culture found themselves in prison from time to time. The woodblock print artists whose work is so familiar to us today made a living portraying the courtesans, geisha and kabuki actors who were the pin-ups of this alternative society.

As for the glamorous courtesans and rollicking male geisha who were like court jesters to the wealthy guests, the Japanese will tell you that both professions died out at least a century ago. I found differently . . .

And what of modern-day geisha? Very few Japanese have ever met one. In the evening the streets of Gion are crowded with Japanese tourists with cameras poised, waiting patiently like birdwatchers for a maiko to flit into view for a few seconds before darting into a nearby teahouse. Only the very wealthy or their guests will ever get to spend an evening in the company of maiko or geisha. Who are these women and why do they do what they do? In the second part of the book I look at the world of the geisha today: from the rites and rituals of geisha life and how a geisha does her make-up and kimono, to how she learns to charm at geisha parties. It is a journey in search of the last remnants of a dying tradition, to record some of these colourful personalities, their customs, their stories, their memories, their present and their past.

Inevitably I find myself looking at what it means to be a woman in Japan. What is the dividing line between geisha and prostitutes and between wives and geisha? And what of the men who spend their time with geisha? Almost all the people who recorded the geisha and their lives in stories, novels and woodblock prints were men. In the few surviving writings and paintings by geisha, they portray themselves very differently, not as siren queens but down-to-earth women.

In Japan in the heyday of the geisha, relations between men and women operated very differently from the way we do things in the west. Until recently, all but the lowest classes had arranged marriages. The purpose of marriage was to create an alliance between families; to go against one's family and marry for love would have been quite unthinkable. It was also – hard though it is to imagine – considered shockingly improper to enjoy sex with one's wife. The function of conjugal relations was to produce children to perpetuate the family line. As for pleasure, men were expected to find that elsewhere.

Rather as in France, there is still little stigma against having a wife to take care of the home and household affairs and a mistress or two to provide charming conversation and sexual pleasure. As far as Japanese men are concerned, the job of all these women is to mother them, pamper them and please them. Japanese women conversely have grown adept at using their silken charms to wind their men around their little fingers. Outsiders may see Japan as a male-dominated society. Japanese women know otherwise.

I also look at the Japanese attitude to love and sex, untouched until recently by either the European notion of romantic love or Christian sexual morality. This is a culture in which hedonism, sensualism and the art of the erotic, not at all the same as sex, were uninhibitedly developed in very sophisticated ways. In the floating world of the geisha, it was love, not sex or sensual pleasure, which was taboo.

But perhaps for the very reason that love was beyond the pale, it became all the more powerful and devastating a force. Long before geisha there were women in Japan skilled at weaving a web of romance to entrap men . . .

I

COURTESANS AND GEISHA

PRELUDE

THE ART OF LOVE

*Because they fall
we love them —
the cherry blossoms.
In this floating world,
does anything endure?*
Tales of Ise, Ariwara no Narihira (AD 823–880)[1]

Purple Hills and Crystal Streams

More than a thousand years ago, long before geisha were even thought of, there lived a woman so beautiful, proud and passionate that she has never been forgotten. She is considered the most beautiful woman of all time, the emblem of female beauty in Japan. Her name was Ono no Komachi and she was a lady-in-waiting in the court of the emperor of Japan in the mid-ninth century AD, the early years of the Heian period, which stretched from 794 to 1195. She was a historical poet and a famous siren of her day though the details of her story have become hugely embellished over time, with many apocryphal stories surrounding the few known biographical facts. Several moving plays of the classical Noh theatre have been written about her irresistible allure and tragic end.

In her day the capital had only recently been moved from Nara to a new and more auspicious location, a wide bowl-shaped valley surrounded by tree-clad hills, with sparkling rivers bordering it to each side. The official name was Heian-kyo, the Capital of Peace and Tranquillity. Poets called it the City of Purple Hills and Crystal Streams; we know it as Kyoto.

There a city grew up of vermilion-painted palaces, slender-pillared temples and spacious mansions of wood with wattled roofs. Noblemen and princes rumbled up and down the broad mud-paved boulevards, in the shadow of the overhanging willows, in lavishly decorated ox carts with huge wheels, attended by retinues of liveried outriders. Under the rule of the emperor and his all-powerful ministers of state, the Fujiwara family, the country basked in three centuries of peace and prosperity. For the pampered aristocrats of the Heian court, it was a time of unending leisure which they filled with the pursuit of art, beauty and love. They spent their days moon-viewing, writing poems, mixing incense, playing elaborate games and honing love itself into an art form.

Long after the Heian nobles themselves had disappeared, the wonderful refinement of their culture echoed down the ages in Japan. People looked back with nostalgia to a time when the worst one had to fear was the shame of committing a social gaffe or writing a bad poem. And when, centuries later, men began to seek out alternative worlds where they could transcend their everyday lives and imagine themselves noblemen of leisure, the courtesans and geisha modelled the dreams which they sold on the hothouse culture of the Heian princes.

Lady Komachi drove the noblemen of her day to distraction. According to the legend, she had raven tresses that cascaded to the floor, a face like a blossom and eyebrows painted into perfect crescent moons. She would glide through the cedar-scented halls in her multi-layered gauze and damask robes, oblivious to the thousands of love letters which lay discarded about her chambers. At night she slept in a room bright with tortoiseshell where golden flowers decorated the walls and strings of crystal beads hung in the doorway. When she passed the cup at banquets, people said it was as if the moon lay on her trailing sleeve.

But she was not just a pretty face. She was brilliant, accomplished, powerful and tough-minded, a woman of burning passions which she wrote about in *waka* (jewel-like 31-syllable poems) which are read and loved to this day.

Of the fickleness of men's love she wrote:

A thing which fades
With no outward sign
Is the flower
Of the heart of man
In this world![2]

Unlike the maidens of medieval Europe, waiting passively for a knight in
shining armour to come courting, she herself burnt with fiery passion:

This night of no moon
There is no way to meet him.
I rise in longing –
My breast pounds, a leaping flame,
My heart is consumed in fire.[3]

She was only available to a man who could prove himself worthy of her.
For the most lovelorn of all, a commander of the imperial guard named
Fukakusa no Shi'i no Shosho, she devised the sternest of ordeals. He was
to come to her house for a hundred nights and sleep outside on a bench
used to support the shafts of her chariot before she would even consider
his suit. Night after night he hitched up his stiff silk trousers and donned
his tall lacquered hat or put on a wide-brimmed wicker hat and straw rain
cape and ventured out into the elements. Evading the nightwatchmen
and the barrier guards he walked through wind, rain and snow, made a
notch on the shaft bench, then waited through the night there shivering.
Ninety-nine days had passed and the last joyful day was dawning when
suddenly he died, of heartbreak, perhaps, or exposure.

For her hard-heartedness, Komachi suffered the cruellest punishment
of all – the loss of her beauty. Instead of dying young and beautiful like
Cleopatra or Helen of Troy, she lived to be a hundred. After the death
of Captain Shosho she was spurned and driven from court and ended
up a tattered, crazed beggar woman. In folk legend and Noh plays she
is portrayed as an ancient withered crone, hideously ugly, haunted by
the unsettled spirits of the men who died for love of her. Like the cherry
blossoms, beauty is all too fleeting; and this is what gives her story its

poignancy. The beauty of women can drive men to distraction and to their deaths but in the end men get their revenge: such women die old and alone. Komachi's tragic end made her all the more the perfect precursor of the geisha. Like her they too came to be regarded with ambivalence. They were sirens, so beautiful that men could not resist them – yet to yield and to fall in love with one was to court disaster. At least in legend, if not in real life, Komachi had to be punished for her fearsome powers.

Around the time that Komachi was breaking hearts, a louche young nobleman named Ariwara no Narihira (823–880) was cutting a swath through the womenfolk of the Japanese court and countryside. While she was a true femme fatale, he was the all-time great lover, charming, sensitive and passionate. If his book of prose and poetry, *The Tales of Ise*, is to be believed, his life was driven entirely by affairs of the heart.

Early on he embarked on a relationship with one of the emperor's concubines, putting himself and her in great danger. When their affair was found out, he was exiled and she imprisoned and tortured; but he found a way to creep to her prison at night and would play his flute and sing to her. Thus the two were able to exchange poems, the most essential element of a love affair in those days. Then he seduced the Vestal Virgin at the Grand Shrine of Ise, bringing about her ritual defilement and thereby breaking every ritual taboo of the time. He had his way with everyone, from imperial consorts to a 99-year-old who yearned for a night with him, and he wet his sleeve with bitter tears over many others.

His beauty and charm made him irresistible. But the quality that singled him out above all was his ability to turn out a heart-wrenchingly perfect poem. With each of the many women with whom he briefly engaged, he wrote of love as if he really felt it. Narihira's passionate *waka* played a key part in setting the conventions for the feelings to be expressed and how to express them:

> Through the blackest shadow
> Of the darkness of the heart I wander
> In bewilderment –
> You who know the world of love, decide:
> Is my love reality or dream?[4]

The Cult of Beauty

For love was becoming an art form. More than sexual desire or gut-wrenching passion, it was an opportunity to put brush to paper, to immortalise the moment in a literary gem.

With war a distant memory, the Heian noblemen were able to devote themselves to the pursuit of beauty and love. While the peasants sweated to produce the rice that fed them, they developed an extraordinarily effete, decadent and promiscuous culture which reached its apogee a century after Komachi and Narihira pursued their affairs of the heart.

Like Komachi, the women of Heian society were articulate, literate and highly educated, well able to turn a well-honed poem or a witty riposte. One, Murasaki Shikibu, was the author of the world's first novel, *The Tale of Genji*, written around the year 1000, which recounts the romantic adventures of the charismatic Prince Genji. Several of these women kept diaries in which they recorded their thoughts and feelings in extraordinary detail, leaving us very intimate accounts of what life was like for the aristocrats of those days.

It was a world in which women lived their lives away from the sight of men, hidden in a kind of purdah in windowless unheated houses, shadowy by day and lit with oil lamps and tapers by night. When men came to visit they received them sitting behind latticed screens draped with silk curtains or opaque hangings, and when they went out, they travelled concealed behind the closed window blinds of their ox carriages, though they made sure that there was always an exquisite silk sleeve trailing outside to hint at the beauty within.

In this small becalmed world, beauty and fashion were all-important. A court lady was more likely to suffer censure for a lapse of taste in the colour of her robes than for having numerous lovers. Heian women wore silk kimonos, as many as twelve at a time, one on top of the other, each cut a little shorter than the one below and draped so that the layers were visible at cuff and throat, taking care to orchestrate the colours according to the latest fashion.

Given their indoor lives, a pale complexion was considered beautiful.

They whitened their skin with dried ground nightingale droppings (presumably the lime had a bleaching effect; nightingale droppings are still sold as a form of organic skin care in Japan). They accentuated their pallor still further with white powder made from rice husks, convolvulus seeds or white lead, though the lead, which geisha also later used, meant that their skin became prematurely aged. Using a paste of crushed safflower petals they rouged their cheeks and painted a spot of bright red in the middle of their lower lip to turn the mouth into a tiny pouting rosebud. They shaved off their eyebrows, replacing them with two smudgy charcoal-grey dots high on their foreheads and painted their teeth black with a dye of powdered gall-nut and iron dissolved in vinegar or tea; to Heian eyes gleaming unpainted teeth looked unspeakably barbaric.

But their most prized asset was their hair, which hung long, loose and glossy, cascading in a gleaming black curtain to the floor and often sweeping behind them like a train as they walked. Few men ever had the chance to see the results of all this preening, though they did their best. They were not averse to lifting a hanging screen and peeking inside or standing on tiptoe to look over a fence. And sometimes they were rewarded with a tantalising glimpse of a tiny figure with acres of black flowing locks, engulfed within layer upon layer of kimonos.

The men were rather pale, tubby and effeminate. They too powdered their faces and blackened their teeth, sported little tufts of beard and smeared liberal quantities of scent on their hair and clothes. When they were not polishing their poetry-writing and calligraphy skills, they spent their time moon-viewing or blossom-viewing, going on trips to hear the first cry of the cuckoo or playing float-the-saké-cup-down-the-river. The most prized skill was the art of perfume-mixing. A favourite pastime, still played in refined circles in Japan, was incense guessing, where players passed around an incense burner, snuffed the smoke, guessed the name of the incense and finally voted for the best.

But the main activity was love. For the men of Heian-kyo, the field was wide open. They were all married; that went without saying. But, following the Confucian precepts which governed society, marriage was a purely political affair arranged by the parents when both partners were young in order to create an advantageous alliance between families. Usually the husband and wife spent very little time together and met only to procreate. Love and marriage had nothing to do with each other, though the number one wife's position at the top of the hierarchy had to be respected.

Besides a wife, a man rich and powerful enough to afford it had concubines, anything from four to eight. These were women of high rank whom he had to woo according to the proper procedures and marry in a formal ceremony. In addition, there was nothing to stop him carrying on casual affairs with other men's wives or concubines, ladies-in-waiting, lower-class women (with whom he could not, of course, make a formal bond) and women of pleasure. Promiscuity, in fact, was expected. A man who was faithful to one woman was considered an oddity and told to pull himself together.

But what made the Heian period extraordinary was not the promiscuity (though it was probably one of the most lax societies the world has ever seen) but the way in which art and the cult of beauty were bound up with love. The courting process was exceedingly ritualised and bound by strict codes of etiquette. And, as with the incense ceremony, the pleasure was as much in the playing of the game as in the final consummation.

Having heard that a certain lady was very beautiful or, even more titillating, had beautiful handwriting, the nobleman sat down to compose a *waka* and brushed it, in his finest calligraphy, on delicately hued scented paper. He attached a sprig of willow, a cherry blossom or plum blossom, depending on the season, rolled the letter up and gave it to his messenger to deliver. On receiving it, the lady assessed the handwriting and colour of the paper as well as the wit and appropriateness of the poem; one would only wish to form a relationship with a person of the utmost refinement. She then brushed a reply. The nobleman, meanwhile, was waiting with bated breath to see whether her handwriting and poem lived up to expectations.

If the exchange of poems was satisfactory, the man continued the correspondence and eventually assayed a visit. He crept in at night and, immediately, in the pitch darkness, removed his clothes, lifted the silken counterpane, lay down on the hard straw mat next to the lady and – without further ado – consummated the relationship. The maids studiously affected total ignorance of his presence, though (as each nobleman wore a distinctive perfume) not only did they know he was there, they knew who he was by his scent.

Leaving before dawn, the nobleman immediately penned an eloquent morning-after poem, bewailing the rising of the sun or the crowing of the cock announcing the hour of farewell. The lady, in her turn, penned a reply and thus through their poems each communicated their decision as to whether to continue with the affair or not. Very often it was not so much a matter of real passion as an opportunity to play again and again the classic role of the lovelorn suitor, finding elegant new conceits to repeat the well-worn laments about the transience of art, life and beauty.

Such an effete society could not last forever. Long before the end of the Heian period, the wondrous city of Kyoto had already begun to fall into disrepair. Bands of armed priests and their hired mercenaries took to raiding the capital. Tracts of land in the south and west of the capital became wasteland, where thieves and beggars roamed, and travel outside the city was very dangerous. With all the focus on poetry writing, incense mixing, dancing and drinking, the supposed rulers of the city scarcely knew any longer how to ride a horse or wield a sword. The warrior arts were quite forgotten. It was hardly surprising that, in 1156, a couple of rival military clans based in the outlying provinces overran the capital and seized power. The delicately featured heads of the last Heian noblemen were skewered on pikes and displayed around the city.

There followed more than 400 years of instability and intermittent warfare. There were bursts of cultural activity but nothing sustained until the country was united again and peace was enforced at the beginning of the seventeenth century.

Shirabyoshi Dancing Women

Even at the height of Heian promiscuity when noblemen had no problem finding a companion for the night and flitted merrily from one aristocratic woman's chamber to another, there were also prostitutes who offered a different sort of pleasure. At one end of the scale were ordinary prostitutes who wandered the streets, waterways, hills and woods and were referred to as 'wandering women', 'floating women' and 'play women'. At the other extreme were cultivated, refined professionals who in English we might call courtesans.[5] Some were of good family, fallen upon hard times; others were noted for their beauty, brilliance or talent. Skilled musicians, dancers and singers, they were often the invited guests and chosen companions of aristocrats. These high-class courtesans were the original precursors of the geisha.

The most popular of the courtesans were the *shirabyoshi* dancing women. They dressed in white male clothing and manly court caps, carried swords like men and performed highly charged erotic songs and dances to rhythmic music. Like today's supermodels or rock singers, they were stars and the chosen companions of the country's most powerful men.

The most celebrated of all was Shizuka Gozen, the concubine of the twelfth-century hero Yoshitsune. (Shizuka, alas, is probably legendary though the great warrior who was her lover is a very important historical figure.) She was renowned throughout the country for her extraordinary beauty and also for the power of her dancing – so magical that once, when the country had been suffering from drought for a hundred days, the gods sent rain as soon as she began to dance. This is not as extraordinary as it sounds. Dance began as a way of supplicating the gods in Japan and the women who worked in Shinto shrines[6] often combined the roles of shamaness and prostitute. Centuries later, when the first geisha appeared they claimed the beautiful and spirited dancer as their ancestor.

After the demise of the effete Heian nobles, the country was swept into civil war as two rival warrior clans battled for power. In the end the Minamoto clan utterly routed their enemies, thanks to a couple of brilliant victories won by the dashing 21-year-old general Yoshitsune (1159–1189), one of which involved a reckless cavalry charge straight down a steep cliff in an area near present-day Kobe. Yoshitsune's elder half-brother, Yoritomo, forthwith established himself as the country's first military ruler or shogun, a word best translated as 'generalissimo'. But instead of being grateful to Yoshitsune for his help, he was fearful that his brother would use his popularity to supplant him and secretly ordered him to be killed.

Getting wind of the plan, Yoshitsune fled the capital with a few followers. Thus far is history though many legends grew up after his death to embellish the story of his heroic journey and tragic end. He was, by all accounts, something of a lady's man. There were, say the stories, twenty-four women with whom he was on intimate terms. Of those he took eleven with him – six noblewomen and five *shirabyoshi*, including his favourite, Shizuka. But he soon realised that they were slowing him down and sent them all back, even Shizuka, who was pregnant with his child.

Betrayed by Yoshitsune's followers who were supposed to guard her, goes the story, Shizuka found her way back to Kyoto where she was arrested and taken off to Yoritomo's court. There she was interrogated as to Yoshitsune's whereabouts. But being plucky as well as beautiful – two characteristics which later came to distinguish the geisha – she refused to give anything away. Far worse was to come. The cruel Yoritomo, discovering that she was pregnant, ordered that the child be killed if it was a boy. He could not afford to let any son of Yoshitsune's live. The baby was barely out of Shizuka's womb when Yoritomo's retainers snatched him from her arms, took him down to the beach and dashed his brains out against a rock.

Before letting her go, Yoritomo was determined to see the most celebrated dancer in the country perform. Oblivious to her feelings, he sent an order for her to dance before him. She refused but was then persuaded to dance to petition the gods at Hachiman Shrine. Realising that she had been deceived and that Yoritomo was watching from behind a blind, she declared that she could only dance if she had the proper accompaniment. Three court nobles stepped forward, all famous musicians. One carried a sandalwood drum covered with sheepskin strung with six cords; one a pair of silver cymbals embossed with gold chrysanthemums and suspended from a multicoloured cord, which he rattled to produce a sound like the chirrup of an insect; and one, the famously handsome Hatakeyama, a long bamboo flute.

There was no escape. She would have to dance.

Shizuka's legendary dance is still performed on the Japanese stage. Wearing an exquisite garment of Chinese damask over long white skirts which swirled around her feet like a train and a voluminous long-sleeved overgarment embroidered with diamonds, and with her floor-length hair swept into a loose knot on her head, she unfurled her crimson fan and stepped forward. First she performed one of the erotic *shirabyoshi* dances after which the dancers were named, singing and dancing with such grace and beauty that everyone who watched was utterly bewitched. Then – when she was sure she had them in the palm of her hand – she burst full-throatedly into a defiant love song, singing passionately of Yoshitsune and her deep yearning for him and jibing that he had successfully managed to evade Yoritomo. Yoritomo was torn between rage at such effrontery and pleasure at the beauty of her voice. But as she was, after all, a mere woman and therefore harmless, he was persuaded to let her go unpunished.

She was still only eighteen. Back in Kyoto she cut off her floor-length tresses, shaved her head and became a nun. A year later, goes the story, she died of grief. The historical Yoshitsune too was tracked down and killed.

1

The Floating World

Living only for the moment, giving all our time to the pleasures of the moon, the snow, cherry blossoms and maple leaves. Singing songs, drinking saké, caressing each other, just drifting, drifting. Never giving a care if we have no money, never sad in our hearts. Only like a plant moving on the river's current; that is what is called ukiyo – The Floating World.

Tales of the Floating World, Ryoi Asai, c.1661[1]

Music of a Bygone Age

Even before I arrived in Kyoto I began to hear about *tayu*. They were not geisha, as far as I could understand, but something even more splendid, a vestige of a bygone age. And there were very few left – only five or six. At a party in the Swedish Embassy in Tokyo I met the veteran fashion designer Junko Koshino, a small, imperious woman. 'You are going to Kyoto to study geisha?' she asked me. 'In that case you must go to Wachigaiya and see the tayu.' There and then she took my mobile phone, called the owner, made an appointment for me and commanded him to treat me well.

Wachigaiya was, I gathered, a geisha house of sorts in a part of town called Shimabara; but Shimabara was not on my map of Kyoto. I took a taxi, wondering where I was going. It was only later that I learnt that Shimabara had once been the most glittering of pleasure quarters, licensed and sponsored by the government.

Driving through a maze of narrow back streets lined with dingy shops, we suddenly came upon a massive wooden gateway overhung by a tall willow tree. With a gleaming tiled roof and enormous gates shoved wide open, it was set in an earthen wall with a bamboo fence and a moss-covered water barrel in front. It was a surreal sight – the entrance to some splendid medieval castle out of a Kurosawa film thrown up in the middle of a rundown inner-city neighbourhood.

'Shimabara,' announced the taxi driver as we inched our way through. On the other side were more shabby streets lined with nondescript houses. But on one corner, occupying an entire block, was a building like an ancient coaching inn with thick dark beams and buttresses – Wachigaiya. The enormous entrance hall had a ceiling three storeys high with smoke-blackened rafters and wooden doors that grated and screeched in their grooves.

Mr Takahashi, the owner – a jokey, laid-back man – was, it transpired, a distinguished actor and dancer. He showed me around, led me to the bar and offered me a drink, then showed me photographs of himself dressed as a woman, performing *Nihon buyo*, the traditional dance form of geisha and kabuki actors.

The building evoked an extraordinarily lavish age. In the banqueting halls the walls were sand-sprayed with a maple leaf design, the windows and screens were fretted and latticed, and the paper door panels were painted with exquisite scenes. In one room a courtesan's kimono hung like a painting on a bamboo frame. Quilted at the hem, it was of rich purple silk embroidered with two dancing figures dressed in multi-layered Heian robes, pink, pale blue, orange, white and gold.

Wachigaiya, Takahashi-san told me, had been in his family for generations. The house had been built some 300 years earlier, when it housed *tayu*, the highest rank of courtesans, who predated geisha. In their heyday they had been concubines and courtesans to the princes of the imperial palace. Unlike other courtesans they were permitted inside the palace; and in their leisure time the princes would travel on horseback or by palanquin to amuse themselves at the famous Shimabara pleasure quarters. Thus, little by little, I began to piece together the story of the courtesans and the pleasure quarters, the world out of which the geisha sprang.

Geisha, he said, specialised in shamisen, singing and various different

41

types of drum. *Tayu*, conversely, cultivated different arts: the writing of *waka* poetry, the incense-guessing ceremony, the shamisen, the classical zither – *koto* – and the tea ceremony. Perhaps, he suggested, I might like to meet a *tayu*. Hanakoto was due to perform for a group of executives from Fuji television. I could come along early, talk to her, then watch her performance. Full of excitement, I agreed.

A couple of weeks later I was back at Wachigaiya, eagerly waiting for the *tayu* to appear. Finally a tiny fairy-like creature slipped into the room, barely visible beneath her voluminous layered kimonos. Her face was chalky, her eyebrows and eyes etched in black and her underlip an intense peony red. Her hair was swept into loops and coils, as bulky as a Restoration wig. On it she supported an enormously ornate head-dress studded with tortoiseshell and silver hairpins and decorated with silk flowers and foliage, with dangling mother-of-pearl ornaments and strings of coral weighted with gold-leaf blossoms.

She was wrapped in layer upon layer of priceless antique kimonos. At her throat was a thick collar of beige brocade embroidered with a swirling pattern of irises. On top of that came a red kimono with a quilted hem which swept the floor and swung heavily as she walked, and above that an exquisite robe of thick black silk glistened with lustrous gold flowers, swirling around her feet like a train. The obi, a swath of orange silk brocade with a gold-thread design of chrysanthemums and maple leaves, was tied in the front in an enormous knot which hung in great folds from her waist to her knees. Later I learnt that this was a symbol of her availability. In theory it might be untied – if you happened to be rich and fortunate enough to be permitted to do so.

'The head-dress weighs 10 pounds,' declared Takahashi-san with a proprietorial air, 'and the costume 60 pounds.'

The *tayu* knelt next to me, adjusting her skirts. Underneath it all, she had a cheeky, elfin face with a tiny nose and pointed chin. How long had she been a *tayu*, I asked, then gasped when she opened her small mouth to answer. In the chalky-white face with the blood-red lips, her teeth were painted black. It was macabre, like looking into a black hole.

Four years was the answer. She was twenty-four and she was interested in the particular styles of dance and music which the *tayu* performed, quite different from the dance and music of the geisha tradition. She was fascinated, she said, by the history and traditions of the *tayu* and the stories of the great *tayu* of old. She loved the world of darkness and shadow in which the *tayu* moved. It was, she said, more *shibui* than the geisha tradition. The word *shibui*, which literally translates as 'astringent' or 'sober', evokes a mood of old gold, glimmering shadows and rust.

I listened, trying not to be distracted by the well of darkness in the middle of her face, until she was called away. She was, I suspected, just a modern young woman with an unusual job. There was one *tayu*, I had heard – maybe it was her – who came to work by motorbike and went back to her boyfriend and her modern flat in the evening. Another, in more traditional style, had lived for years with a *danna*, a much older man who supported her, furnished her flat and paid for everything. In this day and age, of course, they could not be real courtesans; they were certainly not for sale, even to the highest bidder. They were simply preserving the forms of a long-lost tradition.

In the banqueting hall the guests were waiting, cross-legged on the floor. The women among them knelt demurely. Dusk had fallen. The room was lit by huge smoking candles set in tall golden candlesticks. Dimly visible in the gloom of an alcove was an ancient scroll bearing a poem brushed with exquisite skill.

The *tayu* had disappeared. Two child attendants – *kamuro* – appeared in red kimonos, their chubby faces painted white, their lower lips cherry red. With a rustle of silk and a tinkling of the bells which hung from their sleeves they settled themselves gravely on their knees. The candles sputtered and smoked. The guests waited expectantly.

Then the *tayu* appeared, framed in the doorway like a visitation from another age. She was transformed, she was a shamaness. Aloof, withdrawn, self-contained, she did not speak, smile or glance at the guests. She was to be looked at, not to look. As she swept gracefully into the room, deftly swinging the heavy quilted train of the kimono, more layers became visible, rippling at the sleeve and hem.

Solemnly she knelt between the children, lifted a shallow red-lacquered bowl brimming with saké and put it to her lips. Then, having served bowls of foamy green tea which the *kamuro* passed around to the guests, she picked up a *kokyu*, an instrument shaped like a small shamisen with a square base and long narrow neck, and rested it on her knees. Taking a bow strung so loosely that it looked as if it could not possibly produce any sound, she scraped it across the strings to coax out a thin scratchy melody, turning the instrument so that the bow touched each of the three strings. It was an extraordinary, archaic sound. It lifted the hairs on the back of your neck and took you back across the centuries to a time when, one could imagine, rakes and dandies dissipated fortunes in places such as this. Lastly, rising to her feet, she danced, mesmerisingly slow and stately, while the guests and I, sitting in the shadows, watched, entranced.

But the most unforgettable thing was that under the layers and layers of brocade and silk, her tiny feet were bare. It was the most erotic sight, it sent a shiver up the spine. They peeked from beneath the heavy finery, the only reminder that underneath the painted face, the priceless head-dress, the three layers of under-kimono and four layers of over-kimono, there was a real woman. It must have been even more poignant in the old days, if anyone then ever stopped to think about it. For in those days, for all their sumptuous finery, their robes embroidered with gorgeous landscapes and their velvet and damask bedding, the courtesans did not own their own bodies. They were chattels, to be bought and sold.

Renaissance in Japan

Had you arrived in Kyoto at the turn of the seventeenth century, you would have found yourself swept along with the mob to the sprawling entertainment district beside the River Kamo, stretching as far as the massive red gates of Yasaka Shrine at the foot of the Eastern Hills. One of the chief attractions was the burgeoning pleasure quarters packed with teahouses and taverns where women – who a century later would become known as geisha – sold tea or saké and might, for a consideration, entertain you with singing, dancing or more, depending on the depth of your purse. Here and there on open-air stages, under wooden roofs, were groups of women performing lively dances to the plink plonk of the shamisen or the tootle of the flute while their audiences lounged on red felt rugs or low platforms, tucking into picnics.

Kyoto was the official capital of the country and, along with the bustling mercantile city of Osaka, the centre of commerce and culture. Artists of the time painted people in festive robes dancing through the streets between red-painted temples and tile-roofed wooden houses, and crowding to see performances of dance, music and drumming. Outside the wattle fencing surrounding the stages were stalls selling food. Inside, women in rich kimonos, men with wicker hats or samurai swords, even a couple of Portuguese with big collars, bulbous noses and tall hats, stood watching the shows.

You could gawk at puppets, wrestling, jugglers or sword swallowers, laugh at the clowns and jesters, admire the rare animals in cages, try your skill at target practice, shoot darts in the blowpipe parlour, or while away the day in singing and dancing. There you would have felt sorely tempted to fritter away the rest of your life in fun. There was everything a person could want, enough to distract and delight him for the rest of his days. It was an entertainment mecca, a non-stop medieval carnival such as Chaucer might have enjoyed.

After more than 400 years of warfare and upheaval, there was peace again such as had not been seen since the halcyon days of the decadent Heian aristocrats. Japan had changed beyond all recognition. As the medieval knights – the samurai – fought their bloody civil wars, Kyoto had been burnt to ashes time and time again. Now all that was over. The country was unified and the people could turn their attention to becoming prosperous and developing the arts of peace. It was the beginning of an extraordinary renaissance.

The man who brought all this about was the great general Ieyasu Tokugawa who defeated the last of his rival warlords in the Battle of Sekigahara in October 1600 and declared himself shogun and ruler of all Japan in the emperor's name. He chose the little fishing village of Edo, an area of marshland and rivers where he had established his castle a decade earlier, as the seat of his military administration and it gradually grew in size and importance. Eventually it was to become the great city of Tokyo.

Determined that the country would never again descend into civil war, Tokugawa and his successors set about fencing in the population with rigid systems of control. Among other measures, they sealed off the country from the outside world to ensure that no subversive ideas entered to disturb the delicate balance. Foreigners and in particular Catholics were not allowed in and Japanese were not allowed to leave. Anyone breaking these rules was liable to execution. Only one small window was left open – the remote southern port of Nagasaki where Chinese junks brought their goods and a few Protestant Dutch merchants were allowed to trade. For the next two and a half centuries the Japanese were to develop a unique culture and lifestyle, largely free from outside influences.

To create a well-ordered society in which there would be no room for the slightest possibility of rebellion or upheaval, the shogunate adopted neo-Confucianism, as expounded by the twelfth-century Chinese philosopher Chu Hsi, as the state philosophy. Confucianism, with its rigid codes of behaviour and emphasis on hierarchy and respect for authority, had coloured Japanese society for centuries, alongside the austere beliefs of Buddhism and the joyous life-affirming practices of Shinto. Under the House of Tokugawa it became the official basis of government and the underlying ethical code for all levels of society. The system remained in force throughout the Tokugawa period after which in theory it began to change. But many of the attitudes which it engendered remain in place to this day.

Society was divided into rigid classes, with a different set of laws governing each. Sumptuary laws were issued decreeing what each class could and could not wear, what they should eat, how they should wear their hair, where they could and could not live, whom they could marry and how they should decorate their houses.

At the top of the hierarchy were the daimyo, provincial princes who governed their own domains but had to pledge fealty to the shogun. Then came the samurai, the military class who had grown in numbers mightily during the years of warfare and were now to be the army, police and administrators of the new system. They lived in garrisons, received a stipend and were allowed to carry two swords. They were also – in theory, at least – permitted to test their razor-sharp blades on the necks of any members of the lower orders who displeased them.

Below the samurai came the farmers, who ranked high because they were responsible for producing the rice by which everyone lived, though in fact they had miserable lives. They were followed by the artisans who were also producers: they were craftsmen and builders. Right at the bottom were tradesmen and merchants who, so the argument went, produced nothing. They just passed goods around from the producers to everyone else, skimming off a profit along the way, and were thus considered worthless parasites. In reality, of course, they were absolutely essential to the life of the country, ensuring that goods were shuttled from the provinces, where they were produced, to be sold in the cities.

In practice the main division was between the samurai and the rest, lumped together as 'townsmen'. But the trouble with relegating merchants to the very bottom was that the samurai desperately needed and wanted the goods which the merchants sold and quickly spent their miserable stipends on them. Over the centuries their stipends never increased at all; they were rigidly prescribed. So the merchants started lending money, first to the samurai, then the daimyos and eventually to the shogun himself and thus became richer and richer.

Thanks to the peace which the shogunate had brought about, the country was quickly becoming prosperous. An end of warfare meant that all hands could be turned to production, developing arts, crafts and trade. Just as in the years after the Second World War, there was a population boom. More and more people meant that there was more and more food being produced and also an explosion of culture. Seeking a share of the growing pool of wealth, people flocked to the rapidly expanding cities.

The people who benefited the most from all this were the merchants. But no matter how rich they became, they were prohibited from using their wealth to improve their status by, for example, marrying into a samurai family or moving into the samurai section of town. And the wealthier they became, the more likely it was that the government would confiscate everything they had. Merchants did not pay taxes, as that would have given them rights; instead, every now and then, the shogunate found a pretext to confiscate their riches. Therefore it made ample sense to squander as much of one's money as possible, as quickly as possible, on pleasure.

There were a couple of classes so low that they did not even feature in the Tokugawa ranking system. One encompassed popular entertainers – everyone from roving minstrels, musicians, itinerant prostitutes, jugglers, jesters, dancers, tea-serving wenches, saké servers and grand courtesans to actors. They were all lumped together under the term *kawaramono* – riverbed folk – and (unless, like the courtesans, they were lucky enough to have a patron) they lived in ghettos in the dry riverbeds and along the banks, frontier areas of the city which were outside government control, considered unsuitable for permanent habitation because of flooding. Lowest of all were the *hinin* (non-humans), most of whom were beggars or did the work that no one else wanted to do.

One of the most urgent tasks for the new shogunate was to clamp down on vice, which had increased enormously over the years of civil war. Kyoto had become a centre of prostitution, with women who had lost their menfolk, itinerant nuns and unemployed shrine maidens wandering the streets. There were also thousands of prostitutes servicing travellers along the rivers and roads, at ports and in front of shrines and temples where pilgrims gathered. The problem came to a head not long after Ieyasu Tokugawa established peace.

The Lusty Lady of Izumo

The cause of all the trouble was a woman named Izumo no Okuni ('Okuni of Izumo'). Around 1603, when peace had barely been established, she set up an open-air stage in the dry riverbed of the Kamo and, with her troupe of wandering female entertainers, began to dance. Those who saw her were electrified. The populace, who had suffered two centuries of civil war, was hungry for pleasure, diversion and beautiful women in silk kimonos. It was from Okuni and her dance that the geisha, with their irresistible combination of charm, entertainment and eroticism, were to develop.

As word spread, crowds descended on the riverbed to watch Okuni perform. Artists of the time portrayed her dancing wildly, accompanied by singers, a flute-player and people beating hand drums before an eager audience of top-knotted samurai and robed women and children, sheltered by huge red parasols, with the groundlings jam-packed in front of the stage.

Okuni claimed to be a shrine maiden and shamaness from the Grand Shrine at Izumo (from where she took her name) though this may have just been an invention to give her an air of mystery. She was, in any case, a dazzling dancer and by definition a prostitute; in those days, the two were one and the same.

Some of her dances were adapted from ancient folk dances, such as the Buddhist prayer dance, for which she dressed in priest's robes, sporting a conical black hat and baggy black trousers and carrying a bell which she struck with a small hammer. Sometimes she dressed as a Shinto priest and at other times she mimicked a Christian one, wearing a large golden rosary.

But the most thrilling part of her show was when she played a man. Audiences cheered, applauded and roared with laughter when she sauntered out wearing brocade trousers and an animal skin jacket. With a painted moustache like a dashing young man about town, she would mime chatting up a teahouse woman, wooing a courtesan or having an assignation in a bath-house. Okuni's dancing was not just brilliant but cheerfully erotic. It was so extraordinary that a new word had to be coined: *kabuki*, from the verb *kabuku*, meaning 'to frolic' or 'to be wild and outrageous'. Okuni's sexy dancing was the seed of the kabuki theatre and also of the floating world of the courtesans and geisha.

Okuni's fame spread all over the country. In 1607 she and her all-women troupe went on tour to Edo and gave a public performance at the shogun's castle there. Soon there were imitators – troupes of prostitutes and courtesans performing erotic dances and bedroom farces throughout the great cities. It was showbiz; the actresses were stars. But, while the court ladies and townswomen imitated their stylish ways, men were more interested in their bodies. A contemporary wrote, 'Men threw away their wealth, some forgot their fathers and mothers, others did not care if the mothers of their children were jealous . . .'

There was nothing wrong with eroticism. But the shogunate could not risk anything that threatened public order. When men started fighting over the actresses, it was time to put a stop to it. In 1628, after a major brawl, the authorities banned women from performing in public. It was a law that was extremely difficult to enforce. It had to be passed again in 1629, 1630, 1640, 1645, 1646 and 1647. Finally the manager of the last offending theatre was thrown into prison and women disappeared from the public stage, not to reappear for another 250 years.

Banned from public performance, some of the women dancers took up work as prostitutes, licensed or unlicensed. Others found positions in samurai households where they gave private performances or set themselves up as teachers of music and dance. These were the sort of women who a century later were to become known as 'geisha'.[2]

The authorities had banned women's kabuki. But they had said nothing about kabuki performed by young men, which now became hugely popular. The young men incorporated acrobatics and juggling into their kabuki and the most beautiful took on female roles.

But, alas for the efforts of the authorities, these beautiful young men too were prostitutes. Those who played women dressed the part off stage as well as on. They lived in little shacks near the river banks, notably in the area of Kyoto called Miyagawa-cho, now one of the geisha districts, and used their performances to attract customers. Most of them were under fifteen, the age of adulthood, which probably made them all the more attractive.

For Buddhist priests who had abjured the company of women it was perfectly acceptable thus to work off their frustrations with a clean conscience. The youths also appealed to samurai, among whom homosexuality was considered the purest form of love. In any case, in this society – free of Christianity's guilt-inducing notions of sin – love was simply love. Homosexual and heterosexual love were seen as different sides of the same coin. Both, as far as the authorities were concerned, were equally liable to lead to public disorder. Eventually in 1652, after the death of a shogun who had himself been partial to young men, this variety of kabuki was also banned and replaced by kabuki played by adult males, as it is today. Thereafter kabuki and the women's world of courtesans and geisha together made up the heart of the demi-monde.

Home Life

Ironically the geisha and the whole culture of eroticism arose out of the rigid strictures of Confucianism; the walled cities of pleasure which were to become the heart of the counter-culture in Japan were created with whole-hearted government approval. Like everything else in the highly regulated Confucian society of seventeenth-century Japan, prostitution needed to be organised. The best way to manage it was to control it, to herd as many prostitutes as possible into one place and to make prostitution legal there but illegal anywhere else. Along with the kabuki theatre, the pleasure quarters were classified as the 'bad places' where the lower orders, and anyone else who wanted to, could go to let off steam and exercise their baser instincts. But, 'bad' though they were, they fulfilled a recognised need.

Confucianism required unquestioning obedience to authority. Within the state, this was the shogun, acting in the name of the emperor. Within the household, it was the father, who was to be accorded as much loyalty and respect as one would give the ruler of the country. The basic unit of society was not the individual but the family, which was to be preserved and protected at all costs. A woman was expected to obey her father, then, after she was married, her husband, and finally, if her husband predeceased her, her son.

Marriage was nothing to do with love. It was a political matter, an alliance between families which was arranged by the head of the household with the help of a go-between. It was far too important to be left to the will of the individuals concerned. A woman married into the household. She became a *yome*, which means 'daughter-in-law' as well as 'bride', and moved into her husband's house with her in-laws where she was more like a glorified domestic servant than the usual concept of a wife.

The function of conjugal sex was to produce a male heir who would ensure the continuance of the family line and carry out the ritual respects due to the ancestors. Apart from that, sexual gratification was not supposed to take place within marriage. In other words, you were not supposed to love your wife, enjoy sex with her or give her sexual pleasure. That was the

51

theory; though in reality many a Japanese mother provided her daughter with a 'pillow book' of sexual techniques to try and lure her husband away from the sirens of the pleasure quarters and the manifold other temptations available to him.

Just so long as a man did his duty by his family, supported it financially and produced an heir, he was at liberty to amuse himself in any way he pleased. As François Caron, who was in Japan with the Dutch East India Company in 1639, observed, 'One Man hath but one Wife, though as many Concubines as he can keep; and if that Wife do not please him, he may put her away, provided he dismiss her in a civil and honourable way. Any Man may lie with a Whore, or common Woman, although he be married, with impunitie; but the Wife may not so much as speak in private with another Man, without hazarding her life.'[3]

Besides enjoying oneself with the wife and concubines, there was no disgrace in visiting the 'bad places'. The options, of course, were not limited to the pleasure quarters or the female sex. In fact, a man who chose to stay home with his wife and children would have seemed a bit of a wet-blanket goody goody, probably tight-fisted and certainly far from a stylish man-about-town.

The Shimabara Pleasure Quarter

The viceroy told me that in the City of Miyako [Kyoto] alone there were 5000 temples of their gods, as well as many hermitages. He also said there were some 50,000 registered public women, placed by the authorities in special districts.

Relacion y noticias del reino del Japan, Rodrigo de Vivero y Velasco (1564–1636, shipwrecked off the coast of Japan in 1609)

Japan's first pleasure quarter opened in Kyoto even before Ieyasu Tokugawa's great victory of 1600. In 1589, when Tokugawa's predecessor, the enlightened warlord Hideyoshi Toyotomi, was governing the country from his castle in Osaka, one of his favourites, a stable hand called Saburoemon Hara, asked permission to open a brothel. Hideyoshi granted him a licence and he built a small walled-in quarter with a single gate, not far on foot, horseback or by palanquin from the emperor's palace. He called it Yanagimachi (Willow Town). There he set up brothels and teahouses and installed some high-class, educated courtesans to lure the sophisticated gentlemen of Kyoto.

It was an immediate success. Hideyoshi himself used to sneak in, in disguise, with his retainers. It was, however, altogether too close to the imperial palace for propriety and in 1602 was moved to a site further south. In 1641 the quarter was finally established a decent distance from the centre of the city where it would not corrupt upstanding citizens. It was named Shimabara after the 1638 uprising of Christians in a place of that name, perhaps because it was as noisy and rambunctious as that revolt or because its massive wooden tile-roofed entrance gate was as imposing as the Great Gate of Shimabara Castle. Thereafter business continued until it burnt down in 1854. But it reached the apogee of its prosperity and fame in the seventeenth and early eighteenth centuries.

This was the height of the Japanese Renaissance, the glittering Genroku period. By then, money-lenders and merchants had built up stupendous fortunes. Samurai, trying to subsist on their stipends, were forbidden to get a job; not only was there no upward mobility, there was no downward mobility either. There was nothing they could do but borrow from the money-lenders, who got richer and richer. Every now and then edicts were issued forbidding merchants from, for example, wearing silk, living in a three-storey house, decorating their rooms with gold and silver leaf or furnishing them with gold lacquer objects; edicts had to be issued, of course, because that was precisely what they were doing. Initially these supposedly low-class townsmen lavished their money on luxuries, filling their storehouses with fabulously expensive gold screens, ceramics, lacquerware, tea bowls, books, prints and sumptuous kimonos. All this big spending further stimulated the economy by providing a market for the artisans.

Engelbert Kaempfer (1651–1716), who visited Kyoto in this period, wrote of it:

This city serves as the storehouse of all Japanese workmanship and trade . . . It is here where they refine copper, mint coins, print books, weave the most wonderful materials with gold and silver flowers, have the rarest dye works, and produce fine carving, musical instruments, paintings, lacquered cupboards and other utensils, the most meticulous working of gold and of a variety of metals, especially the best steel, and from it the rarest blades and other weapons. It is here where one finds the prettiest clothing, all sorts of fashionable accessories; artificially moving dolls and toys are also made here.[4]

But too much showy spending by these unimaginably wealthy merchants risked confiscation. One of the most famous plutocrats, whose outrageous spending gave the pleasure quarters much of their lustre, ended up losing everything. His name was Saburoemon Yodoya of the House of Yodoya, a great Osaka business dynasty. At the height of his fortune, he had amassed an incredible amount of wealth which he invested in, for example, 21 solid gold hens with 10 chickens, 14 solid gold macaws, 15 solid gold sparrows, more than 700 swords, 480 carpets, a solid gold chess board 3 inches thick, countless hoards of money and precious stones and 250 farms with 1500 tenants.[5]

By 1705 the daimyo warlords were in debt to Yodoya to the tune of 100,000,000 gold nuggets (several billion pounds or dollars in today's currency and several times the total national income of Japan at the time). The shogun peremptorily cancelled these debts and confiscated all Yodoya's property for good measure, declaring that it exceeded the limits proper to a townsman. Overnight Yodoya fell from unimaginable riches to the depths of poverty. No wonder the merchants made a point of spending their money as quickly as possible in the pleasure quarters and turned the notion of transience into a romantic cult.

By the Genroku period the Shimabara pleasure quarter was a splendid place the size of a small village. Surrounded by high earthen walls topped with shiny silver-grey tiles, set in the middle of pastureland with a canal running through the middle, from the outside it looked a little like a fortress or a jail. But inside it was filled with street upon street of elegant, palatial buildings.

Two of these buildings remain to give a flavour of the era. Wachigaiya, owned by the Takahashi family, is just inside the massive gate with its overhanging willow tree. Sumiya, a couple of blocks away, was built half a century later in 1781 and is the premier example of teahouse architecture in Japan.

By then, the merchant class had developed an aesthetic of understatement. The sophisticated man-about-town would wear a rather plain coat-like garment over his kimono; but every now and then one would catch a glimpse of the glittering gold-thread lining. That was the height of chic at that time.

From the outside Sumiya was like a grand merchant's house, large but not too splendid; but the severe exterior of a building belied the sumptuousness that lay within. There were walls covered in lustrous gold leaf, elaborately carved transoms between the rooms, beautiful screen paintings and delicate fretwork on the wooden window screens. Each room had a theme. In the Fan Room the ceiling was gold and decorated with paintings of fans, the metal door handles and window screens were fan-shaped, and the door panels were painted with scenes from *The Tale of Genji*. At one end was a stage where musicians played the shamisen and sang. There was also an exquisite room in the Chinese style with delicate mother-of-pearl landscapes inlaid in the black-lacquered walls and ceiling. Outside was a garden of rocks, raked sand and clipped pine trees with a tea ceremony hut in one corner.

Something had gone badly wrong in the shoguns' plans. The idea had been to sweep vice under the carpet, to restrict the perpetrators of vice – the prostitutes and the kabuki actors, their companions in sin – to specific areas of the capital and thus control both them and their vulgar customers, the nouveau-riche merchants. But instead the pleasure quarters rapidly turned into the most glamorous part of town. Everyone from samurai to the imperial princes and even the emperor himself sneaked off for surreptitious visits.

As well as sex, romance and sensual pleasure, Shimabara offered all that a sophisticated man-about-town might demand: elegance, culture and brilliant conversation with beautiful women in an atmosphere of refinement. It was a place where merchants could entertain clients and show off their glamorous connections, basking in the company of these not-quite-reputable stars. As for what happened afterwards, that was practically irrelevant. The show was the thing.

In 1661 a writer called Ryoi Asai coined a word for this new way of living: ukiyo (the floating world) from which came the term ukiyo-e (pictures of the floating world) for the woodblock prints which depicted the courtesans, prostitutes and later geisha who were its denizens. In the past, the word ukiyo had been a Buddhist term, referring to the transience of all things. In Ryoi's Tales of the Floating World, it took on a new slant. Life was indeed transient; so what better way to spend one's time than in the pursuit of pleasure, like a gourd bobbing lightly along the stream of life!

For men it was a topsy-turvy world of pleasure which was the reverse in every way from the world of work and family outside its gates. Even the layout of Shimabara was the opposite of the proper city layout, as determined by feng shui (the Chinese science of topography). In the city of Kyoto, the top people lived in the north of the city, where the emperor lived; while downtown was in the south. But in Shimabara, downtown was in the north and uptown in the south. Every convention, every rule, was turned on its head. There, it was said, a man would forget what time of day it was, what period of history and even his own wife. There the outcast courtesans and prostitutes could play at being queens and the low-grade merchants kings. As for the samurai, who were supposedly at the top of the tree, they were dismissed as bumpkins.

For the women, however, it was no dream. It was where they lived and worked. Even if they wanted to leave, their wings were clipped. Gorgeous though they were, the inhabitants of the pleasure quarters were caged birds. They had been brought to the quarter as small children and had grown up entirely in this hothouse world of women. They knew nothing else. For all their finery and glamour, they were virtual slaves, indentured to the brothel owners.

Almost all were from the lower classes, the beautiful children of impoverished rural families or debt-ridden townsfolk. There were professional procurers – pimps – who scoured the countryside and poorer sections of the city. When they found a suitable child, they would offer the parents a set sum of money. Buying or selling of persons was illegal so the child would be bound with a contract for a fixed period of time, usually ten years.

For the parents, sending a child off to the pleasure quarters was nothing out of the ordinary; it is still done to this day in Asia. Apart from the much-needed money and the brutal necessity of reducing the number of mouths to be fed, they probably felt they were giving their daughter a chance in life. Going to Kyoto to eat fine food, wear fine clothes, meet fine people and be educated offered far more hope than staying in the countryside hoeing the soil for the rest of her life. As for the child, according to the Confucian code it was her filial duty to put the well-being of her family ahead of her own. Girls who were sold to the pleasure quarters were considered virtuous and admirable for having sacrificed themselves for their family.

Most were recruited when they were six or seven and had only the haziest memories of life outside the walls of the pleasure quarter. While peasants were lucky if they had millet, the children in Shimabara ate white rice, wore beautiful kimonos and learnt to walk, talk and comport themselves in the exaggeratedly feminine style of the quarter. Shimabara had its own dialect, as did the other pleasure quarters, with distinctive slang that was charmingly polite yet playfully seductive. Any child who managed to escape could thus be immediately identified by the way she spoke and sent back again. For visitors it made the pleasure quarters feel all the more like a dream world, an exotic foreign land.

The children were the property of the brothel owner. Before they even arrived, they had already incurred an enormous debt: the outlay involved in buying them from their parents. Their food and kimono were provided by the brothel; but every grain of rice and every bolt of silk only served to increase the burden of debt. By the time they were old enough to start working, their debt was so huge that they had no choice but to work day and night in a desperate attempt to repay it.

Initially the children worked as maids. When they were older, if they showed promise they became *kamuro* (child attendants to a courtesan). The courtesan taught them how to behave and ensured that they were trained in accomplishments such as calligraphy, tea ceremony and music. There were many little secrets to be absorbed: how to lure men, how to wind them around their little fingers with tears or protestations of undying love, how to write love letters, how to hold men off long enough to drive them mad with desire, how to pleasure them in the bedchamber and how to fake an orgasm while conserving one's energy for the next customer. The key rule was to play at love but never, never to allow oneself to feel it. That way lay disaster.

At thirteen or fourteen, when the child reached sexual maturity, there was a grand celebration accompanied by a rite of passage which the girl had to accept with gritted teeth – *mizuage*, ritual deflowerment, conducted by a patron who had paid mightily for the privilege. If she was uncommonly lovely she might be designated a *koshi*, the second rank of courtesan, though there were many that slipped through the net and ended up as lower-grade prostitutes, sitting patiently behind the latticed windows of the teahouses waiting to be picked out by a customer.

At the very pinnacle of the hierarchy of prostitutes and courtesans were the *tayu*. If a man wanted to enjoy the company of one, the first step was to go to an *ageya*, a house of assignation (the precursor of the teahouses of the geisha districts) to apply for a meeting. If he was a sophisticate, he would ask for one of the *tayu* by name; some were so popular that it might take months before a day became free in their calendar. The owner of the *ageya* would write a letter to the bordello where the courtesan lived, roll it up and give it to a messenger. While the customer was waiting, he would enjoy the services of jesters and dancing girls and ply them with food and drink, all of which, of course, would be added to his bill.

Hours later, the *tayu* would sweep in, dressed in layer upon layer of gorgeous kimonos and accompanied by a flotilla of child attendants and dancing girls, having progressed at snail's pace along the boulevard with her entourage. They would while away the evening playing music, dancing, exchanging poems, enjoying tea ceremony and incense ceremony – exactly as if they were ladies and gentlemen of the Heian court. Sex did not automatically follow. After all, it would lower the courtesan's worth if she were too easily available. A proprietor who owned a beautiful *tayu* would want to increase the value of his or her investment by making her as exclusive as possible.

If the man wanted to spend the night with the courtesan, he would have to engage in a long and very expensive courtship. The earliest that one could hope to experience her luxurious silk bedding was at the third visit. And even then, if the *tayu* was not satisfied with the man's performance, she could decline to sleep with him. If she did agree to spend the night with him, the cost was 90 silver nuggets (*momme*) which equalled 1½ gold nuggets (*ryo*), in modern currency about £420.[6] It was costly but, for a wealthy man, the only sort of person whom a *tayu* would consider, hardly prohibitive.

The *koshi*, the second-rank courtesans, charged 60 silver nuggets, and the *sancha* (teahouse waitresses-cum-courtesans) charged 30. At the Shimabara even the lowest class of prostitutes, the *hashi*, whom one could buy for just 1 silver nugget, were said to be elegant.

But no matter how famous the courtesans became, they were still slaves of debt, constrained to work out their ten-year contract. In fact the system ensured that, no matter how hard they worked, their debts only increased. There were always new costs being incurred – the purchasing of the splendid kimonos necessary to carry on their trade, the costs of bedding and of clothing and supporting their retinue of retainers, the tips that had to be paid to the bordello staff. They had just three days off a year. If they missed a day's work for any reason at all they had to pay the bordello the sum they would have earned, out of their own pocket. Most carried on working until they were twenty-seven, the usual retirement age. Those who were successful would have plenty of supplicants begging to marry them after that.

They probably accepted the hardships with stoicism. That was the way it was in the floating world and, in any case, any other life would have had its hardships too. Within the narrow confines of their gilded cage they were queens. The one chance of escape – if they wanted it – was to find someone prepared to buy out their contract and make them his wife or mistress. As the old saying went, the courtesan's favourite lie was 'I love you', the customer's 'I will marry you'.

The names and rankings changed over the centuries but everyone agreed that the greatest courtesans of all time were the *tayu* of seventeenth-century Shimabara. *Tayu* were also known as *keisei* (castle topplers) because, it was said, they could overthrow a castle with a single flutter of their eyelashes or, like Helen of Troy, bring an entire kingdom to ruin. Their looks fitted the canons of beauty of the day and they were accomplished and gracious paragons of every virtue (except, of course, chastity). They were superstars, celebrated in woodblock prints and written about endlessly in guidebooks to the pleasure quarters. The most famous of all the castle-toppling courtesans was the peerless Yoshino.

The Tale of Yoshino

In the early days of the Shimabara quarter, there were seven celebrated *tayu* courtesans in Kyoto. Of these, Yoshino was the most adored. To this day, people still go to pay their respects at her grave on the anniversary of her death. Like the geisha who were to follow, Yoshino exemplified an ideal of womanhood of her day. She was a star, one of the few women in this rigid Confucian society who could rule over men. Her story also illustrates the ambivalence with which such women were regarded. They were both hugely desirable yet not at all respectable, an edge which made them all the more irresistible.

Yoshino was, of course, incomparably beautiful. No descriptions survive but we can imagine that she had the melon-seed-shaped face of the ideal beauty of the day, with large eyes, startlingly black pupils and eyebrows close together. Her hair, like Ono no Komachi's, was a glossy black curtain that swept the floor, loosely tied with a ribbon; courtesans had not yet started wearing their hair in the elaborate coiffures of later years. Her fingers and toes tapered delicately, her waist was tiny and her legs were long and slender. She was refined, cultured and endlessly fascinating, able to charm the city's wealthiest millionaires into emptying their purses for a few precious moments in her company. But the quality that made her truly legendary – and that appears again and again in the tales of the great courtesans – was her humanity.

Many legends have gathered around her, not least that she was the lover of Miyamoto Musashi, the greatest swordsman of all time and author of *The Book of Five Rings* (a Bible for practitioners of the martial arts and more recently for businessmen). He learnt his secrets, so the story goes, from the gentle but insightful Yoshino.

Yoshino was entertaining him and his friends in the pleasure quarter one snowy night when he slipped quietly out of the room. She was the only one to notice him leave. He returned a few minutes later. But there was a splash of red on the hem of his kimono.

'What is that?' asked one of his friends.

'Just a peony petal,' said Yoshino and quickly wiped it away with a napkin.

When the party came to an end, she suggested lightly that he had better stay there with her. With her unerring instinct she had guessed that he had been engaged in a duel to the death in the few minutes he had been away. The retainers of the two men whom he had killed, several dozen of them, were waiting right outside to ambush him and exact revenge.

Sitting in her chamber he was silent, tense in anticipation of the hopeless battle that lay ahead. Suddenly Yoshino picked up her *biwa*, a priceless lute, took a knife and smashed the curved sound box to pieces. From the ruined instrument she picked out the cross-piece, a single piece of wood, and showed it to him.

This, she explained, was the heart of the instrument; all the sound came from this. If the cross-piece were as taut and unyielding as he was at that moment, a single stroke of the plectrum would break it. But if he could be as flexible and responsive as it was, no one could defeat him. Inspired by her words, he bounded out into the snow and, with a few nonchalant slashes of his sword, decimated the dozens of men gathered outside. For the rest of his sword-wielding career, he never forgot her or her advice.

The historical Yoshino was born on the third day of the third month 1606, just three years after Izumo no Okuni had thrilled the populace with her erotic dancing. Her father was a *ronin*, a masterless samurai from the southern island of Kyushu, who died when she was very young. She was sold to the pleasure quarters at the age of six and at fourteen was so beautiful and accomplished that she was promoted to the rank of *tayu*, a rare and extraordinary honour. By now, following in Okuni's footsteps, courtesans from the pleasure quarters were performing kabuki and dancing on stages around the city. Yoshino became one of the most celebrated.

So famous and so hugely desired was she that she had no need ever to bestow her favours on anyone. Her wealthy and adoring patrons made sure that her income was high enough to be able to pay all her annual expenses in advance. But no matter how much they paid her, she kept them at a distance, hopelessly yearning for her. If they were not the equivalent of Narihira, the great lover – if they were not refined, sophisticated, handsome, witty and able to turn a stylish poem at the drop of a very expensive hat – she would not look twice at them.

Samples of her calligraphy, still extant, show that she had a beautiful hand. Her loveliness and talents were celebrated as far away as China. One Ming courtier dreamt that he had met her and was so enthralled that he sent her a poem which ends with the romantic lines:

> Longing for a glimpse of such beauty,
> I gaze eastward as the geese fly across the sea.[7]

A year later a request arrived from the Chinese court for a portrait of her. Her patrons had one painted and sent via Chinese merchants in Nagasaki. The court, apparently, was well pleased.

Yoshino had been called to entertain at a gathering of Kyoto's most influential literary coterie, presided over by the emperor's fourth son, when she met Joeki Haiya, a merchant's son. Not only was he handsome, refined and accomplished enough to satisfy the most demanding courtesan, he was an adept of the tea ceremony which he hosted with wonderful finesse. Born into a family of indigo dye merchants, he was also extremely rich. He was younger than her by four years; at the time he was twenty-two, she twenty-six. He fell hopelessly in love, so much so that he laid out the enormous fortune necessary to buy out her contract for – beautiful, accomplished and celebrated though she was – she was still the property of the bordello keeper. Having bought her freedom, he married her.

Thus far is history. The rest may or may not be legend. Joeki's adoptive father, goes the story, was furious that the boy had brought the family into disrepute and disowned him. After all, Yoshino might be a superstar but until she married she had been a glorified prostitute who made her living by selling her body. Reduced to poverty, the love birds retired to a humble house on the outskirts of Kyoto. Joeki began to sell off his much-loved collection of tea ceremony utensils to support them.

Then one day Joeki's father, far from home, was caught in a rainstorm and sought shelter under the eaves of an unprepossessing house. Through the window he heard a gentle, refined voice inviting him to rest inside. He walked across the stepping stones of a humble but perfectly arranged garden and into a house where everything, though poor, was of the most exquisite taste. On a wall was a single piece of calligraphy by the most accomplished master of the day.

The lady of the house appeared, dressed in a plain, humble kimono which could not dim her radiant beauty. Dignified and gracious, she knelt and performed a tea ceremony for him, whipping up a bowl of foaming green tea. On returning home he recounted the tale of his adventure to friends and discovered that this vision was none other than Yoshino. He summoned his son immediately, was reconciled with him and took the couple back into his family.

Yoshino died in 1643 at the age of thirty-eight (very young in modern terms but not so extraordinary in those days). Joeki grieved for her for the rest of his life. Without her, he declared, the magnificent city of Kyoto, with all its luxury and culture, was nothing but a desert.

The Nightless City

Closing time is midnight –
So why do I now hear
The wooden clappers
Strike out four times?

In Yoshiwara, even the
Wooden rhythm sticks are liars.
Geisha song[8]

Meanwhile over in the rough north-east of the country, in the shadow of the shogun's castle, a pleasure quarter was developing which would put all the others in the shade. This was where the culture of love was to be taken to its zenith and the geisha were to flower.

When Saburoemon Hara was petitioning to start a brothel in the great city of Kyoto, Edo was nothing but a few fishermen's shacks in a marshy area where three rivers met. But once Shogun Ieyasu established it as his capital it became a boomtown such as the world had never seen before. People flocked from all over the country to help in the building of the new city and make their fortunes. It was like a gold rush.

There was work for a multitude of architects, artists, labourers, craftsmen, artisans and builders in the enormous programme of landfill, waterworks and construction projects that the shogun initiated. Mansions, palaces, temples, shrines, shops, stalls and houses sprang up, while alleys, roads and a maze of canals that made the city an eastern Venice spiralled out from the walls of the shogun's castle to the newly reclaimed land beside the river. In 1500 Edo had a population of 1000; in the early 1600s it was an urban centre of 150,000. By the end of the seventeenth century it was the largest city in the world with a population of one million.

It was a man's city, a frontier town akin to those of America's wild west, with just as many bars, brothels and brawls. More than half the population were samurai, retainers of the daimyos (the ex-warlords who governed the provinces). This was a direct result of the shogun's policy of *sankin kotai* (alternate attendance), established in 1635, which required all the daimyos to maintain a mansion in Edo as well as their provincial seat. Every alternate year they had to make the arduous journey from one to the other, accompanied by hundreds of retainers, bannermen, halberd-bearers, soldiers and servants in a splendid procession which stretched along the roads for miles. The idea was to use up all their time and money so that they would have no chance to even think of organising a rebellion.

The daimyos' families lived permanently in Edo, effectively as hostages, together with a huge staff of vassal samurai. Most of the samurai were unmarried; they could not afford to support a family on their stipends. To add to this multitude of men there were thousands of merchants and tradesmen from Kyoto, Osaka and points west, who arrived to set up businesses and send money to their wives and children back home. As the great comic novelist Ihara Saikaku wrote towards the end of the century, it was 'a City of Bachelors'.

All these frustrated men provided fertile soil for prostitution. Among the flood of people hoping to make fortunes or at least stay afloat in the new city were a goodly number of harlots, not to mention procurers and brothel-keepers who came from all over the country. Even before anyone had been given a licence to open a pleasure quarter, professional brothel-keepers from Kyoto who had spotted an irresistible opportunity were erecting a red-light district with streets and beautiful wooden houses in a broad grassland dense with rushes near the coast. Just as in later years, when the geisha areas became cultural centres, the district offered far more than sex. There was also plentiful entertainment: kabuki, shrine dancing, temple dancing, the spider dance, the lion dance, wrestling, singing and twanging *joruri* music. 'How these conspiring courtesans allure men without resorting to force is beyond our comprehension,' wrote a commentator of the time disapprovingly.[9]

Following the initiative of Hara, who had founded Shimabara, a wealthy brothel-owner named Shoji Jinemon petitioned the shogun for a licence to establish an official pleasure quarter. Like Shimabara, the Yoshiwara was built, rebuilt, moved and burnt down in a fire before it was finally established in 1656 in a reed plain (*yoshi wara*) a decent hour's journey from the city.

By the end of the century it was far larger than the country's other famous pleasure quarters. Shimabara women were said to be the most beautiful; Shinmachi, where the playboy merchants of Osaka went to enjoy themselves, had the most sumptuous buildings and luxurious facilities; the women of Maruyama in Nagasaki wore the most gorgeous kimonos; but the Yoshiwara girls outdid them all with their *hari* ('attitude' or 'style'). At its height there were more than 3000 courtesans in the Yoshiwara, though only a few held the rank of *tayu*.

For the people of Edo, the Yoshiwara offered non-stop drama. The vast majority, who could never even dream of being able to afford an evening with a courtesan, could still follow their exploits in print. For the pleasure quarters together with the kabuki theatre were the heart of a cultural renaissance, both democratic and subversive, produced by, for and about the townsfolk and treated with great suspicion by the shogunate who made periodic attempts to clamp down on it. The courtesans and their clientele were the prime subject matter of woodblock prints, kabuki plays, and the courtesan critiques and *tayu* biographies which poured off the newly developed printing presses. Like the lives of the rich and famous today, they offered endless fascination and vicarious excitement.

The stories of the time are full of grand guignol – passion, love, debauchery, men ruined for love, suicides, deaths – and also of ribald humour. Like the great *tayu* of Kyoto, the courtesans of the Yoshiwara stood the usual customer/merchandise relationship on its head. They were at liberty to turn down any client, no matter how wealthy or aristocratic. Many of the sizzling stories of the day, much appreciated by the townsfolk, concern courtesans who rejected lovesick nobles and fell in love with handsome but low-born and impoverished clerks.

Much as the groundlings loved such bodice-ripping melodramas, the real lives of the courtesans tended to be a lot more down to earth. Besides the elegant, high-class courtesans of the official pleasure quarter, there were also many unlicensed and distinctly lower-class prostitutes operating illegally. In the mid-1600s, a few years before Takao's shooting star career, many of these were to be found in bath-houses. These were a little like the Turkish baths of today, with large reception areas where customers could lounge, drink tea and be entertained after bathing. As far as the Yoshiwara brothel-keepers were concerned, this was unwarranted competition. They frequently petitioned the shogunate to have it stamped out.

Katsuyama was a real-life prostitute who appeared at a bath-house called Tanzen in 1646. She was a beauty with a warm, open face and a cheeky, larger-than-life personality. But what the customers loved most was when she dressed up as a man. There had been nothing like it since Izumo no Okuni took to the stage dressed as a man back in 1603 and stunned the populace with her wild *kabuku* dancing. Wearing a wicker hat, man's kimono and two swords like a samurai, Katsuyama would bring the house down with the *Tanzen-bushi* dance, named after the bath-house, strutting and swaggering in jaunty macho fashion. Like all such dances, there was an erotic coda.

Katsuyama became so popular that she outshone all the *tayu* of the Yoshiwara. In 1653, after a brawl between a bunch of townsfolk and some rival samurai, the authorities closed down the bath-house. Katsuyama was head-hunted by one of the top Yoshiwara bordellos who gave her instant promotion to *tayu*. When she made her first grand procession down the main boulevard of the quarter to an assignation with a client, the great courtesans were so curious about this upstart that they all turned out to watch. They were so impressed with the cocky way in which she kicked out her feet in the 'figure of eight' walk and with her distinctive topknot that the 'Katsuyama gait' and the 'Katsuyama knot' continued to be in vogue for a century afterwards.

In his rollicking tales, the great novelist Ihara Saikaku (1642–1693) paints a vivid picture of the floating world. Born in Osaka, probably of a wealthy merchant family, he himself was exactly the kind of sophisticated, irreverent and flamboyantly talented man who frequented the pleasure quarters. He enjoyed flashy tours de force such as turning out record-breaking numbers of linked verse poems in a single day and took nothing very seriously, particularly the demi-monde. Despite the fact that his novels have inspired mountains of po-faced literary criticism, he probably dashed them off in order to earn a few silver nuggets and go back and enjoy himself again.

In his hilarious tale of a harlot's fall, *Life of an Amorous Woman* (1686),[10] he describes the ideal patron dressed in the height of fashion, fanning himself nonchalantly in the reception room, patting the sweat from his forehead with tissue paper, far too suave to pay any attention to the singing of the third-rank courtesans. He might turn to one of the *taikomochi* jesters and start talking with studied cool, casually dropping the names of top court officials and mentioning conversations he has had with them about classical poetry, so that everyone can see how cultured and well-connected he is. But even a character as suave as this would have had to follow the proper procedure before he could enjoy the favours of a courtesan; and she still might turn him down.

The whole thing was a game. Like any game, you had to play it to the best of your ability and you had to stick to the rules; but in the long run it was not to be taken too seriously. And whatever went on in the licentious night-time dreamworld of the Yoshiwara was always forgotten the next day. It never infected the world outside those enchanted walls. That tradition carried over into the world of the geisha. Mystery was of the essence.

It was all showbiz. But in the floating world, nothing could continue unchanged for long. By the eighteenth century, the pleasure quarter culture had been thriving for over a hundred years. The courtesans, with their stilted conversation and layer upon layer of starchy clothing, were beginning to seem a little passé. It was time for something new.

Gradually the number of women worthy to be designated *tayu* began to decline. The term itself, which had been used exclusively in Shimabara, disappeared as the focus of culture and life shifted to Edo. The last recorded *tayu* was in 1761. (The *tayu* of Wachigaiya, sadly, are not a continuation of the line but actresses, playing out a charade, a re-creation of a lost era.)

It was then that a new breed of woman first began to step out not just in the pleasure quarters but in the town: a woman who was not a caged bird, who dressed with understated sophistication, not showy glitter, and who sold not her body but her arts.

2

DRUM-BEARERS, TEA-BREWING WOMEN AND DANCING GIRLS

Wine and women
Balm for the soul,
This floating world is
Women and wine.
Geisha song[1]

Shichiko, the Male Geisha

The first time I met Shichiko he looked like a very conservative Japanese man. He wore the traditional outfit of baggy trousers and a cotton jacket, all in moss green, immaculately pressed, and carried a fan which he tapped prissily on the table whenever he wanted to make a point. But then I happened to glance at his feet. He was wearing *tabi*, toed linen socks which Japanese men traditionally wear indoors. *Tabi* are always white – except for Shichiko's. His were an intense shade of royal blue covered with dragonflies. And, despite all his attempts to look serious and solemn, a smile or even a laugh kept breaking out across his horsy jut-jawed face.

Shichiko had come to tell me about *taikomochi*, of which he was one. *Taikomochi*, he explained, were the first geisha – and they were men. They played the same music as the females, they danced and, instead of being up on stage like kabuki actors, they were down there chatting with the customers, in every way just like their female counterparts. But, historically, male geisha had been around long before.

The word *taikomochi* means drum-bearer, in reference to the small hand drum which some of them carried. Back in the seventeenth century, the pleasure quarters supported not only courtesans and prostitutes but an enormous population of brothel-keepers, owners of houses of assignation, cooks, maids, bouncers, cleaners and assorted hangers-on. The *taikomochi* were the party masters who kept the fun and games going. They were the ones for whom the term *gei-sha* ('artiste', 'entertainer' or, literally, 'arts person') was coined. Like court jesters, they sang, pranced and told jokes and stories. When a bunch of men went out drinking, they would call a *taikomochi* to entertain them. *Taikomochi* and saké went together.

Shichiko told me an old quip: 'Mess about with taikomochi and you'll end up a taikomochi yourself.'[2] If a rich man spent all his time with *taikomochi*, he explained, his business would go bankrupt and his wife would throw him out. In the end he would be totally ruined. There would be nothing for it but to become a *taikomochi* himself. In the old days, he added with a toothy grin, that's how a lot of men got to be *taikomochi*.

I asked him whether *taikomochi* were gay.

'Nah,' he said firmly. 'You want to have fun that way, you go to Shinjuku [Tokyo's famous gay district]. You don't mess about with taikomochi.'

This was a little disingenuous. Of course, no one ever talked about that sort of thing any more, but nevertheless, at least until the end of the war, it was understood that the selling of sexual favours was part of any traditional actor's job.

But *taikomochi* had almost died out. At present, Shichiko told me, there were only five or six left in the whole of Japan, working almost exclusively in Asakusa in Tokyo's East End, which was where I had met him. He himself had started life as an actor in contemporary Japanese theatre until one day he was asked to play a *taikomochi*. There and then he decided he wanted to know more. He was fortunate enough to be taken on as an apprentice by Yoneshichi, who had studied under one of the last great pre-war *taikomochi*.

Some weeks later I went to watch him perform. It was at one of the regular dance displays which geisha give; though, this being downtown Tokyo, the atmosphere was very different from a Kyoto dance meeting.

The room was crowded with elderly shop-owners and bigwigs, squashed together on cushions on the tatami floor. The plump, prosperous women wore matronly kimonos, while the men were in grey suits. Before the performance started, geisha fluttered among the audience, chatting and laughing. They had all clearly known each other for decades. In western terms it was a bit like a garden party at the local parish church.

By then I had seen many dance displays. The best, like this one, were in a small space where one could sit close to the stage, akin to the intimacy of a geisha party. The band – five old women on shamisen and five women singers – struck up and the geisha came out in ones, twos and threes to show off their skills. They performed dances of the seasons – spring, summer, autumn, winter – and miniature dramas. By now my eye was attuned to the subtle differences in performance – the soft, fluid, feminine style of the younger geisha, who had not been learning for long, and the crisp, defined movements of the star performers.

Then came intermission and out came a slender young man in a turquoise-coloured men's kimono. He was the warm-up act. The person everyone was waiting for was Shichiko.

He burst on stage in a maroon men's kimono, announcing, 'We're male geisha – but we don't wear white paint!' Then came a series of impersonations of, as he announced, Asakusa geisha. Balancing a folded scarf comically on his head to imitate a geisha's wig, he undulated along, pigeon-toed, eyes cast coyly down, then knelt in front of an imaginary mirror and mimed applying make-up, boasting in a fluting falsetto, 'I've got an important danna who takes care of me'. I had, I thought, worked out what *taikomochi* were all about. They were stand-up comics, doing mime and impersonations to the accompaniment of shamisen and song.

But then things began to go quite a bit further. In a corner of the stage was a large white folding screen.

'Gay? No, sir, not me,' said Shichiko, back in his own persona now, addressing an imaginary customer – *danna* – behind the screen. 'Absolutely not. I don't do that kind of thing. I've called a geisha for you. She'll be here any minute.'

By now he had advanced until he was half hidden behind the screen.

Suddenly there was a hand on his ear, grabbing at him, tugging him, while he struggled fiercely to escape. (It was, of course, *his* hand, though it looked as if it belonged to the fictitious *danna*.) Then a hand wrapped around his face, then his sleeve was tugged, then his kimono, until he was dragged out of sight behind the screen. He burst out again.

'Danna, wait,' he protested. 'Stop, stop! I'm not the geisha.'

Again he was dragged bodily behind the screen by the imaginary *danna*, again he escaped. Finally he groaned, in tones of exaggerated resignation, 'Okay, danna, okay. But just once, okay? From the back?' With that he pulled up his kimono skirts, revealing a pair of blue baggy trousers. He turned to look behind the screen, pointing derisively, scoffing, 'What's that? Is that all? Is that yours?'

Then he turned so that his rear end was concealed behind the screen and proceeded to mime being penetrated extremely realistically with yelps of pain, rolling his eyes in comic anguish. Finally he made great play of wiping himself clean with tissues, an essential conclusion to the sex act in Japan. He even gave the floor a swab.

I was utterly shocked. Given the conservative nature of the audience, this struck me as being way over the top. But I was the only one. No one else was shocked in the slightest. The shop-owners and their matronly wives laughed heartily and clapped enthusiastically as if it were a familiar everyday skit, skilfully carried out. The geisha returned to the stage for the second part of their performance. I later discovered that the 'gay sketch' is indeed a set piece and a standard part of the *taikomochi* repertoire (there are other, even more outrageous sketches) – a classic, in fact.

Later, when I met Shichiko again, I asked him about it. 'It's just a joke,' he said, impatient at my tedious western literal-mindedness. 'It's a symbol of how far we'll go to please our customers, if you like. We treat the customers like kings. Whatever they ask, we can't say No.' It was just a game, not real life; and in games anything goes.

The First Geisha

Right from the founding of the pleasure quarters, there were jesters prancing about, playing tricks, doing risqué sketches and singing ribald or melancholy songs to the accompaniment of the shamisen. They kept the mood upbeat and the jokes coming. The canny old brothel-keeper Shoji Jinemon, the founder of the Yoshiwara in the great city of Edo, was particularly fond of one of these talented young men and allowed him to wear his crest. He is said to have been the first to dub them *geisha*.

There were jesters of all levels of distinction, from serious musicians and accomplished dancers to *nodaiko* (talentless *taikomochi*), just hangers-on who boosted the numbers in a merchant's retinue so that he could appear important and lived off tips and scraps from his table. Talented or talentless, they were an important and popular feature of the quarters and their numbers increased steadily over the years.

The instrument that marked out the geisha, male or female, was the shamisen. A three-stringed banjo-like instrument, introduced from the tropical kingdom of Okinawa in the mid-sixteenth century, it was made of red sandalwood, mulberry or quince wood. Originally it was made with snake-skin stretched over the sound box. Snake-skin being hard to find in the colder climate of Japan, it was replaced with dog- or cat-skin which is used to this day. Traditionally the best shamisens are made from the immaculate soft white pelt of a young female virgin cat which has not yet been mounted and therefore scratched by a tomcat. Played with a large plectrum of wood or ivory, the instrument makes a melancholy sound, perfect to accompany plaintive love songs. The shamisen became the definitive instrument of the pleasure quarters; it was said that its sound could stir erotic yearnings where none had existed before.

Initially the courtesans, too, entertained with the shamisen. But after a while it became such a commonplace skill that the higher ranks began to leave it to the lower orders. Instead of entertaining their clients by singing and dancing, the top courtesans would sit regally in their sumptuous robes surrounded by their entourage of child attendants and junior courtesans. Male geisha and younger courtesans took over the job of performing. Around the end of the seventeenth century male geisha began to specialise. Musicians and dancers kept the name 'geisha', while clowns and professional fools were *taikomochi* or jesters.

Some of the jesters travelled around with troupes of dancing girls; some worked in teahouses, entertaining customers during the interminable wait

73

for the courtesan to arrive; and some joined the entourages of wealthy merchants. Some, like Shakespeare's fools, were the best friends of powerful men, dispensing advice and flattery along with songs and buffoonery. Others were distinctly tricky.

Ejima Kiseki (1667–1736) succeeded Saikaku as the most famous chronicler of the demi-monde of his day. Like Saikaku, he wrote from experience. The son of a wealthy Kyoto shopkeeper, his early years were a rake's progress through the pleasure quarters. Having squandered the family fortune on high living, he reluctantly took up writing. His novels, like *The Courtesans' Amorous Shamisen* and *Courtesans Forbidden to Lose their Tempers*,[3] were best-sellers, as acidic and entertaining as Saikaku's tales.

Male geisha often feature in his tales of life among the demi-monde. In one of his stories, the *taikomochi* reflect on the hardships of their life:

> We jesters have to drink when we'd rather not. We have to praise the tiresome little songs of our patrons, hear ourselves called fools by real blockheads, force a smile if we're offended and tell a roomful of people what even a woman would keep secret. No, there's nothing so bitter as to entertain for a living. If you happen to please, you may be hired five times and get only one bu [£75 in today's money] or two at most. In this wide world, is there no country where it rains hard cash?[4]

The Tea-Brewing Women of Gion

From the start, it was a hopeless task to try and keep pleasure restricted to the pleasure quarters. For young gallants, there were plenty of places other than the quarters, with their stilted conversation and over-dressed courtesans, where they could go to enjoy an evening of witty repartee culminating, with luck, in sex. The most fashionable of these was Kyoto's glittering and sophisticated quarter of Gion, soon to become famous for its geisha.

Gion was not walled in; neither was it officially sanctioned. Unlike Shimabara and Yoshiwara, it was not the result of an administrative decision to keep prostitution in one place. Instead it had been created by free enterprise, operating in response to demand, which made it all the more vibrant and lively.

While the castle-topplers of the nightless cities were spinning ever more complex webs of romance to ensnare the wealthy and privileged, there were less arcane and more affordable alternatives springing up outside the gates. Wherever people gathered there was a never-ending supply of unlicensed prostitutes. At coaching inns along the post roads linking city to city, at inns and taverns in the post towns, at the bustling points where the highways entered the cities, at bath-houses and in hot-spring resorts – wherever there were men in search of pleasure, there were women to serve their needs.

As in medieval Europe, people tended to gather at places of worship – temples and shrines. They would go to pray and then stay on to have fun and take refreshment. As it was for Chaucer's pilgrims, visiting a holy place or going on pilgrimage was the closest anyone in those days ever got to going on holiday. There was certainly no requirement to be solemn or earnest about it. Under the peaceful and prosperous rule of the Tokugawa shoguns, entrepreneurs began to build stalls and shops in and around the shrine precincts to serve the needs of pilgrims.

Gion grew up around Yasaka Shrine, on the opposite side of town from Shimabara. Dedicated to a local deity who took particular care of cotton merchants, the temple was one of the most famous and popular in the country. When nouveau-riche travellers arrived from rough and ready Edo to the east to sample the sophisticated delights of Kyoto, they would lighten their purses there first.

Screen paintings of the time show a sprawling complex of large and small shrine buildings with delicate vermilion pillars supporting sweeping cypress shingle roofs, with a squat red pagoda behind. Visitors would arrive on foot or by sedan chair, passing through the enormous *torii*, the red-painted wooden gateway, shaped like one of the Stonehenge monoliths, which marked the entrance. The grounds were the scene of much merriment. Paintings show pilgrims dancing exuberantly in circles, flourishing fans, accompanied by drummers and shamisen players and groups of people playing shuttlecock, while women conducted tea ceremonies among the trees and palanquin-bearers snoozed. Flanking the main gate of the shrine were tile-roofed stalls where women brewed tea and steamed round white *dango* (skewered rice flour dumplings).

These were the first teahouses. Gradually they took to serving stronger beverages and more substantial food and the women began to sing and dance for their customers. They also provided other, more personal services, though this was strictly illegal. But the name 'teahouse' (*ochaya*) remained.

There was never any lack of candidates among local women to be *cha-tate onna*, tea-brewing women. Women had always played an important part in Shinto ritual. To this day shrine maidens in red and white robes, with long glossy hair like Heian court ladies, act as intermediaries, communicating with the gods on behalf of supplicants. Such maidens had to be virgins; purity was the very essence of Shinto. A woman who had lost her virginity was ritually impure and could no longer officiate.

Under the shoguns nothing could get far without official permission. Teahouses, like brothels, smacked of the salacious and had to be licensed. The first teahouses in Gion appeared in 1665 but it was not until 1712 that the authorities sanctioned their establishment and officially designated the area a teahouse quarter. Teahouses now began to mushroom throughout the entertainment zone that stretched between Yasaka Shrine and the River Kamo.

Besides Gion the authorities also licensed two other teahouse quarters, both of which would later become famous geisha districts. One was Pontocho, alongside the River Kamo, on the opposite bank from Gion. The other was Kamishichiken, up in the north-west of the city at the entrance to another great shrine, Kitano Tenmangu. More than a century earlier the then-ruler, Hideyoshi Toyotomi, had presided there over the biggest tea ceremony of all time, inviting the entire population of the city to celebrate his decisive defeat of the last of his great rival warlords.

Kamishichiken was rather exclusive; it drew its patrons largely from the silk merchants who lived in the same area. But Gion, the most famous and fashionable, welcomed any men wealthy and stylish enough to know how to enjoy themselves there, be they Osaka merchants, Edo parvenus or Kyoto playboys.

The Dancing Girls of Edo

While the tea-brewing ladies and dancing girls of Gion rapidly turned into courtesans every bit as accomplished and seductive as the caged birds of the licensed quarters, Edo, the 'City of Bachelors', was developing its own breed of freelance prostitutes. And it was in Edo, in a rather disreputable section of town called Fukagawa, where prostitutes and courtesans did business out of small wooden houses along the side of the River Sumida, that the first woman to call herself a 'geisha' appeared. It was around 1750. Her name was Kikuya and she was a prostitute who had made a reputation for herself with her shamisen-playing and singing and decided to make entertaining her full-time profession.

Fukagawa ('Deep River') was to become the most renowned of the unlicensed pleasure quarters, famous for the stylish bravado of its women. Back in 1683, three decades before the first licences were issued for teahouses, it was already thriving. That year a poet and author named Mosui Toda (1629–1706) wrote a guidebook to the Edo of his day entitled *A Sprig of Purple*. In this he described a shrine to the god Hachiman in a place called Eitai Island, shortly to become known as Fukagawa.

Like Yasaka Shrine in Kyoto, this was an important place of worship in a rather remote part of town. In fact it was so out-of-the-way that it might have had to close for lack of business were it not for the fact that the authorities 'took mercy and tempered the stringency of the law' against unlicensed prostitution. By Mosui's time the approaches to the shrine were occupied entirely by teahouses, each employing 'ten women of remarkable beauty' who were more than happy to 'comfort the pilgrims'. As a result, the area bloomed and became prosperous.[5]

There were illegal red-light districts all over Edo but Fukagawa had the most, seven in all, known as the *oka basho* ('hill places'). It was a kind of suburb, conveniently outside the jurisdiction of the city magistrates, lined with wharves and warehouses belonging to the wealthy timber merchants who also had villas there. A famous big-spender named Kinokuniya Bunzaemon had a villa there and, when he was not busy taking over the entire Yoshiwara for the night, he often enjoyed sampling the local talent.

Some time in the 1680s, some daimyos and upper-crust samurai began hosting parties at which dancing girls – *odoriko* – were hired to perform before the guests. For the lower orders this offered a great opportunity to obtain gainful employment for one's daughter or, with luck, settle her in a position in a good household. So townsfolk started sending their daughters off for dancing classes.

A few decades on, the dancing girls had expanded their repertoire. By then Edo – and in particular the outlying district of Fukagawa – was overflowing with young women who called themselves *odoriko* but were really prostitutes. Every now and then the authorities would swoop down on unlicensed areas, round up working girls and send them off to the licensed quarters where they would be forced to work for three years without pay. Some were out of their teens, too old to be *odoriko*, which literally means 'dancing child'. These older *odoriko* began to call themselves 'geisha', after the male geisha of the pleasure quarters.[6]

The first female geisha, Kikuya, must have been one of these – and she must have been a star, for her name has been remembered through the centuries, though nothing is known of her beyond her reputation as a brilliantly accomplished singer and dancer. Around the same time that she was strutting her stuff in the teahouses of Fukagawa, across the country in Kyoto, in the walled city of Shimabara, the first female drum-bearer sauntered in to a party. She was referred to as a *geiko*, 'arts child', which is still the word used for geisha in Kyoto. Soon geisha were all the rage. Tea-brewing women, dancing girls and drum-bearers took to calling themselves 'geisha', insisting that they were not mere prostitutes but artistes. A new profession was born.

The female geisha were an instant success. Unlike the courtesans and prostitutes of the pleasure quarters, they were independent, smart women who made a living by their skills and their wit and who were not bound by traditions that forced them to behave in certain ways. They did not have to engage in endless formality and could take sexual partners as and when they pleased. They were women of the world. And although the geisha quarters were clustered in particular parts of town, they were not walled in. The women could come and go freely. They were not caged birds.

While Shimabara quickly embraced the new trend, the Yoshiwara held out against it for a decade. At last, finding their business threatened by the popularity of this new breed of woman, the brothel-keepers there started to hire freelance female geisha to compete with the dancing girls, geisha and *geiko* outside the gates. These geisha worked as entertainers, like the male geisha, in the Yoshiwara, on one condition: they were not allowed to steal the courtesans' clients by sleeping with them. The geisha of the 'hill places' had no such restrictions.

The first geisha in the Yoshiwara was recorded in 1761. Called Kasen of the Ogiya house, she was a prostitute who had earned her freedom and set up in business as an entertainer. Thereafter the number of female geisha swelled until they completely overwhelmed the male geisha. In 1770 there were 16 female geisha in the Yoshiwara and 31 men; in 1775, 33 female geisha but still 31 men; and by 1800 there were 143 females as against 45 men.[7] By that time the word 'geisha' primarily meant a woman, not a man. As the last of the grand *tayu* courtesans disappeared, the geisha moved centre-stage.

Times were changing. The peak of prosperity had passed, the Genroku period – when one commentator wrote of the pleasure quarters that 'their splendour was by day like Paradise and by night like the Palace of the Dragon King'[8] – was over. The great economic slowdown of the 1750s – which was to inspire the building of places such as the beautiful Sumiya teahouse with its austere external walls concealing a lavish interior – was underway. Inflation was rampant, the population boom of the early years of the Tokugawa peace had slowed and, crippled by corruption and incompetence, the shogunate was incapable of improving matters.

Two classes, in particular, suffered: the peasants, who were largely dependent on a single crop – rice; and the samurai, who received their fixed stipends in rice, which then had to be handed over to the merchants in exchange for pitiful amounts of cash. While the townsmen hoarded rice, the samurai declined into genteel poverty. The economic malaise was made all the more oppressive by a calamitous barrage of natural disasters. Fire levelled the flimsy wooden structures of Edo again and again. There were storms, earthquakes, volcanic eruptions, tidal waves and a string of bad harvests leading to devastating famines in which half a million peasants died. The mood of the country grew darker.

The townsfolk, however, were not suffering at all. In fact, they were growing ever wealthier. Many profited from the misery by lending money and selling their goods at extortionate rates. Sporadically the shogunate tried to clamp down on ostentatious spending. There were regular edicts that 'Townsmen and servants may not wear silk', 'Townsmen may not wear cloth mantles', 'Townsmen may not live extravagantly' and 'Townsmen may not give lavish entertainments'. Those who were too obviously prosperous also ran the risk of having their riches confiscated and redistributed into the shogun's coffers. In any case, affluence was no longer a novelty. Many merchant families had been prosperous for several generations and no longer needed to flaunt it.

Thus arose the new aesthetic of restraint. Townsfolk, nervous of having their fortunes impounded, took to wearing sober robes with a sumptuous lining, only visible when they flung off their jacket, and spent their money on tiny but inordinately expensive items like intricately carved *netsuke* toggles of wood or ivory, tobacco pouches and the like. By the mid-1700s, the courtesans of the pleasure quarters, in their showy kimonos, were beginning to seem rather passé. They continued to have their aficionados. But modern young men-about-town were starting to prefer the more understated attractions of the geisha.

While the courtesans tied their obi in front, geisha tied theirs chastely at the back like ordinary townswomen. Instead of flamboyant multi-layered kimonos, they sported plain monochrome ones with the narrow white collar of the under-kimono visible at the throat. Their coiffure was relatively simple, decorated with two or three hairpins and a single comb, rather than an armoury of tortoiseshell pins, combs, ribbons and dangling decorations like the courtesans. Some of the understatement which gave the geisha their special flavour was the result of official ordinances. They were forbidden to wear elaborate kimonos even if they wanted to.

By now no one could deny that the geisha were a profession in their own right. The brothel-keepers of the Yoshiwara were becoming more and more worried by their success and popularity. In 1779 a man called Shoroku, the proprietor of the Daikokuya, one of the oldest establishments in the quarter, proposed setting up an inspection station, a *kemban*, to regulate and control them. With the backing of the other brothel-keepers, he promptly retired and appointed himself comptroller. Installed at the Great Gate of the Yoshiwara, he sold 100 permits to geisha. He had a staff of two inspectors and dozens of clerks who processed all requests that geisha be sent to entertain.

The *kemban* took 30 to 50 per cent of the geishas' fees. They also kept an eye out to ensure that the geisha did not engage in prostitution and interfere with the business of the Yoshiwara. Wherever a geisha went, she was accompanied by a man who carried her shamisen. It was also his job to keep an eye on her and make sure she did not try to run away. As for Shoroku, he ended up a very rich man with an enviable collection of fine art and antiques.

Shoroku established rules of conduct to distinguish geisha from courtesans and prostitutes and ensure that they did not steal their customers. Geisha were to be recruited from among the less beautiful women. They were to wear a severe kimono and simple hairstyle. They were to work in twos or threes, never alone, so as to discourage propositioning, and they were not to sit too close to guests. If a prostitute accused a geisha of interfering with her customers, there would be an inquiry. A geisha found contravening the regulations was liable to lose her licence for several days or even permanently.

Such constraints only applied to those who wished to work in the pleasure quarters. There was never any doubt that the geisha of Fukagawa, stylish and talented as they were, slept with whomever they liked, whenever they liked. But prostitutes were prostitutes and geisha were geisha. If a geisha chose to enter into a relationship with a client, that was legally classified as misconduct, not prostitution. And such activities were the free choice of the geisha. Prostitution was never something they were forced to engage in.[9]

Iki *Geisha*, Tsu *Gallants*

The geisha of Tatsumi goes walking,
Bare white feet in black lacquered clogs.
In her haori *jacket, she's the pride of Great Edo.*
Ah, the Hachiman bell is ringing.
Geisha song (Tatsumi was another name for Fukagawa)[10]

The Fukagawa geisha were particularly famous for their sex appeal. Above their plain, understated kimonos they wore a *haori*, a loose, square-cut jacket with huge sleeves originally worn by men. This gave them a raffish air reminiscent of the kabuki actors who played women's roles who, on leaving the theatre, would toss a jacket on over their women's costume. The geisha never wore *tabi* (toed linen socks). Even in the dead of winter, they always went barefoot, their red-painted toenails framed against the black of their lacquer clogs peeping out from under the hem of their kimonos. The word for this casual, effortless chic was *iki*, which the Fukagawa geisha – more than any other – embodied.

In those days Fukagawa was by the sea, though nowadays, after centuries of landfill, the sea has been pushed a long way away. Young blades who wanted to enjoy the company of geisha would take a roofed houseboat down the river and along the seashore. There were temptations even before they disembarked. There were boats owned by cut-price prostitutes known, in the slang of the time, as *funa-manju* ('boat dumplings'), ready to offer their services then and there on board. On land there were *kekoro* (literally 'kicks') and *maruta* ('logs') ready to waylay them, and right at the bottom *yotaka* ('night hawks') who carried out their work in the open air; as to exactly what these colloquialisms referred to, that has been lost in the mists of time and will have to be left to the imagination. In Fukagawa the lowest grade of prostitute were called *ahiru* ('ducks'), perhaps because they lived near the water; Ahiru became the name of the quarter there.

As the young man reached the Fukagawa area, he would be beguiled by the strumming of shamisen and the sound of singing from the restaurants and teahouses along the waterfront. The geisha were fine musicians who had spent years studying their art. Even though they might choose to augment their income with prostitution, they had a skill with which they could support themselves for the rest of their lives. In comparison with the chic, independent geisha, the courtesans of the pleasure quarters seemed stuck in a time warp.

The young man who wanted to win himself one of these stylish modern women had to be a very cool character himself. While the ideal woman was *iki*, the equivalent for men was to be a *tsu* – a sophisticate, a connoisseur.

The word arose around 1770 and quickly became an enormous fad. Being a *tsu* meant knowing one's way around the demi-monde, knowing the rules of the game so thoroughly that one was completely at ease. Every self-respecting Edo man wanted to be thought a *tsu*, certainly not a *yabo* ('a boor', the opposite) or a *hanka-tsu* ('a half-baked *tsu*', a pseud).

As it happened, the typical *yabo* was likely to be a samurai, an uncouth provincial type who had no idea how to dress stylishly and talked in stiff out-moded language. A *tsu*, in contrast, had no need to be rich or to have high social status. If he looked good and had savoir faire, he was welcome. Thus the countercultural values of the demi-monde, which focused obsessively on style, dress and appearance, seeped through to permeate society at large.

One of the most brilliant figures of the time was a man called Santo Kyoden (1761–1816). A poet and comic novelist, he was also a famous artist who worked under the name Kitao Masanobu and practically lived in the Yoshiwara. Both his wives were second-rank Yoshiwara courtesans. At twenty-four, he published a book called *Romantic Embroilments Born in Edo* (1785). Told cartoon-style in drawings, with the dialogue and narrative festooning every available space, this is the story of Enjiro, the spoilt son of wealthy parents.

Enjiro fancies himself as a great lover (*iro-otoko*), and wants the whole world to know it. Sadly, being ugly, this is rather difficult for him to achieve. So he pays a geisha 50 pieces of gold to pursue him as publicly as possible. She throws herself at his feet and declares that if he will not take her as his wife she will happily be his maid, and if he still won't have her even as that, she will kill herself. But she hasn't said this loudly enough, so he slips her another 10 gold pieces to say it again and make sure the neighbours hear.

But the only way in which he can become really famous as a great lover is if he commits love suicide with a courtesan. He buys the freedom of a woman called Ukina, paying a lot of money to have a window in her brothel broken. The two scramble down a ladder, feigning elopement, though the brothel staff ruin the effect by cheerfully waving them off. Still, he sets off into the woods with her, having arranged for friends to arrive and stop them before they actually commit the act.

Unfortunately at this stage two robbers turn up, waving swords and wearing the Japanese equivalent of balaclavas, sinister black scarves tied around their faces revealing only their eyes. They set upon the helpless pair and offer to help them die. 'We didn't mean to kill ourselves when we set off to commit suicide,' groans Enjiro.

In the end the robbers make off with their clothes, leaving them naked but for their loincloths and an umbrella. Enjiro has become famous, though not in the way he intended.

Kyoden's story caused great hilarity and was hugely successful, with the scene of the pair walking along miserably, practically naked, reproduced on innumerable woodblock prints and paper fans. Clearly there were plenty of Enjiros to be found around Edo and in the pleasure quarters.[11]

The licensed and the unlicensed districts, the two worlds within and without the walls, frequently mingled. Whenever there was a clamp-down on illegal prostitution, the unfortunate women were shipped off and dumped in the nearest licensed quarter. Given that the walled cities were never allowed to expand a single yard, there must have been terrible overcrowding and considerable squalor. Moreover, each influx of untrained, unqualified prostitutes dragged standards in the quarters down another notch.

Every now and then there was a devastating fire. In the hundred years following the first appearance of the geisha in 1760, the Yoshiwara burnt to the ground ten times and there were several other fires which destroyed sections. When this happened, the brothel-keepers were permitted to relocate temporarily to one of the unlicensed areas until the walled city was rebuilt. The unlicensed quarters were by now so much more lively, popular and accessible than the licensed that it was a great opportunity to advertise their wares and increase their profits.

One such upheaval took place in 1787, when some brothel-keepers set up temporary houses in a fashionable riverfront zone called Nakasu Island after a fire. The area had been known as Three Forks in the heyday of the Yoshiwara, when the doomed courtesan Takao was murdered there by her disappointed suitor. After the shogunate instigated a programme of landfill, it developed into the most sophisticated and exciting entertainment district in the country, packed with famous and exclusive restaurants and teahouses, with resident geisha to take care of guests.

At its height there were 18 restaurants, some of which catered only to the deputies of the provincial lords, 93 teahouses, 14 boathouses and at least 27 geisha, not to mention brothels, theatres and assorted food stalls. The most famous restaurant of all, depicted in many woodblock prints, was the Shikian (the Four Seasons Hermitage). Nakasu was an eighteenth-century equivalent of London's Soho, within easy reach of the city centre, with fun for ordinary folk too, where people could go for the day to enjoy side-shows, jugglers, freak shows, mimes and street theatre.

For the women of the Yoshiwara who were transported to this lively environment, there was a far greater degree of freedom than usual. Here no one worried about formalities like the first and second meetings, where clients and courtesans exchanged cups of saké. Instead they could jump straight to consummation, which was supposed to be withheld until the third meeting. Likewise, there were fewer staff around who needed to be tipped, which made it easier on the customers. Conditions were so crowded inside the small temporary brothels that sometimes a girl's feet touched someone else's head and everyone could hear the noisy carousing of the drunken customers and the courtesans' insincere declarations of eternal love to each and every one of them.

Morality was not the only thing which was slipping. For, while privileged debauchees sang, danced and frittered away their time in the company of geisha and courtesans on Nakasu Island, the poor were starving to death. In 1787, after seven years of bad harvests and famine, rioting peasants broke into the shops and storehouses of the wealthy rice merchants, first in Osaka, then in Edo and Kyoto, wrecking, destroying and making off with sacks of hoarded rice.

Despite the economic woes of the rest of the country, it was still a golden age for pleasure. At the Yoshiwara and the other government-recognised licensed quarters (of which there were about 200 throughout the country), the partying never stopped. For the man-about-town there was unlimited choice. He could trawl the unlicensed quarters with their edge of illegality, enjoy himself at the less risky licensed quarters and take his pick between courtesans, geisha and straightforward prostitutes.

The Yoshiwara was still unquestionably the most famous pleasure quarter in Japan. Artists depicted its beautiful, languid women in woodblock prints which rolled off the presses to be snapped up by an eager populace. Guidebooks, like the fanzines of modern times, listed their attributes and special skills. Ambitious young men, eager to be recognised as *tsu* sophisticates, studied the manuals describing the latest fashions, desperately checking that they had the right undergarment, silver pipe and tobacco pouch, could drop the right names and could spot the most celebrated courtesans and geisha.

They did not realise that their elaborately hedonistic lifestyle would soon be threatened. For cataclysmic events were about to overtake the precious world of Edo, the Yoshiwara and Tokugawa Japan. And the women who would dominate the brave new world which was to follow would be the geisha, not the courtesans.

3

ALL FOR LOVE
HEROINES AND PATRIOTS

Drunk, my head pillowed in a beauty's lap;
Awake and sober, grasping power to govern the nation.
Pre-Restoration popular ditty[1]

The Black Ships

One fateful day in 1853, four warships bristling with cannon and trailing clouds of smoke appeared on the horizon, steaming towards the coast of Japan. They dropped anchor in the shadow of Mount Fuji, threateningly close to Edo. Fishermen at work in the placid waters fled panic-stricken for shore.

The Japanese called them the Black Ships. Their commander, Commodore Matthew C. Perry (1794–1858), carried a golden casket containing a letter from President Millard Fillmore of the United States of America demanding that Japan open its doors to trade and friendship forthwith. He sent a message that he would speak only to the highest-ranking man in the nation. After waiting a week he finally stepped ashore. Bedecked with medals and gold braid, flanked by two burly black sailors and accompanied by an escort of marines and a brass band, he presented his letter. He would return the following year for an answer, he declared, and with a much larger fleet.

The night of Perry's arrival, a comet flashed across the sky like a harbinger of doom. Until that moment, it might have seemed to the

Japanese as if nothing would ever change. For a quarter of a millennium Japan had been able to develop a rich and idiosyncratic culture almost entirely free from prying eyes and unwanted influences. One of the cornerstones of the shoguns' policy was isolation, keeping the country sealed against the many dangers – both literal and ideological – which the outside world might present. Apart from a tiny enclave of Dutch and Chinese traders, who were forbidden to leave the foreigners' compound in the distant city of Nagasaki, Japan had been closed to foreign contact. The flower and willow world of the Yoshiwara and the geisha had bloomed in this hothouse atmosphere.

But the last years had been marked by a growing sense of malaise. The country was wracked by economic crises and famines, sparking riots among the peasantry.

In the Yoshiwara courtesans and prostitutes continued to ply their trade but the balance had shifted decisively. The real heart of the demi-monde was now the spirited women of Fukagawa, not Yoshiwara; and in Kyoto, Shimabara had long since yielded in popularity to Gion. In 1811 one observer wrote that 'the Yoshiwara has fallen on hard times nowadays. . . . It seems to me that the courtesans are fewer and the number of famous ladies halved.' There were, he said, only two women of *yobidashi* rank (the top rank which had replaced *tayu*); in fact there were almost no high-ranking courtesans at all.[2]

Another batch of reforms in 1841 only hastened the Yoshiwara's decline. Once again several thousand prostitutes and geisha were rounded up from the unlicensed districts. The prostitutes were then dumped in the Yoshiwara, thus filling it to overflowing with untrained low-grade women. But the geisha were allowed to return to work so long as they promised to restrict their activities to music and dancing. It was the first time that geisha had been officially recognised as different from prostitutes. By 1851 the Yoshiwara, once the exclusive domain of the super-rich, was reduced to trawling for trade with discounts and special offers. The writer who chronicled this with disgust added grimly that veritably it marked 'the end of the world'.[3] The arrival of the foreigner was the last straw.

Early in 1854, half a year after his first visit, Perry was back, this time accompanied by a squadron of eight well-armed vessels. Hopelessly out of touch with western technology and modern warfare, Japan did not even have a navy. The government had no option but to sign a treaty opening two ports to American ships. That same year an earthquake levelled Edo and the shogun who had signed the treaty died shortly after his brush left the paper. The omens were bad.

Okichi, the Foreigner's Concubine

As they depart,
Passing the sampans and spreading their eight sails,
They think of beloved Shimoda
And let their tears fall.

Whilst along the river side
The dirty water flows from the hovels,
Behind the doors the sound of the prostitutes' voices rises:
'Oh! how grateful we are to the honourable foreigner
Who gives two dollars for the one dollar whore.'
'The Black Ships', Shimoda Boatmen's Song[4]

The key had been turned and the western boot was firmly wedged in the door. Across the Pacific, a man named Townsend Harris (1804–1878) saw an opportunity to make his name and, with any luck, his fortune too. As the Americans saw it, the 1854 treaty signed by the shogun provided for a consul general to take up residence on Japanese soil. Harris petitioned the American president to give him the post. In August 1856 he arrived at the newly opened port of Shimoda, to the dismay of the Japanese who had read the terms very differently.

His brief was to conclude a proper commercial treaty. But he was in for a long hard battle. A couple of weeks after he had arrived he finally raised the Stars and Stripes above Gyokusenji, a beautiful old disused temple set among the terraced paddy fields and rugged hills of Kakisaki, a small fishing village on the peninsula at Anegasaki, just outside Shimoda. There he settled with his interpreter and secretary, an ebullient twenty-three-year-old Dutchman named Henry Heusken.

Harris was fifty-two, a portly, rather curmudgeonly businessman with

89

a fleshy face, mutton-chop whiskers and grey collar-length hair. He had helped found New York's City College but in recent years had fallen into difficulties with a series of trading ventures. As he wrote in his letter of application to the president, he had the most essential qualification for the job: he had no wife or children, he was without ties 'to cause me to look anxiously to my old home or to become impatient in my new one'.[5]

Harris's first few months in Japan were filled with wrangling, interspersed with long periods of inactivity while the negotiators awaited instruction from Edo. Often ill and with only Heusken for company, Harris needed some way to alleviate the boredom and gloom. The red-blooded young Heusken knew the answer. What they needed was women.

Heusken lodged the request for 'nurses' with the burghers of Shimoda. Perfectly natural, they all agreed once he had left. But where was the woman of whom they could ask such a sacrifice? Who would ever voluntarily consent to be fondled by a hairy barbarian who reeked of meat and butter? (The Japanese ate no meat or dairy products and referred to foreigners as *bataa-kusai*, 'stinking of butter'.) Who would want to take on the stigma of being a *rashamen*, 'foreigner's concubine' (a word whose alternative meaning was 'sheep')? The visits of Perry's American sailors and a Russian fleet had resulted in a rash of pale-skinned babies, all of whom had been clandestinely disposed of in a graveyard in an isolated little valley.

More weeks passed. If no women were forthcoming, Heusken announced ominously, Harris might be minded to annul the agreements made so far. In Shimoda there was much worried sucking in of breath.

Heusken had specifically asked for two of the town geisha: Okichi for Harris, Ofuku for himself. The elders informed the women of their decision. They were to attend the temple forthwith.

Okichi has become a legendary heroine in Japan. She is revered, practically deified – there is a temple dedicated to her in Shimoda – as the first lamb to be sacrificed on the altar of foreign relations. Harris and Heusken, no doubt looking to their place in history, made not a single reference to the women in their diaries. But there is plenty of Japanese documentation.

Okichi was seventeen or eighteen, an adult by the standards of those days. She was a beautiful and popular young woman, famous for her sweet voice and in particular her unforgettably lovely rendition of 'Raven at Dawn', a plaintive ditty about a Yoshiwara courtesan and a merchant's son who had committed love suicide back in 1769. The story has it that Harris noticed her one day as she was walking home from the bath, looking fresh and comely. As for Ofuku, Heusken had seen her when she went to the consular residence to take lunch to her mother's common-law husband, who was repairing the paper doors there.

Okichi was reluctant to take on the assignment but the town elders were insistent. In the end she was promised a salary which by local standards was a fortune, beginning with the staggering sum of 25 gold coins (more than a Shimoda workman could make in a year) for her 'trousseau'. The figure was entered in the Shimoda municipal accounts, dated the 24th day of the 5th month, Ansei era (1857). It would have set Harris back about $34 (in contemporary currency about £8000), a lot of money in 1857.

On 13 June the consul's large black-lacquered palanquin, specially made to fit his long legs, arrived to carry her to his residence at Anegasaki. She jolted off on the shoulders of the bearers, escorted by equerries and samurai who cleared a way through the crowds. As she sat inside, hidden behind the bamboo window blind, she could hear the townsfolk jeering, 'Here comes a sheep for the consul!'

The cross-roads at Madogahama was the point of no return. Shimoda children still sing a ditty evoking the fear and indecision which Okichi must have felt:

> Shall we go to Anegasaki?
> Shall we return to Shimoda?
> Here is Madogahama. We must decide!

Harris had had carpenters in to turn the disused temple into a western home, throwing away the rice straw tatami matting which had become infested by American beetles from the Black Ships and replacing it with western carpets and furniture. To Okichi it must have been unimaginably alien, full of strange and repellent odours – woollen carpets instead of the familiar new-mown-hay smell of tatami, the whiff of polish on the heavy wooden furniture and, worst of all, the reek of searing animal flesh from the kitchen. Then there was the consul himself with his big, hairy, smelly body; though in the end there was not much difference between what he did on the large uncomfortable western bed and what other men had done to her in the past.

As for Ofuku, she was not at all reluctant to be the lover of the dashing young Heusken. There was no palanquin for her. But, while Ofuku became a regular nightly visitor to the temple, after three days Harris discovered that Okichi had a suspicious skin eruption and told her not to visit again until it was cured. She carried on receiving a sizeable allowance. But even after the sore had disappeared, whenever the subject of a visit was broached, Harris always decided he was unwell. Two and a half months later he terminated the contract.

For Okichi the experience must have been utterly traumatic. She had had to sleep with an old and repugnant barbarian, she had had to abrogate her right as a geisha to choose her customers, and then she had been publicly humiliated and found wanting. On top of all this, as her widowed mother pointed out in a letter to the town council, she was ruined. Having been polluted by the touch of the barbarian, no Japanese man would ever touch her again. Not surprisingly, she turned to drink. As for Harris, he had forgotten her very existence.

It was not until November 1857 that Harris finally succeeded in obtaining an audience with the shogun. Apart from the Dutch, he was the first representative of a western power ever to do so. Resplendent in a uniform which he had designed himself and had made up in Paris – a gold-embroidered frock coat, blue pantaloons, cocked hat with gold tassels and a pearl-handled dress sword – he travelled up to Edo to meet him. Back in Shimoda he applied to the town council for another 'nurse' and the following year government officials in Edo arranged a liaison for him with an eighteen-year-old there. He sailed back to Brooklyn in 1862, never having seen Okichi again.

As for her, she became a beggar, ravaged by drink and syphilis, and years later drowned herself in the river. In the only extant photograph of her, taken ten years after her brief encounter with Harris, she looks worn, grim-faced and rather haunted, though her features are delicate and pretty still. She looks sadly at the camera, her hair pulled back into an unadorned bun.

The legend which grew up after her death is much more romantic. She was the most famous geisha in Shimoda, goes the story, and ravishingly beautiful. When Harris first saw her, flushed and pink, on her way home from the bath, he was immediately smitten. But she had a lover, a lusty young fisherman named Tsuru-Matsu (Crane Pine). Before they dared approach Okichi with their outrageous request, the town elders first had to buy him off, which they did by giving him samurai status and packing him off to Edo to work in the shipyards there. As for Okichi, they made her a *dono*, a Lady, an appropriate status to be the 'wife' of the consul general.

The legend conveniently omits the small matter of the skin eruption. Instead we are told that Okichi lived with the consul for months. Little by little, becoming used to his strange hairy body and foreign mode of lovemaking, she fell in love with him. He, meanwhile, never saw her as anything more than someone to use and discard. Back in Shimoda, after his momentous trip to meet the shogun in Edo, he found American Black Ships at anchor in the bay. Horrified at the notion of flaunting his native floozy before his countrymen, he ejected Okichi from the temple.

Poor Okichi was distraught. Rejected by this man whom she had come to love, she also found herself despised by her own people and in her misery turned to drink. But in later months she was back at the temple, nursing him through illness and even obtaining that loathsome drink, milk, for him. In 1862, having accomplished his mission, Harris set sail for home, carelessly leaving her behind.

Harris may have forgotten her but the Japanese never did. If you visit Shimoda today, there is a temple dedicated to Okichi Kannon (Kannon being the mother goddess), complete with a sex museum. Here you can see the cliff from where, according to the much-embellished legend, Okichi jumped into the sea, having done her bit for international relations.

Long before Harris had packed his bags to leave Shimoda, representatives of other western nations were already appearing on Japan's coast, demanding equal or greater concessions. The Russians came, the

Dutch appeared, the French, Swiss and Portuguese sent representatives. Meanwhile Queen Victoria's special envoy, Lord Elgin, fresh from victory in China, steamed imperiously straight past Shimoda and right into Edo Bay where he dropped anchor, to make sure the Japanese were well aware of his superior status.

The barbarians were not just at the gates, they had burst through. To the Japanese, it must have seemed like Armageddon. The shogunate, grown old, complacent and irrevocably decadent after two and a half centuries of peace, could not withstand the assault of the hated foreigners. A few independently minded warlords, daimyos of far-flung provinces like Choshu (now Hagi) to the west, and Satsuma (present-day Kagoshima) in the deep south, became more and more convinced that radical change was the only solution. There were spontaneous outbreaks of patriotic violence against the intruders, during one of which Henry Heusken, Harris's cheery young companion-at-arms, was ambushed and cut down with a samurai sword as he rode his horse down a Yokohama street. He had not yet turned thirty.

The Victorians Go East

And west you'll sail and south again, beyond the sea-fog's rim,
And tell the Yoshiwara girls to burn a stick for him.
Rudyard Kipling, 'The Rhyme of the Three Sealers', 1893

The westerners who poured in to populate the foreign settlements in the country's growing number of treaty ports ranged from diplomats, missionaries and scholars to adventurers, misfits, roisterers and sailors. They had all heard rumours of the legendary geisha and of the walled city of delights, the Yoshiwara.

One of the first to see this twilight world with his own eyes was a dashing young London University graduate of Swedish extraction called Ernest Satow (1843–1929). A brilliant linguist, he was the interpreter for the British representative in Japan. One night in 1865, having shaken off their minders, he and his Japanese aide set off on foot through the streets of Osaka on an expedition to meet 'the most celebrated singing and dancing girls of the city' – in other words, geisha.

'The streets were by this time quite deserted, and we hugged ourselves with the consciousness of an adventure,' he wrote in his memoirs, *A Diplomat in Japan*. 'No European had yet been abroad in the streets of a Japanese city at night as a free man.'

They went not to the pleasure quarters but to a house in the unlicensed district, the Osaka equivalent of Gion or Fukagawa, where some Japanese had arranged a party for them. No one, no matter what the circumstances, would ever succeed in meeting geisha without a proper introduction and in the company of a customer well-known to the house.

Served tea by some very ancient females, he was afraid that the promised meeting would not come to pass. Then flasks of saké were brought in and a group of women appeared. Satow was not entirely convinced of their charms. 'Some of them were certainly pretty, others decidedly ugly, but we thought their looks ruined in any case by the blackened teeth and white-lead-powdered faces,' he wrote.

At that time married women, courtesans and geisha still practised teeth-blackening, using a mixture of gall and vinegar. A few years later, in 1873, the empress decided to show how progressive she was by initiating a revolutionary new fashion for teeth au naturel, in the western barbarian style. By then, Satow wrote, he was so used to it that he was as shocked as any Japanese to see ladies baring gleaming white fangs.

Satow also found the geishas' dancing 'extremely uninteresting' and their music so much of an acquired taste as to be probably not worth acquiring. 'No foreigner, unless he be an enthusiast, would ever take the trouble to educate himself to appreciate this form of art,' he wrote. In any case, by then his official escort had tracked him down and at 11 p.m. he was packed off back to the British legation.

The quarters still beckoned. A couple of years after his first adventure, Satow and his great friend, a blond, moustachioed Old Etonian Oxford graduate named Algernon Mitford (1837–1916; grandfather of the famous Mitford sisters – Nancy, Jessica, Unity and Diana) found a gap in the wall of the British legation and sneaked out to reconnoitre the Osaka version of the Yoshiwara. Keeping out of sight of the guards at the gates, they headed off at a crouching run, sticking to the shadows of the houses and zigzagging from street to street until they had shaken off all possible pursuers.

A bold young Japanese friend had taken a room in his own name where some girls, 'bepowdered and berouged', knelt expecting to meet a party of Japanese. They screamed with fear on seeing these extraordinary-looking intruders, fled the room and could not be persuaded to return. 'But even the slight glimpse we had of the native beauties seemed to compensate for the risk run, for here in Ozaka [Osaka] no foreigner had ever been admitted to the quarter,' concluded Satow with satisfaction.

He made it to the Yoshiwara in 1868, crossing the rice fields to get there and passing through the Great Gate. There he and his party sent for geisha and spent the evening strolling from teahouse to teahouse, enjoying singing, dancing, drinking, and guessing games where the loser had to down a cup of saké. Three of the geisha accompanied the party home.[6]

Mitford too was a sympathetic observer of the Japanese scene and wrote a wonderful evocation of the Yoshiwara after nearly three centuries of glory:

> The time to see the Yoshiwara to the best advantage is just after nightfall, when the lamps are lighted. Then it is that the women – who for the last two hours have been engaged in gilding their lips and painting their eyebrows black, and their throats and bosoms a snowy white, carefully leaving three brown Vandyke-collar points where the back of the head joins the neck, in accordance with one of the strictest rules of Japanese cosmetic science – leave the back rooms, and take their places, side by side, in a kind of long narrow cage, the wooden bars of which open onto the public thoroughfare. Here they sit for hours, gorgeous in dresses of silk and gold and silver embroidery, speechless and motionless as wax figures, until they shall have attracted the attention of some of the passers-by, who begin to throng the place.

Consulting the up-to-the-minute *Official Guide to the Yoshiwara* of 1869, he recorded a total of 394 teahouses serving as houses of assignation and 153 brothels containing 3289 courtesans of all classes, 'from the Oiran or proud beauty, who, dressed up in gorgeous brocade of gold and silver, with painted face and gilded lips, and with her teeth fashionably blacked, has all the young bloods of Yedo [Edo] at her feet, down to the humble Shinzo, or white-toothed woman, who rots away her life in the common stews.'[7]

There were also 39 *taikomochi* jesters and 55 famous singing and dancing girls (geisha), plus a host of minor stars. 'These women are not to be confounded with the courtesans,' he warned, though from time to time one might be persuaded to sell her favours; and 'to be the favoured lover of a fashionable singer or dancer is rather a feather in the cap of a fast young Japanese gentleman'. On another occasion he found it necessary to remind his readers that although unsophisticated westerners might at first have assumed that geisha were prostitutes and vice versa, as everyone now knew, they were completely different. 'In song and in story the geiko of old Kioto is celebrated as an artist,' he wrote.[8]

He also mentioned the Flower District at Fukagawa and several other population hubs in Edo where the hotels contained 'women who, nominally only waitresses, are in reality prostitutes'.

'On the whole,' he concluded, 'I believe the amount of prostitution in Yedo [Edo] to be wonderfully small, considering the vast size of the city.' The ports were another matter. 'Yokohama at night is as leprous a place as the London Haymarket,' he wrote sternly, giving his readers a useful reminder that vice was by no means confined to the Orient. Victorian London was swarming with prostitutes, an estimated 80,000–120,000 of them, living in situations of squalor and violence, while in 1894 New York there were 40,000 prostitutes turning over an estimated $40 million (£26 million) a year.[9]

Nonetheless missionaries and other upstanding members of Victorian society, not to mention the few Victorian women who set foot on Japanese soil, continued to exclaim in shock and disgust at such practices as mixed communal bathing and general loose morals as the west understood them. Foreign bachelors were less squeamish. Those billeted in the treaty ports cheerfully got 'married' for as long or short a time as they happened to be in Japan. In 1860 when Bishop George Smith of Hong Kong visited, he was outraged not so much at the number of foreign men with native 'wives' but at the fact that the go-betweens for such liaisons were the local Japanese customs officials whom one would have expected to uphold law, order and common decency.

No doubt Japanese women felt equally shocked and horrified at the notion of being pawed or worse by 'hairy unwashed barbarians'. But pragmatism and a decent financial settlement could usually be trusted to overcome such scruples.

In 1885 a languid, rather unpleasant French naval officer who wrote under the pen-name of Pierre Loti (1850–1923) sailed into Nagasaki harbour with the express intention of marrying a Japanese wife and writing about it. He had already titillated the world with tales of his exotic love affairs in Turkey and Tahiti. Now, for his Japanese period, he wanted 'a little yellow-skinned woman with black hair and cat's eyes. She must be pretty. Not much bigger than a doll.'

He spent a mere five weeks in Nagasaki, quite long enough to marry, gather the material for his opus, become bored and leave again. The object of his brief affections was Kiku ('Chrysanthemum'), a teahouse girl whom he called Madame Chrysanthème and married for a price of 20 piastres a month. They seem to have had a relationship of mutual contempt. Loti described his wife's irritating habits, the incessant tap of her tiny pipe-bowl against her porcelain smoking box, her bored yawns and mirthless laugh. Asleep, at least, he wrote, she did not bore him.

'A Japanese woman,' he added acerbically, 'deprived of her long dress and her huge sash with its pretentious bows, is nothing but a diminutive yellow being, with crooked legs and flat unshapely bust.' As he was making his farewells, he was horrified to find her cheerfully counting the coins he had tossed to her and hitting them with a mallet to test that they were real silver.[10]

Unromantic though Loti's account was, he had touched a chord. The western world was thirsty for tales of sweet, gentle Japanese child-women who gave themselves adoringly to western men, even if the reality was a good deal more mercenary and sordid. John Luther Long's tragic 'Madame Butterfly' of 1903, pining away for the caddish Lieutenant Pinkerton, was exactly the heroine that Victorian readers had been waiting for. The story was immortalised in Giacomo Puccini's opera in 1904 and the western myth – or should we say cliché – of the 'geisha' was born. As for the real geisha, living their lives out in Japan, they were made of considerably sterner stuff.

Plotters in Gion

Back in 1612 when the wily brothel-keeper Shoji Jinemon petitioned the shogun for permission to open a licensed brothel district, his most potent argument was nothing to do with public morality. As the shogun well knew, he wrote, the newly established frontier city was awash with masterless samurai (*ronin*), self-styled 'street knights', the infamous 'six gangs of Edo', ruffians, brawlers, vagabonds and assorted mischief-makers. All these dangerously subversive elements found a natural home in houses of ill-repute, where they might even start plotting a rebellion. The solution was to concentrate brothels in one place so that the brothel-keepers could keep an eye on the customers and report any undesirables.

This was the kind of argument the shogun understood, and, as we know, Jinemon was given the go-ahead. In a way the real purpose of the wall and the Great Gate of the Yoshiwara and the Shimabara was not so much to fence in the enslaved courtesans as to keep an eye on everyone who came in and went out.

Two and a half centuries later, Jinemon was proved more prescient than anyone could ever have imagined.

The coming of the barbarians threw everything into chaos. First there was Perry, then Harris, with his interminable and infernal demands, and behind them the menacing Black Ships lurking just across the horizon. What on earth was to be done? As far as the newly installed twelve-year-old shogun, his regent, councillors and court in Edo were concerned, there was nothing for it but to concede on every point. Rusty samurai swords and antique muskets were useless against the might of the foreigner's firepower.

It was a matter of national survival. But national pride was also at stake, and for the first time in centuries a sizeable proportion of daimyo warlords chose to disagree with the shogun. Some called for war, others argued that the country's seclusion must at all costs be maintained. The matter was so critical that the emperor himself – normally utterly outside politics

– took a stand, in favour of continuing the policy of isolation. The real reason why Harris was left twiddling his thumbs in Shimoda for so long was because the emperor refused to sign his treaty.

In the end, under intolerable pressure, the shogun's regent signed the document and those presented by the other western powers without the emperor's consent. This act sparked outrage amongst samurai of all ranks and men of other classes too.

Disaffected samurai, particularly from the distant provinces of Satsuma and Chofu, followers of the dissident daimyos and others who opposed the shogunate, began to gather in Kyoto. They united under the double slogan 'Restore the emperor, expel the barbarian'. Many abandoned their families and headed for Kyoto without their lord's consent, thus turning themselves into *ronin*, lordless men with nothing to lose. For centuries the political centre of the country had been the shogun's capital, Edo. But now there were two hubs, not one. Kyoto was abuzz with passionate political debate.

For these young blades, mainly in their twenties, the natural place to meet, argue, plan and eventually foment revolution was Gion, with its rabbit warren of tiny lanes lit with glowing white lanterns and lined with teahouses and geisha houses. There they could pretend to be wastrels, drinking their lives away. Many also fell in love with geisha who returned their love and were to prove every bit as brave and stubborn as they.

The young braves on the shogun's side, meanwhile, spent their evenings carousing in another of the geisha quarters – not Gion but its arch-rival, Pontocho, on the other side of the river. It would have been far too risky for both sides to have had their plots and secrets overheard by the same geisha, even though the geishas' code of secrecy theoretically prevented them from ever divulging what they had heard.

These were desperate times. When the shogun's crack troops came marching through Gion, conducting house-to-house searches, it was the geisha who confronted them, arguing with them while their lovers hid in closets or on false floors under the tatami matting or sneaked away out of back doors. Some of the geisha were threatened or even tortured but they would never give away the rebels' hiding places. At least they were able to stall for time, to give their lovers the precious few extra minutes they needed to make their escape.

One of the rebel leaders was a romantic, driven young samurai called Takayoshi Kido (1833–1877). Photographs show a handsome, thoughtful youth, frowning purposefully, with his hair oiled into a topknot, wearing two swords, the mark of the samurai, wide *hakama* trousers and a wide-sleeved jacket, his hands on his thighs, ready for action.

Kido was from Choshu, to the far west of the country, the most radical province of all. He studied swordsmanship in Edo and was serving in the Choshu coastal defence forces when Commodore Perry and his fleet steamed across the horizon for their fateful second visit. He became a devoted follower and student of Yoshida Shoin, the Karl Marx of Japan, one of the key thinkers behind the Japanese revolution. When Shoin was executed for his extremism in 1859, it was Kido and a swashbuckling eighteen-year-old named Hirobumi Ito, later the country's first prime minister, who risked their lives to retrieve his body from the execution ground and give it a decent burial.

By the 1860s, Kido was a leader on the Choshu side. In Edo he plotted revolution in the teahouses of Yanagibashi and in spring went boating on the River Sumida with his geisha friends to admire the dazzling displays of pink cherry blossoms along the banks. In Kyoto he held rabble-rousing meetings in Gion, where he fell in love with a beautiful and spirited geisha named Ikumatsu.

In August 1864 fighting broke out on the streets of Kyoto. A desperate band of Choshu men, 2000 strong, tried to storm the imperial palace and capture the emperor to make him the figurehead of their struggle against the shogunate. Finally the shogun's troops succeeded in driving back the rebels. Many of their leaders were killed and the rest fled or went into hiding. There are still deep gashes in the beams and corner-posts of some of the Kyoto teahouses to testify to the fierce fighting that went on.

Kido was not on the battlefield that day. But the shogun's men knew that he was one of the leaders and came hammering on Ikumatsu's door in search of him. She stood in the entrance, arguing with them long enough to give him time to sneak out and escape across the tiled roof. By the time they shoved past her, swords glittering, he was gone.

For five days, disguised as a beggar, he hid among the down-and-outs who lived on the riverbank under Nijo Bridge. Ikumatsu crept out by night to take him rice balls, given to her by a loyal Choshu merchant. After that he disguised himself to try and shake off his pursuers. One day he was a shampooer, the next an attendant at a public bath-house or a porter at a coaching inn on the highway out of town. Finally, with Ikumatsu's help, he escaped from the city and lived under a false name as a shopkeeper in a country town.

Meanwhile the western nations had realised that there were two powers in Japan, not one, and that a cataclysmic power struggle was going on. The British decided that the future lay with the rebels, not the shogun, and began supplying them with arms. Young Ernest Satow went so far as to take aside the legendary rebel leader Takamori Saigo, a great bull of a man from the southern state of Satsuma, and tell him in no uncertain terms that the time for a coup d'état was now. As Satow phrased it in his memoirs, 'the chance of a revolution was not to be lost'.

By now Kido was out of hiding and, together with Saigo, had become one of the leaders of the movement. The final push came in 1868. The old emperor had died and been succeeded by his fifteen-year-old son, Mutsuhito, known to history as Emperor Meiji. In Japan the years are named after the reigning emperor; it was Year 1 of the Meiji Era, the beginning of a new age. Kido, Saigo and the other rebel leaders, backed by a large military force, seized the imperial palace and declared an end to the rule of the shoguns. Hereafter the emperor would be their titular head and the figurehead of the nation.

On the outskirts of Kyoto, there was heavy fighting. In the evenings the youthful rebels – who were now the imperial army – would be back in Gion, relaxing in the teahouses, arguing, singing and dancing with the geisha. One night a geisha plucked out a rousing tune on her shamisen. A Choshu samurai, Yajiro Shinagawa, composed the lyrics:

> *Miya-sama, Miya-sama, o-uma no maeni*
> *hira hira suru no nanja ya ya!*

> Your Highness, Your Highness,
> What can that be, fluttering before your horse! . . .

It's the imperial brocade banner
that attacks the enemies of the court.

We'll shoot down the scoundrels
who would raise their hands
against the Mikado,
emperor of the firmament.

When the shogunate's samurai hear the noise
which way will they run?
They'll throw away their castle and their spirit
and flee eastward.

The next day Shinagawa handed out copies of 'Toko Ton Yare Bushi', as he called his song, meaning something like 'To the Death!' or 'Go for Broke!', and the samurai marched into battle singing lustily. It was Japan's first war song. Seventeen years later, in 1885, it was hijacked in its entirety by W.S. Gilbert and Sir Arthur Sullivan to use as the overture and the song of the Mikado's troops in their operetta *The Mikado*, in which it is sung in the original Japanese.[11]

From Kyoto the imperial troops marched east, heading for Edo, where the townsfolk waited in suspense to see what would become of them. The shogun had already fled. Shortly afterwards the young emperor was installed in the shogun's palace which would hereafter be the imperial palace. Edo became the new capital and was renamed Tokyo, the 'Eastern Capital'.

The young men who had led the rebellion were now the leaders of the new government. They settled in Edo and many brought their geisha lovers to join them. Kido was one of the most powerful men in the Meiji administration where his greatest achievement was to abolish the feudal social structure of the shogun's era. He did not forget his brave and devoted geisha lover, Ikumatsu. First he arranged for her to be adopted into a samurai family, a traditional procedure to make a geisha into a respectable woman, essential in a society where marriage was a matter of creating an alliance between families rather than of individual preference. She was given a new name, Matsuko, and shortly afterwards he made her his wife. (To this day when a man wishes to marry his geisha lover, he has first to find an older man from a respectable family who will agree to 'adopt' her and act as her 'father' at the wedding.)

Algernon Mitford met her in 1869 and described her as 'a bonny little lady, though eyes less familiar with the custom than mine would have objected to the disfigurement of shaved eyebrows and blackened teeth'. He commented on her 'ease and grace' as a hostess and added that as a former geisha, she had 'none of the shyness which I have usually met with in Japanese ladies'. She sang and played the shamisen for the party while a friend accompanied her on the flute. 'A very happy couple they seemed to be,' concluded Mitford of Kido and his wife.[12]

Thus a Gion geisha rose to the pinnacle of Japanese high society to become, if not First Lady, at least the woman behind one of the most powerful men of the realm. Many other rebel leaders married their loyal geisha lovers and all of them, from the bull-like Saigo to Hirobumi Ito, the country's first prime minister, kept geisha mistresses.

The geisha had proved their mettle and, with their unique ability to span the social hierarchy, were poised to become the leading women of their day. The courtesans in their gorgeous cages and the wives of rich men, trapped in their homes, offered no competition. The years that were to come would be the heyday of the geisha, when they were at the forefront of society as trend-setters, fashion leaders and the companions and confidantes of powerful men.

4

LOVE NEVER CHANGES
TOKYO GEISHA AND THEIR
POWERMONGER LOVERS

In the floating world where all things change
Love never changes by promising never to change
Geisha song[1]

The party at the riverside house is over, the lamplight dim;
The crowd of painted ladies, tipsy, is departing now.
Their delicate hands have trouble opening snake-eyes umbrellas —
On the banks of the Ryogoku Bridge the rain is mixed with sleet.
On a geisha party at Yanagibashi by Yodo Yamauchi (1827–1872),
former daimyo of Tosa[2]

Tokyo Teahouse Politics

For the Edo-ites who turned out in their tens of thousands to watch the emperor's grand entry into the city in his palanquin, the Phoenix Chair, on 26 November 1868, it must have seemed as if the world had turned topsy-turvy. Was the future to consist of rule by country bumpkin samurai married to geisha lovers? It was as if these queens of the counterculture, who had hitherto played at being great ladies so that merchants could play at being gentlemen, had suddenly turned respectable.

Still, business was business. In recent years the Yoshiwara, with its population of imprisoned courtesans, had fallen far behind the times. Fashionable young men-about-town much preferred the chic geisha of the illegal quarters; it was geisha the new oligarchs married, not courtesans. By now all but one of the Yoshiwara houses were small and low-class, offering little more than sex. Still, seeing a new market in the influx of provincial males flocking into the new capital, the Yoshiwara brothel-keepers quickly upgraded 120 courtesans to the top *yobidashi* rank, thus enabling them to charge far higher fees than for a humble prostitute.

The enthusiastic young samurai who ran the new government recognised the needs of the city's growing populace by designating six areas which had been semi-licensed as licensed. Whereas the illegal quarters had sprung up around shrines and temples, the natural gathering places under the shogunate, these new licensed quarters were in the bustling population hubs of the new order, at the points where roads from the provinces entered the city, soon to become railway termini: Shinagawa, Shinjuku, Itabashi, Nezu and two at Senju. Hereafter the quarters were to be taxed at the rate of 10 per cent of their revenues. The first ever hospital for venereal diseases in the Yoshiwara opened that same year.

They also, rather touchingly, attempted to provide for the many foreign gentlemen who were expected to come and work in the city. For, despite the slogan 'Revere the emperor, expel the barbarian', it had become apparent not only that the foreigner was here to stay but that he had a myriad of interesting things to teach the fledgling state.

Shortly after the emperor arrived in Edo, he put his signature to a memo from the leading daimyos recommending that Japan abandon the attitude of 'the frog looking at the world from the bottom of a well' and resolve instead to learn from the foreigners, 'adopting their best points and making good our own deficiencies'. The Japanese forthwith embarked on a love affair with all things foreign which far outdid anything that the shoguns could ever have imagined. Young Japanese steamed off on P & O liners to the west to study and the Japanese hired foreign experts – British engineers to share the secrets of the industrial revolution, French to teach them law and military affairs, Germans to teach them about their parliamentary system, and Americans to teach commerce, agriculture and technology. A British engineer arrived to build the first railway, the Tokyo–Yokohama line, which opened with enormous fanfare on 12 October 1872.

One of the first of the Meiji government's projects was a pleasure quarter for foreigners. Named the New Shimabara, after the famous quarter in Kyoto, it opened not far from the imperial palace, near present-day Ginza, in 1869. It operated according to the Yoshiwara system, with teahouses serving as houses of assignation for clients to make appointments for the grander brothels. A total of 1700 courtesans and 200 geisha, including 21 male geisha, moved in from the Yoshiwara to populate its 130 brothels and 84 teahouses.

Unfortunately all these brothels and teahouses remained largely empty. Foreigners, it became apparent, preferred more illicit pleasures. Many came to sightsee but few stayed on to enjoy themselves. The project was particularly over-ambitious given the small size of the foreign settlement at the time and the fact that a large proportion of the foreigners were missionaries. As for the Japanese, the military – who had formed a staple of the Yoshiwara's clientele – stayed away from the New Shimabara, though a few townsmen tried it out. In 1870 an excuse was found to close it down.

By now the Japanese were beginning to get the measure of the foreigner's prudery. They had already discovered, to their astonishment, that foreigners not only thought there was something wrong with male on male sex but punished it with death. It was utterly different from the Japanese notion that, when it came to sex, anything went.

Shortly after the ignominious closure of the New Shimabara, an extraordinary event occurred which focused Japanese attention on the gulf between foreign attitudes and their own. In June 1872 a Peruvian ship, the *Maria Luz*, dropped anchor in Yokohama Harbour for repairs. A Chinese coolie jumped overboard, to try and escape, revealing that the ship was carrying a cargo of 230 Chinese slaves. Thirteen were children, including one, a little girl, who was under ten. There was international uproar and the captain was arrested and put on trial. The slaves were finally declared free and sent back to Hong Kong.

In the course of the furore the Peruvians pointed out that the Japanese too trafficked in slaves – the women of the Yoshiwara. This was not strictly accurate. The sale of human beings had been declared illegal in 1612 and services in the Yoshiwara were known as 'term employment'. Nevertheless, the women were not free even to leave the quarter, let alone give up their 'employment' there.

Having been a closed society for so long, the Japanese now squirmed under the eyes of the world. The Meiji government was anxious to persuade the western powers that Japan was every bit as civilised and modern as they. Four months after the *Maria Luz* incident the government passed the Prostitute and Geisha Emancipation Act, prohibiting the sale and trade of human beings. 'Said prostitutes and geisha,' went the wording, 'have lost their human rights and are treated no differently from cows and horses. Human beings cannot logically demand payment of obligations from cows and horses. Therefore the said prostitutes and geisha should not pay debts or the balance of instalments.' The act became known humorously as 'the Cattle Release Act'. (The Japanese, incidentally, were early by international standards in this respect. In Britain, for example, the Public Prostitution Law was only repealed in 1886.)

Many prostitutes went home and brothels were forced to close, though, as the individual members of the government knew perfectly well, there were plenty of 'cattle' who did not wish to be emancipated and had no idea how to make a living if they were. Many brothels quickly reopened for business under the designation 'rental parlours'. Before emancipation, according to the census of the time, there were 5759 prostitutes and 280 geisha in the seven licensed districts. Afterwards the figures show that the number of prostitutes had quartered, to a mere 1367. Geisha, conversely, had increased to 417.

The act, in fact, gave a fillip to the geisha, who were already far more popular and chic; there were always fewer geisha than prostitutes because of the stringent artistic requirements for the geisha. The government also recognised a distinction between geisha and prostitutes. Hereafter prostitutes who wished voluntarily to carry on their trade were required to have a licence. Geisha who also practised as prostitutes had to have two licences, one for the sale of *gei* ('entertainment'), the other for *iro* ('sex').

The Yoshiwara continued to do business right up until prostitution was made illegal, in 1958. But it had long since ceased to be the cultural centre it once was. It had become a splendid relic of a bygone age, the sort of place where Victorians went to gape and the hoi polloi went for sex.

At the height of its glory, as a Japanese playwright noted in 1911, the natural setting for the great dramas of the kabuki theatre had been the Yoshiwara. In those days it had been the vibrant heart of society, where grand passions were played out and a chance encounter at the Great Gate might well involve an unimaginably wealthy daimyo and a gallant old-style robber baron. Nowadays, he wrote acerbically:

the courtesan has degenerated into a tasteless chalk drawing, the stylish clientele has given way to workmen's jackets, flat-top haircuts and rubber boots and . . . a chance encounter under the lights of the beer hall at the main gate would most likely involve a person with a north country accent and a home-made cap and his uncle, in the city with a petition to the Ministry of Commerce and Agriculture.[3]

A decade after the Cattle Release Act, in 1883, cognoscenti were dismissing the geisha of the Yoshiwara as low-class compared to their sisters in the unlicensed districts. By then all the most fashionable geisha were to be found in Yanagibashi (Willow Bridge) and Shimbashi (New Bridge), while the second rank of geisha were those of Sukiyacho and Yoshicho. The Yoshiwara geisha came a poor third.

In 1908 the great novelist and mythologiser of the geisha world, Kafu Nagai, was to write nostalgically of the decline of 'Fukagawa of the waters'. Even before the swashbucklers of the Meiji Restoration had transformed Japanese society for ever, Fukagawa – once the haunt of the coolest, spiciest geisha of them all – had already passed its peak.

The final blow had come between 1841 and 1843, during the last of the shogunate's great clean-ups. The anti-vice police had targeted the chic anti-establishment women of Fukagawa, rounded them up and bundled them off to the Yoshiwara or ordered them to leave the area and engage in other occupations. Then, even before the coming of the Meiji government, early modernisers decided to turn Fukagawa into Edo's first industrial zone. Today it is the home of shipyards and cement works, though there is still a small community of Fukagawa geisha who entertain aficionados.

A couple of decades before Kido was plotting in Gion, the romantically named Yanagibashi (Willow Bridge) on the other side of the river had already supplanted Fukagawa. This was an area of boathouses along a tributary giving on to the River Sumida whence the *chokibune* – light swift boats with a single long oar – set off to carry customers to the Yoshiwara. Enterprising boathouse-keepers turned their properties into stylish teahouses and restaurants so that customers need not even bother with the journey. When the geisha of Fukagawa were evicted from their brothels, they crossed the river and found employment there.

Yanagibashi took on the mantle of Fukagawa as the home of the most elegant and witty geisha who entertained the merchants of old Edo. In 1836, when the curmudgeonly seventy-year-old novelist Bakin Takizawa decided to throw a grand party, he chose one of the splendid Yanagibashi houses as the venue. It was the party of the year. Everyone who was anyone was there, including the most celebrated writers, scholars, publishers, booksellers and artists of the day, 800 guests in all. The famous woodblock print artists Hokusai Katsushika, then seventy-six, and Hiroshige Ando, who at thirty-nine was at the height of his career, both put in an appearance and there was drinking and carousing, presided over by the area's famous geisha, from one morning until the small hours of the next.

Yanagibashi too had its chronicler, a man famous for his inordinately long nose, who wrote under the pen-name Ryuhoku, 'North of the Willows'. The last of the great *tsu* sophisticates, he wrote of rakes and dandies and the decadent lifestyle they enjoyed in the Yanagibashi teahouses in the waning years of the shogunate. He also wrote scathingly of the uncouth ways of the country bumpkin samurai who succeeded them, of ghastly post-restoration parties where people were so boorish that they talked politics or even spoke in English and ignored the geisha and their singing and dancing. He complained of modern geisha – little better than prostitutes – who were more interested in money than art and bought copies of the official gazette to find out how much their clients were earning. The new men of the Meiji administration did not take kindly to such vitriol. One instalment of Ryuhoku's writings was banned and he ended up spending time in prison.

But in fact he was right. Yanagibashi was too thoroughly imbued with the decadence of old Edo under the shogunate. The men who had spent their youths rabble-rousing in the teahouses, the industrialists, politicians, bureaucrats and businessmen who ran the brave new Tokyo, now found Shimbashi (New Bridge) more to their taste. With all things western coming into vogue, Shimbashi had the advantage of bordering on the Ginza, where the first street of brick buildings with a long colonnaded arcade was built in 1872. And, as it happened, it was also where many of the Gion geishas who had followed their lovers the 250 miles to Tokyo had set up teahouses.

There, men like Hirobumi Ito, the country's first prime minister, and Taro Katsura, one of his successors, would spend the evening – after a day of wrangling over the fledgling constitution in the Diet, the country's new parliament. And there, in their crass, forthright, country samurai way, they would discuss matters of state between nibbling on delicacies, exchanging banter with the geisha and showing off their own skills at singing and dancing.

The larger-than-life women whose names were on every tongue, like the models, movie stars and rock stars of today, and whose stories gripped the popular imagination of the time, were mainly Shimbashi geisha. Connoisseurs of the old school, nevertheless, continued to favour the Yanagibashi geisha, who were much admired for their elegance and stylish femininity.

The most celebrated geisha of the era was Sadayakko Kawakami who rose to become the concubine of the country's first prime minister and later the first woman to tread the boards as an actress. Her story casts light on the women who became geisha, the life they led and the way in which becoming a geisha opened doors that would otherwise have remained firmly shut. It was the only way a woman could hope to take control of her own destiny.

The Story of Sadayakko

Sadayakko or Sada (as she was known at the height of her career) was born in the Nihombashi district of Tokyo just four years into the new era, in 1872. Her father had been a successful businessman but when she was six his business collapsed. Desperate, the family took her along to a geisha house in the Yoshicho geisha district and arranged for her to be adopted by the proprietress, a woman named Kamekichi who became her geisha 'mother'. Undoubtedly money changed hands and the family finances benefited from the transaction. Still, it was an adoption, not a 'sale of persons', considered a perfectly normal way in those days to ensure the future of one's child.

Mother Kame too did well out of the deal. Not only was the child 'of good family', which would make her more saleable as a geisha, she was also strikingly lovely, with translucent white skin, lustrous black tresses and extraordinary eyes. The left was flat like an Asian eye, the right had a crease like a western one. And she was very quick; she could 'learn one thing and pick up ten' as the saying went. At the age of ten she demanded to learn to read and write, an outrageous request for a young girl training to be a geisha. The first high schools for women had opened only in 1870 and they were certainly not for the likes of Sada.

Had it been any other child, Mother Kame would have said, 'What are you trying to do? Reading and writing is for men!' But she had high ambitions for Sada. She could win, she thought, not just a good *danna* but the very best in the country. To groom her, she arranged classes in riding, swimming, billiards and martial arts as well as reading and writing.

The word *danna* means 'master' in the sense of 'patron' or 'husband', though the geisha's patron will almost always already be married to someone else. Until the enormous changes brought about in Japan by the Second World War and its aftermath, it was a matter of prestige, a mark of a man's wealth and success in the world, to be known as the patron of a beautiful and famous geisha. Even the dashing rebel samurai leader Kido, devoted as he was to his wife the ex-geisha Matsuko, was the patron of a Gion geisha named Okayo who had been one of Matsuko's friends. And, as he wrote in his diary, he also spent much time carousing in geisha quarters.

For the geisha house 'mother' and 'older sisters' who had the future of a young geisha in their hands, their most important task was to find her a suitable patron. In the course of her career, a geisha would probably have several. The first would have the unique privilege of deflowering her, of introducing her to the ways of love in an initiation ceremony known as *mizuage*, 'raising or offering up the waters'. For this he would pay a large sum of money, and possibly a fortune if the woman was considered a jewel; it was a way in which a geisha could repay at least part of her ever-growing debt to the geisha house.

A relationship with a *danna* was equivalent to marriage. Just as Japanese parents chose a husband for their daughter, so the geisha house mother would select an appropriate *danna*. And, as with marriage, the young woman usually had little or no choice in the matter. Then a legal contract was drawn up between the geisha house and the *danna*, specifying that, for example, he would buy the geisha's freedom by paying off her debt and deciding the exact monthly allowance he would pay. Unromantic though this might seem, a normal Japanese marriage was more pragmatic still. Many wives were little better than glorified domestic servants, seldom left home and did not even enjoy a sexual relationship with their husband. In comparison, a geisha retained a large degree of independence. The man who supported her was not usually able to visit very often and in his absence she was free to do as she pleased.

The *danna* system was specific to the geisha; courtesans did not have *danna*. A good *danna* paid for everything. He might set up a home for the geisha and would shower her with handsome gifts, paying the exorbitant cost of the annual new kimonos and obis which she needed for her work, financing her public dance performances (geisha had to pay to perform in public, they did not receive a fee) and supporting her for as long as the relationship suited both, which often meant throughout his life. (A man was usually fairly old by the time he was able to afford to support a lovely young geisha and invariably died long before she did.) If she wished to give up being a geisha, he might set her up in her own teahouse, bar or restaurant.

When he visited, she would cancel all other engagements to entertain him and his guests and would be available for sex whenever he required it. If she wished to sleep with others, she did so discreetly though she did have some leeway; the last thing a sophisticated *danna*, a *tsu* among *danna*, would wish to appear was jealous or possessive. Many older geisha to this day are supported by a *danna* and confess that it would be extremely hard to survive otherwise.

At sixteen, Sada, who, as a virgin geisha, had been given the name of

Ko-yakko (Little Yakko), was an exquisite girl with feathery eyebrows, delicate features and those extraordinary mesmerising eyes. As the proprietress of a top geisha house, Mother Kame had many connections in high society. One day she met up with Eiichi Shibusawa, a great industrialist, property magnate and banker who lived in a splendidly baroque faux-Moorish mansion. To him, Mother Kame confided her ambition for Sada. He suggested the prime minister himself, Hirobumi Ito, and said he would put in a word on Sada's behalf.

Like Kido, Ito (1841–1909) had been a swashbuckling gallant from Choshu. Under the stern rule of the dying shogunate he risked execution by smuggling himself aboard a British ship in 1863 when leaving the country was still a capital offence. (According to another version of the story, it was actually the shogunate that sent him and his colleagues on a secret mission to find out how things were in the west.) With four friends he sailed via Shanghai to London where he lodged in Hampstead and studied at University College for a few months. Reading one day in *The Times* that an international coalition led by the British was planning to attack his home province, he rushed back to Japan to mediate. By 1880 he was the leading figure in the government and in 1885 became the first person to take the title of prime minister. He was instrumental in developing the country's constitution and served four different terms as prime minister.

A short, stout man who loved to strut around sporting a chest covered in medals, he had a broad forehead, turned-up nose and straggling goatee beard. He was a notorious libertine. Pompous in public, in private he loved nothing better than the company of a group of charming geisha, whom he would regale with an endless flow of improvised songs, finally driving all but the one who struck his fancy out of the room with a favourite ditty like 'Oh, what a boor and nuisance are you!'.[4]

A great dancer, he once hosted a magnificent masked ball at his western-style mansion, to which all the foreign diplomats in the city were invited. He went as a Venetian nobleman but the evening degenerated into ribaldry and bawdiness, after which his cabinet became known, rather unflatteringly, as 'the dancing cabinet'. Of his incessant love affairs, the most scandalous involved a Japanese nobleman's wife.[5]

On his raffish nights out in the geisha districts, Ito had already noticed

A *tayu* courtesan in the Shimabara pleasure quarter uses a loosely strung bow to play the *kokyu*, the classic instrument of the *tayu*. Her headdress and kimono are far more ornate than those of geisha or maiko. (LESLEY DOWNER)

The main street of Miyagawa-cho geisha district, too narrow for cars. (LESLEY DOWNER)

The Great Gate of Shimabara. The willow tree outside marks the flower and willow world. (LESLEY DOWNER)

Stone Wall Alley with its high walls, where rich men used to house their concubines. (LESLEY DOWNER)

Harumi, the maiko, in her room in Haruta geisha house. The mirror is lined with photographs of famous geisha. (LESLEY DOWNER)

Ready for a night out. Harumi in full maiko regalia. (LESLEY DOWNER)

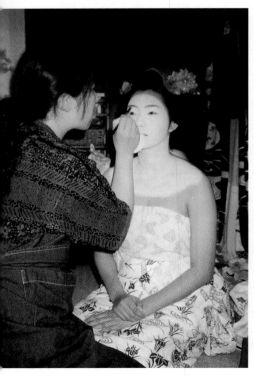

Masami preparing Kanosome for her *misedashi* debut. (LESLEY DOWNER)

Kanosome in black ceremonial kimono, ready for her debut. Only her bottom lip is painted. (LESLEY DOWNER)

Mr Imanishi resets a wig. (LESLEY DOWNER)

Koito, the geisha with the website, prepares to put on her wig. (LESLEY DOWNER)

A young maiko in the 'home bar' of a geisha house reveals the titillating fork of unpainted flesh at the nape of her neck, which Japanese men find the most sexy. (LESLEY DOWNER)

'Harem', a soapland in the old Yoshiwara quarter, modelled on an old geisha house, offers 'baths' for ¥20,000 (£100). (LESLEY DOWNER)

The author (in wig) with Mr Imanishi, the wigmaker, and family. (LESLEY DOWNER)

The author in geisha mode, tending to a customer. (LESLEY DOWNER)

The beautiful Katsuno, star of the Kyoto geisha. (CHRIS STEELE-PERKINS/MAGNUM)

The *maikosí* room in a geisha house. Maiko can be as young as thirteen or fourteen. (CHRIS STEELE-PERKINS/MAGNUM)

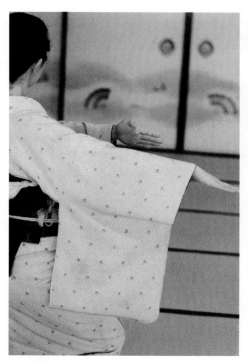

The Nihon buyo dance form is as controlled and precise as ballet, though not so athletic. (CHRIS STEELE-PERKINS/MAGNUM)

A maiko on high clogs, her obi reaching her ankles and her hair in the maiko coiffure, carries a red oiled paper umbrella. A geisha, on lower clogs, wearing a wig and with her obi tied into a knot, follows behind. (CHRIS STEELE-PERKINS/MAGNUM)

Teahouse party. A maiko with swinging sleeves and a geisha dance before the customers
(CHRIS STEELE-PERKINS/MAGNUM)

Geisha musicians perform for the annual Cherry Dances. (GIDEON MENDEL/NETWORK)

Two maiko on their way home after a hard night's partying. (CHRIS STEELE-PERKINS/MAGNUM)

the ravishing, precocious child who shyly filled his saké cup. He was not the sort of man to turn down a proposal to deflower a girl like this. However, he explained, his wife was something of a dragon, and therefore suggested that the encounter should take place at his villa on an island outside Tokyo. He also handed over a very substantial amount of money to Mother Kame.

As for Sada, she was already in love with a swarthy thickset farm boy turned student but knew well that, as a woman, her private feelings were utterly irrelevant. One summer afternoon in 1888 she boarded a boat for Ito's palatial villa where she had a bath and carefully applied her make-up. The tubby, bewhiskered Ito, who at forty-seven must have seemed like a grandfather to her, arrived in time for dinner. Knowing her charmingly eccentric interest in reading and writing, he had brought with him, so the story goes, a Chinese book full of extremely explicit instructions on lovemaking. He read to her before putting the instructions into action.

Having now officially become a woman, Sada was entitled to wear the kimono of an adult geisha and took the name Yakko to mark her change in status. Given his wife's no-nonsense attitudes and the need to avoid scandal, explained Ito, he could not openly keep her. But he bought her the latest fashions, new-fangled western items like a bathing suit, riding costume, boots, and spurs of 14 carat gold. Whenever he could, he arranged clandestine visits to continue his lessons in sexual techniques. When a policeman questioned her for swimming in the Sumida in her glamorous bathing costume, she tossed her black tresses and said, 'I am Yakko, Count Ito's concubine.'

As Ito's mistress, Sada was a celebrity, one of the most famous faces in the country. When she went to meet her student lover, she had to go in disguise, hiding her face in her shawl. She in her turn initiated him in the arts of love. But he, like her, could not afford to be ruled by sentiment. Offered the chance to marry into one of the country's most powerful and wealthy families, he took it and was sent to the United States to study.

Sada knew there was no point pining. Beautiful and famous, she took a succession of lovers, including two kabuki actors, heart-throbs of their day, and a mountainous sumo wrestler. Then one fateful day in 1892 she was summoned to entertain Ito and his guests, among them the property tycoon Shibusawa who had introduced them. He had brought along a young man who was the talk of the town, an actor and satirist named Otojiro Kawakami.

Eight years older than Sada, Otojiro came from a rough rural background and had spent time in prison because of his scurrilous tongue and subversive speeches. Making a living by his wits on the streets, he had become a *rakugo* comedian, a teller of funny stories, the Japanese equivalent of a stand-up comic. He quickly became famous for his savage but very entertaining satires in which he targeted pretentious city-dwellers who followed the fashion for all things western, right down to western government, but somehow always got it wrong.

Shibusawa expected Otojiro to do his piece in front of the prime minister but the young man refused. 'If you want to see my performance, you'll have to come to my theatre and pay for a ticket,' he said cheekily. It was the kind of effrontery that Ito, who had been a rebel himself, rather liked.

Entranced by this brusque young man, Sada saw him to the door, introduced herself and a few days later went to see him perform. The result was a love affair which was to last for the rest of their lives.

It was the end of Sada's career as a geisha. It was one thing for a geisha to have a professional relationship with a *danna*, quite another for her to have an all-engrossing personal relationship. It gave her a different flavour. Men could no longer enjoy the pleasures of an innocent flirtation with her. Thus if a geisha wished to marry, she had to leave the profession immediately.

As for the *danna*, the only course was to respond with a good grace. Normally he would offer to be the official go-between, a key part of the formalities of marriage in Japan. Given Ito's position, he could not do so; instead he did the next best thing and arranged for a friend of his – a man of rank – to perform the role.

Otojiro became a famous (some would say infamous) actor, director and impresario and built his own theatre, while Sada busied herself in time-honoured Japanese fashion being his wife. Some years later he started planning a world tour in which, as was usual in Japan, *onnagata* – male actors – would take the female roles. Ever since Izumo no Okuni and her followers had been banned from the theatre in the seventeenth century, women had been forbidden to perform as actresses in public. Not that this meant there were no actresses. Geisha and courtesans were, as it were, 'parlour actresses', performing on a small stage to a select audience, and just as famous and celebrated as if they had performed on the public stage.

But, said the promoter, in order to attract an audience in the United States Otojiro would have to have a female star – and who better than his own deservedly celebrated wife, the beautiful Sadayakko!

So Otojiro, Sada and their troupe of twenty actors set sail for San Francisco. It was 1899, the cusp of the new century, and Sada was twenty-seven.

The west which they were on their way to seduce had been enjoying a love affair with olde worlde Japan ever since Commodore Perry opened the doors of this extraordinary feudal society. *Japonisme* was all the rage. In Britain Victorian artists, notably James McNeill Whistler, were painting in the Japonesque style and collecting Japanese art; Arthur Lasenby Liberty spent much time in Japan studying fabrics and buying goods for his shop on London's Regent Street; and Victorians avidly bought kimonos, fans, and blue-and-white porcelain to decorate their homes. 'In fact, the whole of Japan is a pure invention,' commented Oscar Wilde in his supercilious way. 'The Japanese people are simply a mode of style, an exquisite fancy of art.'

In England *The Mikado* had been a smash hit, with 1000 performances over an eleven-year run. Across the Atlantic on one particular night in 1886 there were 170 separate performances going on simultaneously all over the North American continent. A pin-up that same year of the much-adored star Marie Lloyd showed her dressed as the westerner's notion of the geisha in a red long-sleeved kimono open like a coat, waving a fan, with hairpins in her hair and an enormous bow on her back. The chorus to her song was inscribed beneath the picture:

Every little Jappy chappie's gone upon the Geisha –
Trickiest little Geisha ever seen in Asia!
I've made things hum a bit you know, since I became a Geisha,
Japanesey, free and easy Tea house girl![6]

In those politically incorrect times, such lyrics seemed utterly inoffensive.

But no one, apart from those who had been posted to Japan and certainly no one in San Francisco, had ever seen a real geisha. When they arrived Sada was astonished to find that her fame had preceded her. There were posters, not of the famous actor but of his humble wife, all over the city.

The troupe performed a melodramatic piece called *The Warrior and the Geisha*, fusing together a couple of different kabuki dramas and ending with a death scene derived from *Musume Dojoji* ('The Maiden of Dojo Temple') in which a maiden, maddened with jealousy and rage, dies of a broken heart. Sada's dancing thrilled audiences across the country. 'Mme. Yacco's death scene at the end of the play revealed tragic force,' enthused the *New York Times* of 6 December 1899 after the troupe performed in Boston.[7] (Western writers of the day, unused to Japanese names, referred to her as Sada Yacco – romanised thus rather than the more modern 'Yakko' – and assumed mistakenly that Yacco was her surname.)

Then they sailed for London where they played at the Coronet, the leading theatre of the day. The artist William Nicholson painted a portrait of 'Sada Yacco' as an old-style courtesan with foot-high lacquered pattens and a splendid coiffure spiked with hairpins. She looks sombre and dignified, utterly unlike the pin-up of Marie Lloyd.

In France their visit coincided with the Paris Exposition of 1900 where Japanese arts and crafts excited huge interest. A journalist called Louis Fournier conducted a lengthy interview with Sada and later described her long black kimono and 'delicate and childish melancholy face'. He asked her: 'What is love in Japan?'

She replied: 'Different – so different . . . In this country men and women love each other freely; it is the custom. Japanese girls do not declare their love so frankly. Often they will die rather than confess it . . . Ah! to me, my friend, love in Japan is very noble, sublime and sacred!'[8]

The young artist Pablo Picasso did a painting of her in india ink and gouache, entitled *Sada Yacco*, in which he portrayed her dancing in a rather wild and abandoned way, her arms flung over her head, wearing a kimono and obi, with a sinister black cloak coiling, serpent-like, around her.

In Washington President William McKinley had commandeered a box to see the troupe; in Paris they performed at the presidential palace, where President Emile Loubet personally presented Sada with a bouquet; and in London the Prince of Wales requested a command performance on a specially built Japanese stage inside Buckingham Palace. Japanese government officials, however, were outraged that their country was being represented by these geisha and actors. As far as snobbish, traditional-minded Japanese were concerned, such people were riverbed folk, no different from prostitutes and beggars. To have fun with them and use them for pleasure was one thing. But for such people to be adored and treated as symbols of the mysterious Orient by westerners, whose opinion the Japanese were very sensitive about, was a scandal. In the long run it just went to show that westerners would never be able to grasp what Japan was all about. It was a matter for national shame.[9]

Abroad Sada played a geisha or a courtesan in productions specially tailored to suit western taste. But at home, along with Otojiro, she was instrumental in introducing Shakespeare to the Japanese public. She played Ophelia, Portia and Desdemona, among other roles, and also founded a school for actresses.

On one memorable occasion the troupe gave a performance of *Othello* before a packed house. At the time Otojiro was engaged in an intense affair with a Shimbashi geisha, Kyoka, whom he had seated in the front row. When the time came for Otojiro, as Othello, to smother Sada, who was playing Desdemona, she refused to die. 'I don't want to die, I'm innocent,' she screamed.

'Please die,' whispered Otojiro desperately. 'I swear I'll never see her again.'

He kept his word. The couple remained together until Otojiro died in 1911. Later Sada re-met her student lover, the thickset farm boy, now a successful businessman, and lived with him until his death in 1938. She lived to see the Second World War and the devastation that followed and died in 1946 at the age of seventy-four. Thus, thanks to her beauty and talent and the doors opened to her as a geisha, Sadayakko was able to rise from impoverished beginnings to become Japan's first actress and real star. She is celebrated as such to this day.[10]

Honourable Carp and her Prime Minister Lover

While the west raved about all things Japanese, the Japanese were mad about all things western. The great symbol of westernisation, which they referred to as 'Civilisation and Enlightenment', was the Rokumeikan (a name which translates romantically as 'the House of the Cry of the Stag' or 'Deer Cry Pavilion'). Designed by the young British architect Josiah Conder, it opened right in the middle of Tokyo, diagonally across the moat from the imperial palace, in 1883. It was a rather showy Italianate mansion of white-painted brick with colonnaded verandas, set in landscaped gardens. That sardonic Frenchman, Pierre Loti, who visited a couple of years later, wrote that it reminded him of a provincial casino.[11]

There the crème de la crème of Japanese society – the gentlemen in frock coats, the ladies in bustles, bows, corsets and bonnets – gathered to engage in outlandish activities like banquets, balls, concerts, billiards and charity bazaars. It was the perfect place to entertain western diplomats, who recorded in their diaries balls with thousands of guests, where the food, menus and chefs were French, and Japanese husbands and wives twirled about the dance floor in the close embrace of the waltz, a dance form which had shocked the aristocracy of Europe only half a century earlier.

Dancing was far from the forte of the retiring Japanese wife, no matter how high-class; any public show of affection, let alone physical contact, between married couples was simply not done. So no doubt there were men who quietly took along their geisha instead to such occasions. Geisha, after all, were professional dancers who would have been the first to pick up the complicated steps of the waltz and the quadrille. They would certainly not have felt any embarrassment at dancing cheek to cheek, added to which they were adepts at charming and entertaining conversation.

Having always been in the vanguard of fashion, there were geisha who took to western dress and even wore their hair in the 'shampoo coiffure', a rather unkempt style which resembled nothing so much as hair let down for shampooing and not put up again, as opposed to the traditional waxed pompadour. Teeth-blackening disappeared decisively, at least in sophisticated Tokyo, when the empress gave it up in 1873. And anyone with any pretence of being up to date carried a western umbrella and was to be seen taking the occasional meal of beef in the city's à la mode sukiyaki restaurants. The word for the look was *bankara* or *bai-kara* ('high collar'), a modish, effortless, slightly rumpled chic.

The first sign that the Japanese had learnt their lessons well was when they went to war with China in 1894, laying claim to the Korean peninsula, and roundly trounced their gigantic neighbour. The victory was greeted with public rejoicing (though, to the chagrin of the Japanese and their government, the western powers immediately put heavy pressure on them to give up most of their spoils). Celebrating in a Shimbashi teahouse, a leading politician, Taro Katsura, was struck by a graceful young geisha-in-training who performed a dance which she had choreographed herself with the Rising Sun flag as a prop. In his diary he commented approvingly on her patriotic spirit.

The girl's name was Okoi ('Honourable Carp'), and she was fifteen. Born in 1880, like Sada she was the child of a good family fallen on hard times. Her mother, the daughter of a lacquerer, had fallen in love with a nobleman and eloped. Cast out by society and devastatingly poor, the couple had had to sell their four-year-old child for adoption into a geisha house. There her training began. She showed such promise that at thirteen she was taken on by one of the top Shimbashi geisha houses and given the name Okoi. For her presentation as a fledgling geisha she wore a deep blue kimono embroidered with an intricately patterned scene of orange carp and silver waterfalls.

As photographs show, Okoi had an unusual, distinctive and very intelligent face with full lips, a pronounced chin and a slender nose with a slightly aristocratic curve. She was also determined and ambitious – like her namesake, the carp, a fish admired not only for its sensual grace and intense colouring but for its fortitude and strength. She clearly had a glittering future ahead of her.

At eighteen she took a *danna*, a middle-aged stockbroker named Heizo

Yajima who paid off her debts and set her up as an independent geisha with her own teahouse. The most generous of patrons, he acted as her mentor, teaching her how to comport herself in the often jealous and spiteful flower and willow world and allowing her the freedom to spend as much time as she liked at her teahouse before returning to spend the night at the house he had set up for her. Soon the cream of fashionable Tokyo, wits, rakes, writers, artists and politicos, were vying for invitations to her teahouse salons.

According to Okoi's memoirs, it was her toothless old hairdresser, who had spent a lifetime in the demi-monde, who advised her on the secret way to the heart of each of the great men of the day. Prince Yamagata, for example, was a great performer of *ko-uta* (short lyrical songs), and had a stern eye for the tiniest hair astray in a coiffure. Viscount Inoue, on the other hand, was a connoisseur of silks and dyes; one should therefore wear only the most distinctive and elegant kimonos in his presence.[12] As for Count Ito, now promoted to Prince Ito, the only question was how to be the one who won his heart for the night.

Around this time Okoi was thrown together with a kabuki actor named Uzaemon Ichimura. Part Italian on his mother's side, he had that boyish leading-man beauty which Japanese women adore, with a thin intense face and aristocratic Roman nose. Despite his popularity, he had recently been jilted in favour of another kabuki actor by a geisha known as the 'loose-haired beauty', who wore her hair in the modern 'shampoo' style.

So his fan club decided to set him up with a new wife. This was a perfectly normal procedure; there was always a go-between in a Japanese marriage. A couple would expect love to blossom after, not before, the ceremony, if at all. It was, in fact, not remotely romantic but much more of a business proposition. And the perfect choice of wife for the handsome actor was, of course, Okoi, the city's most famous geisha.

It was an offer no one could refuse. Her kind *danna* (who had his own wife and children) if anything rose in status by being supplanted by such a glamorous rival. He did the proper thing and acted as the official go-between for the couple who duly married.

But from the beginning the marriage was bedevilled by the lack of love. No matter how famous Okoi might have been when she was a geisha, as a wife she was expected to become, like all Japanese wives, a combination of manager, business partner and maid for her husband and a serving wench for her mother-in-law. She reverted to her pre-geisha name of Teruko and went to live with her husband's parents.

While Uzaemon became the heart-throb of his day, Okoi was reduced to counting pennies. His lifestyle involved lavish entertaining and gifts to patrons, most of which had to be paid for out of her hard-earned savings; household and other expenses are always the responsibility of the wife in Japan. But worse than his neglect of her was his serial infidelity. Women threw themselves at him. A couple of years on he had a much-publicised affair in which he was discovered in bed with a banker's wife. Okoi packed her bags and asked for a divorce.

She had left the glittering life of Shimbashi in triumph, having captured the city's most desirable man. Since then Uzaemon's incessant infidelities had been blazoned across the press and filled the teahouses and geisha houses with malicious gossip. Many of her fellow geisha were pleased to see the proud Okoi laid low. To crawl back, miserable and broke, would be the ultimate humiliation. But what else could she do?

However, Okoi was not called 'the Carp' for nothing. Like the fish which was her namesake, she was proud and resilient. Pulling herself together, she took out a loan of 1000 yen and set up shop in another teahouse. She tried to conceal her pain under a flinty façade but sometimes it overwhelmed her. At times she drank so much that she passed out in the gutter and earned herself the nickname 'Madame Bacchus'. Boorish customers made fun of her. In the end, after all, geisha were simply their playthings. If she needed their custom and money, she had to give them whatever they wanted. What she needed was a good *danna*.

Then one day a wealthy brewer and patron of the arts hosted a dinner at which he summoned her to entertain his distinguished guests. Every dish was carp, prepared in a different way as a tribute to her. There she came to the notice of Hitachiyama, one of the sumo grand champions of the day. The mountainous wrestlers were (and still are) like gods in Japan; not so much sporting heroes as representatives of the Japanese spirit, and considered mightily sexy to boot.

Barely had he begun his courtship, plying her with gifts of bolts of silk,

123

when his arch rival, Araiwa, also fell for her. Once again Okoi was the darling of the town. It was a story to pique everyone's interest, featuring the three symbols of romantic Old Edo – the geisha, the actor and the wrestler.

The backers of the two wrestlers decided to stage a duel with Okoi as the prize. On the day crowds poured into the stadium. The referee in his brocade robes launched the proceedings and the two man-mountains lumbered into the ring. They faced each other, stamping the ground, glaring and throwing salt contemptuously over their shoulders in time-honoured fashion before lurching together with an earth-shaking thud. The match was over within seconds. Araiwa was the winner of the purse and the geisha. That night, it was said, he poured the coins into her lap and offered all his winnings to her.

Beneath his voluminous flesh and silky oiled skin beat the heart of a simple man. He loved her, he told her, and begged her to marry him. But she had had her fill of marriage to public idols and gently turned him down.

Shortly afterwards, now once again the most famous geisha of her day, she was called upon to entertain at a banquet hosted by the prime minister, that same Taro Katsura who had admired her dancing nearly a decade before. It was summer 1903 and relations between Japan and another gigantic neighbour, Russia, had reached breaking point. The issue was Russian expansionism – a matter which also concerned Britain which had recently signed the Anglo-Japanese Alliance – and the old question of control of the Korean peninsula.

Katsura (1847–1913), a Choshu man, was a war hero who had distinguished himself during the fighting that had followed the establishment of the emperor in 1868. He had risen from the rank of general to become prime minister in 1902 and, like Kido and Ito, his predecessors, he was a bon viveur who loved nothing better than playing host at a geisha party. When the Russian war minister, General Aleksei Nikolaevich Kuropatkin, arrived in Japan to try to negotiate a diplomatic solution to the crisis, he determined to give him a rousing and memorable welcome, no matter what the outcome of the talks.

Fifty geisha were called upon to entertain, gliding into the room in white-socked feet, the long sleeves of their brilliantly coloured kimonos reaching to the ground. The banquet consisted of thirty-eight courses, served individually, each a tiny culinary work of art arranged on the most fragile porcelain. Okoi was personally presented to the bearded general, his chest sporting rows of medals, who held out his hand to take hers. She records in her memoirs that she was frightened by this physical contact with the 'hairy barbarian'.[13]

By the following year the two countries were at war. Prince Yamagata, the elder statesman famous for his proficiency at singing and his admiration of a fine coiffure, decided that the prime minister needed to relax. He invited him to a geisha party, to which he summoned his old friend, the beautiful Okoi. Later he asked the proprietress of the restaurant to be the intermediary between the two. Okoi was twenty-four; Katsura, at fifty-seven, easily old enough to be her father – a perfectly normal age gap.

Katsura handed over 2000 yen to pay off Okoi's debts and once again she left the geisha world. Hereafter she was no longer seen in public or at geisha parties. Instead she devoted herself completely to him. The house where he settled her, not far from his official residence, became a place where the great men of the nation would drop in to rest, relax and enjoy anything from a game of go with the prime minister and his charming companion to a hot bath and a flask of saké. More and more the house became the venue for long discussions into the night on the conduct of the war. No matter what she saw and heard, Okoi remained 'silent as a carp', though rumour had it that in the privacy of the bedroom he discussed politics with her and listened respectfully to her opinion. Perhaps at first she saw the liaison as a job. But in time, as she records in her memoirs, it came to provide her with the first real happiness she had known. As the prime minister's lover, confidante and friend, she was fulfilling the geisha role of legend.

The war ended in the summer of 1905. Japan had won a resounding victory against Russia, culminating in the bloody Battle of Tsushima in which the Japanese navy inflicted a terrible defeat on the Russian Baltic fleet. A couple of generations earlier the country had barely even had a navy. Now, for the first time, they had defeated one of those same western powers which had seemed unstoppable not so long before. Not surprisingly, there was an outburst of patriotic fervour in Japan.

Katsura, as prime minister, was one of the key figures in drawing up the Treaty of Portsmouth which followed the ending of hostilities. Japan did well out of the treaty, increasing its strength in Korea, Manchuria and the Russian-owned islands to the north. But the Japanese public, who had been expecting the Russians to pay a huge indemnity, felt cheated once again of the full spoils of victory.

This time they expressed their fury in violence. Mobs spilled on to the streets and for a couple of days there was rioting across Tokyo. Crowds attacked government and newspaper offices and the American legation; they destroyed ten Christian churches, overturned trams and wrecked police stations. Finally, with a thousand casualties on their hands, the government had to call in the troops and establish martial law.

The mob reserved special hatred for 'the traitor's whore', who, they felt, had distracted the prime minister when he should have been wringing greater concessions from the Russians. An unruly rabble gathered threateningly outside Okoi's house, throwing stones, baying for blood and threatening to burn it to the ground.

Okoi had taken refuge in the prime minister's office. When the streets quietened, she records in her memoirs, she was smuggled home in a closed carriage and ended up hiding in a tool shed in her silk kimono. For the next three weeks she stayed at home with the shutters closed and the lights off, reading in the toilet, the only room that had a skylight, while her gardener brought in food for her.[14]

All this was bearable while she still thought she had the prime minister's love. But her worst moment came when his attendant arrived carrying a note giving her back her freedom. He had enclosed 10,000 yen in crisp 1000-yen notes to help her start up a business.

Katsura, who lived his life in the public domain, had had no choice but to resign and announce the end of his relations with the woman whom the newspapers were referring to contemptuously as 'Katsura's Okoi'. Alone in her house, Okoi wept.

But Katsura was too fond of her to be without her for long. After a few months, when the fuss had died down, he sent for her and installed her in his country villa among the rugged hills and emerald-green paddy fields of the Izu Peninsula, not far from Shimoda where Townsend Harris had had his brief dalliance with Okichi.

The years passed. Okoi was once again lover, confidante and hostess at Katsura's splendid country house parties, her beauty unfaded by the years. She also bore him two children who, in the Japanese way, were given for adoption into wealthy families to ensure them a good and respectable future. Katsura, by now one of the nation's elder statesmen, served a further three-year term as prime minister from 1908.

Then in July 1912 an event occurred which many Japanese feared would bring about the end of the world as they knew it – the death of Emperor Meiji, as apocalyptic as Queen Victoria's death had been a decade before. He was succeeded by his son, the mentally unstable Emperor Taisho. That same year the maelstrom of Japanese politics brought Katsura back into power for a third time but a few weeks later he was forced to resign again. (There were mobs rioting outside parliament that time as well.)

By now his health was in decline. He died shortly afterwards at the age of sixty-six. His wife forbade Okoi to be present during his last illness, though he was allowed to see their two children. She was also barred from attending his state funeral. As his concubine, she grieved in private and alone. She was still only thirty-three.

Five years later she made a rather splendid comeback. With her geisha's instinct for the mood of the moment, she opened not a teahouse but one of the first bars in the Ginza, the most fashionable street in town, abutting on to Shimbashi, her old home. The period which history has come to know as the Taisho Era was rapidly becoming a rather decadent time, when frail, languid Taisho beauties in modern kimonos wasted their days in Gin-bura ('hanging out in the Ginza'), arm-in-arm with cool young men with modern haircuts and American suits. Given the fame and contacts of its glamorous owner, Okoi's bar, the National, quickly became the haunt of a fashionable and rather exclusive set.

But for Okoi disaster always seemed to be just around the corner. In 1923 her bar was destroyed, along with the rest of the city, in the Great Tokyo Earthquake. Later she rebuilt it but it never regained its popularity. By now she herself was a figure from a bygone age. Most of the men who remembered her in her youth and beauty were dead. In 1934 – when she was fifty-four – a last remaining friend from the old days opened a teahouse in the Akasaka district which by now threatened to rival Shimbashi as the most elegant geisha district in town. He invited Okoi to manage it. For a while things went well. But then the teahouse became involved in a political scandal. Okoi was summoned to appear in court as a witness.

She had had enough. As soon as she got the chance, she took the course chosen by many geisha in the past. She had her thick, beautiful hair cut off, took the tonsure and became a nun. For a geisha who had lived her life outside the norms of society, and as part of a community of women, it was not such an extraordinary choice; indeed in Japanese terms it was perfectly normal.

Her life was still not over. She went to live in a dilapidated temple in the quiet Tokyo suburb of Meguro where she worked to raise money to restore its 500 statues. And, when war broke out, she made a long journey around China, offering prayers for both Chinese and Japanese soldiers killed in action.[15] She died at the age of seventy-seven in 1948. She is remembered as the last of the great Tokyo geisha.

5

IN LOVE WITH GION
KYOTO *GEIKO*, MILLIONAIRES
AND SALONS

No matter what happens
I am in love with Gion
even when I sleep.
Beneath my pillow
the waters ripple.

Poem inscribed on a stone beside the Shirakawa stream at the
site of Daitomo teahouse by Isamu Yoshii (1886–1960), writer of
geisha songs[1]

Cherry Dances

While Tokyo bloomed, a deathly hush fell over Kyoto. Throughout the centuries of the shoguns' rule, there had always been two hearts in Japan. Although Edo was the centre of power where the shogun had his castle, Kyoto-ites could console themselves with the thought that theirs was the emperor's city, home to the imperial court. They were the upholders of taste, class and the aristocratic old ways.

For a few years, as valiant young samurai crowded the teahouses of Gion, plotting and roistering, the city had seethed with passion and politics. Then suddenly the emperor, the courtiers, the princes, the lords, even the flunkies had gone. Dust began to gather on the white-walled imperial palace with its red pillars and silent expanses of raked sand. The swashbuckling samurai and their geisha mistresses, the merchants, writers and artists packed their possessions, hired palanquin bearers and headed for the glittering streets of the new capital.

What was to become of Kyoto? What role did the ancient capital have to play in this brave new world? For a while a pall of gloom hung over the beautiful valley with its purple hills and crystalline rivers. Then the city fathers put their heads together.

They came up with the idea of an international exposition to show off the city's traditional arts and crafts, already much admired abroad, and build up business. The Kyoto Exposition, the first in Japan, took place in 1871 but had only limited success. Something extra was needed to brighten up the city and bring it back to life.

The answer was to bring the geisha (or *geiko*, as they are known in Kyoto) out of the closet. They were, after all, one of the city's chief glories and, having played such a heroic part in the recent struggle, might finally be considered almost respectable. Some had married the country's new rulers; they need no longer suffer the stigma of being branded 'riverbed prostitutes' by polite society.

So the vice-governor consulted the two most powerful people in Gion: the ninth Sugiura, the owner and direct descendant of the founder of Ichiriki-tei, the most famous and venerable teahouse in Japan, where the heroes of the recent revolution had revelled; and Haruko Katayama, the legendary dancer and teacher who, under her professional name, Yachiyo Inoue III, was responsible for establishing the Inoue style as the exclusive dance form practised in Gion. (The Inoue School might be considered the Bolshoi of the geisha world in Japan; the present principal is Yachiyo Inoue IV, now ninety-six.)

Once a year, they decided, the public should have a chance to see the geisha perform their famous dances. The first public performance of Miyako Odori, 'Dances of the Capital' (known as 'the Cherry Dances' in the English-language brochures published for Victorian tourists), took place in March 1872 as part of the second and much larger Kyoto Exposition. They lasted seven weeks and have been repeated in some form annually (increasing to semi-annually in 1952) ever since. Two other geisha districts also performed public dances. Gion's arch-rival, Pontocho (still rather subdued, having been the quarter favoured by the losing side), called theirs the Kamo River Dances, while Kamishichiken, in the north of the city, performed the Kitano dances.

Until then the geishas' charms had been reserved for those who could afford to pay for them. Many, along with courtesans, were famous and adored among the populace. Everyone knew their names and might even own a woodblock print pin-up of a favourite; but few ever had the chance to see them close up. Now, once a year, the dancing which had previously been only for the eyes of a select and wealthy few in intimate tatami-matted rooms was on display for the general public. It was, of course, rather different. It was large-scale, not small-scale, involving many geisha. In the 1872 performance, there were 7 groups each of 32 dancers, 11 singers, 4 hand drum players, 2 flautists, 3 players of smaller drums and gongs and 1 player of the large drum, who performed for a week each, 371 performers in all.[2]

It was the beginning of a new role for the geisha. They were still regarded with ambivalence. They were still on the outskirts of society, being either the children of geishas, part of a demi-monde beyond the pale of the respectable world, or having been sold by impoverished country parents into a sort of servitude. But they were also stars; they had a recognised place in society and an aura of glamour. And every year crowds flocked to buy tickets for their brilliant and colourful dance spectaculars.

Thus both Kyoto and the geisha continued to flourish. When, that same year, the Cattle Release Act was passed, geisha stood in line at Kyoto City Hall to buy their two licences: one for entertainment, the other for sex. The enthusiastic reformers of the young government, out to emulate western ways, instigated various experiments. For a few years there were compulsory workshops for geisha so that they could learn a skill and, in theory at least, be equipped to pursue a decent living. There they sat in glum rows spinning and weaving, or learning reading, accountancy, dancing or music. The only escape was when they were summoned to a teahouse to entertain. Eventually attendance was made optional and classes immediately stopped, apart from dancing and singing. This was the beginning of the vocational schools which each geisha district in Kyoto still runs.

The American Millionaire
and the Icy-Hearted Geisha

One spring day in 1902 a world-weary American named George Dennison Morgan, whiling away a few weeks in Kyoto, went to see a performance of the Cherry Dances. A nephew of the millionaire financier J. Pierpont Morgan, he was wealthy enough that he would never have to work. Disillusioned with New York society after a soured romance, he moved to Japan and settled in Yokohama where he started collecting antiques.

No doubt he thought of taking a Japanese concubine. For a western man it was the simplest of financial arrangements and one Japanese girl was much like another, or so the average western chauvinist might have thought. But then at the Cherry Dances he saw a geisha so beautiful, so feminine and so graceful that he had eyes for no one else. Another, only slightly less romantic version of the story is that he met her at a Gion geisha party. In any case, he fell utterly and incurably in love.

It was a story which was to set tongues wagging and newspaper presses whirring furiously on both sides of the Pacific. To this day, if you ask a Kyoto geisha to name the most famous geisha of all time, she will say 'Oyuki Morgan'. (Tokyo geisha, of course, opt for Okoi.)

O-yuki ('Honourable Snow') was an exquisite young woman of twenty-one. In photographs she looks like a porcelain doll, with a long, strikingly aristocratic face, fine nose, delicate mouth, tapering almond eyes and a disdainful lift to her eyebrows. She is the eternal feminine, woman personified, remote, aloof and mysterious. As far as Morgan could see, she was completely perfect.

In fact she was not at all aristocratic but the daughter of a Kyoto swordsmith. There being less and less call for swords in the bright new Japan, the family business had gone disastrously into decline when she was in her teens. For a good-looking young Kyoto girl, it was the most natural thing in the world to go and work in Gion to help her family out. Missing out the trainee maiko stage (she was too old for that), she went to live at a geisha house run by one of her relatives.

George was thirty-one, not handsome but impeccably groomed and rather stolid in appearance, with a faintly lugubrious spaniel air. He wore his hair with a neatly combed centre parting, in the fashion of the time, and had a bristly moustache which covered the sides of his pursed, rather stubborn mouth. His deepset eyes were a little sad, his nose slightly bulbous.

To western eyes he looked unremarkable enough. But in the Kyoto backwoods, where westerners were a rarity, the round-eyed long-nosed foreigner seemed like a visitor from another planet. When Oyuki was summoned to the teahouse to entertain him, she was shocked and repelled by his pallid skin, coarse compared to silky Asian skin, and colourless hair. Maybe he wooed her through an interpreter, maybe he had picked up a few words of barbarically accented Japanese. In any case, at the end of the evening he asked the maid of the teahouse to arrange for him to spend the night with her. Oyuki was aghast.

'Sleep with a foreigner? I'd rather die,' she exclaimed in the privacy of one of the teahouse's back rooms.

But George had no intention of giving up. Even though she rejected him, he gave her an outrageously extravagant tip – 20 yen – at a time when a 1-yen tip was unheard of and a ticket for the Cherry Dances cost 10 sen (one-tenth of a yen). So Oyuki, having a family to support, accepted him as a regular customer.

She had other financial pressures too. As it happened, she was in love with a student named Shunsuke Kawakami. One of the customs among geisha until well into the modern era was to invite university students to have fun at the teahouses after hours without charging them *bana-dai*, 'flower money', the geishas' fee; they only paid for their drinks and sometimes not even for those. After midnight, when the formal geisha parties were over and the customers had been packed off home to their wives, the dashing students of Kyoto's Imperial University would pile into the teahouses to chat, drink and carouse.

The geisha loved the company of these handsome young gallants. They also knew that one day they would undoubtedly be among the country's elite. The first universities had only recently been founded and the gilded young men (it was only men) who succeeded in entering were guaranteed powerful positions, whether in the financial, bureaucratic or political spheres. When they were rich and powerful, they would automatically continue to patronise the teahouses where they had been so kindly treated as students. Japanese society worked (and still works) on the basis of loyalty. Once a man had set up a relationship with a teahouse, he would maintain it throughout his life; indeed, he would probably pass it on to his son.

Thus Oyuki was able to meet her student. She also, very secretly indeed, broke all the rules by sleeping with him when she got the chance. It was strictly counter to the geisha code to sleep with someone who was not paying for it.

Shunsuke had promised to take her out of the geisha world and marry her when he finished his studies. But in the meantime he was struggling to find the money to pay his fees. George, knowing nothing of all this, persisted in his suit. By now, he wanted more than just a night of sex. He wanted to possess this exquisite creature; he wanted to marry her. Night after night he went to the teahouse and asked for Oyuki to entertain him, then plied her with gifts and tips. Oyuki smiled her cool mysterious smile, icily played her shamisen and the antique bowed *kokyu*, danced with grave but unmistakable eroticism and accepted his money, most of which ended up in Shunsuke's pocket. Beyond that, she kept poor George at arm's length.

By now the story of the fabulously rich foreigner and the icy-hearted geisha had become big news. The *Osaka Daily News* published a series of sixteen articles under the title 'The Lovelorn Foreigner', reporting breathlessly on events as they unfolded and padding the story with colourful details, some true, some distinctly dubious.[3] There was, for example, the matter of the 40,000 yen (about £250,000 in modern currency) which, rumour had it, Oyuki had demanded of George in order to fend him off, telling him that she needed it to pay off her *danna* (the *danna* was, of course, fictitious). But, far from giving up at being asked for such an exorbitant sum, he set off for New York to raise the money. True or false, Oyuki became known as '40,000 Yen Oyuki' and a stage play entitled *A Single Night's Dream for 40,000 Yen* was a great success.

George became more and more desperate. He also, say Japanese sources, whiled away the time by visiting other teahouses and even became the *danna* of a Shimabara courtesan named Hinamado whom he set up in a house with her mother. He was, after all, only a man. But although he found sensual satisfaction with others, his heart was Oyuki's.

Then Shunsuke graduated and took himself off to Osaka where he immediately got a fast-track job in a bank. Suddenly his love for Oyuki evaporated. The last thing an ambitious young man wanted was a scandalous relationship with a geisha, let alone a geisha as notorious as Oyuki had become thanks to George's much-publicised attentions. As for marrying her – that did not even bear thinking about. When she went to see him in Osaka, he offered to pay back the money he owed her.

For Oyuki it was a terrible shock. Suffering the pangs of rejection, she was also overwhelmed with remorse at the way she had exploited the lovelorn foreigner on behalf of this perfidious lover. It was like karmic retribution for her cruelty to him. Even while she had been using him, she herself was being used. George had been so constant in his devotion no matter how cruelly she treated him; surely the proper thing to do was to give him what he wanted and marry him.

So she did. The 40,000-yen story pops up at this point too. George, it was said, handed over this outrageous sum – enough to start a bank – to Oyuki's family for the privilege of marrying their daughter. George himself denied any such rumours, as did Oyuki's family. But even American papers reported that he had paid $25,000 (about £250,000 in modern currency) 'according to Japanese tradition'.[4]

In 1904, the year that the Russo-Japanese war began, the couple had a very quiet wedding in Yokohama. Shortly afterwards they boarded a steamer for New York. During the voyage, he taught her a few words of English and explained how she would be expected to comport herself as a member of one of America's most powerful and snobbish dynasties.

George's immediate family was on the quay to meet them, together with the American press, buzzing with curiosity about this outlandish match. The family, his stepmother was reported to have said, was far from happy with George's choice. The woman was, after all, Japanese and not even a Christian. In those days westerners were unabashedly chauvinist when it came to other races. No matter how clever their fans and pretty their kimonos, the Japanese were still non-whites and therefore inferior; it was only after the Japanese armed forces had shot a few Russians in the ongoing Russo-Japanese war that, as one Japanese diplomat commented with heavy irony, the west began to concede that they might be remotely civilised.[5]

The prodigal son and his Madame Butterfly bride who could barely speak a word of English found themselves ostracised not only by the Morgans but by New York polite society. There were no invitations to Mrs Astor's balls or to soirées with the Vanderbilts or dinner with the Goulds. After a few uncomfortable months, the couple set sail for Paris. By 1906 they were back in Japan, with the intention of settling there. But in the aftermath of the Russo-Japanese war, anti-foreign sentiment was running high. The slut who had given herself to a barbarian was far from welcome. Finally they took a house in the Champs Elysées in Paris, a city both relaxed and Bohemian enough to welcome a wealthy American and his geisha wife into chic society.

There they lived happily for a decade. Madame Morgan, famous for her porcelain-like Oriental beauty, learnt French, studied the piano and was regularly seen at the salons of the top couturiers. She was never dressed in anything less than the height of Paris fashion. With an ample purse at their disposal they visited Oyuki's family in Japan several times; though, when George had to go to New York to settle financial matters, he went alone. Still, his family, who summered in Europe and there spent time with George and his wife, gradually came round to the marriage.

Then came the First World War. In Japan it was a distant war in far-off countries whose main effect was to provide bottomless markets for Japanese munitions, ship-building companies and other industries. Foreign businesses having tied up all their resources in the war effort, it was an unprecedented opportunity for Japanese companies to gain the edge — a bonanza, in fact.

George and Oyuki, however, were caught up in the middle of it. When war broke out, George was in New York where he had gone to deal with family affairs. Trying to get back to Paris, he discovered that the direct route was impassable because of German submarine warfare. So he boarded a ship for Gibraltar. After a long and circuitous journey he was travelling overland towards Paris when he had a sudden massive heart attack. It was 1915 and he was forty-four.

Utterly shocked by his death – he had never even been ill before – and all alone in a foreign country in the midst of a major war, Oyuki waited as bravely as she could for the body to be sent back for cremation. When the will was read it transpired that George had left enough to support her, in considerable style, on the interest alone for the rest of her life.

The legend of Oyuki Morgan has it that she then returned to New York bearing his ashes where, as his widow, she was more kindly received than when she had been his wife. She settled down there, goes the story, and became a prominent figure in fashionable society, entertaining her guests with her eloquent piano recitals.

A Japanese journalist, however, looked into Oyuki's life, studied her letters and diaries and came up with a completely different end to the story. In fact, it seems, she stayed on in Paris where she lived with a French legionnaire who had been sending her love letters from China for some time before George's death. Oyuki had complained that she was 'a widow' even then. So perhaps, ponders the journalist, George, having captured his prey, lost interest and went in search of new lands to conquer. Perhaps he had reasons other than business for going to New York. In any case, Oyuki was only thirty-four when he died, very beautiful still and enormously wealthy, a most eligible prospect.[6]

In 1938, the ex-legionnaire (by then an elderly academic) having died, Oyuki decided it was time to go home. She was still such a celebrity in Japan that long before she got there, when her ship docked at Shanghai, Japanese journalists were crowding the quay to get a glimpse of her. Back in Kyoto, she settled near the teahouse where George had first gone to woo her, in the oldest section of Gion, north of the River Shirakawa. By then she was practically a foreigner herself. She could barely speak Japanese and wore her outlandish Parisian hats even inside the house. When the Second World War broke out a few years later, people in Gion joked that they would not be bombed 'because Oyuki Morgan lives here'. She died in 1963 at the age of eighty-two. Even before that, in 1961, her extraordinary life had been celebrated in a Japanese musical entitled *Morgan Oyuki*.

Katoro, the teahouse run by her cousin's family, is still there on the corner of a quiet cobbled street shaded with willows beside the Shirakawa stream. In the evening a white lantern glows outside and the wooden doors slide open and close again as customers come and go. The plangent notes of the shamisen, plucky but somehow sad, can be heard faintly from inside.

Taka-jo, the Literary Geisha, and Her Salon

Where is she now,
the woman with the hydrangea heart?
Only the river knows.
Poem by Junichiro Tanizaki on the death of Taka-jo, 1948[7]

At the same time that Oyuki was breaking George Morgan's heart in Gion, a few doors away along the Shirakawa stream another young woman was establishing a different sort of reputation. Old-timers in Gion still remember how their parents used to talk about Taka-jo ('Miss Taka') and the glittering society that passed through her doors. If you went to Taka-jo's, the locals used to say, there was a good chance of bumping into the great and the famous. Those were the days when geisha and maiko were as famous as the movie stars of today and when Gion shops could make a fine living just selling photos and prints of them or even souvenirs, like their delicately perfumed name cards.

In its day, Taka-jo's teahouse could rival any salon in Paris, London or Tokyo. Two of the giants of Japanese fiction, Junichiro Tanizaki, author of *The Makioka Sisters*, and Soseki Natsume, the greatest novelist of the Meiji period, author of *Kokoro* ('Heart') and *Botchan*, were regular visitors at Taka-jo's cultural gatherings. Soseki for one fell briefly and rather tetchily in love with her. While other women loved sensitive poetic flowers like roses and camellias, in Taka's garden she grew the garish hydrangea which changes colour seven times in a season. Her fickle heart, she liked to say, was just as inconsistent, attaching first to one man then to another.

Unlike Oyuki, Taka Isoda was that much-admired creature, a 'Woman of Gion'; born in Gion to a Gion family and raised there. As such, her destiny was bound to lie within the flower and willow world. For her there was no other. Born in 1879, she was near enough a contemporary of both Oyuki and Okoi. But, as the 'child of a teahouse', born to the owners of the Daitomo house, she would never have to ponder what to do for a living.

Small and dumpy, Taka was no beauty, though that did not matter; her future was still assured. She had, however, startling eyes, large and black. 'I could see her brilliance blazing through her eyes,' Tanizaki later wrote, describing his first meeting with her. 'It was her eyes which distinguished her from all the other denizens of the flower and willow world.'

Taka's parents set her on the path towards a successful career as a Gion geisha. At the age of six years, six months and six days, following standard practice in the geisha world, they packed her off to the Inoue School to learn not reading, writing and arithmetic but the far more important skills of singing, dancing and playing the shamisen, taught by the formidable Haruko Katayama. It was not unlike being the child of a star of the Ballets Russes and starting barre work at the earliest possible age under the strict eye of Diaghilev.

Taka, however, had her own ideas. She was a fey, introverted child, not at all the sort of person one would think of as a geisha. Between classes, she read voraciously and one day surprised her father by begging him to arrange for her to study *waka* (classical poetry written in 31-syllable stanzas). Her mother, who had been a geisha herself until her marriage, was against; geisha did not need such skills, she grumbled. But Taka was insistent.

She also held out against *mizuage* (ritual deflowerment). One by one her schoolmates stopped wearing the virginal hairstyle of the trainee geisha and stepped out flaunting the more restrained kimono and coiffure which marked them as women initiated in the ways of love. Only Taka still walked around in a little girl kimono.

Her mother was worried. Reading and writing poems was all very well; but if she did not get a *danna* soon, what on earth would become of her? Worse, she was making the Daitomo teahouse look ridiculous. Tongues were wagging all over Gion. Still a virgin at eighteen? People were starting to whisper that there was something wrong with the child.

So her mother had a word with a middle-aged male acquaintance, who was happy to pay the requisite fee and take on the job. Later Taka wrote about the experience. The man said not a word to her except, 'Don't be afraid.' She lay stiffly on the silk futon, thinking hard about something else, aware of him panting and heaving as if in a dream. In the dim light she barely saw his face. The ordeal did not last long. She felt only a stab of pain in her abdomen.

Later her mother gave her a lecture: 'You are a Woman of Gion, your body counts for nothing. Your arts and your honour, those are the things to value. Whatever you do, never blacken the name of the Daitomo house.'

Thus Taka became a geisha, though a rather odd one. She did not drink, she did not flirt, though she was rather good at punning and joking. But usually she sat very gravely at parties, listening intently, or applied herself assiduously to her dancing. So it was a surprise to everyone when, some time after her initiation, a customer, Mr Nakajima, applied through the teahouse owner to be her *danna*. The teahouse owner, in the proper way, passed on the request to the proprietress of the geisha house where Taka lived. In those days the geisha herself had no say in the matter. But Taka, being Gion-born and bred, was lucky in this respect. The proprietress was her own mother, who asked this strange daughter of hers what she wanted to do. Would she stay on the registry of geishas available for business or would she go and live in the house which this man wanted to set up for her?

Taka was not particularly interested in a career. She had a vague recollection of having met a pale, sickly-looking man at a party and thought he seemed unobjectionable. So she accepted. Carefully bundling up some hydrangea bushes from her mother's garden, she moved to a small house not far away. Mr Nakajima footed the bills and paid regular visits. He was not married but she was a geisha, so it was out of the question that they would live together. And in the daytime she tended her hydrangeas.

There for a couple of years she experienced something which felt a lot like love. But Nakajima's pallor had been a symptom of the dreaded tuberculosis, which caused 50 per cent of deaths from illness in Japan in those days. Gradually his visits decreased, then he died. At twenty-three, Taka felt as if her life too had ended. In the small house, now hers, she threw herself into reading and writing. She had tried the path of emotion and it had yielded only pain. From now on, she decided, she would devote herself to the life of the mind.

But emotion had not finished with her yet. At a teahouse gathering she met Chu Asai, a well-known designer, ceramicist and artist in the European style. The two recognised each other as kindred spirits. He started visiting the little house where they would compose poetry, play shamisen duets and chat about music. He also began teaching her how to paint in charcoal ink with controlled Zen-like flourishes of the brush.

Then they came up with the idea of going into business. Once again Taka gave up attending geisha parties and they set up a small shop stocking Asai's ceramic pieces at prices which the unworldly pair set ludicrously low. But the place was always more of a salon than a shop. The great men of the artistic and literary worlds, poets, painters, novelists and professors, would drop in to look at the wares and stay to while away the hours in argument, raucous talk, laughter and gossip.

Then three months after the shop opened, Asai had a sudden heart attack and died. Taka was horror-struck. Could it be that she was cursed, that she had only to love someone and they would die? A few nights after his death, she went to commiserate with his wife. She put on his nightwear and the two grieving women shared a futon for comfort.

For a while she ran the little shop alone, then, saddened, moved back to Daitomo to take over the running of the teahouse from her ageing mother. It was 1910 and she was thirty-one. As a Japanese woman, she had always assumed that her life would revolve around men. She would serve them, and one might support her as a *danna* or even marry her and take her out of the geisha world. In any case, her role would be to do whatever they wanted. But now she had her own teahouse and had become the centre of a brilliant and talented circle. Let men, by all means, fall at her feet. She no longer needed any of them to lead the way.

Daitomo was a ramshackle dimly lit old house, with dark corridors leading to rooms with blackened ceilings low enough to bang your head on and crazily leaning wooden pillars to hold them up. There the small, round-faced geisha with the piercingly intelligent eyes held court. She was still rather plain with an unfashionably sun-touched complexion which she did not bother to paint white like other geishas. At the time those geisha who were most ahead of the crowd were experimenting with modern kimono styles and even (though rarely) western clothes and western hairstyles. But Taka always wore the same conservative style of kimono. There were some in the Gion geisha world who disliked her and accused her of arrogance.

Yet somehow all the men who gathered at Daitomo were fascinated by her. She would sit swapping poems, joking, punning, reciting old poetry, singing or simply listening to them. She was also a wonderful storyteller. Word quickly spread that, among all the fashionable teahouses of Gion, this was the most brilliant by far.

Among the regular visitors was Kisen Okamoto, an eccentric aesthete with considerable private means who lived in the inn which he had inherited in an unconventional but cheery menage à trois with his wife and mistress. On hearing of Asai's death, he had rushed to the ceramic shop where, as he talked earnestly to Taka, he casually picked up a small teapot and five teacups. A minute later he had turned on his heel and fled from the shop so precipitously that he left his umbrella behind. Taka could only laugh at such cheek and later wrote an essay about it entitled 'Pilferers with Style'. Thereafter their names were linked, though Okamoto never did pay for the teapot.

One day in 1913 Okamoto turned up at the teahouse with a thickset, rather thuggish-looking young man and introduced him to Taka with a knowing smile. It was Junichiro Tanizaki (1886–1965), the Martin Amis or Bret Easton Ellis of his day, who at twenty-seven had already made a name for himself with a couple of sensational story collections. Now, his pockets stuffed with money from top newspapers, he had set off for Kyoto and Osaka to write a series of columns on his experiences; and where better to start than Taka-jo's literary teahouse?

Of Okamoto, Tanizaki wrote, 'Coming from Tokyo, most of the so-called *iki* – stylish – people in the Kyoto area seem pretty out of touch. But Kisen is the exception. He is the kind of man you read about in old books – a true sophisticate, a man of *tsu*.'

As for Taka, 'The second she laid eyes on me, she said, "Tanizaki, my friend, you're a terrible man." Our eyes met for a second before she quickly looked down. I could feel a frisson of attraction. Then she smiled and said, "How could you describe me as an old geisha?"' Abashed, Tanizaki suddenly remembered that he had written that he was looking forward to meeting Kyoto's famous 'old geisha'.[8] She was, he confirmed unkindly, rather old-looking for her years.

Tanizaki soon became a familiar face around Gion. The geisha protested that his name was too difficult to pronounce and called him Tanuki-han, 'Mr Badger'. At parties, after he had downed some saké, he would play up to the snobbish Kyoto-ites' notion of the brash, anything-goes *Edokko* ('child of Edo'), put his hands over his face and ape the kabuki stars of the day, singing in a high-pitched voice.

He too fell under Taka's spell. As you stepped out of the street into the entrance lobby where you left your shoes, you could not fail to notice the voluptuous scent of aloe which she burnt all day long. It seeped into every corner of every room and permeated the folds of her kimono. Wherever she went, the faint musky fragrance wafted along with her. 'I had never before been driven mad with desire by the scent of aloe,' he wrote.[9]

One night, a futon was laid out for him in the room next to Taka's. It was summer and the paper doors between the rooms were open to let the breezes waft through. Taka was lying on her futon, looking very intellectual, reading the *Kokinshu*, a collection of *waka* poetry that pre-dates Chaucer. Tanizaki lay covertly watching her, trying to pluck up courage to make some comment or, even better, creep into her room. But in the end he was too much of a coward. 'I didn't even have the courage to make a single pun. I just lay there rigid like a board and drifted off to sleep.'

Soseki Natsume (1867–1916) was a much older man when he met Taka but he fell even more uncontrollably in thrall to her mysterious fascination. It was early in 1916. At forty-nine, he was a hugely successful author whose novels, such as the best-selling and much-loved *I Am a Cat*, *Botchan* and *Kokoro*, captured unforgettably the insecurities and ambiguities of the changing times. He was a gloomy, angst-ridden man, plagued by ulcers, and had been advised to go to Kyoto for the sake of his health. In photographs he looks painfully sensitive, with a thin face, high cheekbones, haunted eyes and a droopy moustache.

Taka brought out a different side of him. The two had met before, five years earlier, when the great man had passed through Kyoto and been introduced to the 'Literary Geisha'. Shortly after he arrived, one snowy March day, he asked his innkeeper to call her and book her for a geisha party. That evening they met up in a teahouse beside the river with a couple of other geisha and whiled away the hours in witty conversation, capping each other's quips and engaging in clever wordplay at which, Taka recorded in her diary, she and Soseki utterly outshone the others.

'He's not as stiff as I expected,' she wrote of the great man. 'In fact he's rather sweet [*yasashii*]; but he has an inner strength.'[10] Later she added, 'He has a crooked smile and when he laughs his eyes crinkle up at the corners.'

The next night he asked her to meet him privately and they had dinner together. In the course of the evening, Taka suggested a trip to Kitano Shrine to see the famous plum blossoms which were just bursting into flower. So the following morning, full of anticipation, he slid open the door of Daitomo. But Taka was out. She had gone away for the day with a glamorous young financier and was not expected back.

In fact it was all a misunderstanding. Taka had not named the day when she would take him plum-blossom viewing; she had simply meant that she would take him some time. But Soseki was mortified. He stormed off in a tremendous sulk and tramped the streets aimlessly, ending up back at his inn where he threw himself on his futon, declaring that his stomach was hurting. Outside his window, he could see Daitomo across the Shirakawa stream. He composed a poem:

> Divided
> by the springtime river
> a man and a woman.[11]

The next day Taka, knowing nothing of all this, arrived to suggest a plum-viewing expedition and discovered that he was indisposed. 'When I don't see you, it makes me ill,' he told her. A few days later, when he was visiting Daitomo, his ulcers really did begin to trouble him so badly that she telegrammed his wife, who came immediately from Tokyo. For a couple of days both Mr and Mrs Natsume stayed at Daitomo.

Soseki did not forget the slight. Back in Tokyo, he bombarded Taka with scathing letters. He had forgotten, he wrote, that she was 'that kind of woman' and that 'that kind of woman' always tells lies. When she promised to take him plum-blossom viewing, he had thought she meant it. He had thought their relationship was not just customer-geisha. But then she lied to him. 'If you tell me lies, I won't see you next time I'm in Kyoto,' he concluded brusquely. 'That's it. Kinnosuke.' (Kinnosuke was his real name, Soseki his pen-name.)

That December he died. Taka visited his wife to offer condolences and in the years that followed, whenever Mrs Natsume visited Kyoto, she looked Taka up. The two – the geisha and the wife – became close friends.

The years passed and writers continued to gather at Daitomo teahouse. Taka had the place rebuilt with fresh wood, higher ceilings and straight pillars, though it was still suffused with the scent of aloe; and at some stage she gave birth to a daughter. Then came the Second World War. Fearful that the city would be bombed, the council ordered evacuations. In one night in March 1945, 17,000 firebombs fell on nearby Osaka. Three days later the council ordered that 10,000 of the old wooden houses to the east of the city should be demolished to prevent fire spreading if Kyoto in turn was bombed. Among them were the teahouses along the Shirakawa stream.

At first Taka, who was sixty-six by then, refused to move. Her son-in-law packed everything up and took her off to a safer part of town. Two months later, in May, she died. It was as if she had died when she left Daitomo. Kyoto was not bombed but it was too late to save the teahouse. The bank of the stream where it used to be is still crowded with hydrangea bushes which blossom, bright blue, in early summer.

6

DREAMING OF GEISHA
BETWEEN THE OLD WORLD
AND THE NEW

The bamboo was withered and the stalks were eaten at the base by insects. Chokichi thought they would probably disintegrate if he poked them. An emaciated willow tree drooped its branches, barely touched with green, over the shingled roof of a gate. The geisha Yonehachi must have passed through just such a gate when, of a winter's afternoon, she secretly visited the sick Tanjiro [hero of *The Plum Blossom Calendar*, an early nineteenth-century romance]. And it must have been in a room of such a house that Hanjiro, telling ghost stories one rainy night, dared to take his sweetheart's hand for the first time. Chokichi experienced a strange fascination and sorrow. He wanted to be possessed by that sweet, gentle, suddenly cold and indifferent fate.

The River Sumida, Kafu Nagai (1909)[1]

The Writer Who Yearned for Old Edo

In 1909 a young writer named Kafu Nagai (1879–1959) published an achingly lyrical short story entitled 'The River Sumida'. It established him as a master of exquisite prose and defined him as the chronicler par excellence of the demi-monde – the last remnant of the misty world of old Edo which was being blasted away by the cold winds of westernisation.

It is a slight but evocative story, the literary equivalent of an *ukiyo-e* (a woodblock print depicting the floating world). The mood of nostalgia is so powerful that when it was published critics assumed that it was set twenty years earlier; but Kafu denied this. He himself chose to live his life as far as possible in this half-remembered, half-imagined Edo twilight, endlessly inveighing against the brutal new world of trains, streetcars, automobiles and tawdry modern houses. Looking for some romanticised past, he found it above all in the shadowy world of the geisha, prostitutes, strippers, bar girls and chorus girls.

Kafu could afford to slum it. Born in the same year as Taka, 1879, he was the son of a successful Meiji businessman and bureaucrat. But, instead of following in his father's footsteps, he spent most of his youth in the Yoshiwara and the Yanagibashi geisha quarter. When he was not furtively devouring old romances like *The Plum Blossom Calendar*, not to mention the pornographic works of Saikaku, which he hid inside his school textbooks, he was studying English and French or, most shocking of all, writing fiction, an activity which he did his best to conceal from his family. (In old Japan, writers and artists had been considered as disreputable as the geisha, actors and prostitutes they portrayed, an attitude which persisted among conservative families such as Kafu's.)

Despairing of his son's feckless lifestyle, his father packed him off to the United States to learn banking. But he ended up living with a Washington prostitute named Edyth whom he picked up in a bar. Photographs from those years show a young man who could almost be a Japanese Oscar Wilde. Somehow too pretty, with floppy hair, a long jaw and a full-lipped, sensual pout, he stares languidly at the camera with an arrogant, rather louche arch of the eyebrows.

Kafu spent four years in the US and went to Kalamazoo College but longed for France which he was sure would prove to be his spiritual home. Finally managing to shake off Edyth, he arrived in Paris in 1907 at the age of twenty-eight. There he had a rather lonely time of it, and ended up in a bank in Lyon, working among Japanese expatriates whom he hated. But at least he was able to breathe the air which had inspired the writers he most admired: Baudelaire, Zola, Verlaine and Maupassant.

A few months later he was back in Tokyo, pouring out – in a torrent of writing – his horror at the brutal new Japan. The only place where he glimpsed anything akin to the beauty and passion he had found abroad was among the denizens of the demi-monde who still lived the life of old Edo. His diatribes against the loss of the old ways and his swooningly

147

elegiac tales full of decadence and overblown passion soon won him a huge following.

Urged on by his father, he made a respectable marriage to a merchant's daughter. But for love he went to geisha. In 1910 he had a brief romance with a geisha named Tomimatsu. She soon left him for a man with more in the way of wealth and prospects, but not before he had a tattoo inscribed in her honour. Then he met an elegant, beautiful and sophisticated Shimbashi geisha named Yaeji. When his father suddenly took ill and died, he was away at the mountain resort of Hakone with her and could not be found.

Freed of parental control, he divorced his wife in a matter of weeks and married Yaeji. They lived in a small ramshackle house with paper screens and doors where they practised the shamisen together and she helped him prepare paper on which to brush his stories; he wrote contemptuously of 'the modern scribbler who does his polemics with a fountain pen on western-style paper'.

But less than a year later, when he got home one day, she was gone. He had never been able to conquer his habit of frequenting 'the streets of the heavily painted'; and his serial infidelity, as Yaeji revealed in a radio programme recorded at his death many years later, had become unacceptable.

He never married again. Instead he lived his life in or near the geisha areas and found his pleasures among geisha, bar girls, dancers and 'waitresses' (who were really unlicensed prostitutes) at the new-fangled cafés. In his fifties he bought a pretty young bespectacled geisha out of indenture and set her up in a little house which became a gathering place for journalists and literary people. Later he bought her a house of assignation with, rumour had it, peepholes through which the ageing Kafu could watch the customers and geisha at play.[2]

In many ways he was a strange, misanthropic, rather unattractive character. Apart from his girlfriends he professed to hate everyone except for one writer friend who turned down a top position on a newspaper in order to have more time to drink himself to death, an ambition which he duly achieved.

Nevertheless Kafu was a magical writer. He captured better than anyone the disappearing romance of Edo. The work which most vividly portrays the suffocating claustrophia and desperate passions of the geisha world is *Rivalry*, published in 1917.[3] In it, a Japanese critic wrote, Kafu 'attempted to evoke the essence of pure Japanese-style romance, with a strong note of loneliness and submission to fate'.[4]

Set in the classy Shimbashi geisha quarter, *Rivalry* is the story of Komayo, a gentle, guileless young woman – very different from the stylish, sophisticated Shimbashi geisha of legend. Utterly at the mercy of her feelings, she seems to live life balanced precariously on the edge of disaster. When the story starts she is twenty-six, in geisha terms past her peak. She has already been married, to a provincial man who paid off her debts, bought her freedom and took her back to his family home in the distant north. When he died, she decided to return to Tokyo and the geisha calling, rather than staying on in the middle of nowhere among people with whom she had nothing in common.

One day at the theatre she bumps into a man called Yoshioka who, when he was a student many years before, had been her lover. He has become a successful, rather cynical businessman and is already the *danna* of a senior and celebrated geisha, as well as an ex-waitress whom he has set up in her own house of assignation. Meeting the lovely, child-like Komayo, he remembers the innocent days of his youth. Smitten with unaccustomed and unexpected passion, he determines to make her his own.

Yoshioka has every intention of doing the decent thing by Komayo – in other words, buying her. He offers to pay off her indenture, buy her her freedom, set her up in a villa and become her *danna*. But, to his astonishment and rage, Komayo does not leap at this proposal. Is it worth losing her independence again, she wonders, for a man who, like all the others, will only prove to be unreliable and leave her in the end? For Yoshioka is, of course, not offering her marriage. He has a wife and children, as we discover in a passage where he decides to spend a few days leading a sober and respectable life. But soon he is overcome by the urge to live life to the hilt again, to seize 'every pleasure that the world offered, leaving not a single one untasted'. Such a life has nothing to do with wife or children.

Komayo, meanwhile, has committed the one mistake which is fatal for a denizen of the floating world: she has fallen in love. Successful geisha make men fall in love with them; but if they lose control of their own feelings, they are doomed. Seduced by Segawa, a handsome young *onnagata* (a kabuki actor who specialises in women's roles), Komayo finds herself utterly obsessed with him. Recklessly she throws herself into the emotion. At last, she feels (or Kafu imagines that she feels), she knows the essence of what it is to be a geisha, to live on the edge, experiencing the extremes of passion and pain. 'Realising now that bitterness and pleasure alike were part of being a geisha, Komayo felt that she had tasted for the first time the true flavour of geisha life.'

She is convinced, against all the odds, that the actor will marry her. Nevertheless, to keep her options open, she agrees to accept as a part-time *danna* a hideously ugly antique dealer whom she refers to as 'the sea monster'. He provides her with money and in exchange satisfies two of his proclivities: to sleep with a geisha who also from time to time buys the love of a famous kabuki actor, and to entertain himself by having sex with a woman who, he knows very well, finds him physically repellent.

Predictably all this ends in tears. As Komayo behaves in a more and more wifely fashion to the kabuki actor, he becomes bored with her and finally rejects her in favour of a statuesque woman made all the more attractive by being the possessor of a large inheritance. It was the senior geisha whom Komayo displaced in Yoshioka's affections who arranged this liaison, thus finally avenging herself on her rival. Yoshioka, in his turn, has taken his revenge on the hapless Komayo by buying the freedom of a rival geisha from Komayo's own house and becoming her *danna*.

Thus Komayo has to pay the price for having broken the geisha code by allowing herself to be swept away by her emotions. She is in utter despair. Her life, it seems, is over. She has lost everything. But the way is still open for the story to have a happy ending. The kind old man who runs Komayo's geisha house wants to retire and decides to pass the business on to her. He gives her the deeds to the house, the use of the name and the business. Once again she has a future. She can run the geisha house and take care of the geisha who live there. She has finally won financial independence, a far greater prize in the geisha world, and certainly much more reliable, than winning a man.

Rivalry is probably the most complete, lovingly observed evocation of the geisha world ever written. Kafu never questions the values of the geisha, though he does point out that the underlying flaw in their lifestyle is their fatal dependence on others. They cannot say 'No' to a customer no matter what he asks. There is a memorable passage which was excised from early versions of the book and only appeared in private editions, describing an encounter which Yoshioka, an insatiable sexual athlete, has with Komayo:

> When, at eleven o'clock, she finally escaped from his embrace, she was breathing great gasps, she could scarcely speak, and she had no will to get up. Entirely satisfied with this state of affairs, Yoshioka sped off into the darkness . . . She sighed, and chagrin and resentment came back with doubled intensity at the thought of the men who had imposed themselves on her in the course of the evening. She was battered to the very core. She wanted only to die.[5]

No wonder the geisha yearn not for Mr Right but for independence. Nevertheless, *Rivalry* is a romanticised and whitewashed account. There is no suggestion in the novel that anyone has been kidnapped or sold into geishadom; the only hint we have of the true state of affairs is when a man offers to pay off a geisha's debt, reminding us that, for all the romance surrounding them, they are still indentured workers. In another, much tougher novel named *Dwarf Bamboo*, which Kafu wrote around the same time, the wife of one character dies of venereal disease, acquired as the result of her husband's nightly excursions; nothing so sordid soils the romantic picture painted in *Rivalry*.

Rivalry and *Dwarf Bamboo* were Kafu's last novels set in the Edo twilight. When he took up his brush again after several fallow years, it was to write about the geisha's less romantic successors: 'waitresses', bar girls, café girls and resolutely cheery prostitutes living in squalid little houses above fetid ditches where mosquitoes swarmed.

151

New Geisha for a New Age

In 1922 the handsome young Prince of Wales, later to rule briefly as Edward VIII, toured Japan on a state visit. At the time Britain was Japan's staunchest ally and he was greeted with boundless enthusiasm. Wherever he went enormous crowds turned out to cheer him. In Tokyo he reviewed the army, took in an opera at the imperial opera house, and viewed the cherry blossom in the grounds of the imperial palace.

One of the most memorable celebrations took place on the small rural island of Shikoku. Here, in the city of Takamatsu, Count Matsudaira, a scion of one of the country's most ancient aristocratic families, had spent more than £10,000 (£258,000 in modern currency, a veritable fortune) to provide suitable entertainment for such an important guest. After a feast prepared and served by a staff of 300, the climax of the evening came when twelve of the city's most renowned and beautiful geisha glided demurely into the room. Clad in specially woven silk kimonos with a design of Union Jacks intermingled with the Rising Sun, they performed a series of elegant dances.[6]

Much had changed since a couple of decades earlier when the conservative Japanese establishment had been horrified at the success of Sada Yakko and her husband Otojiro – a 'riverbed prostitute' and a low-grade actor – on the stages of Europe and America. Having started out as countercultural heroines on the fringes of society, geisha had now reached the acme of respectability, being wheeled out as proud representatives of their country to entertain visiting royalty. To the Japanese, it seemed there was no longer the remotest correlation between geisha and prostitutes. After all, who would dream of entertaining visiting royalty with a chorus line of prostitutes? Or perhaps it was just that Japanese society had finally accepted that, whether they liked it or not, geisha were as potent a symbol of Japan as cherry blossom and Mount Fuji.

Where once the licensed pleasure quarters had dominated the demimonde, it was now the geisha districts that people referred to when they spoke of the 'flower and willow world'. There were still highly accomplished geisha in the Yoshiwara; geisha from all over town went to them for lessons in dancing and music. Nevertheless, in the popular mind the licensed quarters had become little more than red-light districts. For high culture in the traditional Japanese mode, for exquisite shamisen-playing, graceful and subtly erotic dancing and witty conversation, men visited the teahouses and high-class restaurants of the geisha districts. For the geisha it was something of a golden age. At the turn of the century there were 25,000 geisha in Japan; by 1929 close to 80,000.[7] It was a thriving profession.

The 1920s, however, were to be the pinnacle. Already people were asking where exactly geisha fitted into the wild new era of speed, sport and sex, with its fast cars, American movies, gramophones, ice cream, Marxism, *moga* ('modern gals' with short hair and flapper skirts) and *mobo* ('modern boys' with slicked-back Harold Lloyd haircuts).

Geisha had always been fashion leaders. In the nineteenth century, they set the trends in kimono and obi styles which townswomen enthusiastically followed. Geisha had been the first to try western hairstyles, carry umbrellas and learn western dancing. In 1915 the geisha district of Pontocho in Kyoto established a ballroom dancing school and the geisha houses there had on their books 'dance geisha' who could offer the tango and the waltz among their *gei*.[8] Nevertheless the chief pleasure geisha still offered connoisseurs was their mastery of the high arts. As in Kafu's stories, their company could transport the harassed salaryman in his uncomfortable western suit and prickly haircut back to the romantic days of old Edo. With them, he could imagine himself a swaggering samurai, a wealthy merchant or a dashing rake.

Moreover, for men who wished to enjoy the company of women, or possibly more than just their company, there was now a plethora of choices. The roaring twenties spawned cafés (really bars) across the country and, most famously, up and down the Ginza. There young women, in time-honoured fashion, poured men's drinks for them and chatted flirtatiously. Unlike geisha, they did not need years of training to learn their skills. Nor did a man have to be a *tsu* connoisseur to appreciate them. Particularly in the years following the great earthquake of 1923, which levelled Tokyo and destroyed what few buildings remained of the old city, cafés were all the rage.

Kafu's favourite tippling place from 1926 onwards was the Café Tiger. 'The interiors and exteriors of Ginza cafés take me back to the days when I was in Paris,' he recorded nostalgically in a published essay.

In his personal diary he was less diplomatic:

> The cafés that are so popular throughout the city are to all appearances like Parisian cafés. The reality is much different. We try to imitate everything western and we always make a botch of it. The girls go to work every day and yet they do not receive salaries, and they must depend on gifts from customers for their livelihood. It is quite evident, therefore, that they actually live by prostitution. Fearing rumours and the threats of newspaper reporters, they must appear unwilling to surrender to the blandishments of drunken customers.[9]

He had personal experience of 'rumours and newspaper reporters', having had problems with a waitress named Ohisa with whom he must have shared a bed. By then he was a famous author. After newspaper and magazine reports linked their names, Ohisa decided that she was entitled to share his wealth and badgered him relentlessly.

As the ranks of café girls grew, the number of geisha began to fall, until by 1934 there were over 100,000 café girls to 72,000 geisha.[10] It was time for a radical rethink of geisha and their place in society.

What exactly were they? Leaving aside the more dubious country geisha, the grand ladies of Tokyo and Kyoto could in no way be confused with prostitutes, high-class or otherwise. They could hardly be countercultural queens, for, with the neat class system of Tokugawa society shaken out of place, there was no longer a counterculture – or, if there was, it was not the sort that would be ruled by geisha.

Perhaps they should follow the same path as their fellow entertainers, the kabuki actors, who were in the process of undergoing a distinctly ironic transformation from disreputable members of the underclass, frequently prostitutes, to doyens of the public stage. The Emperor Meiji had made history by attending a kabuki play in 1887, though many more years were to pass before acting in the kabuki theatre, as opposed to watching it, became respectable. Until the departure of the shoguns, kabuki had been a living, changing theatrical form. But, with the coming of the modern age, it became a historical relic. When new plays were written, they were always set in a timeless, nostalgically remembered Edo Never-Never Land.

The music and dance of the geisha too had been a living art form, the popular music and dance of its day. Should they now move with the times or, like kabuki, become repositories of the much-loved past? Were they too doomed to live for ever in Edo?

In the mid-1930s, there was much debate on the subject. Geisha, being women, did not contribute. But intellectuals, poets, restaurateurs who employed geisha, politicians, actors and the director of the Shimbashi Association of Geisha Houses all had their say. Their comments were published as a series of essays in a book called *The Geisha Reader*.

In it the poet Sakutaro Hagiwara expressed in a neat paragraph what was to become the accepted definition of the role of the geisha:

Our wives at home are engrossed in cookery and children, and our conversations with them are quietly serious, mostly concerning household affairs. Outside of this, men need a totally different sort of companion: a woman with whom we can talk about affairs of the world, about the arts, about ideas. We need someone who is entertaining, knowledgeable, educated. This is what a geisha should be.

He went on to say that they should wear western clothes, give up the shamisen and learn the piano. The ideal for the modern geisha, it seemed, was to be the Japanese equivalent of the Ancient Greek *hetaera*, an accomplished companion for gentlemen.[11]

But there were more serious things to worry about than the role of the geisha. Japan had plunged deep into an era which people later spoke of as 'the Dark Valley'. The army had grown more and more powerful. Defying the ineffective and corrupt civilian government, troops had invaded China and occupied Manchuria. There they set up a puppet state and, as a matter of course, shipped out geisha and prostitutes to entertain the soldiers.

As army and politicians clashed, there were several attempted coups d'état and a rash of assassinations. In 1932 naval cadets marched into the residence of the moderate Prime Minister Tsuyoshi Inukai (who happened to be married to a geisha) and shot him in the head. Then in February 1936, 1400 men of the elite First Division and Imperial Guard took over the Diet (the parliament buildings), the Ministry of War and the police headquarters and sent death squads to execute leading members of the government. The coup was contained and the leaders executed but thereafter the senior army officers argued that they needed still greater powers to maintain order.

In the growing mood of patriotic fervour, the 'thought police' were out in force, clamping down on anything that smacked of subversion. The infatuation with all things western evaporated. Speaking English and playing the piano were frowned on, while the geisha, a potent symbol of the old days when Japan was great, found business booming once more. Politicos and the military gathered in the grand geisha restaurants of Shimbashi and Akasaka to discuss policy and celebrate victories.

While intellectuals like Kafu kept their heads down, and sales declined in the grand department stores of the classier sections of town, in the back streets on the wrong side of the river – which had been the heart of the old city of Edo – life went on much as before. There the great event of 1936 was the apprehension of a woman called Sada Abe, known to history as O-sada, who was found wandering the streets with her lover's severed penis wrapped in a *furoshiki*, a large kerchief. A low-grade geisha, she had fallen in love with her employer, a restaurant owner, and spent a week with him in a house of assignation. According to one version of events, the grand climax to a week of fevered love-making came when she strangled him. Another has it that he was a philandering pimp and that she strangled him to ensure that he would remain eternally faithful to her.

In any case, hers was judged to be a crime of passion and she was sentenced to a mere five years' imprisonment. The public, tired of gloomy news, latched joyfully on to her story and she became something of romantic heroine. Freed in 1941, she opened a bar in the old city and some years later, in traditional fashion, ended up in a nunnery. Her story was made into one of Japan's most famous films – *Ai no Corrida* ('In the Realm of the Senses') by the celebrated director Nagisa Oshima.

Kiharu, the English-Speaking Geisha

One of the star geisha in the years leading up to the war was a young woman named Kiharu who worked in the Shimbashi quarter. She recorded her life story in her autobiography, *Edo Geisha – Kiharu Nakamura, the True Story*.[12] (The Japanese title is *Edokko geisha*, an *Edokko* being a 'child of Edo'.) In those days, Shimbashi was the favoured gathering place for naval officers, while the Akasaka geisha houses were the haunt of the army. Navy men tended to be cosmopolitan types who had spent time abroad and were against becoming involved in a war with the west which they could not possibly win. Army men, conversely, were boorish country types who favoured an aggressive foreign policy. All the nice girls, she wrote, wanted to marry a navy man, not an army man.

Kiharu's is a very different story from those of the many thousands of unfortunate women from poor families whose parents, at that time, were still selling them into geishadom. She became a geisha out of choice and was one of the elite. The bright, headstrong daughter of a wealthy family who owned a private hospital, she loved dancing and performing. As an only child, her parents wanted her to marry a doctor who would take on the family name and business (in Japan families who have no son often 'adopt' a son-in-law in this way). But she insisted on joining a geisha house despite her parents' disapproval.

Born in 1913, Kiharu was the epitome of the Shimbashi geisha – smart and sassy, rather than cute and girlish like Kyoto geisha. In photographs she is exquisitely pretty, with a bright-eyed, lively face and full, expressive mouth. She looks like a modern woman, very different from the languid, withdrawn, expressionless beauties portrayed in the previous century's woodblock prints. She was even smart enough to avoid *mizuage* (the customary deflowering).

When she was sixteen, she records, the mistress of Tombo Ochaya ('Dragonfly Teahouse') took her aside and told her that she had had a lucky break. The mistress had found a *mizuage danna* to perform Kiharu's *mizuage* – not just any *mizuage danna*, but one of the most important men in the country, a senior government minister who had taken a liking to

157

her. Kiharu nodded submissively; privately she was wondering what on earth importance had to do with it.

The next night she was summoned to a party at Dragonfly Teahouse. On inquiry, she discovered which of the guests was the minister in question. He was older than her grandfather, with purplish blotches all over his face. But before she could do more than register horror, the party came to an end and the minister disappeared. A few minutes later the head maid led her off to a small secluded room at the top of a staircase, pushed her in and left. The minister was waiting there.

The room was a kind of ante-chamber with another behind. Having swallowed a few cups of saké, he slid back the doors between the rooms and sat down on the futon which was spread on the floor. 'Come here,' he coaxed. 'There's nothing to worry about. Take off your kimono.'

Kiharu had been thinking hard. 'I'm not a child any more,' she told him, bursting into tears. 'I know what's going to happen. If you do this to me, I'll hate you for the rest of my life. Do you want that to happen?'

The minister told her not to be so childish. After all, everyone had an arranged marriage and slept with people they had never met before. There was nothing strange in that. But Kiharu was stronger-willed than he.

'I've never before had anyone give me a lecture at mizuage,' he laughed finally, admitting defeat, and sat and chatted to her instead.

Kiharu had been learning English. In the daytime she plaited her hair, put on a uniform and took the train to school. In the evening, she changed into a kimono to attend geisha parties. She wanted to be able to talk to the western guests she met there. They always brought an interpreter; but usually the interpreter knew as little about the geisha world as they did. When the geisha started performing their dances, instead of explaining the meaning the interpreter would just mumble the English words 'Japanese dance' and down a few more cups of saké. Now she was saving up, she told the minister, for a typewriter. So he gave her 100 yen, enough to buy one. He was, she conceded, actually rather a kind man.

Kiharu became known as 'the English-speaking geisha'. In the mid-thirties a stream of celebrities passed through Tokyo, and Kiharu was always summoned to entertain them. She met the silent-screen star Charlie Chaplin, the baseball legend Babe Ruth and the French film director Jean

Cocteau, who wrote a poem about her. There was wild speculation about the two of them in the Japanese press, despite his reputation for being gay. 'Some people are like Miyamoto Musashi,' she commented dryly in her memoirs, referring to the great swordsman who was adept with two swords, not just one. She was also invited by a German film director to star in a film. But, had she taken up his offer, she would have had to give up her profession as a geisha, so she declined.

In her spare time she slipped away to a flying school outside Tokyo and got her pilot's licence. In her memoirs there is a picture of her standing with her hand on the propeller of an Abro, wearing a helmet, goggles and flying suit, smiling winsomely.

She was in no hurry to find love. Then, in 1935, when she was twenty-two, she was summoned to entertain at a party for the great Russian opera singer, Feodor Ivanovitch Chaliapin who, during his stay in Japan, had become one of her regular customers. Among the guests were the distinguished politician Prince Fumimaro Konoe and his debonair younger brother, Hidemaro. The Konoes were aristocrats, related to the imperial family. But Hidemaro, something of a maverick, had taken the decidedly eccentric course of becoming a conductor at a time when musicians were still considered nearly as disreputable as actors. He had also scandalised society circles by leaving his wife, a woman of suitable rank and bloodline with whom he had had an arranged marriage; as a member of the imperial household, he was not at liberty to divorce.

In other words, he was the perfect match for a bright, sassy, modern woman like Kiharu. It was love at first sight. The two used to slip away to Yokohama to the glamorous New Grand Hotel where all the international travellers stayed. From the stone pillars and sweeping staircase in the lobby to the ornate headboards in the bedrooms and huge western-style baths, it seemed wonderfully exotic. Five years on, he invited her to go with him to the United States and live there as his mistress. But her mother and grandmother were desperate for her to marry, not live out her years as a concubine, and appealed to his brother, who by then was prime minister, to intervene. Thus Hidemaro disappeared from her life.

It was 1940. No one could doubt any longer that Japan was at war. The intervening years had seen Japan's invasion of China and the massacre of a quarter of a million civilians at Nanjing. The government had signed the Tripartite Pact with Germany and Italy and Japanese troops, having occupied much of China, were marching through the jungles of South-East Asia. For ordinary people at home in Japan, their main experience of the war was rationing. Every possible resource was needed to support the military and already the goods on the shelves of shops were pitifully scarce. As part of the general clamp-down, the government banned the use of alcohol in brothels. The measure applied to prostitutes but not to geisha, who were an entirely different profession and also serviced the very people who had imposed the ban. For them business continued as usual.

Besides army and navy geisha, there were also geisha who served the military police, geisha patronised by the ordinary police and geisha who took care of the civil service bureaucrats. More than most, they must have known what was going on, for the most confidential discussions often took place at geisha parties. As not only the war but arguments between the government and the military grew more intense, geisha were called in and asked to play a part in intelligence-gathering. Many agreed. As a result, geisha formed a considerable part of the intelligence network.[13]

A few months after Hidemaro had sailed out of her life, Kiharu was called to the police station to help them deal with some bizarre pornographic photographs taken by an American whom they suspected of being a spy. There the chief of police took her aside. He had a proposal for her. Just as the dashing geisha of the Meiji period had supported their samurai lovers, so she too should work for her country. She knew many powerful westerners, top executives and the chairmen of major companies, who frequented the Shimbashi teahouses when they were in town. All he asked was that she should make a note of the westerners she met and their companies. He would visit her regularly to collect information. In other words, he wanted her to spy. At the time this was routine. Anyone who came into contact with westerners was expected to watch their every move.

However, for Kiharu it was a terrible dilemma. If she did as he wished, she wrote, she would have to betray the trust of her customers and break the fundamental geisha tenet of confidentiality. If she refused, she might be jailed; and she would be guilty of disloyalty to her country. The only solution was to give up being a geisha. At twenty-seven she was no longer young; it was time to get married. She also had an inkling that it might be a good idea to leave the country.

At the time there were three suitors eager to marry her: the heir to a button fortune, a singer of traditional Japanese ballads, and a man called Kazuo Ota, a 33-year-old career diplomat recently returned from England whom she had met at a tea ceremony gathering. Of the three, he seemed the best choice. He was clever, he could speak English and, having just returned from abroad, knew nothing of her background as a geisha. Having calculated the pros and cons, she settled on him.

When they married in 1941, she asked the president of Nissan Motors to stand in as her surrogate 'father' so that she would seem properly respectable. Two weeks later the young couple were on their way to India, where Kazuo had been posted. In September the following year he was sent on an extended posting to Burma, which had been conquered by Japanese troops that June. Kiharu had returned to Japan with her baby son. She went back to Shimbashi and worked as a geisha for as long as possible, then fled to the countryside with her mother and grandmother. By the time Kazuo reappeared, in 1948, he had a new wife and family. Kiharu sued for divorce and a few years later moved to New York, where she lives still.

Armageddon

Kiharu came home to a country embroiled in war. Japan had launched a surprise attack on Pearl Harbour in December 1941. The first retaliatory bombing raids by American B-25s came the following April, damaging and demolishing swaths of buildings around the edges of Tokyo.

Still the splendid restaurants, where Tokyo's 9000 geisha entertained, stayed open for business, despite the swingeing new tax which the government, desperate for funds, had imposed on such luxurious activities. Anyone who could afford it had every intention of carrying on their hedonistic lifestyle. As for the military, they were still partying at teahouses in the spring of 1943 when – for everyone else – rationing was biting hard. Kafu's chosen companions were now the youthful chorus girls of Asakusa in the city's East End. 'In this world apart, there are no ashes of war,' he wrote in his diary.

Finally even the geisha had to go. On 4 March 1944, Kafu recorded regretfully, 'From tomorrow restaurants and teahouses are to be banned . . . Geisha have not yet been banned, but they appear to be moving into other trades for want of engagements. Without theatres and geisha, the music of Edo, based upon the shamisen, will perish.'[14] It was not a matter of morality but of desperate need. The country was on the brink of collapse and every woman and child had to be conscripted to help with the war effort.

On their last night the geisha restaurants stayed open almost until dawn. Then the geisha took off their silk kimonos, folded them carefully and wrapped them in sheets of crisp hand-made paper for storage. They put on smocks and *mompe* (baggy cotton indigo-dyed peasant trousers) and went to work in ammunition factories or to labour through the night sewing uniforms and parachutes. The canniest managed to avoid such a fate by finding someone to marry them, becoming concubines or persuading their patrons to include them on their lists of company employees. And if, of course, your *danna* was a member of the military, he would ensure that you were properly cared for.

Worst of all was 1945, the last year of the war. People sold everything they had and fled to the countryside. In Tokyo, the air-raid sirens whined nearly every night as swarms of B-29s cruised the skies, raining down firebombs in such quantity that the snowflakes turned soot black. The rundown wooden city stood no chance. In a single night, on 9 March, some 78,000 people burnt to death and one and a half million were left homeless. The city was reduced to a sea of ashes, rubble, twisted metal and charred, broken stone walls. The pleasure quarters were utterly destroyed and the theatres (including the beautiful art deco Shimbashi Embujo Theatre, built in 1925 for the geisha to perform their annual dances) were reduced to blackened shells. The Yoshiwara, still functioning in defiance of government orders, was burnt to a cinder together with hundreds of women who had been locked inside by the brothel-keepers, anxious not to lose their investment.

Kyoto fared better. Thanks to the intervention of American scholars who argued that it was a place of irreplaceable cultural heritage, it was barely touched by bombing.

As the war intensified, the patriotic geisha of Gion decided to do their bit. They bought two planes for the extravagant sum of 65,000 yen each, had the names 'Dai ichi Gion Kogo' ('Number 1 Gion plane') and 'Dai ni Gion Kogo' ('Number 2 Gion plane') painted with a flourish on the flanks and presented them to the army. The ceremony took place at a nearby military airstrip, where the troupe of beautiful young geisha, clad patriotically in peasants' working clothes and straw sandals and with their famous glossy black locks tied up in bonnets, drew much press attention. Being practical women, the geisha also instigated evacuation training at the teahouses, practised relaying buckets of water to put out possible fires and observed a curfew so that the quarters fell into darkness after nightfall.

The last annual dances, entitled 'Ko-koku no miyabi' ('Elegance of the Japanese Empire'), took place in spring 1943. Shortly afterwards the Gion Kobu Kaburenjo, where dance performances and classes took place, was commandeered and transformed into a munitions factory where those geisha and maiko who had not fled to the countryside were conscripted to sew parachutes and uniforms for the army. From late in 1944 they were also ordered to produce incendiary balloons (enormous hydrogen balloons containing bombs and incendiary devices) which would, in theory, drift across the Pacific on the jet stream and set America's cities ablaze. After 17,000 firebombs fell on Osaka, the city council, fearful that Kyoto would suffer the same fate, ordered swaths of houses, 10,000 in all, to be evacuated and demolished to make fire breaks. Among them were the beautiful old teahouses of Shimbashi, the northern part of Gion, including Daitomo, the much-loved house where Taka had entertained writers and artists.

The end came on 15 August 1945, after the cities of Hiroshima and Nagasaki had been obliterated by atomic bombs. A few days later, people gathered round their radios, expecting to be exhorted to fight the enemy, with bamboo spears if necessary, to the death. Instead, for the first time ever, they heard the reedy voice of their emperor, crackling over the air waves. His words were convoluted and the language archaic but the meaning was clear. His people, he said, would have to 'endure the unendurable and suffer the insufferable'.

After the Deluge

When the American and other Allied occupation forces, under the command of General Douglas MacArthur, arrived in the country a couple of weeks later, many were shaken by the scenes of utter devastation which they saw. They had been expecting violent resistance. Instead they found a nation of shell-shocked, half-starved people, ragged and dirty, who stared at them, blank-eyed, as they drove through the dusty, rubble-strewn streets. Some seemed positively – and astonishingly – pleased to see them.

For the Japanese the first winter was, if anything, even grimmer than the bombing had been. Then they had had wartime spirit to buoy them up. Now they were a nation in defeat. Life had been reduced to the barest essentials – keeping warm and scavenging, thieving, smuggling or begging for food. In Tokyo 60 per cent of the housing had been destroyed. The few buildings that still stood were unheated, and the miserable shelters people put together out of broken bits of wood and rubble offered little protection against the icy winds and snow. Many died of exposure or pneumonia or of the plagues which swept the stricken city – typhus, smallpox and cholera. Malnutrition and beriberi were rife.

Those geisha who had fled to the countryside used their kimonos for barter. One by one they gave them away – a priceless silk kimono with an exquisite gold-thread design in exchange for pumpkins, aubergines and sweet potatoes; a heavy brocade obi worth tens of thousands of yen for some cabbages, spinach and radishes. Rice was like gold dust, almost never to be found. The farmers got richer and the geisha poorer, but at least they were able to eat.

For the women who remained in the cities, whether geisha, prostitutes or destitute women who had lost their families, there were other ways of staying alive. The victorious GIs might be well-fed with clean uniforms but there was one commodity they lacked. And there were plenty of

Japanese men with lengthy experience in the field ready to ensure that this gap in the market was promptly filled.

Mark Gayn, one of the first American journalists to arrive in the country, recorded a 'curious tale' reported to him by an American colonel. Barely two weeks after General MacArthur flew into Atsugi air base, on 9 September 1945, the American First Cavalry Division was poised to march into Tokyo. The GIs were nervous about how the Japanese military might react when their capital was invaded and had set up a road block on the edge of the city. Well after nightfall, they heard the rumble of an approaching truck.

'Halt!' yelled the sentry when it was within hailing distance. The truck stopped and a Japanese man stepped down. Behind him followed a flock of young women. Warily they walked towards the troops. When they were quite close the man stopped, bowed low to the soldiers, gestured to the women and announced, 'Compliments of the Recreation and Amusement Association!'[15]

It was a bizarrely comic moment which pointed up the enormous cultural gulf between the invaded and the invaders. The Japanese, convinced that the Americans were beasts who would rape their wives, mothers and daughters, had taken the precaution of sending their women as far away into the countryside as possible before the troops arrived. As an alternative, brothel-owners from the Yoshiwara, which had been burnt to the ground in the bombing, together with the presidents of the seven major entertainment guilds in Tokyo including the restaurant, cabaret, geisha and brothel associations, had been commissioned by the Metropolitan Police, under government auspices and with government funding, to set up the RAA. Long before the first American set foot in the country, they started recruiting from among prostitutes, geisha and bar girls. They were looking for 5000 women, though only 1360 initially responded to the poster they had pasted up in the Ginza.

To sternly puritanical conspiracy theorists like Mark Gayn, the RAA was 'the world's biggest white-slave traffic combine' and a prime 'item of evidence in the damning record of Japan's efforts to seduce the Army of Occupation away from its purposes'.[16] But to the Japanese, it was not unlike the New Shimabara, the licensed quarters set up at the time of the Meiji Restoration for visiting foreigners. Conquering army or not, the Americans were men and had the same needs as any others.

There were plenty of GIs who did not suffer from Gayn's moral scruples. By April 1946, as his doughty researches revealed, there were 668 known brothels in Tokyo alone, with 8000 prostitutes who did not, one assumes, suffer from lack of customers. But none could compete with the RAA which, thanks to government sponsorship, offered the prettiest women working in thirty-three 'houses of entertainment'. The most famous was the Oasis Dance Hall in the Ginza, which featured an 'army prophylactic station' in a Nissen hut. The RAA ran two hospitals for its women and had a network of agents recruiting through Japan.

Gayn also investigated the International Palace, a large ugly factory on the outskirts of Tokyo which had started life producing clocks and watches for the Seiko Corporation, then became a munitions plant and after the war, on the advice of the Tokyo Police, was transformed into 'the world's largest brothel'. Five concrete-walled dormitory buildings which had housed workers now functioned as brothels. The women Gayn interviewed there told him they had lost their families in air raids, though there were also some who described themselves as geisha. All, he noted grimly, had been forced to buy clothes and cosmetics from the company and were heavily in debt.

Kafu too went to see this new pleasure quarter (which he knew as the Tokyo Palace) and told a rather different story. It was populated, he reported, by whores from Kameido, one of Tokyo's unlicensed districts, who had packed their bags and moved in en masse. At first the main clientele had been American soldiers; but from October 1946 onwards the American traffic stopped and the only customers were Japanese. Painted across the walls were large signs in English reading 'Off Limits – VD'. He noted, in his dour way, that the women seemed more like factory girls and students than bona fide whores.[17] Perhaps the truth fell somewhere between the two versions.

General MacArthur, whose powers were so all-encompassing that the Japanese called him the 'last shogun', was determined to clamp down on this dangerous and unhealthy trade. He declared all brothels off limits to GIs and issued a directive banning contractual prostitution.

This was followed a year later, in 1947, by an imperial edict, drafted by the Americans like everything else at that time, outlawing officially sanctioned prostitution. Like the Prostitute and Geisha Emancipation Act enacted by the Meiji government in deference to western notions of propriety, it was full of noble intentions but utterly unenforceable. Worse, far from ending prostitution, it made life harder for the women.

No longer publicly recognised and government-sponsored, the Yoshiwara, which had been hastily rebuilt and was operating out of barrack-like shacks, was privatised. The masters and mistresses of the old bordellos became 'special purveyors of beverages' and the women became 'waitresses'. As freelancers, they received a percentage of the brothel earnings and in theory could leave whenever they wished. The law required that they should all be over eighteen, though many were not. The problem was that the proprietors of the new, illegal Yoshiwara required firm assurances that the women would not run off without repaying their debts. They took to using *yakuza* – members of the Japanese mafia – to enforce this.

Added to which, officially recognised red-light zones were only the tip of the iceberg. Besides the unlicensed quarters which had always existed side by side with the licensed ones, the ranks of prostitutes had been massively swollen by thousands of desperate women who had lost their families or were waiting hopelessly for husbands who would never return from the front. These women had no means of supporting themselves except for prostitution. The most visible were the streetwalkers or *panpan* girls ('bang bang girls', referring to the speed of the transaction). At their height there were as many as 500 young women thronging the area around the railway arches near the Ginza and within spitting distance of General MacArthur's headquarters, grabbing passing GIs, pulling them into the shadows. For payment they begged for cigarettes, chocolate, chewing gum or, most pitifully, food.

Using a term the GIs could understand, they called themselves 'geisha gals'. Among westerners, 'geisha girl' became the catch-all term for anyone of dubious morality, from hostesses at bars, cabarets and dance halls to the lowliest streetwalkers.

The authorities, nevertheless, were perfectly aware that geisha were a different species. They were excluded from the directive and the imperial edict and on appropriate occasions top American officers enjoyed geisha parties. The government discreetly sponsored the Shinagawa quarter which was popular with Americans. They also offered a subsidy to the Shimbashi quarter, though the proud Shimbashi geisha refused it.

Bars, teahouses and geisha houses were officially permitted to reopen on 25 October 1945. Little by little, those who had fled to the countryside began to make their way back. Kiharu, once the star geisha of Shimbashi, found herself on a rickety train jammed between scavengers and sacks of illicit rice on their way to Tokyo's black markets. Once in the city, she found work as a translator for a British journalist and every Sunday took food to her son, mother and grandmother whom she had left in the countryside. From time to time she appeared at geisha parties. She also began teaching English to young geisha so that they could talk to their foreign guests.

With the war, the number of geisha had been reduced practically to zero. Now they gradually began to rise again, though it was a long time before the profession returned to its pre-war prosperity. In 1947 there were 1695 geisha in Tokyo and 2478 in the whole country.[18] And in March 1948 the Shimbashi geisha were ready to perform their first post-war dance spectacular, *Azuma Odori* (the Dance of the East), in their own Shimbashi Embujo Theatre, which had been restored to its pre-war art deco glory.

During the seven years in which the American and other Allied forces occupied Japan, they revolutionised society in a myriad of ways, some expected, some less so. Their brief was to instil democracy and to bring Japan into line with the modern world. One way in which the country was way out of line was in its treatment of women. The new constitution of 1947, hastily drafted by American officials, recognised men and women as equal in politics, law and education, which was, in Japanese terms, utterly revolutionary. It introduced universal suffrage, thereby giving women the vote for the first time. Henceforth women – who had been banned in the late nineteenth century from participating in politics at any level – were to be as free as men to run for parliament. Article 24 stated, even more radically, that 'marriage shall be based only on the mutual consent of both sexes'. The occupying forces also instituted compulsory education for boys and girls up to the age of fifteen and stipulated that all national universities were to be open to women.

A more unexpected development was the introduction of public kissing, on stage and screen. In Japan kissing was very much confined to the bedroom; it was one of the most esoteric of the geishas' repertoire of outré sexual techniques and considered almost as intimate as the sex act. But if the Americans wanted Japan to imitate their ways, imitate they would. The first on-stage and on-screen kisses took place in 1946, to the considerable embarrassment of the actors called upon to perform them. Traditionalists were shocked but audiences were entertained. Kissing, however, was only the beginning. The following year saw another innovation: the introduction of striptease. What with all these raunchy American imports and the traditional Japanese laissez faire attitude towards such matters, the way was open for Japan to develop a no-holds-barred sexual culture – which, indeed, it has. Could there be a place for the delicate arts of the geisha in such a world?

Less than a century had passed since Commodore Perry and his men had roughly booted open the door of Japan, exposing its hothouse culture to the cold winds of change. The geisha, who had started out as the stylish queens of a raffish underground, had survived the transition, though, as skirts got shorter and lifestyles wilder in the twenties, they were already beginning to seem like something of an anachronism. Then in the patriotic years before the war, with traditional Japanese values being reasserted, they found themselves back in favour. Like it or not, it seemed, they were identified in people's minds with Edo and old Japan. No matter how western the country became, while that core of Japanese-ness remained they would survive. But how long could it remain, as Japan moved inexorably into the modern world?

7

MODERN TIMES

After the war two things became stronger — women and nylon stockings.
Popular post-war Japanese saying

Street of Shame

As the clocks struck midnight on 31 March 1958, in the thirty-third year of the reign of Emperor Hirohito (known to history as Emperor Showa), prostitutes and their customers in brothels and bordellos across Japan rose to their feet, linked hands and, swaying rather boozily, broke into the nostalgic strains of 'Auld Lang Syne', known in Japanese as 'Hotaru no Hikari' ('The Firefly's Glow'). It was one of those moments of exquisite poignancy which the Japanese love to savour. An era had come to an end.

By then, to general rejoicing, the occupying forces had climbed into their aeroplanes and gone home. In the aftermath of the Korean War, Japan was thriving again, becoming wealthier with each year that passed. New buildings had sprung up on the rubble of the old. It was a country of worker ants busy rebuilding their economy and their lives. In many ways things had not changed much since the pre-war days. Many of the same old faces were to be found running the country and its businesses and hobnobbing in geisha restaurants in the evenings, though they wore modern suits and voiced updated sentiments about democracy and the like. Even so, inside their conservative jackets and ties, these men were serving their companies with the same single-minded devotion with which the samurai had served their feudal lords. That old core of Japanese-ness was still there.

But there was one legacy of the occupation which could not be shuffled aside so easily. General MacArthur and his cohorts had given women a voice. It would be generations before Japanese women became as independent as western women, if they ever even wished to do so. But they had the vote and, after the 1946 elections, there were thirty-nine women lawmakers in the Diet, the Japanese parliament. In the early 1950s militant women's groups, aligned with the Salvation Army, the Japanese Christian Women's movement and anti-slavery organisations, lobbied tirelessly to bring to an end, once and for all, what they saw as the pernicious, humiliating and barbaric practice of licensed prostitution. The imperial edict of 1947 had been singularly ineffectual. What was needed, they argued, was a law to abolish socially recognised prostitution and make it as unacceptable as it was in the west.

Kenji Mizoguchi's moving 1956 film, *Street of Shame*, stirred the national conscience and provided powerful ammunition for the anti-prostitution lobby. In it he depicts life in the Yoshiwara as the law is being debated in the Diet. There the rapacious brothel-keeper of Yume no Sato ('Village of Dreams') plays the bluff, fatherly old man as he counts his earnings. 'We're social workers,' he argues, insisting that he is doing good, providing a home and work for the girls. But the film also shows the desperate lives the women lead: the ageing mother, too old to appeal to any but the most drunk or undiscerning of clients, who has sacrificed herself to support her ungrateful son; the bespectacled wife working to support her sick husband who kills himself when he discovers how she has earned their money; and the young women already hardened in a life of vice, heartlessly fleecing men to set themselves up in business.

There were plenty of people struggling to maintain the status quo, who argued that prostitution was a social necessity. Brothel-keepers hastily got together the All-Japan Association for the Prevention of Venereal Diseases to show how responsible they were and also smuggled sizeable amounts of cash into the pockets of Diet members in an attempt to buy their votes. One was arrested for accepting bribes from them. And thousands of women at risk of losing their jobs united to form the Tokyo Federation of Unions of Women Workers.

But there was never any doubt that the voices raised in outrage against socially recognised prostitution would carry the day. The Anti-Prostitution Law, outlawing public solicitation and management of prostitutes, was passed in 1956 – with a year's leeway before it came into force and another before prostitution became a punishable offence. The women who had supposedly been liberated joined hands and lifted their voices in a soulful rendering of 'Auld Lang Syne' before going home to pack their bags. Some half a million had either to go back to their families, look for other work, or – most commonly – find a new job title under which to operate.

After 350 years in business, the Yoshiwara and its ilk were to close their doors for ever – at least in theory. Respectable, controllable, government-sanctioned prostitution was at an end. The licensed quarters had, for all their faults, been clean, well-organised and safe for both the women and their customers. Hereafter there would only be unlicensed prostitution which rapidly became the domain of the *yakuza*. Some of the most famous old houses of the Yoshiwara did indeed close. But most simply carried on under another name, setting up signboards advertising themselves as 'Toruko' or 'Turkish baths'. (Later, after protests by the Turkish ambassador, these became known as 'soaplands'.) Despite the illegality of prostitution, the number of prostitutes actually rose in the years following the passage of the act. After all, as western observers (invariably male) delighted in pointing out, the day on which the bill went into force was April Fool's Day.

Geisha, of course, being considered an entirely different profession, were exempt. Yet, for them too, the Anti-Prostitution Law of Showa 33 was a watershed. Despite the many pious words which had been spoken and written to the contrary, there had always been grey areas where the geisha and prostitute worlds crossed. In the poorer unlicensed districts such as Miyagawa-cho and Gion Otsu in Kyoto, geisha houses were side by side with houses where prostitutes lived. Geisha and prostitutes were part of the same community.

172

After the bill was passed, the geisha moved several steps closer towards respectability – though they never made it all the way; the ambivalence remains to this day. Prostitutes who had lived in the same areas faded into the shadows. Some went back to their families in the countryside, some became *nigo-san* (mistresses or 'second wives'), while the lucky ones found someone to marry them. Others who were skilled at playing the shamisen stayed on as musicians. Red-light districts developed where illegal prostitution flourished under the vigilant eyes of the *yakuza*, completely separate from the geisha districts.

Many women who became geisha before the war had been sold by their parents as children. Long after the bill was passed, such practices continued. Despite the law, as late as the mid-seventies, children from impoverished rural villages were still ending up as maids in geisha houses, attending primary school in the daytime, and cleaning and helping the geisha with their make-up and kimonos in the evening. But attitudes had changed. Such practices were coming to seem more and more unacceptable, and the country's growing prosperity meant that soon no one would be in such straits that they would need to sell their children.

Likewise, anyone who had become a geisha in the pre-war years had taken for granted that the rite of passage by which one blossomed into a fully fledged adult geisha was *mizuage* (compulsory deflowering). After the Showa 33 bill, this too became strictly illegal. A geisha might continue to have a *danna* or *dannas* to support her, but if she did she kept quiet about it.

The institution of compulsory education up to the age of fifteen also undermined the profession. Before the war, budding geisha had begun their dancing and shamisen lessons at the age of six years, six months and six days. They became maiko at eleven and had *mizuage* to become adult geisha around fifteen. But now that they had to attend school, they could not become maiko until the age of fifteen, which meant that their rigorous training as professional musicians or dancers had to be curtailed. Standards, it seemed, were doomed. Could geisha still be geisha when everything that made them unique and distinctive was changing?

By the 1960s, Japan's post-war recovery period had come to an end. The country was rapidly becoming more prosperous than ever before.

Gleaming skyscrapers sprouted on the Tokyo horizon. New boulevards and the first bullet train lines were put in place for the 1964 Tokyo Olympics, which showed the world that Japan was again a force to be reckoned with. By then almost every family in the land possessed the 'three treasures': a television, a washing machine and a refrigerator.

But astonishingly, the geisha continued to flourish. The number of geisha never returned to their pinnacle in the twenties but by the mid-1970s there were a healthy 17,000.

For the men who ran Japan, the geisha world was something they had grown up with. To support a beautiful and famous geisha was still a measure of a man's success. Industrialists and politicians took it for granted that, after a hard day at work, they would spend the evening at a familiar teahouse which was practically their second home. There they could get a feminine perspective on the events of the day by talking them over with their favourite geisha in an atmosphere of intimacy and trust. Their wives, who lived in a much narrower domestic world, bounded by home and children, could not understand such things, they felt, whereas geisha were used to mixing on equal terms with powerful, articulate men. Lesser men might use bars and hostess clubs for the same purpose. But the top men of the nation had earned the attentions of women that they considered the nation's most sophisticated and accomplished. Teahouses, in fact, were very much akin to the gentlemen's clubs of the west, luxurious, ruinously expensive and closed to all but the elite.

The evening sessions at the teahouse were also where movers and shakers would deepen their bonds with their colleagues, wrangle over business or political matters and conclude deals which had been barely broached in the formal daylight meetings in the boardroom. When there was a guest to be impressed, rewarded or entertained, they would call the teahouse, secure in the knowledge that the highly professional geisha would ensure that the party went without a hitch.

Two great scandals shook the 1970s and 1980s: the Lockheed scandal, which culminated in prime minister Kakuei Tanaka's disgrace when he was indicted of accepting more than $2 million (£3 million) in bribes from the American Lockheed corporation; and the Recruit shares-for-influence scandal. Many of the key meetings between the plotters had taken place in the teahouses of Shimbashi and Akasaka where discretion was guaranteed.

But society was changing. Japan was entering the modern world at an unprecedented pace. The men for whom geisha were an essential part of their lives were growing older. A new generation was coming into power which no longer understood or appreciated the gracious old ways. Gradually the numbers of geisha began to fall.

The oil crisis of 1973 was probably the beginning of the decline. Thereafter, although Japan's economic fortunes rose again, the country had changed beyond all recognition. In the new world of big money, fads, fashion, schoolgirl prostitution, host clubs and a bacchanalian world of sexual titillation, the geisha retired deeper and deeper into the shadows, jealously guarding their ancient culture.

In 1945 Shigeru Yoshida, soon to become prime minister and a towering figure of the post-war years, was released from house arrest, where he had been kept in the last days of the war for advocating peace talks with the Allies. He went straight to Shin Kiraku, the famous geisha restaurant in Shimbashi, to see his mistress Korin and stayed there for several days. At the time, such behaviour was not even worthy of comment; it was to be expected. Within the Yoshida family, the great man's relationship with Korin was completely open. When he died in 1967, she was an official guest at his funeral. But by then everything was changing. Yoshida was the last politician who could afford to be so splendidly insouciant about his affairs.

The Short, Fat Prime Minister Who Wanted to Save Money

In June 1989 a woman who described herself as a former geisha sold a kiss-and-tell story to the Japanese media. Her name was Mitsuko Nakanishi and she had, she revealed, had an affair with the prime minister, Sosuke Uno, several years earlier while she was working as a geisha in the Kagurazaka district. He had kept her as a paid mistress for a few months, then ditched her.

In Japan such a story was far from newsworthy. Everyone knew that politicians, along with any other man who could afford it, kept mistresses.

Newspapers scrupulously refrained from scrutinising such matters. 'There's no personality below the navel,' went the saying; in other words, what goes on beneath the navel is a man's private business and nothing to do with his public persona. But Nakanishi – who by now had a lowly job in a law office and was short of cash – persisted. The editor of the *Mainichi* newspaper finally decided to print the story, arguing that in the late twentieth century the public ought to know about the peccadilloes of its leaders.

Uno was not at all the kind of man one could imagine having an affair. At sixty-six, he was short, fat, bespectacled, jowly and extremely unprepossessing. His alleged paramour, Nakanishi, was forty. Uno had become prime minister for want of anyone better to do the job. At the time the seemingly invincible Liberal Democratic Party (LDP) was embroiled in one of its periodic corruption scandals. Uno, then foreign minister, was virtually the only person who had not been accused of accepting bribes and had thus been thrust into the notional top post by the real behind-the-scenes powerbrokers. He became prime minister on 2 June and immediately Nakanishi started plotting a way of getting her own back and supplementing her income.

As well as the *Mainichi* article, Nakanishi also appeared on television to hold forth in excruciating detail on their relationship. The story was blazoned across the western press, thrilled to be in on Japan's first ever sex scandal. At last, wrote western journalists, traditional attitudes were changing. Japan was falling into line with the rest of the world (or at least the Anglo-Saxon part of it) in condemning men who had extra-marital affairs.

In reality, though a few women Diet members and vocal representatives of women's groups made great play of Uno 'treating women as pieces of merchandise', what shocked and amused most Japanese was his meanness. He had paid her, Nakanishi complained, the paltry sum of 300,000 yen (£1000 at the exchange rate of the time) per month when the going rate had been a million yen. Then she had phoned him on the night that he became prime minister and suggested he pay her to keep her mouth shut. Ten million yen would have shown proper respect. Instead, he gave her three. Infidelity on a grand scale showed that a man was a man; mean-mindedness was the very opposite.

In the geisha world there was fury, not against Uno but against Nakanishi, who had brought shame upon the profession by speaking out. Obviously she was not a real geisha, for no geisha with an ounce of self-respect would dream of breaking the fundamental code of silence; indeed, it transpired, she had not done the geisha training and had worked in the Kagurazaka district for only a few months. Uno was guilty not only of meanness but of having had an affair with a geisha so low-grade that she would talk about it. 'That woman is nothing but a prostitute!' raged Kiharu ('the English-speaking geisha') who by then, at the age of seventy-six, was living in New York but happened to be passing through.

Then a geisha from Akasaka broke cover to reveal that she too had had an affair with Uno. On the tenth anniversary of their relationship, she had asked him for a small financial memento. Instead of paying up, he walked out. She had been brooding ever since. She revealed every detail of the affair – his penchant for pornographic videos, his refusal ever to give her a raise – to the *Weekly Shincho* magazine.

As for Uno, he remained silent, choosing neither to confirm nor deny the reports. Before the Upper House elections a few weeks later, his wife took to the podium at a meeting in Yokohama. What she had to say was rather different from the betrayed western wife's response of 'standing by her man'. She did not apologise for her husband's deed nor express anger. Instead, before a largely female audience of 6000, she offered 'heartfelt apologies for the controversy surrounding my husband'. An election was due and the most important thing was to win it. Many things were at stake, including all the benefits and respect due to her as the wife of a top politician. She was a good Confucian wife, like the long-suffering wives of the Tokugawa era. It would certainly not do to let personal feelings intrude.

In the election, the opposition Socialist Party took an unprecedented number of seats and several of the appointees were women. Uno resigned. He had been in office for just over two months.

The Japanese take on the business was instructive. It was clear that Uno was incapable of managing his women. And if a man couldn't manage his women, how could he be expected to manage the country?

If a man did not take care of his geisha properly, he was not to be trusted. It was 1989; but among the movers and shakers who ran Japan Inc, attitudes were still firmly entrenched in the old Never-Never Land of Edo; that old Japanese-ness was still in place.

From time to time since then, geisha scandals have broken in the press. One very famous geisha is renowned for having had an affair with a louche Japanese heart-throb. But in general the geisha world remains secret and impenetrable.

But these women are still the stuff of romance in Japan. They still shape the Japanese self-image. Novels and films endlessly re-create the romantic age embodied by the geisha, when it was better to die rather than be dishonoured and men paused regretfully at the Willow of the Backward Glance, at the boundary of the Yoshiwara, before returning to the real world.

II

THE FLOWER AND WILLOW WORLD

8

PUTTING ON THE MASK

When I see the first new moon
Faintly in the dusk
I think of the moth eyebrows
Of a girl I saw only once.
Anonymous poem[1]

Present and Past

Once I had become an accepted part of the geisha world in Kyoto, I took to spending my days and evenings in geisha houses and teahouses with maiko, geisha and the 'mothers' of the houses – *okami-san* – or chatting to the motley collection of individuals who populated the geisha world. Elderly barmen reminisced about their favourite maiko of decades past and showed off their collections of signed photographs, scented business cards, fans, and the towels which maiko handed out to mark rites of passage in their careers. Men who boasted of being regular customers dropped the names of maiko they were friendly with and talked of taking them bowling on their days off. Shopkeepers along Shijo Street whose families had served the geisha community for generations regaled me with stories of past and present maiko. And whenever I had a spare moment I pored over books on geisha history or read novels written in the days when any love story had a geisha as the heroine and ended not 'and then they got married and lived happily ever after' but 'and then they committed love suicide'.

Clearly, there was an enormous gulf between the way maiko and geisha had lived even in the recent past and their present-day lives. The watershed, as everyone always told me, was Showa 33 (1958), the year that prostitution had been made illegal. Yet some of what gave the geisha their special flavour still remained. In the past, love had been the forbidden fruit, made all the more romantic because it was illicit. But today too the geisha were somehow beyond the pale – respectable yet not respectable. On the one hand, they were the symbol of Kyoto; posters of maiko inscribed 'Welcome to Kyoto!' greeted travellers as they arrived at the central railway station. People on the edges of the geisha world would happily describe their customs and rituals and boast about the geisha they knew. But when I asked if they would let their own daughter become a geisha, they always looked askance and mumbled, 'Well, it's a difficult question.'

It was also clear that there had been a devastating decline in numbers. Old people – both geisha and shopkeepers – remembered the days when the whole area between the River Kamo and the Eastern Hills, from north of Fourth Bridge down to Fifth Bridge, had been a special world. Every dwelling had been a teahouse or geisha house and every shop had served the geisha community. In the 1920s, at the height of the geisha era, there had been 80,000 geisha throughout the country. In Gion alone there were 2500 geisha and 106 maiko.

When the teahouses reopened after the war, around 1948, there were still 1200 geisha and 160 maiko in Kyoto. In those days the flower and willow world was a thriving industry, governed by pro-tocol and ritual, with geisha clattering on their wooden clogs from teahouse to teahouse every day to pay their respects to the teahouse mothers and sometimes entertaining from the morning of one day to the small hours of the next. But by 1999 there were just 195 geisha and 55 maiko left in Kyoto, of whom 90 geisha and 22 maiko were in Gion.

I wondered if I was seeing the end of a way of life or if the geisha would somehow survive. What did it mean to be a geisha today? Could they still be called 'geisha' when so much of what had made them geisha had disappeared? In modern Japan, they were no longer the heart of the entertainment industry, nor, as they had been, sirens and idols, the most desired women of their generation. What role could they play when they had become almost an anachronism?

The kabuki actors, once their fellow leaders of the demi-monde, equally disreputable 'riverbed folk', had turned respectable. Stuck in an unchanging Edo-period time warp, they now put on costume dramas for the populace to enjoy. But even if the geisha had wanted to follow this course, it was not open to them. The essence of the flower and willow world was its secrecy. It was open only to a few well-heeled initiates. If the geisha became popular entertainers, their seductive mystery would be lost. But if they did not, how could they survive?

And what of the geishas' past? Was it a distant memory? In fact, as I discovered early on, it was still very much alive.

'When I think about the old days I always remember them as dark,' said young Mr Kato one day. I had spent hours in his small printing shop in one of the geisha districts planning the wording for some business cards he was making for me. When I went to pick them up he invited me into the cluttered kitchen at the back to have tea with his mother and father. A fresh-faced, handsome man with a moustache and a penchant for oversized T-shirts, he was in his late thirties, so he must have been referring to the seventies, when he was a boy. He and his parents were in the geisha world but not of it; so they had no axe to grind. Unlike many geisha I had met, they were not worried about creating a pretty image of the geisha and their lives. They simply told it as it was.

'The buildings were lower, the ceilings were lower – everything was low and dark. When I think of the street then, it was all blacks and browns and reds,' he said. 'Those slatted screens that hang in front of the windows so no one can see in – they were all dark brown.'

There were, he said, plenty of daughters of geisha in his class at primary school. Sometimes there would be rumours: so-and-so's father is the owner of such-and-such construction company, so-and-so's father is a doctor or a dentist or an actor. In the rest of Japan people might have thought it was strange; but here in the geisha districts one-parent families were normal. The children certainly never suffered prejudice; in fact no one thought twice about it. The only trouble was, they were spoilt. Every now and then you'd hear them saying, 'Uncle's coming today!' You knew that whenever their father turned up, they got whatever they wanted.

'But there was also a girl from the country. Her parents must have received a "preparation fee".'

'"Preparation fee"?' I queried.

'For having made her and brought her up until then,' he explained as if it was the most normal thing in the world. 'They had sent her off to a geisha house to be raised. I felt sorry for her. I remember she was always crying in class. She was the only maid in the house. When she got back from school she had to clean and help the maiko and geisha with their kimonos and make-up. She was busy all the time; she didn't have any friends. She got two days off a month, the 7th and the 20th. That was twenty-five years ago. There were quite a few like her at school with me, but she was the only one in my class. I don't know what became of her. She probably ran away. She's certainly not around now.'

'Your grandad used to mess around with geisha,' rumbled Mr Kato's father unexpectedly. In his sixties, he had recently been ill and his son had had to take over the business. We all settled into deferential silence. 'My mother, my real mother, that is – I had three or four "mothers" – used to have a geisha house. She'd been a geisha herself.'

'Grandma was a geisha? You never told us that before!' gasped Mr Kato and his mother in unison.

'Your grandad ran a Chinese restaurant,' Mr Kato senior went on imperturbably. 'In the war there was no food here so he used to go out to the country to get supplies. My last "mother" was the owner of the inn where he stayed. She was the mistress – the "number two wife" – of someone important. In those days guys had children all over the place. That was normal. No one ever asked who anyone else's parents were. You didn't go round asking that kind of thing.' Young Mr Kato and his mother were murmuring and tut-tutting together at these revelations.

In Mr Kato senior's time (before the occupation, the imposition of universal compulsory education to the age of fifteen and the 1958 watershed), *zegen* – somewhere between talent-spotters and pimps – used to go out and scour the poorer parts of the countryside for pretty young girls whom they would take back to Kyoto to be trained. In those days maids might arrive in Kyoto at the age of six or seven and, after a period of servitude and training, became maiko at eleven. That was why they wore 4-inch-high clogs, to add to their height, for they were not yet fully grown. Modern-day maiko teetering down the street on their clogs sometimes towered above their clients.

There had been many other changes. In pre-war days, the majority of the maiko in Kyoto were from geisha families; their mothers, grand-mothers and sometimes great-grandmothers had been geisha. The girls from the countryside were on the bottom rung of the ladder. But in modern times, many daughters of geisha wanted to take up another career or marry a 'normal' man and have a 'normal' life. At least one elderly ex-geisha I spoke to begged me not to refer to her by her real name, because none of her family, not even her son and daughter, now grandparents themselves and highly respected members of society, had any idea that she had been a geisha.

Modern maiko, conversely, were mainly not from Kyoto and, even if they were, were not from a geisha background. The first criterion was that they had to be pretty; like modelling, this was a career where social background counted for nothing and a pretty face was all. They also had to be fit and healthy, for the maiko training involved hard work and long hours. But the biggest difference was that they had all become maiko out of choice. Some had seen maiko, perhaps on television, perhaps on a school trip to Kyoto, and had been starstruck by these fairytale creatures. Others had studied traditional Japanese dancing and wanted to pursue the art more deeply. In most cases their parents had been horrified at the idea; but the girls wanted so badly to become maiko that they reluctantly gave their consent. It was the exact reverse of the bad old days, when children had been sold by their parents out of desperate poverty.

As far as the old ladies of the geisha community were concerned, the result had been a disturbing drop in standards. Before the war the daughters of geisha began their dancing classes at the age of six years, six months and six days. In those days it was a serious profession and children started young, like students of the Bolshoi Ballet. Modern-day maiko did not even begin their training until they were fourteen or fifteen – by which time they had had so much so-called education that, instead of listening obediently and repeating again and again, as was expected, they were prone to question every instruction they were given.

As an elegant seventy-year-old, the fourth generation of a family of geisha, told me with a disdainful lift of the eyebrows, 'In the old days at least you could expect girls to have basic manners.' Now, she huffed, they knew nothing: how to put on a kimono, how to walk in one, how to kneel and rise elegantly with one knee just an inch or two above the other, or how to open the sliding paper *fusuma* doors with a discreet motion of the hand, fingers and thumb held straight and pressed together. Some had never sat on tatami before and didn't even know how to use chopsticks. 'You have to teach them everything!' she concluded with an extravagant sigh.

The Professor of Hairstyling

Whenever I had a spare moment I dropped into Professor Ishihara's hairdressing salon to the north of Shijo Street, in the oldest part of Gion (his Japanese title is Ishihara Sensei, 'Teacher Ishihara'). He knew everything one could ever want to know about geisha, maiko, their history and their hair. His wife, I had heard, was from a family that ran a teahouse, though that was the one thing he would never talk about.

A laid-back, humorous, dapper man, always dressed in an elegant pin-striped suit, he had penned three books on the history of maiko and *tayu* hairstyles and was working on a fourth. He was the only person left in Japan who knew how to create the ornate hairstyles of the *tayu* courtesans.

'In Edo times you could tell everything about a person just by looking at their hair,' he told me one day. 'In those days there was a different hairstyle for each class of person. You could tell from someone's hairstyle what class they were, what kind of work they did and what part of the country they came from. The geisha world is the only place where that still goes on. There are different hairstyles for each stage of the geisha's career, different hairstyles for geisha in different parts of Japan and different sorts of kimono.

'This,' he explained, showing me a picture of an ornate hairstyle, decorated with ribbons, ornaments and silk flowers, with a bagel-shaped rolled knot of hair worn high on the head, 'is ware-shinobu. It's the maiko's first hairstyle. It means that she is young and cute.

'And this,' turning the page to show me a less heavily decorated hairstyle with the knot lower down, 'is the maiko's second hairstyle, ofuku. It means that she is to be congratulated, she is no longer a virgin. Maiko used to start wearing their hair like this when they were thirteen.'

'Thirteen?' I queried, aghast. It was hard to get to grips with the idea that the old geisha I knew had lost their virginity – in other words, been deflowered whether they liked it or not – at the tender age of thirteen.

'They all had it,' he said carelessly. 'They all had mizuage. If you listen to the old grannies at the teahouses, they'll tell you, "We were children, we didn't know anything, what could we do?" In those days Kyoto was full of rich silk traders and kimono merchants. The danna would pay for mizuage, buy the girl a house and pay her an allowance. The wives? They were like employees, they just thought it was normal. Nowadays they'd ask for a divorce! For three hundred years it was perfectly normal for men to pay and for women to give sex. All that's stopped now, of course. Ever since 1958 it's been completely different. It's much more serious now. The maiko all concentrate on their dancing. The ofuku hairstyle just means she's more senior.'

Once you became a senior maiko, he said, there was no further to go. You wore your hair in the *ofuku* style, though there were a couple of other styles worn for special occasions: *yakko-shimada*, a sweeping elegant style worn for the New Year celebrations, decorated with sprigs of dried rice for fertility and good luck; and the *katsuyama*, named after the seventeenth-century bath-house attendant who became a great courtesan famous for her splendid topknot. The maiko's last hairstyle, which was very ornate indeed, was the *sakko*, which she wore for her last month before graduating to become a geisha.

The door opened and a young woman came in, piping in a fluting falsetto, 'Ohayo-dosu! Sensei, o tanomo shimasu!' ('Good morning! Professor, could you please . . . ?'). In the mornings maiko were always pale and subdued after the previous night's parties. Without further ado, this one, in an everyday cotton *yukata* and with her long hair loose and shaggy, sat down, picked up a teen magazine and started leafing through it.

One way to spot an ex-maiko is the perfectly round little bald patch on the crown of her head. Having been tugged and pulled by the hairdresser week after week for five years, the hair never grows back. Watching Professor Ishihara at work, it was easy to see how this could happen. He was like an artist struggling to create beauty out of his chosen material – hair.

Heating curling irons over a portable charcoal brazier, he stretched the hair until it was crimped, shiny and perfectly straight. Then, combing in globs of white pomade and oiling his comb with *bintsuke* oil (the same oil used to keep sumo wrestlers' topknots rigid), he parted and sectioned it. Beginning with the hair at the crown of the head, he tugged it firmly into a ponytail, tied in a roll of handmade paper to give bulk and swept it forward to form the central knot of the entire edifice. He sculpted the hair at the back of the head up and over it, coiling it into a stiff loop, with a thin frame of lacquered wood to hold it in place. The front of the hair meanwhile was rollered. Then he set to work on the two side pieces, stretching them round, with plenty of *bintsuke* oil, and tying them with string to the central knot so that they formed two wings, one on either side of the face. He slipped a thin lacquered wooden band like a hairband through the two wings to hold them firmly in place and tucked a wad of artificial hair inside each.

Then he took a hairpiece, a ponytail of coarse black hair from the Tibetan yak, and tied it on to the central ponytail of the maiko's own hair. He combed the whole lot together, folded it forward, looped it back, opened it out and – lo and behold! – there was a bagel-shaped knot. Finally he teased the front of the hair into an arch and attached it too to the central knot. He added a hairpin to conceal the centre of the bagel, some pieces of stiff black paper to keep the shape of the wings precise, and a couple of crinkly red ribbons. The whole masterful creation took about forty minutes and the end result was a sleek, shiny coiffure with not a single hair out of place, firm enough to survive a week's working, playing and sleeping.

'Oki-ni,' said the maiko, transformed from a shaggy-haired young woman into a creature bearing such an immaculate pompadour that a man would be terrified to touch her in case he mussed it; bowing and smiling, she slipped out of the shop.

A Maiko's Debut

Most of what goes on in the geisha world happens behind closed doors. It is a little like Hollywood. Every now and then you might spot a geisha or maiko on the street as she flits from teahouse to teahouse or, if you are the guest of someone very wealthy, meet one entertaining at a geisha party. But you only ever see the public face, immaculately made-up, eternally composed and gracious. As for the private life of the geisha, that is an entirely different matter, utterly closed to outsiders.

So when I was invited to sit in on the backstage preparations for the debut of a maiko called Kanosome, it was an enormous privilege. The debut – *misedashi*, literally 'store opening' – is one of the most momentous rites of passage in the geisha's career, when she steps out for the first time as a fully fledged maiko on the geisha stage. It would also be an opportunity to witness the putting on of the mask, the moment of transformation when the fresh-faced teenager became a denizen of another world.

It was the rainy season in Kyoto by the time Kanosome's debut came up. Standing on the rickety balcony of the small room where I lived, I looked in dismay at the rain pounding on the roofs, sluicing through the gutters and sweeping in great sheets along the street. The River Kamo, usually a calm little stream with paths along both banks populated by joggers and courting couples, had turned into a savage brown torrent. Mammoth waves, big enough to surf on, surged along with frightening speed.

Nothing, however, would prevent me from going out. Huddled under an umbrella, I splashed past the dark, shuttered and screened wooden houses of Gion and along the covered pavement of Shijo Street. At the end of the road, behind the red-painted gateway and giant pagoda of Yasaka Shrine, the forested slopes of the Eastern Hills were swathed in mist and driving rain. Dripping, I found the house, slid open the door and went inside.

Upstairs, Kanosome was kneeling on the floor, her cotton *yukata* folded

189

down so that her shoulders were bare. The room had the orderly chaos of a theatre dressing room, with kimonos hanging around the walls and bowls, brushes and tubs of make-up spread across the floor. At fifteen, she had the face of a classic Japanese beauty such as one sees in woodblock prints, a perfect melon-seed shape with a slightly protruding lower jaw, large wide apart eyes, well-shaped eyebrows and a mouth neither too big nor too small. Without make-up she was just a nervous, excited teenager. Despite the waxed medieval hairstyle with its red ribbons, tortoiseshell combs and decorations, one could imagine her in jeans or school uniform, riding her bicycle, satchel on her back.

Patient, obedient, she sat motionless on her knees while Masami, the senior geisha of the house, massaged her shoulders, then took a knob of soft white wax and rubbed it thoroughly into her face. One of the most popular geisha in the city, Masami was normally to be seen in white face, kimono and wig. She was lively, entertaining and beautiful with a wide face and full laughing mouth. But that day she had a different role to play. In simple ponytail and jeans, she applied herself very seriously to the magical business of transmuting the girl before her into a work of art.

Taking a tub of white make-up, Masami put some into a dish, mixed in a trace of pink, then carefully applied a layer to Kanosome's face with a wide flat goat's hair brush, leaving a clean line of unpainted skin at the hairline. It was an extraordinary transformation, as if the girl had put on one of the beautiful but expressionless masks which actors wear in the classical Japanese Noh theatre. She had lost the idiosyncratic features of a teenager and become an icon from another age.

In the old days, the make-up was white lead and it had a disastrous effect on the skin. Women quickly aged and their skin became yellow-tinged and prematurely wrinkled from applying it every day. Sometimes young geisha died from the poisoning. Nowadays maiko and geisha use a gentler make-up, produced by Kanebo, the Japanese cosmetics manufacturer — though modern women, as well as geisha, still swear by nightingale droppings (sold by the bottle in organic cosmetics shops in Japan) to cleanse the skin and give it a pearl-like pallor. To get the luminous white of the face, Masami explained, she mixed a little pink into the white; true white would give a sallow tint on Japanese skin. But for the throat and shoulders, she used pure white to set off the brilliant red of the collar.

Next Masami puffed on a layer of white powder, patting until Kanosome's face was as smooth as alabaster and as pristine as an artist's canvas. She filled in the eye sockets and the sides of the nose with pink, then brushed a layer of white around the girl's neck and shoulders, puffing powder over the top.

Kanosome's family and a couple of her school friends had travelled from the city outside Tokyo where they lived to witness this rite of passage. They crowded into the room, whispering nervously. Squashed in a row along one wall, they sat formally on their heels. Her parents looked ridiculously young to have such a grown-up child. Her father, in a brown suit, shuffled to his feet, took out a video camera and started filming. It was like a wedding except that there was no groom. They were seeing their child for the last time. Even more than it would have been for western parents, it was a hugely emotional occasion. For in Japan girls usually live at home with their parents until they marry, then move straight from their parents' home to their husband's.

Taking a narrow brush, Masami shaded in the eyebrows in feathery strokes, painting them very straight like moths' wings, then outlined the eyes in red, extending the line out at the corners. Finally she painted in a line of black around the eyes.

'The trick is to get the face the same every time,' she said. 'When they first try and do it themselves, it's a mess. Our other maiko has a different face every day.'

'She'll never be able to do this herself!' tut-tutted Kanosome's small round grandmother.

'Sshh!' whispered Kanosome, motionless as an artist's canvas.

Then Masami took a silver template and placed it against the girl's back, adjusting the position at the nape of her neck. With a large flat brush she painted the back in white, up behind the ears and down to the centre. She removed the template, revealing a titillating three-pronged tongue of bare skin. Usually a maiko would paint her own face, using two mirrors to paint her back and leaving a two-pronged V of unpainted flesh. The shape supposedly hints at a woman's private parts.

191

Two *otokoshi* bustled in, middle-aged women in skirts and white gloves. There have been *otokoshi*, literally 'male staff' or 'boys', ever since there were geisha. They were the geishas' assistants. They helped them dress, carried their shamisen boxes as they went back and forth from geisha house to teahouse, and were often their confidantes, privy to the tastiest items of gossip. But these days there were only five of the original male 'boys' left, all rather old. Their job had largely been usurped by women.

Chatting and laughing, the *otokoshi* helped Kanosome into her under-kimonos, first a filmy red petticoat, then a white cotton under-blouse with a red collar and long red sleeves, then a floor-length red petticoat, tying them all in place with silk ribbons. Then they laid a brocade collar, embroidered in red, white and silver, around her neck. Kanosome stood like a tailor's dummy while the women tugged, readjusted and tied.

Hanging on the wall was a sumptuous black kimono with a stream in white and pale turquoise swirling across the hem and shoulders. Blossoms and leaves floated along it and there was a stylised bridge across it. There are appropriate kimonos for each season and each event. This was a formal kimono used only for ceremonial occasions. It was made of a light almost transparent silk gauze with a very loose weave called *ro*, worn in summer.

Helping Kanosome into the garment, the women tugged the collar and back of the kimono right down to the middle of her back to expose the familiar breathtaking expanse of white skin and the three-pronged tongue of unpainted flesh at the nape of her neck. Tying it in place with ribbons, they took the obi, a weighty band of sumptuous gold brocade, and wrapped it round and round her. Then they inserted a cushion to pad the back and tied it all with silken strings so that the two long ends dangled to the floor. They were heaving and tugging so vigorously they had to stop for breath and wipe the sweat from their brows.

For the final touch, Masami took a small stick of intensely red safflower paste, moistened a thin brush and carefully painted a tiny petal of red in the centre of Kanosome's lower lip. The upper lip she left white; it is only after a year that the maiko begins to paint her upper lip. Then, tucking two silver dangling combs into the girl's coiffure, she handed her a mascara brush and mirror. To everyone's horror, a black dot appeared on the immaculate white of the face. Masami touched up her handiwork, laughing cheerfully. After all, under all the paint, Kanosome was still a child.

'What a pretty maiko . . .' said Kanosome's mother in uncertain tones.

The teenager had disappeared. In her place was a beautiful painted doll, all lips and eyes etched on the pure white canvas of her face.

'It's your own daughter,' smiled the *okasan*, the proprietress of the house, elegant in a dark blue kimono. *Okasan* means 'mother'; from now on Kanosome would address *her* by this title. The two mothers could not have been more different. The *okasan* of the house was slim, elegant and rather icy, like a nightclub hostess; whereas Kanosome's real mother was plump, comfortable and homely. She was giving up one for the other.

Preparations completed, we swept off to the teahouse, owned by the *okasan*, where Kanosome was to celebrate the beginning of her professional career as a maiko. The narrow entrance was decorated wall to wall with enormous colourful paintings of the gods of good luck with 'Kanosome' brushed in huge black characters on each. Here the family bade her 'Goodbye', watching rather wistfully as she stepped into her high wooden clogs and out into the night.

'Oki-ni, oki-ni,' she piped, using the Kyoto word for 'Thank you'. It must have sounded disturbingly affected to her parents' Tokyo ears. Somehow her demeanour had changed, along with her appearance. What on earth had happened to their little girl? She was not even talking the same language as them any more.

Bowing, she set off with her new mother, clattering down the road, her obi swinging heavily behind her. The two would parade through the neighbourhood so that Kanosome could be formally introduced to all the teahouse owners. Usually it was a grand parade, the maiko's moment of glory when, like a Hollywood starlet, trailing a pack of photographers and the odd TV cameraman, she showed herself in all her finery to her public. But the rain had kept the photographers away.

'You must be proud of her,' said Kanosome's grandmother to the young father, filming their retreating backs with his video camera.

'Hmm,' he said slowly. The bland Japanese mask, conveying the illusion that everything is eternally fine, slipped just for an instant. He looked down sadly. 'Well,' he said finally. 'She really wanted to do it.'

At the far end of the alley two small figures were silhouetted for a moment, sheltering under a huge oiled paper umbrella, before vanishing from sight around the corner.

Flower Money

One balmy night I went for a stroll along the River Kamo. Behind the teahouses of the Pontocho geisha district, below the platforms where drinkers caroused with geisha in the heat of summer, right at the edge of the water there was a broad stony esplanade lined with cobbles, popular with sunbathers, cyclists and courting couples. That evening it was crowded with the city's youth in shorts and trainers, letting off fireworks, laughing and jostling.

Walking along, I came to a group which seemed to be from another world; though, to a seasoned Kyoto-ite, they were such a common sight as to merit barely a second glance. The men were in business suits but looked as if they had been enjoying a well-lubricated evening out, ties askew, faces flushed and glistening with sweat. They yelled with as much abandon as the youths in shorts. With them were four or five maiko, their painted faces glowing white in the reflected neon light, the decorations in their hair sparkling and swinging, their brilliantly coloured kimonos absurdly cumbersome, like fancy dress. Some of the men were chasing the maiko, brandishing sparklers. The maiko ran about adroitly on their high clogs, shrieking and giggling.

It was just innocent fun, young men and women enjoying a summer evening together. But there was one thing that made that group a little different from all the others. The maiko were being paid for every second of their time.

There was a story I heard about a businessman who had been on his way back to Tokyo. Happening to meet three maiko at Kyoto Station, he invited them to join him in the Green Car, the first-class carriage in the bullet train. Geisha and maiko always travel first-class on any mode of transport and stay only in five-star hotels. It is part of the flower and willow lifestyle. Even an ageing geisha who is no longer in huge demand at parties and has limited means would not dream of travelling economy class. She has to keep up appearances even if it bankrupts her.

Charmed to find himself in such delightful company, the businessman bought the maiko snacks and drinks and enjoyed their girlish chatter. The three-hour journey passed like a dream. When they arrived at Tokyo Station, he bade them 'Farewell', wished them all the best and went off to his meetings.

Several days later – when, no doubt, he had almost forgotten the encounter – a letter arrived in the post. Puzzled, he opened it. It was from a Kyoto teahouse and contained an enormous bill for the time spent with three maiko: three hours each, plus additional charges. It was, said the geisha who told me this story, nothing to do with greed. It was not that the teahouse mistress wanted money. In the geisha world, things have to be done properly. Time spent with a maiko or a geisha has to be paid for, even if it is distasteful to have to ask. It was a matter of doing things with style.

Another story in the same vein concerns an elderly professor who was strolling across Shijo Bridge one day when he happened to meet some maiko he knew. They were off duty, pattering along in cotton *yukata*, their glowing young faces unpainted.

'Big Brother,' they greeted him. Geisha and maiko always address their *danna* as 'Father' and other customers as 'Big Brother', no matter how old they are. 'Where are you going?'

'I'm going to have lunch,' he beamed. 'I don't have any classes today.'

'We haven't had lunch either,' chorused the maiko.

Thrilled at the prospect of several hours in the company of these charming young women, he took them to the best French restaurant in Kyoto, wined and dined them. But alas, for all his generosity, he suffered the same fate as the unsuspecting businessman.

A man who 'knew how to spend money and have fun with geisha' – that was the kind of man a geisha liked. Quite apart from the no-strangers rule, this meant that the geisha world would be eternally exclusive, the realm of the very, very rich. For no one else could possibly keep up with the spending required.

In modern times, elderly geisha grumbled, standards had slipped badly.

These days you got vulgar types throwing around not their own but company money and who were so déclassé as to ask for a receipt. 'The receipt society,' they called it, wrinkling their elegant noses in disdain.

Back in the eighties, when the Japanese economy was on a roll, big spending was all the rage. In those days there was a coffee shop, legendary in Tokyo, where you could get a cup of coffee for $200 (£125). You could buy exactly the same cup of coffee in the same shop for $5 (£3) but that was no fun. The thrill was in spending $200 on a cup of coffee. In the geisha world, that mentality continued. As in the days of the courtesans, it was a world where money spoke.

From the moment a maiko or a geisha slipped her dainty feet into her clogs and slid open the geisha house door, she was at work. The meter clicked on. It continued to run as she moved from party to party, until she was back in the geisha house at the end of the evening. Whether you took a geisha out for dinner, for a trip to the theatre or a day of golfing, no matter how relaxed and informal the occasion, she was still at work, earning an hourly wage.

Geisha were quite unembarrassed to talk about money, though of course one never called it 'money'. The word for the maiko's or geisha's fee was 'flower money' – *hana-dai* or *o-hana*, 'honourable flower'. In the old romantic days, when Japanese clocks pursued a rather eccentric course and the pleasure districts ran on a different time to other parts of the country, a geisha's or a maiko's time was measured by the number of incense sticks which burnt down while she was working. The incense sticks in different areas were different lengths. In Gion, twelve sticks equalled an hour; in Pontocho an hour was four sticks. The nomenclature continued, even though the practice had ended. In theory all geisha in any particular area earned the same. There was no sliding scale for seniority. In other words, as geisha were at pains to point out, being a geisha was not a career. It was a calling.

As for the actual rate, it varied area by area but was in the region of 10,000 yen (about £50) an hour. For an evening's work, a geisha might average 30,000–40,000 yen (£150–£200). On top of that there were tips, invariably lavish. No one would dream of insulting a maiko or geisha by giving her less than at least 10,000 yen (£50). Often by the end of a single evening she would have slipped 40,000–50,000 yen (£200–£250) into the collar of her kimono.

As one maiko told me with a candid smile, she made a far better living than her schoolmates who had taken jobs as OL – 'office ladies' or secretaries. At the geisha house, everything was paid for. Her kimonos, her fans, her bags, her taxi fares and the costs of her trips to the hairdresser were all supplied by the house. The house mother kept all the maiko's earnings as repayment of what was effectively her debt, though she did give her pocket money in the region of 30,000–40,000 yen (£150–£200) a month. And the tips were hers to keep (although in some houses the maiko were required to hand over their tips too). For both the maiko and the house mother, it was a very profitable business.

But if the maiko were to decide to stay on and become a geisha, she would move out of the geisha house and set up on her own after a year or two. Unlike a maiko, she would no longer be in such enormous demand. Men loved the company of the doll-like maiko in their brilliantly coloured kimonos, giggling artlessly; that was why they came to Kyoto. The geisha, however, had a serious profession. A geisha's success depended on her skill in conversation, music and dancing; it was not enough just to have a pretty face. As a geisha, she would keep all her own earnings; but she would have to try to make a living from that alone. Life, in fact, would be much easier if there were a *danna* around.

The amount a customer paid, of course, bore little relation to the amount a geisha received. When a customer wanted to organise a geisha party, he began by calling the proprietress of the teahouse where he was a regular customer. Customers were expected to observe teahouse loyalty. Most businesses, particularly those in Kyoto and Osaka, always used the same teahouse, as did many families. It was like being a member of an exclusive private club. Fathers would take their sons to their teahouse when the boys were in their teens and introduce them to the teahouse mistress and their regular geisha. 'Teahouse crawling' was frowned upon – though, if you were the customer of the venerable Ichiriki teahouse, you had such kudos that you were welcome in any teahouse in Gion.

Most probably the teahouse mistress had known the customer for decades and could plan the perfect party for him on the basis of his tastes and requirements. That was why he had entrusted the job to her. Teahouses were not restaurants. If he had asked for food, she ordered it in from one of the outside caterers.

Then she set about planning the best mix of geisha and maiko. There would have to be geisha who could dance, geisha who could sing and geisha who could play the shamisen. The shamisen, in particular, took years to learn. The best shamisen players were old and were in huge demand. Then there would need to be shy pretty maiko to sit around looking decorative and filling saké cups. The union office at the large concrete Kaburenjo was the centre of operations for the whole district. There they pored over detailed charts, showing where each geisha and maiko would be at any particular time in the evening. There was frequently feverish juggling of names as last-minute calls for geisha came in.

The system varied district by district. Sometimes the teahouse mistress called the Kaburenjo to sort out geisha for the evening, at others she would call the geisha house direct to book a particular geisha.

The first party of the evening was from 6 to 9 p.m. Invitations in Japan usually tell you what time the party will end as well as what time it begins and formal parties invariably end precisely when they say they will; geisha are being paid by the hour and running over would be extremely costly. Popular geisha might not stay for the whole evening but might flit from party to party. After the party was over, everyone relaxed. A guest might take a maiko or a geisha out for dinner or to a karaoké bar and later on they might come to some private arrangement for the night. But no matter how relaxed the evening became, the meter ticked relentlessly on.

On such occasions, nothing so crass as a bill would ever appear; neither would money ever cross hands – unless it was a tip proffered to a maiko or geisha. At the end of the evening, the customer thanked the geisha for their hospitality, they thanked him for his patronage and he left. From time to time a bill from the teahouse covering the last few months would arrive discreetly at the accounts department of his company. He would probably not even see it. If he did, he would not dream of checking it, let alone – perish the thought! – asking for a receipt.

In any case, there would be no itemised charges, no hint as to how the final figure had been arrived at, though one could be sure that that final figure would be earth-shatteringly huge. Quite apart from the costs of the geisha, there was the fee to the teahouse owner for organising the party. Each titbit or sip of liquor that passed a guest's lips cost a fortune and the expense, if a meal was ordered, can barely be imagined. A geisha party I attended along with two other guests, which included four geisha and a light meal for the three of us, cost the host more than £2000. I heard of parties costing £5000–£10,000, as much as a new car. But then again, the kudos for the party-giver was to show that for him this was a mere nothing. As in the old days, when a dashing young fellow would happily ruin himself for pleasure, it showed that he was not only a man of means but of style.

When the payment arrived, the teahouse mistress took a percentage that included the cost of paying the caterers who had provided the food. She also sent an agreed sum to the union to cover the costs of the maiko and geisha. The registry office would take a percentage of that and send the requisite fee on to the geisha house.

The *Danna*

The geisha world was always awash with gossip and rumours. There was the house a few doors up from mine, of shiny new wood, half-hidden behind a bamboo fence, with a permanently closed gate pressed almost up against the front door, adding a symbolic extra barrier against intruders. The houses to each side were bustling with life. Maiko would slip in and out in their cotton *yukata*, the house mothers would emerge and bow to passers-by as they went to tidy the small shrine across the road or went off to the coffee shop for breakfast. I would hear the plangent notes of the shamisen as the same riffs were practised uncertainly over and over again. But the house in the middle was always silent and the door firmly shut.

'That was her danna had that house built for her,' people told me.

'Is it a geisha house?' I asked.

'Nah, she doesn't have to work at all. Doesn't do a thing.'

Then there was the story of the beautiful geisha who had had an affair with the popular singing star which had been blazoned all over the weekly magazines (the Japanese equivalent of the tabloids). And there was the oil

199

magnate who had given his mistress – complete with her house – to a government minister as a 'gift', in exchange for which the minister had turned a blind eye to some illicit activity he was engaged in. All these stories were impossible to confirm and, like most such tales in Japan, probably true.

The geisha I knew were canny, down-to-earth, working-class girls. But, once they put on their make-up and the last cord of their obi was in place, they became fantasy creatures in a dream world which existed solely for the pleasure of men. There they were expected to be the epitome of femininity, dizzy doll-women who understood nothing of the harsh realities of life. As one ex-geisha told me, if a man asked about the cost of anything, she would say – smiling a sweetly helpless smile and speaking in a breathy Marilyn Monroe voice – 'Oh, I really don't know anything about that!' Though, of course, she added, she knew perfectly well.

Until recent years, most geisha had not had to bother their pretty little heads with such distasteful matters as money because almost all of them had *danna* who supported them. Tips from customers, entertaining at parties, running a teahouse, all that had been mere pin money. The real financial backing had been provided by the *danna*. All the older geisha had had a *danna* as a matter of course. Love did not come into it. It was a practical arrangement.

My 79-year-old neighbour, a gracious and still beautiful woman with lacquered white hair and a twinkling smile, had been a geisha before the war. 'If you didn't have a good danna, you couldn't live,' she told me. The mistress of the teahouse where she worked had arranged a *danna* for her when she was twenty-three.

'You could tell immediately,' she said, 'if someone would make a good danna. They'd approach the teahouse mistress. You could refuse if you wanted.' In those days a *danna* was almost like a husband except, of course, that he already had a wife. The geisha would be his concubine, his number two wife, or, if he was a wealthy man, his number three or even number four wife. My neighbour's *danna*, who was in the ceramics business, supported her for thirty years and she bore him two children. She also at one point had a lover. Once, she recalled, they talked about marriage.

'But I told him, "I can't get married." It's part of being a geisha. If you become a geisha, you don't think about marriage. I never think now, "I wish I'd got married."'

A Tokyo geisha I met, who was seventy-three, lived alone, rather sadly, in a small house where she subsisted by giving shamisen lessons. 'You have to have a danna,' she told me. 'You need money.' Her *danna* had been the president of an iron company. 'Some people kept their relationship secret,' she said. 'But ours was open. His wife met me; she understood.

'He gave me a monthly allowance of 200,000 yen [£4000 in modern currency] plus money for kimonos and classes, and bought me presents. It was about the same as you'd make in your first job after leaving university. I lived in the geisha house. I often used to visit his house. He took me to the cinema and to restaurants and to see kabuki and we travelled together to Hokkaido and Kyushu.

'I saved up and bought a house for myself. He said he'd have it repaired for me, but the economy was bad. If the economy had been good he would have bought it for me just like that.

'I remember one day he said to me, "It'll be fifteen years we've been together soon." Soon after that his health got worse and he stopped visiting. Then he died. He was in his sixties, I was in my thirties. At least I got to go to his funeral. I was lucky. A lot of women I know couldn't go to their lovers' funerals. The wives wouldn't allow it. That was always a painful thing.'

The patronage or *danna* system was the essence of the flower and willow lifestyle. The first requirement was a man who had a sizeable amount of money to spare (extra, that is, after he had paid all his living expenses, his mortgage, provided for the needs of his family and dependent relatives, paid for school fees, holidays abroad, pension plans and regular investment commitments). Such a man was likely to be at the pinnacle of his career and rather elderly. Most likely he owned his own business and could do as he pleased with his money, rather than being a salaried president, at the beck and call of the shareholders. One businessman reckoned that it would cost 20–30 million yen (£100,000–£150,000) a year to keep a geisha.

Following the proper route, he would approach the proprietress of the teahouse where he was a long-standing and trustworthy customer and mention his interest in a particular geisha. The proprietress would discuss the matter with the geisha and her house mother. If all were in agreement, the 'mothers' would settle the practical details with the patron and agree the level of financial assistance he was prepared to give.

Usually the *danna* paid a monthly allowance to cover the geisha's rent and living expenses and also bought her kimonos and obis. He paid all the tuition fees for her lessons in dancing, shamisen and singing. When she appeared at a public dance performance, he covered the considerable costs. He would be given the seat of honour and a batch of tickets to distribute to his influential friends and colleagues. If he summoned her to entertain for him at a banquet, he took priority over other guests; though he still had to pay the usual hourly rate for her services. She was also available for sex if required; though, being rather elderly, it was not a foregone conclusion that he would exercise his rights.

As to whether geisha or maiko ever slept with customers for money, as prurient westerners like to imagine: 'Geisha don't do that,' one maiko told me firmly when I dared to ask her. 'A danna and a customer are quite different. The danna is like your husband. You have a proper arrangement with him.'

Maiko, she pointed out, lived in a geisha house watched over by a strict *okasan*; they did not have the opportunity for freelancing of that sort. In any case, they were too busy with their classes and work even to have boyfriends. The maiko confessed that for a short time she had had a boyfriend, not a customer but a young man of her own age. But she had not had the time to see him and eventually the relationship collapsed. Such affairs were strictly against the rules. In the old days, sex had to be arranged through the proper channels and paid for in the proper way; freelance sex was out of the question. The customer had to approach the teahouse mistress who would consult the geisha house mistress before informing the young woman in question. These days, of course, licensed prostitution was illegal.

'Some geisha have dannas, some don't,' the maiko added. 'It's much easier if you do. It's too expensive otherwise.'

Men with the wealth and leisure to become *dannas* were often highly cultured, with a keen interest in the traditional arts practised by the geisha.

They would spend a considerable amount of time and money educating her with tender care so that she became the male ideal of accomplished and talented womanhood. As its most exalted, it was not so much 'Lolita' as 'Pygmalion', with the *danna* as a kind of Professor Henry Higgins, choosing his Eliza Doolittle and putting her through finishing school to create the perfect woman, with no ulterior motive other than the pleasure of seeing her grow and develop. Or he might be a sort of connoisseur, a collector of beautiful items with her as his prize possession, demonstrating his wealth, taste and status.

There is a very simple reason why the geisha world is under threat. The Henry Higgins generation, who saw becoming the *danna* of a geisha as a mark of success and an ideal to strive towards, is dying out. For a start, no one has the money any more. In modern Japan there are very few family-owned businesses left. Most top executives are employees of large impersonal corporations and cannot help themselves to several million yen of the company's money in order to spend it on a geisha. Added to which, the baby-boomers are rapidly growing into society's grand old men. But these are modern Japanese men in their fifties. They have grown up in a world where people go to the ballet and the opera or listen to jazz or techno, rather than the melancholy plink-plonk of the shamisen. They spend more time in French restaurants or hostess bars than teahouses. Many have never even seen a geisha. Far from objects of desire, they think of them as gorgeous fossils or cultural dinosaurs, if they think of them at all.

Nevertheless, teahouse mothers told me that a good proportion of geisha were still supported by *danna*, maybe one in five. But no one I knew would ever admit to it. It was too sensitive a matter. Geisha knew very well what their image was outside the confines of their small enchanted world. One very popular geisha told me, in tones that brooked no argument, that in the old days maiko had had enormous debts to pay off and that was why they needed a *danna*. Now there were no debts – the 1958 bill had seen to that – so there was no need for patrons any longer.

That was not strictly true. Constructing a world where men could live out their dreams was not a cheap matter. To play her part to the full, a geisha had to be a walking work of art, gorgeously attired, her wig, make-up and kimono all of the most exquisite quality. Yet to buy the most basic kimono could cost anything from 200,000 yen (£1000) up to several million (£10,000 upwards); the average kimono cost 350,000–500,000 yen (£1750–2500). And it had to be worn with an obi of equal value. Added to which, one kimono was far from enough. Teahouse customers were regulars who came again and again and it would certainly not do to be seen in the same kimono too many times.

All the geisha adored kimonos and collected them with passion. My white-haired neighbour confessed to having 200. As a famous Japanese saying goes, a native of Osaka will bankrupt himself for a great meal, but for a Kyoto-ite the fatal weakness is fine silk. None of this was a problem for a maiko who lived at a geisha house where the house mother laid out her kimono each evening. But for a newly hatched geisha setting up on her own, the initial costs might run as high as 20 million yen (£100,000). Geisha needed three kimonos a month – one to wear, one to send to the cleaner's, and one spare, in case a customer spilt his drink over your priceless silk. And each month they needed different kimonos. All in all, it came to about 3 million yen (£15,000) a year for kimonos alone.

Then there were classes, which might come to 100,000 yen a month, plus the exorbitant costs incurred for the various ceremonies marking the rites of passage in a geisha's life – the debut and the changing of the collar, when a maiko graduated to become a fully fledged geisha. Those cost hundreds of thousands of yen for the proper kimono, fans, bags and other equipment, for tips to the dressers and other helpers and gifts to members of the community. There were also enormous costs whenever a geisha took part in one of the grand public dance performances like the Cherry Dances. Far from being paid like a professional dancer, she had to pay for the honour of appearing, for her costumes and equipment, plus enormous sums in tips for all the helpers and assistants and monetary gifts to her teachers.

In recent years customers had started offering to sponsor part of the cost. One would pay for the kimono and obi, another for the wig for the new geisha, another for the cost of printing the scarves with the geisha's name which she handed out to everyone. One very popular maiko who had decided to give up before the turning of the collar had had promises from sponsors to pay for everything for the ceremony and been showered with expensive bags and gifts. Nevertheless, well into the 1990s there were still men who maintained the tradition of the big spender. Those who could afford it prided themselves on being the sole sponsor for a maiko's debut or turning of the collar. As to whether the maiko chose to reward her benefactor in the traditional way, that was strictly between her and him.

9

INSIDE A GEISHA HOUSE

Waiting anxiously for you,
Unable to sleep, but falling into a doze –
Are those words of love
Floating to my pillow,
Or is this too a dream . . . ?
My eyes open and here is my tear-drenched sleeve.
Perhaps it was a sudden rain.
Geisha song[1]

From 'Egg' to 'Learning by Observation'

Harumi was in her second year as a maiko when I met her, even though she was only fifteen. She had wanted to become a maiko so badly, she had left home when she was thirteen to move into Haruta geisha house, and had finished her schooling at the same time as she was beginning her maiko training. I used to see her clip-clopping past my house in her maiko regalia. With her heart-shaped face, large limpid eyes, tiny retroussé nose, and mouth like a bow, she was as perfect as a china doll, and the epitome of maiko prettiness.

I bumped into her when I sat in on classes at the Kaburenjo, the 'Dance and Music Practice Place', which housed a theatre, tatami- and wood-floored classrooms and the offices of the district geisha union. Fresh-faced, without her make-up, in a plain indigo and white cotton summer kimono, she had a simple red ribbon in her waxed hair. She shone in the drumming class where she played the *tsuzumi*, a small, rather beautiful, hourglass-shaped drum of gold-painted lacquered wood with a skin made from the hide of a young horse. Looking straight ahead impassively in the prescribed fashion, she rested it on her right shoulder, held it in place with her left hand and beat out a rhythm with the fingers of her right, breaking into a childish giggle when she made a mistake.

There was something irresistibly attractive about maiko with their combination of little-girl cuteness and teenage vulnerability beneath their archaic coiffures. But they were the most difficult of all to meet; regarded as children, they were fiercely protected by the geisha house mothers. It was also difficult to be invited inside a geisha house. After all, these were private homes, where the geisha and maiko lived. Even when I visited a teahouse, theoretically open for business, I never got further than the home bar, the equivalent of a Victorian parlour, at least for the first few weeks.

I was curious to venture a little deeper inside this world. Who were these little girls I saw flitting about the streets like butterflies? Why had they chosen this anachronistic lifestyle when so many other options were open to them? What were their day-to-day lives like? Did they have regrets about what they had given up? But the doors always seemed to be closed and I dared not knock too insistently. It was not until I had become a familiar face in the geisha world that one day a geisha who had befriended me at the local coffee shop suggested casually that I should meet her neighbour. Thus it was that I ended up sliding open the door of the Haruta geisha house.

The Haruta house was a big rambling chaotic house with a yapping lapdog and a constant stream of visitors. Haruta-san herself, the 'mother' of the house, was a large, expansive, open-hearted woman who had had, as she told me, a tough life.

Haruta had been born fifty-two years before, in the rural impoverished island of Kyushu, the love-child of a geisha and a wealthy landowner. Her father took her into his household but from the start she was relentlessly bullied by his seven other children. When she was ten she ran away to look for her mother.

She found her in Osaka. But the mother, who had since married and had children, was far from pleased to see her. She told the child that she had not even wanted to have her. She had fallen downstairs to try to induce a miscarriage when she was pregnant with her. She beat her, treated her like a housemaid and refused to let her go to school, then sold her to a hospital where she was forced to wash filthy rags from morning to night. After four years of utter misery, young Haruta had reached her lowest ebb. She found some pills and swallowed 300, hoping to kill herself. She was found, revived and taken back to Kyushu by her mother's sister. But her life still seemed hopeless. At fourteen, she was barely educated; she had missed four years of schooling. And there was no work to be found in Kyushu.

There was nothing for it but to go back to Osaka and look for work in the 'water trade' (the Japanese term for the sex industry). She found a job in a 'cabaret', a low-grade bar not far removed from a brothel. There she became friendly with a woman who was the girlfriend of a Kyoto textile merchant. She persuaded Haruta-san to try the life of a geisha. With the merchant as her guarantor, Haruta ended up in a geisha house in Kyoto. Once again she was at the bottom of the heap, tormented and bullied. But nothing could be as bad as what she had already gone through. She persevered and in the end inherited the name and the house.

The geisha world was her salvation. When I met her she was the comfortable mother hen to a brood of maiko and geisha, including a couple of children of her own, happily established in Kyoto's world of women.

'I'm very kind to the maiko and geisha,' she told me. 'That's not to say I'm not stern. They have to learn to behave properly. But I would never treat anyone as I was treated.'

Harumi, the youngest maiko in the house, took me upstairs to show me the room she shared with Haruka, her 'older sister'. Japanese rooms are usually cramped and tatty but theirs was large, spacious and airy with fresh tatami matting on the floor, smelling of rice straw. From the open window you could see the tiled roofs of the neighbouring houses and the narrow street outside. The room was full of little-girl clutter – piles of stuffed animals, toys, dolls, a bookcase full of books, magazines and comics, and a large mirror which ran the length of one wall, like in a theatre dressing room, with drawers underneath it filled with brushes and tubs of unguents and make-up. There were photographs of pop stars, famous geisha and several pictures of the Hollywood star Leonardo di Caprio pinned along the top. Filling the wall above it was an enormous poster of Masahiro Nakai of the fabulously popular singing group SMAP, heart-throb to millions of Japanese teenage girls.

Despite her little-girl looks, Harumi was unusually grown-up and confident for her age. Maiko often are, perhaps because they leave home so young. She sat on her heels, cuddling the house cat, a tawny-eyed tortoiseshell, and chatted cheerfully in her piping voice, using the quaint, rather stilted Kyoto dialect and geisha forms of words. The Kyoto dialect, of course, was part of the patina she had acquired when she became a maiko. Originally she was a country girl, from a small town just outside Kyoto, and must have grown up with a rural burr. In her spare time she loved music and films, she told me. She had seen the film *Titanic* on video four times and adored the star, Leonardo di Caprio. Or she went shopping with a schoolmate who had become a maiko at the same time as her.

'Ever since I was ten I've yearned to be a maiko,' she piped, smiling prettily. 'I would see them sometimes on television and once when we came to Kyoto on a school visit, walking along the street. They looked so beautiful in their kimonos! I dreamt and dreamt of looking like them. I've always loved to wear a kimono.'

Her father, a carpenter, was strongly opposed to the notion of any child of his taking up such a profession. It would also mean that she would have to give up her formal education long before high school. But her mother, a taxi driver, thought it was a good idea.

'She thought it would be good for me to learn good manners, like going to finishing school. It would help me when I got married.'

In the past, children sold into the geisha districts often had to work as maids for years. They lived in the geisha house, being treated like dogsbodies but getting the chance to have the patina of the geisha world rub off on them. For Harumi her period as a *shikomi* (literally 'in training') or *tamago* ('egg') lasted just six months. Like the child-maids in the old days, she did a little cleaning, ran errands and helped the maiko and geisha dress. As in any traditional Japanese apprenticeship, the real purpose was for her to absorb the atmosphere of the house, get a feel for how things were done, and get used to the notion of discipline.

But the most difficult thing to get used to was wearing traditional Japanese clothing. Instead of running around in jeans or a skirt, like any modern Japanese child, suddenly she was spending her days in a *yukata*, an ankle-length kimono-like garment that wrapped her knees like a bandage. She also had to hobble around on wooden clogs or tiny slippers while her heels hung off the back. Her hair, which she tied back in a ponytail, grew wild and shaggy as she coaxed it to become long enough to sculpt into the maiko's coiffure. And whenever she made the tiniest mistake, someone would be sure to snap at her.

'Everyone corrects you,' she remembered. 'Every person I spoke to told me off every single time I made a mistake. It was so hard to bear!'

The first thing she had to learn was to speak Kyoto dialect and use the archaic geisha vocabulary. It was like losing all trace of her former self, even the way she talked, which marked which area of the country she came from and what class she was. She also began to learn the gracious ways of the geisha world. Bowing, greeting, speaking in a high-pitched, girlish voice had to become second nature for her. For a start, she had to memorise the names, ranks and position in the hierarchy of everyone in her geisha district. As she flitted down the narrow lanes, she was eternally bowing and greeting each person that she met with 'Ohayo san dosu'. This means 'Good morning', but the words and tone are infinitely softer than the standard Japanese 'Ohayo gozaimasu'.

Every maiko told me the same thing: the worst aspect of the new life was not the dance and music classes, not leaving home and living apart from one's family, but 'human relations' – learning to fit in to the geisha community. They had to learn, as I myself had, to put up with being at the very bottom of the geisha hierarchy and to accept without ever answering back the harsh words and endless sniping of the vinegar-tongued 'older sisters', some of whom were in their seventies and eighties. As they said in the geisha world, if someone told you that grass was black, ordinarily you would say, 'Don't be so stupid, of course it isn't, it's green!' But a would-be maiko had to learn to agree very quietly that it was indeed black, a wonderful shade of black; in fact she couldn't imagine why she had never noticed before.

Throughout the training period the matriarchs – the 'mothers' and the 'older sisters' – kept a close eye on Harumi's progress and on her developing skills in language, manners and the all-important 'human relations'. They also got together with the teachers to discuss her aptitude for the various arts. During the mornings she attended normal school, finishing off her standard education, and in the afternoons went to the classrooms in the Kaburenjo to take her first classes in dancing, singing and playing the drum, flute and shamisen.

Then came a dance test to assess her progress as a *shikomi*. It was the first time Harumi had ever performed in public. Worse still, she had to dance before an audience of the most formidable old ladies of the community. 'I was so nervous,' she remembered with a giggle, 'having to dance all alone before such important people!'

That first hurdle overcome, Harumi was ready for the next – *minarai*, 'learning by observation'. Now, for the first time, she would have the thrilling experience she had been dreaming of for so long. She would put on the mask, she would see the alabaster face which henceforth she would present to the world. First she was taken to the hairdresser to have her locks wrenched, combed and sculpted into the 'cute' *ware-shinobu* coiffure. Then, while she knelt passively, Haruka, the senior maiko, applied make-up and powder to her face until it was perfectly smooth and white, painting a petal of bright red safflower paste on her lower lip. Lastly the *otokoshi*, the assistant-cum-dresser, helped her into the heavy layers of kimono, tugging and tying the obi in place. She was still not yet a maiko. To indicate the lower rank, her obi was only half the length of a maiko's obi, stretching not from neckline to ground but only to the back of her knees. Woven into it was the crest of the Haruta house.

Finally in the entrance hall she stepped into her *okobo*, 4-inch-high clogs made of pale paulownia wood and steeply bevelled at the front, with red thongs. (As her career progressed, she would move on to pink and later purple thongs.) Teetering along unsteadily, clinging on to the arm of the dresser, she set off for her first-ever *o-zashiki* engagement. (O is an honorific, *zashiki* literally means the tatami room where the party takes place; geisha talk about going to 'the honourable room'. Ordinary Japanese, in other words the customers, refer to a geisha party as an *enkai*, a 'banquet'.)

'I was so nervous when I went to o-zashiki for the first time,' she said in her little-girl falsetto, stroking the cat and tickling it under the chin. 'I wondered what I should say to the customers. The older sisters helped me. They told me I must pay attention to the customers' saké cups and fill them quickly so they were never empty. I was so nervous I just sat still, I dared not say a word. The customers told me I looked like a doll! The hairstyle felt so strange. My head was heavy, I could hardly keep it balanced. The kimono felt so heavy too. It was hard just to walk. And when I had to walk in okobo, I thought I would fall! Now I'm used to them. Now I can run in them.'

She showed me the bolster-shaped lacquered wooden pillow, rounded on the bottom and padded on the top, on which she had to rest her neck to prevent her hair getting mussed. It looked like a medieval torture device. In the past, house mothers used to spread brown flaky rice husks under the pillow. If a girl's head slipped even for a second during the night, the brown flakes would stick to her hair, providing incontrovertible evidence. She would be scolded or worse until she had learnt.

'I hate the pillow worst,' she said. 'I can't sleep properly. I have to sleep on my side, I can't sleep on my back. Then I have to wake up to turn over and change sides.'

For Harumi, minarai lasted a month, the standard length of time for modern maiko; in the past it might have been a year or more. Every night as she slept her head rolled off the high wooden pillow and ruined her hair. Every day she struggled to paint her face, trying to get the surface alabaster smooth and the features perfectly symmetrical; and every day the face turned out different. Whenever she got something wrong, Haruka, the senior maiko, or Haruta, the house mother, snapped at her.

Finally, dressed in her minarai kimono, she would set off for the teahouse, the minarai-jaya, where her training in proper party behaviour took place. All evening she attended at parties, watching and listening, learning how to sit, how to behave, how to chat, how to keep the conversation light and entertaining, and assiduously filling saké cups and changing ashtrays. There was little verbal instruction. In the Japanese way, she was expected to watch carefully and learn by observation, absorbing every detail of this new world. The older sisters and teahouse mother did, however, ensure that she was introduced to customers who, in future, might ask specifically for her or even decide to become her patron.

Joining the Geisha Family

Meanwhile Harumi was pondering the first serious decision of her career. Should she go through with the three-day *misedashi* debut and become a fully fledged maiko or should she leave? Until that point the costs the house mother had incurred in training and housing her were not exorbitant. But the debut itself was expensive; and thereafter the costs of classes, kimonos, make-up and regular trips to the hairdresser, not to mention pocket money and other living expenses, would amount to a huge sum. If she wanted to drop out, this was the moment to do so. Otherwise she would be committed to the maiko life for the next five years. It was a big decision for a child of fourteen to make.

Many of her friends had already discovered that it was not the glamorous life they were expecting and had dropped out. As Haruta, the house mother, put it, 'The flower and willow world runs according to strict rules, like Japan in the old days. At home, children are free. Here they are not free. I tell them, try it for a year, but most of them give up within three months. They're children, they don't understand properly.'

'It is much tougher than I expected,' said Harumi. 'From the outside maiko look so pretty. But when you have entered this world, you discover what a hard life it is. Ten of us started at the same time. Six have left. I feel lonely without them.'

For Harumi there was never any question. If she had been planning to leave, she would have left long before. Besides, she had already been enchanted by her first taste of stepping out, painted and dressed like the epitome of feminine beauty. Despite all the discipline and hard work, it was still every girl's dream, an eternity of dressing up.

Before her debut, there was an important rite of passage to be undergone. In order to be initiated as a full member of the geisha family, Harumi needed to be adopted by an 'older sister', a senior maiko or a geisha who would be her mentor, teach her the basics of the geisha lifestyle, keep an eye on her progress with dancing and music, and, most importantly, shoulder the responsibility if she made a mistake. For a maiko it is a weighty deterrent against breaking the rules if she knows that it is her 'older sister' rather than herself who will take the blame.

She would also be given a professional name; until then, she had been called by the name she had been born with. Like a surname, which shows one's link to the family of one's birth, her professional name would show which geisha family she belonged to and in particular her relationship with her 'older sister'. The older sister of Haru-mi – whose name means 'Spring Beauty' – is Haru-ka, 'Spring Flower', the senior maiko of the Haru-ta, 'Spring Field', house.

Women who were maiko thirty or forty years ago can remember petitioning a particularly famous maiko or geisha and begging to be taken on as her younger sister. Those who succeeded in being adopted by a ravishingly beautiful geisha or one of the top dancers could be sure that they would be introduced at the best teahouses, where they could bask in her reflected glory. For an ambitious maiko, this is still the way to ensure a brilliant career. Similarly, geisha might watch out for promising maiko, either particularly lovely or particularly talented at dancing, and take them under their wing.

Most maiko, however, are content to leave the choice of older sister to their house mother. Haruta, the mother of Haruta geisha house, told me, 'You need someone who has common sense. It's like bringing up a child. She has to be strict with her, like a parent. Sometimes I choose a maiko, sometimes a geisha; but I always choose from the girls I've reared myself at the Haruta house.'

The moment of transition was marked by a ceremony which took place on an auspicious day chosen by a fortune-teller au fait with the omens. Called *san-san-kudo*, 'three times three, nine times', it is exactly the same as the most solemn and binding part of the Japanese wedding ceremony, a bit like the exchange of rings in the west. It was almost as if Harumi was marrying into the geisha community, in the same way as a nun marries into the church. Like a nun, henceforth if Harumi wished to marry she would have to give up her geisha vocation.

Dressed in all her finery, her hair tricked out with combs, ribbons, hairpins, ornaments and silk flowers, her face painted to doll-like perfection, wearing a formal black kimono, she knelt solemnly beside Haruka in a tatami room in the geisha house. First Haruka took a small red lacquered saucer brimming with saké and drank it in three sips, then passed it to the maid to refill. Next Harumi drank from the same cup. Then the ceremony was repeated with a middle-sized saucer, then a large one – three saké cups, three sips from each.

The following day was the beginning of Harumi's debut. For three days she was the star of the entire district. Every waking second she was on display as she paraded the streets trailed by photographers, meeting everyone, sliding open teahouse doors, bowing again and again, piping, 'Tanomo, okasan, oki-ni . . .,' 'Asking your favour, mother, thank you . . .' The house mothers gave her gifts of money in envelopes which the dresser or Haruta – whoever happened to be with her – tucked away in a capacious sleeve. Each contained 10,000–20,000 yen (about £50–£100). Multiplied by the number of houses in the district, this came to a sizeable amount of money, though it was still only a small contribution towards the exorbitant costs of the *misedashi*. In the evening there was party after party and most of the customers too gave her sizeable tips. By the end of all the meeting, greeting and partying she was completely exhausted.

Living in the same house, Haruka really was like an older sister to Harumi. At eighteen, she had nearly completed her maiko training. She kept an eye on Harumi's progress, helping her master the minute rules and customs which determine every second of life in the geisha districts. A few days earlier, there had been a small concert at the Kaburenjo where the maiko displayed their musical skills, particularly in drumming. It was an important occasion for Harumi. In the morning, Haruka took her from teahouse to teahouse to greet the teahouse owners, and the ancient 'older sisters' who would make up the audience, and beg their indulgence.

'The timing is so hard,' piped Harumi in her little-girl voice. 'If you arrive too early they scold you. If you speak too softly, they scold you. Haruka taught me about that.'

'If I become a geisha and have my own apartment, Harumi will come every two or three days to visit,' Haruka told me in firm, responsible, big-sister tones. 'It's not like being friends. It's a special relationship.'

Erikae: Changing the Collar

Downstairs in the living room, the nerve centre of the house, the witching hour was fast approaching. The lapdog, now confined to a large cage, yapped hysterically, the television blared and a roomful of ex-geisha sat laughing and chatting. One, in her thirties and married, bounced a large baby on her knee, crooning in English in my honour, 'Hap-pee, hap-pee.' Haruta, the large, gregarious house mother, was on the phone, juggling a timetable covered in multicoloured scribbles and a book of phone numbers.

'We need a shamisen player for tomorrow night,' she barked. 'No, no, she'll be busy . . . No, not that one either, she's not good at keeping up a conversation. We need someone who can play the shamisen and knows how to chat too.'

Harumi disappeared into the kitchen to have a quick meal of boiled beef on rice. Geisha and maiko ate twice a day, at twelve, after classes, and at four, before getting ready for the evening's parties. They might drink with the guests. In fact, they were expected to; a geisha who did not drink was almost a contradiction in terms. But they never ate with them. Thus it was important to eat before starting work so as not to suffer too many pangs at the sight of the mouth-watering dishes being served up. If a maiko was really hungry she might snack at midnight when she got back from her last engagement.

There were no parties that night for Harumi's 'older sister', Haruka. Relaxing in a T-shirt and shorts with her long hair tied back in a ponytail, she was noticeably more mature and confident than the child-like Harumi. She lacked the younger girl's porcelain prettiness but she had an engaging candour of manner. Squashed around a corner of the table that filled the living room, we tried to ignore the noise and bustle as we chatted.

The daughter of a removals man from just outside Kyoto, becoming a maiko had opened doors for Haruka into worlds she could never have imagined.

'My father didn't want me to become a maiko,' she said. 'He was worried about me. He didn't know what I would have to do. But my mother said it was okay. I still go home quite often, but this is my family now; we eat rice from the same pot. I love it. I love classes and I love "work" [the evening parties]. Last night we danced at the International Hotel opposite Nijo Castle. The night before that we were at a restaurant on the river in Takao for an outdoor party. There were jetties out above the water. Three of us were there. We went from table to table, chatting to all the customers. That's how it is most nights in summer, outdoor parties. I love the travelling too, I love seeing new places. I've been everywhere. I've been to Tokyo, I've been to Nagasaki.'

Maiko are in huge demand. Kyoto is the only place in the country that still has them and they are often invited to brighten up a party for particularly important guests at a classy traditional restaurant in another city. They are also often hired to look decorative and be charming at conferences or exhibitions of, for example, kimono fabrics. Added to which, everyone who visits Kyoto and has connections or a bottomless purse wants to meet maiko. They are the symbol of the city. As one self-styled connoisseur put it, 'maiko are the flavour of Kyoto'.

'I meet famous people all the time,' beamed Haruka. 'I've met kabuki actors, TV actors, sportsmen . . .

'You know Masahiro Nakai?' she added, mentioning the boyish heart-throb whose photograph dominated the wall in the room she shared with Harumi. 'I met him! He was starring in a TV drama and came to film in Kyoto. They ended up at a teahouse run by a friend of our house mother. The master of the teahouse knew I was Nakai-kun's fan. He didn't say anything, he just called and asked me to entertain. So I got to meet Nakai-kun. He was really fun, even better-looking than I thought.'

Nevertheless, five years after her debut, her life as a maiko was nearly at an end. She had reached the most important turning point of her career. If she stayed on in the geisha world, the next step was eri-kae, 'changing the collar', when the maiko's thick red embroidered undercollar – eri – was replaced with the geiko's white one, and her long maiko locks were cut in preparation for putting on the wig of the geiko. (In Kyoto gei-sha, 'arts people', are called gei-ko, literally 'arts children' or, to give it a more politically correct translation, 'arts women'.) If she wanted to leave, now was the moment to do so. Otherwise she would be committed for at least two years. It was akin to deciding whether to go on to postgraduate study at university.

Lots of young women became maiko for five years. It was like going to finishing school, acquiring gloss and grooming and also meeting a pool of wealthy and influential men, one of whom might turn out to be a prospective husband. Geisha were much less flamboyant, part of the dark fabric of the place. Instead of the brilliant peacock colours of the maiko, geisha wore simple, elegant kimonos. Instead of the maiko's waxed coiffure, they wore their hair in a bouffant bun except on special occasions, when they would don a wig. They were also in much less demand. Customers would ask for a particular geisha whom they knew; but they would just ask for a maiko, any maiko. If she was not particularly charming or entertaining or a particularly good dancer, a geisha might find herself out of work; and no parties meant no income.

Being a geisha was a vocation. You only went through the changing of the collar if you really wanted to, perhaps because you loved traditional dance and music and wanted to take it up as a full-time profession or because you enjoyed the life and didn't want to leave. But if you did choose to carry on, you would end up spending your most eligible years studying dance and music and entertaining old men at parties. If, after all that, you decided that you wanted to marry, you might well find yourself on the shelf.

'I'm wondering whether to give up,' confided Haruka. 'I like the geisha look; but if you become a geisha, the classes get much more difficult. When you're a maiko, everyone treats you like a child. If you make mistakes, the customers think you're cute. But after erikae you're an adult, you can't make mistakes any more. In any case, I really want to get married. You only have one life. I don't want to go on being a geisha for ever.

'I'd like to marry someone who's not fussy about household stuff, someone manly. An ordinary guy would be fine, I don't need a company chairman's son. The only trouble is, you get spoilt as a maiko. You get used to having presents and being taken to good restaurants. I couldn't marry a poor man. I might not make a good wife.'

Six o'clock was approaching, the magic moment when the first parties always began. Harumi reappeared, poised and ready for the evening's work. The mask was in place. She was no longer a wide-eyed innocent child but a porcelain doll, wrapped like a Christmas gift in layer upon layer of kimonos and obis. Her eyes and eyebrows were drawn in in black, the corners of her eyes defined in red and her lips a perfect bow, startlingly red on the alabaster white of her face. Her kimono, of light, loosely woven silk, was a vivid shade of royal blue with a design of irises. Her thick brocade obi was pale orange and gold with a red and silver under-obi beneath it. Her hair, in the *ofuku* style of the mature maiko, was decked out with a dangling silver comb and a frieze of stylised silk hydrangeas in pale pink and blue, appropriate for the month of June.

She stood rather uncertainly in the entrance like an actress in the wings, composing herself to step out into the spotlight. Outside a taxi had pulled up, almost filling the narrow street with its dark wooden houses. Tucking her wicker-bottomed silk handbag under her arm, she stepped into her high *okobo* clogs and, bells tinkling, slipped gracefully into the taxi, piping 'Oki-ni, oki-ni' as she left. For a moment the geisha soap opera on television was interrupted by the face of Leonardo di Caprio, advertising Orico, a credit card company.

10

MIZUAGE
BECOMING A WOMAN

A hole in the paper wall,
Who has been so guilty?
Through it I hear the breaking of a shamisen string,
Meaning bad luck.

Yet the prediction-seller says
That mine is excellent.
Geisha song[1]

On the Town with Mr Mori

Every now and then a friend of a friend named Mr Mori would phone me and invite me out on a bar crawl. He was a flamboyant character who had taken me under his wing because I was foreign and therefore a guest of his country and, like him, a writer. He was the author of a book on guide dogs for the blind and also ran some kind of major international business. Like many Japanese creative types – academics, artists or writers – he favoured an idiosyncratic style of dress. Rather than the standard issue business suit, he wore multi-pocketed khaki photographer's waistcoats and short-sleeved cotton shirts and occasionally sported a scarf knotted around his bald head like a Sicilian bandit.

He had been a frequenter of the geisha districts for years and was friendly with many maiko and geisha. Maiko, he always told me, were just ordinary girls who enjoyed going bowling on their days off. But he also knew older women who remembered the bad old days when the maiko life was not so innocent or pleasurable, when girls were forced to become maiko whether they wanted to or not. And he knew how to enjoy the company of geisha on the cheap.

One of the defining phrases of the geisha world, passed down unchanged from the days when courtesans entertained merchants in the licensed districts, was the 'no strangers' rule: *ichigen san kotowari*, 'the first-time customer is refused'. Another which I sometimes heard was when an 'older sister' spoke approvingly of customers who were skilful at 'having fun with geisha and spending money'. As in the old days, geisha liked big spenders. If a man was a man, he knew how to spend money.

Mr Mori was certainly not an unknown customer and, in western terms, spent a lot of money; but he managed not to bankrupt himself. The secret was the 'home bar' (*homu baa* in Japanese). A full-blown geisha party was so exorbitantly expensive that, unless one had unlimited means, it was only feasible to throw one when there were very important business guests to be entertained and the whole thing could be paid for on company expenses. In the past, in the heyday of the geisha, men used to drop in to teahouses privately to spend time in the company of a particular geisha or just as a pleasant way to pass the evening. But in modern Japan, to take over a tatami room in a teahouse in order to down a few flagons of saké with a geisha was insanely expensive. If a man simply wanted the company of a woman, there was an enormous number of cheaper, sexier and more up-to-date alternatives. Thus, in order not to price themselves out of the market, most teahouses had developed 'home bars', a small bar with sofas, tables and a karaoké machine where men could go without booking (provided that they were not first-timers) and have a very expensive but still affordable drink. When Mr Mori took me out on bar crawls, that was where we went.

One evening around midnight we ended up at a small bar on a quiet back street behind Yasaka Shrine, right in the lea of the Eastern Hills. From the outside it might have been a private house.

'This is a very special geisha,' Mori-san assured me as he slid the door open, slipped out of his shoes and stepped into the hallway. Polished wooden corridors led to paper-covered doors, some standing open to reveal large empty tatami-matted rooms used for geisha parties.

221

Mori-san had already phoned to announce our impending arrival. The *mama-san* came out to greet us and ushered us into the bar. We perched on one side while she stood on the other before a mirrored wall lined with numbered bottles of whiskey arranged on glass shelves.

A dignified, rather stiff woman, she might have been sixty or seventy. She had a plump round face with even, delicate features which must once have been beautiful. Her hair was swept into the unnaturally black bouffant hairstyle which all the geisha wore and her kimono, crossed high at the neck in matronly style, was a sober dark blue. I felt a little uncomfortable. Her smile was icy. She was perfectly pleasant, yet she seemed to be just going through the motions; she needed our business but in fact would much rather that we had not come. It was as if she was reining in her true feelings with almost noticeable effort.

Mori-san, a buoyant character utterly impervious to subtleties of atmosphere or feeling, was chatting cheerfully about business in the geisha world. Yes, she agreed, it was declining badly as, with a fixed smile, she served small dishes of boiled green soya beans and poured glasses of whiskey for us topped up with water. Then Mori-san's face lit up as two young women appeared. These were not maiko but bar girls, leggy students in tiny skirts whose job was to entertain the customers. While he teased and joked with them, the *mama-san* was left to entertain me.

'Gion must have changed quite a lot since you were first here,' I ventured, carefully avoiding impertinent personal questions. I was amazed at the vehemence of her reply.

'It's completely different,' she exploded. 'Everything has changed. Those days were dark. It was a dark life.'

'Could I ask . . .' I murmured politely, 'would you mind telling me . . . I've heard music and dance classes were much harsher in those days.'

Suddenly the floodgates opened. I didn't need to be polite, I hardly needed to speak. With Mori-san distracted by his two companions and no one but a foreigner, utterly outside the geisha community, to hear her, the *mama-san* poured out her story. Harsh? The classes had been terrible. The older sisters had been tough on her and the house mothers too; and her 'older sister' had died suddenly at twenty-five, so there was no one to stand up for her.

'I thought I'd commit suicide many times,' she burst out. 'My house mother was famous for her cruelty. Everyone knew it. She was always in a rage. I was like the maid. I did all the cleaning in the house by myself. She'd give me a list of jobs, then go out. If I hadn't done them all when she got back, she beat me.'

Her father, she said, disappeared when she was four. Her mother was alone and poor. She hadn't intended to send her child to the geisha district. But her aunt knew of a good position in a geisha house and when she was ten she was packed off to Gion.

'I didn't know anything about it,' she said fiercely. 'I didn't know anything when I was brought here. I lived in Gion, I went to school and I never saw my mother again.'

In the depths of winter she had to climb on to the flat roof where they kept the drying racks for hanging out kimonos. There she would sing, trying to throw her voice until it reached Maruyama Park, half a mile away. The teachers were harsh too. One would whack the drum or the shamisen to show her displeasure and turn her back on the class. If a child committed an offence, she would have to stay on after her own class was finished, sitting shamed on her heels at the back of the room for the rest of the day, until her legs went completely numb.

In those days there were no big decisions about whether to stay on or leave. A child who had been purchased from her parents was effectively an indentured slave. She laboured under an enormous debt – the money used to pay for her purchase, plus the exorbitant costs of the hairstyling and gorgeous kimonos and obis which were an essential part of the job. Until it was repaid, which might be never, she was the property of the geisha house. When the time came for her to go through with her debut and become a maiko, she did so. She had no choice in the matter. And a year later when the time came to change her collar and start wearing the *ofuku* hairstyle, she had no choice in that either. Added to which, changing the collar was not simply a colourful ritual as it is for modern maiko. It meant growing up and becoming an adult in a very literal sense.

'It was against the law to force you to have sex with a patron if you didn't want to, even in those days,' blurted out the *mama-san*. I hadn't even dared mention *mizuage*. 'But no one paid any attention. Of course I had it,

223

we all did. It was horrible, he was a horrible man. He was a specialist, a professional deflowerer.'

Amazed at her outburst, I was burning to ask her what a professional deflowerer was. But she obviously thought she had said enough. Then Mori-san and the two students joined in, chatting blithely, and a few minutes later he decided it was time to leave. As we strolled through the dark streets to our next port of call, a late-night noodle shop, I commented with due politeness on how nice she had been.

'"Nice"?' chuckled the irrepressible Mori-san. 'I wouldn't call her "nice". She's hard – kibishi – tough as an old boot.' There were reasons for that, I thought to myself. I was beginning to understand why so many of the older women of the geisha community were harsh and sharp-tongued.

A Necessary Rite of Passage

The *mama-san* was the first but far from the only 'older sister' to talk to me about *mizuage*. For women who were maiko before prostitution was made illegal in 1958 – in other words, anyone aged over about fifty-five, which included many of the older members of the community – compulsory deflowering at an early age was simply a part of life. It made no difference whether they were the spoilt children of generations of geisha and had grown up in a wealthy geisha house with maids and servants, or whether they were the children of starving peasants, brought in weeping from the countryside. Children in those days did not have choices. The option of leaving before one's debut or before the change of collar was simply not available.

Which is not to say that they were unhappy. Japanese practise *gaman* – 'endurance', 'getting on with things', 'putting up with things'. When it is cold, you are cold, you don't waste energy heating your house. When it is hot, you are hot. Widespread central heating and air-conditioning are recent developments in Japan and older people still do not bother much with them. And if you were told that you had to have *mizuage*, you just put up with it.

One woman, frail but still lovely, had been the child of a famous geisha and remembered the twenties when there were 2500 geisha and 106 maiko

224

in Gion alone. When I met her she was ninety, a little hard of hearing and slow on her feet but imperious still and beautiful, with silky skin as fine as parchment and delicate features. She was perfectly turned out in a kimono of watered silk with a pale grey swirled ink pattern. She spoke not just Kyoto dialect but archaic Kyoto dialect. It was rather like meeting someone who speaks in Dickensian English.

She had grown up in one of the most prosperous teahouses in the district, with maids to serve her. 'Thanks to the money of our patrons,' she said in her thin but piercing voice, 'we ate very well, better than people outside the geisha districts.'

The daughters of geisha and of teahouse owners were in a highly privileged position, very different from girls who had been recruited from outside the geisha areas. They had no debts, they were not in bondage, they had the family house to live in. So she had no need of a patron to support her. In fact, she had no need to become a geisha at all if she didn't want to. She could have simply taken over as the *mama-san* of the teahouse, the family business. But in those days it would have been unthinkable for a beautiful young girl not to have become a geisha, particularly if she came from a geisha background.

People had the misconception that all geisha had had a hard time, she went on; but she had not. The music and dancing teachers had been strict, but that was necessary in order to learn. And when she came out as a maiko at the age of fourteen, she was instantly recognised as a beauty of the first order. She was the superstar of her day. Bromides (as they called photographs in those days) of her exquisitely languid flapper-era features were shown across the country to advertise a brand of saké and she became the instantly recognisable symbol of the Gion geisha and their annual Cherry Dances. At the height of her career she was mixing at the most exalted levels of society. She was an intimate of princes and aristocrats and the model for the great writer Junichiro Tanizaki's depiction in many of his novels of the archetypal black-tressed siren. She finally became the concubine – *nigo-san*, the 'number two wife' – of a powerful daimyo lord, gave up being a geisha and bore him several children.

But even though she came from a privileged background, she had *mizuage*, which suggests that it was seen not as a terrible ordeal from

225

which a mother would wish to protect her daughter, but a necessary rite of passage.

'Mizuage is when you become a woman for the first time,' she said. 'In those days everyone had mizuage around fourteen. I was late, I was fifteen. I was embarrassed. I changed my hairstyle, so everyone knew I had had it. It was like getting married. Everyone congratulated me and I gave celebratory presents to everyone. I gave gifts of food to my teachers and seniors.'

As for the perpetrator, 'in those days it was just a man who makes a woman for the first time. He only did it once. Some customers were mizuage specialists. Mostly they were honourable senior citizens, rich and old. I don't know about nowadays. Young maiko do as they please! Mizuage is really awful; but afterwards you celebrated. The danna paid a lot of money but the family spent it all on celebrating. It certainly wasn't embarrassing. It was normal; it would have been embarrassing to have been late in having it. It would have looked as if you couldn't find a danna.'

When I asked the older women of the geisha community if they had had *mizuage*, they looked at me with astonishment as if they could not imagine how anyone could ask such a stupid question.

'Of course,' they would tut impatiently. 'Otherwise I wouldn't be a geisha.'

Before the 1958 watershed, *mizuage* was not simply something that everyone took for granted but the most crucial step in the maiko's career. Like a young man's circumcision, painful but unavoidable, it was an initiation ritual. It marked the transition from maiko to geisha, from girl to woman, and was a prerequisite for changing one's collar, synonymous with growing up. Until you had had it, you were not a woman. A virgin geisha would have been as much a contradiction in terms as a virgin wife.

From the customer's point of view, of course, the chance to deflower a maiko was an irresistible opportunity. As everywhere, virgins were highly desirable. And a maiko was the apogee of virgins, the crème de la crème, selected for her beauty, highly accomplished and trained to be compliant with whatever a man desired. Men were prepared to pay a small fortune for the privilege of deflowering one. It cost several million yen in today's money, one elderly geisha told me, enough to buy a house.

As for the geisha house, they had invested a lot of money, what with the initial purchase and the costs of raising the girl – classes, training, kimonos, housing and the rest. The first step towards recouping it was *mizuage*, one of the most lucrative transactions in the girl's entire career.

Mizuage began with the courtesans. For the geisha as for them, the cost of the debut was prohibitively expensive. It was simply not possible unless a wealthy sponsor could be found to pay for it. As a bonus, whoever was prepared to lay out the money would have the privilege of being the fledgling courtesan's first patron. The payment was not for deflowering her but to cover the cost of the debut; though for the young woman the distinction must have seemed academic.

Sometimes by the time a courtesan or geisha came to have her debut, she was not really a virgin. Saikaku, the great seventeenth-century chronicler of the pleasure quarters, wrote rollicking stories about girls who were sold for 'deflowering' time and again. The deception could be perpetrated if the girl moved to a new district where no one knew her and she could celebrate her 'debut' for the second, third or fourth time. The customer would not find out the truth until it was too late and would never dream of losing face by broadcasting his humiliation. To this day a sponsor or sponsors have to be found to pay for a maiko's debut; though, post-1958, the position no longer carries the same bonus.

In her charmingly self-deprecating autobiography, *A Drunken Story of Gion*,[2] one of the grand old ladies of the geisha district, Haruyu, who recently passed away in her late eighties, described the terrible embarrassment of being unable to find a *danna*. She was, she wrote candidly, not hugely attractive. In fact, as the photographs in the book reveal, she was downright plain. But she was the daughter of a teahouse owner and, attractive or not, automatically became a maiko. She came from a family of four sisters and two brothers, though her brothers were sent away practically as soon as they were born to be brought up by their father. Otherwise they would have become shamisen players or dressers; those were the only jobs for men in the geisha district.

At eleven she became a maiko. But when she reached fourteen, the magic age when all her contemporaries were losing their virginity and changing from the *ware-shinobu* to the *ofuku* hairstyle, month after month passed and her hair remained resolutely the same. She was so plain that there were no applicants to deflower her. Walking the streets of the geisha districts, wearing the little-girl hairstyle that told everyone she was still a virgin, she felt more and more embarrassed and ashamed.

Eventually her 'older sister' went to one of the professional deflowerers to beg him to perform the *mizuage*. Haruyu reported the conversation: '"I don't want people thinking there's something wrong with her, like a disability or some sort of physical problem. So would you mind . . ." asked Older Sister. "Do you think you could . . . ? Just so people will know she's normal."'

Finally the owner of a big department store agreed to do it. By now Haruyu was fifteen, old for *mizuage*. Afterwards she had the even greater embarrassment of having to walk around with her hair in the *ofuku* – 'just deflowered' – style. The house mothers kept stopping her on the street to congratulate her. She was so embarrassed that she ran home.

At the time, she wrote, there were two 'professional deflowerers' who took care of Gion. She gave them pseudonyms: 'Mr Kawada' and 'Mr Kimura'. Once a maiko was getting past her sell-by date, if she still hadn't been deflowered, the mother of her geisha house would go to one of them and suggest he do the honours.

Once, she wrote, all the maiko of the district were performing at the annual Cherry Dances. There were two pathways like catwalks – *hanamichi*, 'flower roads' – stretching through the middle of the audience from the back of the theatre to the stage. For one piece there was a line of maiko dancing on each. 'This catwalk is Kawada-san's,' yelled a wag in the audience. 'That one's Kimura-san's!'

To a modern woman, the concept of being deflowered on a one-night stand by a rich old man, who paid a lot of money for the privilege and liked to spend his time going around deflowering virgins, is unspeakably abhorrent. But, barbaric though it may seem, it needs to be seen in context. One way or another, most Japanese women who grew up before 1958 wound up having to have sex with someone they barely knew and didn't care about. If they were of the social class that had arranged marriages,

228

often they had met their prospective husband only once or twice before the wedding and most probably had been so shy they had not dared raise their gaze higher than his shoes.

Japanese women in their seventies have told me that the first time they saw their husband's face was at their wedding. For them their wedding night could not have been much different from *mizuage*. They too had no choice but to have sex with someone who was virtually a stranger. The difference was that at least they could expect him to look after them economically in the future. They certainly did not expect fidelity or love. As for the old men who carried out *mizuage*, ghastly though they were, they were quite likely practised and expert. If the fumbling upper-class youths whom respectable women had to marry had any idea what they were doing once the lights were out, it was because their fathers had packed them off to the geisha district to be taught.

Good Days for Men

Daytimes in the geisha district were often quiet but evenings were busy. One night I was out with Sarah, who was Japanese-American, looking for Ishibei Koji, Stone Wall Alley, the small enclosed quarter where, Mori-san had told me, rich men had built houses for their concubines. He had shown me the entrance, a tiny stone doorway, like the entrance to the Secret Garden, hidden in a long wall. We were strolling around the back streets behind Yasaka Shrine when I spotted the discreet sign.

Stepping through the doorway was like walking into a fortress. There was a long paved alley lined with high stone walls ending in a massive gateway which led to the inner sanctum. There, well away from the main road and almost impossible to find unless you knew where to look, was a cluster of imposing houses like miniature castles barricaded behind sturdy buttresses of hewn stones topped with wooden palings or brushwood fences. There were no front gardens, only a few spindly pine trees peeking over the tops of the palings which closed in around the path. It was a strange, isolated, claustrophobic little place, a tiny hidden city. There the concubines must have lived rather a peaceful, sociable life awaiting – with pleasure or distaste,

229

depending on their feelings – the visits of the men who were paying for all this.

As we strolled on I realised that we were just around the corner from the home bar of the formidable *mama-san* in the severe navy-blue kimono. Mori-san had given me her phone number so, on the off-chance, I called. I was sure that, despite his introduction, I would still count as a first-timer and be roughly rebuffed. I was pleasantly surprised when she said, all affability, 'By all means; do come round!'

In the small bar with the rows of whiskey bottles along the mirrored wall, business was a little brisker. Some businessmen, rather the worse for wear, were sitting around a low table, jackets discarded, ties akimbo, enjoying an evening of karaoké. One by one they rose unsteadily to their feet to belt out a sentimental ditty, following the neon words on a video screen.

The *mama-san* was as buttoned-up as ever, smiling glacially, arranging dishes of snacks. I had been hoping to continue our intriguing conversation but was not sure how to set about it. I had been reading Haruyu's autobiography, I told her, trying to break the ice.

'Haruyu-san,' she smiled. 'Everyone knew her. She was "main"' – using the English word – 'she was a very important person in Gion society.'

'There was something we couldn't understand,' said Sarah. 'Did you ever hear of mirare?'

The *mama-san*'s face changed. Yes, she knew all about it.

In her book Haruyu wrote about *mirare* – literally 'being seen' – without ever making it clear exactly what it was. In Ichiriki-tei, Gion's famous terracotta-walled teahouse, there was a small enclosed room called Kako-i where maiko would go 'to be seen'. It was dark and shadowy. Usually four or five maiko were sent for at one time. The customer would look them over and decide on one.

'Mirare was not nice for the maiko,' wrote Haruyu. 'If you were chosen it wasn't nice; and if you weren't chosen it wasn't nice. If you didn't like the person who had chosen you, in theory you could say "No". For a girl born in a geisha house, it was not so difficult to do that. But if you were a maiko who came from far away and were working hard to make money, you couldn't afford to say "No".'

'That was the difference between tayu courtesans in the old days and geisha,' said the *mama-san*. 'Tayu chose who they slept with. They'd say to a customer, "You! I'm sleeping with you tonight!" But geisha couldn't choose. They were chosen.'

'Being seen' was the process by which a customer picked a sleeping partner, either for the night or as a long-term arrangement. First he informed the mistress of his regular teahouse that that was what he wanted to do. She sent for a selection of geisha and maiko who clattered over to the teahouse accompanied, as always, by the 'boy' (the dresser/assistant).

'You always knew it was mirare,' said the *mama-san*, 'when you got one customer asking for a group of maiko and geisha. When we were getting ready, we'd tuck a comb backwards in our hair at the back, where the customer couldn't see it.' She demonstrated slipping a small curved comb back to front into her hair. 'It was like a charm to ward off being chosen.'

It was a little like an audition. After the customer had looked them over, he would inform the mistress of the teahouse or her maid of his choice. She passed the message on to the 'boy'. He took the message back to the mother of the geisha house where the maiko in question lived. Then, when she had given formal consent, he returned to the teahouse and the teahouse 'mother' told the other maiko they could leave. Until then none of them knew which it would be. The chosen maiko was left alone.

In theory she had the right to refuse the customer. In practice, said the *mama-san*, there were times when you could refuse and times when you couldn't. Meanwhile the customer and the mistress of the teahouse would negotiate the price. There was a sliding scale, depending on what the customer wanted, ranging from a single night to some sort of long-term arrangement.

If a customer decided he wanted to become a *danna*, the patron of a maiko or geisha, that was often how he chose her. In those days, as far as a geisha or maiko was concerned, she needed a *danna* in order to survive. Whether he looked like the sea monster of Kafu Nagai's stories or was young and handsome, it would have been absurd of her to refuse. In any case, she could always take a lover in secret or trade him in for another patron if she got a better offer.

If, as the phrase went, she was 'pulled [out of the geisha world] by a danna' — *danna-san hika sareru* — in other words, if she decided to take up his offer and become his concubine, she removed her name from the geisha registry. As a farewell, she handed out dishes of white rice called *hiki-iwai* — 'celebrating being pulled' — to her teachers, seniors, friends and colleagues in the geisha community. The whiteness of the rice symbolised that she would be with that *danna* until her hair was white. If, however, she had had her debts paid off by a *danna* whom she did not love, and wanted to keep her options open, there would be red aduki beans scattered among the white rice, hinting that this was not for ever and that she would most likely be returning to the geisha world one day. The customer, of course, never saw the rice. Most women slipped in a few red beans just in case.

Another permutation popular with the customers was sleeping over — *zakone*, 'sleeping huddled together like small fish'. At the end of an evening's partying, the customers might ask the teahouse mistress to call the geisha house and ask if the maiko could sleep over. The payment was the hourly rate for each maiko's company times twelve — in other words, very expensive.

The dresser arrived with the maikos' nightwear, put all their combs and hair ornaments into a box, then took the combs and kimonos back to the geisha house. He reappeared the following morning with fresh kimonos for them. Meanwhile the maids at the teahouse were spreading futon bedding around one big room. The maiko and customers slept together, spread out around the room, with a pinch-faced old maid awake all night to make sure that nothing untoward took place. Sex, after all, was to be properly arranged and paid for, not stolen. The men could chat to the maiko and the maiko could chat to each other; but the rule was no touching. Still, men loved sleeping surrounded by beautiful young women. For the maiko it was a chance to steal a customer's heart. With luck he might be sufficiently entranced to go through the proper channels and buy her for a night or even become her *danna*.

One elderly teahouse 'mother' I met remembered 'sleeping over'. 'We used to have it in the big room upstairs,' she told me rather indiscreetly, smiling wistfully at the memory of those jolly days long gone by. 'In the summertime. There'd be three or four guests, five or six geisha and maiko and a maid or two. The fun was to try and grab the girls' breasts.'

For the customers it was expensive fun, for the maiko an edgy combination of fun and desperation. The customers, after all, were at play. They had left the real world of home and work behind to enter this world which operated by different rules and where there were no real responsibilities. That was why it was so expensive. But the maiko were not at play. They had a living to make and, until 1958, a frightening debt to pay off. For them it was deadly serious. As for the steely *mama-san* in her dark blue kimono, she had long since put all this behind her. It was a bad memory from the distant past. She had survived. In fact, she had done better than that. She had managed to acquire a teahouse of her own. She had become not just independent but a successful businesswoman. Maybe she had inherited the teahouse from the cruel house mother who had tormented her; or maybe she had had a *danna* to help her out.

'"Being seen", "sleeping over" – all that came to an end in 1958,' she said with an edge of pleasure in her voice. 'Those were good days for men. Now it's good days for women. These days girls become maiko because they want to and leave when they want to.'

With that she presented us with our bill. For a glass each of whiskey and water, a small dish of snacks (dried squid, unappetising crackers) which we didn't touch and about an hour of the *mama-san*'s time, not to mention the cost of sliding open the door and walking in, the bill for myself and Sarah came to 14,000 yen (about £70). Sarah, who knew about these things, said that we had got off lightly.

11

WORLD OF WOMEN
THE GEISHA OF KYOTO

I know she is light and faithless,
But she has come back half-repentant
And very pale and very sad.
A butterfly needs somewhere to rest
At evening.
'Return', geisha song[1]

The Wigmaker

One day, during a break in the weather, I took a bus across town to the other side of the city, near the Nishijin weavers' district and the Kamishichiken geisha district, to visit one of the three wigmakers who between them serviced all the Kyoto geisha. Mr Imanishi had turned a wing of his rambling house behind Myoshinji Zen temple into a busy workshop where he sat on his heels alongside his two sons, his apprentices in the trade. Here and there about the room were what looked at first glance like human heads stuck on poles. They turned out to be wigs, some with long bedraggled locks, others neatly coiffed, set on egg-shaped wooden moulds.

'Wigs used to be all Japanese hair, you know,' grinned Mr Imanishi breezily. He was a roguish man in his sixties with a face like a walnut, a cheeky upturned nose and a mop of curly grey hair. The hair of the wig on the stand in front of him hung in unappetising rat's tails which he was sectioning and combing energetically, slapping on globs of white *bintsuke* wax.

'But these days Japanese girls are rich,' he went on. 'They don't need to sell their hair. So we use imported Chinese hair, plus yak's hair for volume. But Japanese hair is the best. That's what we say, us wigmakers.'

He looped, folded and pinned the tresses in a process very similar to dressing a maiko's hair, until he had created the glossy coiffure of the geisha, with a swatch of hair at the back, held in place with a stiff silver ribbon. Then he handed me the finished wig. The glossy hair was sticky with wax but the wig itself was astonishingly light and hard. Inside was a framework of duralumin, a sort of aluminium, lined with netting, like the inside of a crash helmet. British wigs, conversely, have a rubber base.

'Once they decide to change the collar, that's when we measure them up for their first wig,' explained Mr Imanishi, wiping his hands on his uncannily clean white linen apron. 'I meet the maiko and decide what shape will flatter her face. A round face, I make it look thinner; a thin face, I make it plumper. Those geisha all look pretty, right? That's the wigmaker's art, to make a wig that flatters the face. That's what keeps them coming back.'

Unlike a western wig, a Japanese wig had a widow's peak at the front like Mount Fuji. It took, he said, two weeks to make a wig and required several fittings. For the first five days after the changing of the collar, one of his sons went to the geisha house every day to teach the fledgling geisha how to put it on. Once the first parties were over and she had time for more fittings, she ordered a second wig so that she always had one to wear while the other was being reset.

No geisha would dream of being seen in a wig that had a single hair out of place, let alone one that was a bit flat or misshapen. In order to ensure that they always had that fresh-from-the-hairdresser look, geisha stored their wigs carefully in wig boxes and had them combed out and reset once a month, a job which took half a day (one and a half hours plus fetching and returning the wig) and cost 23,000 yen (£115) a time. Added to that, a wig had a lifespan of about three years, after which a geisha would need a new one. Each new wig cost 500,000 yen (in the region of £2500). All in all, it was a sizeable expense for the geisha and provided a thriving business for Mr Imanishi and his fellow wigmakers.

'In the eighties, during the "bubble economy", I used to work from 9 to 2 or 3 the next morning, seven days a week,' he said cheerfully. 'Now I've got my sons to help, so I can relax. People say Japanese work all the time; in those days I really did!'

Wigs came into vogue well after the end of the war, around the watershed year of 1958. Before then they had been used mainly in the kabuki theatre. Geisha used to go to the hairdresser, as maiko do still.

'My old man was a weaver in Nishijin, the textile area,' recalled Mr Imanishi. 'But after the war the economy was in bad shape. There was no work for weavers. Then I started to hear that there was a demand for wigmakers. They were flying off all over the place, down to Okinawa, up to Hokkaido, there were so few of them and so much demand. That's the job for me, I thought. I knew a wigmaker so I got apprenticed. That was 1955.'

For maiko, who were in the process of being trained, it was essential to live the flower and willow life twenty-four hours a day. But geisha were modern women, adults who had chosen to continue the life while it suited them. In their time off, they preferred to have the option of wearing western clothes and having their hair in a less conspicuous style. Wearing a wig enabled them to switch between the geisha world and everyday life with ease. They could treat being a geisha as a job and the geisha's outfit as a uniform, to be put on when they started work and taken off afterwards. It was a liberation. Thus, as the profession itself changed, wigs soared in popularity.

But how on earth, I asked, could one tamp down the enormous amount of hair which most geisha had to fit a wig on top? Perhaps, said Mr Imanishi, I should try it myself. Without more ado he swept my hair back and twisted a stretchy net over it, then wound a bandage-like tape around the edges. In seconds my head was as flat as the egg-shaped moulds on which the wigs rested. Then he lifted a wig out of its box. After he had tied a few ribbons and made a few adjustments it fitted perfectly. It felt tight, secure and heavy, like wearing a crown. He added an ivory comb and some tortoiseshell hairpins and gave me a mirror to admire his handiwork.

The effect of a black, glossy and absurdly stylised geisha wig perched above my European features was, it has to be said, far from flattering, like wearing an enormous piled-up Louis Quatorze wig without the gown, flounces, powder or perfectly placed round black beauty spot. I hastily dabbed on the reddest lipstick I could find. A good thick layer of white make-up, I could see, would make all the difference. As is normal in Japan to mark the occasion, I lined up with Mr Imanishi and his family, his baby grandson on my knee, for a group photograph.

I had a final question. He had been boasting of how many geisha he knew and how well he knew them.

'What would you say if your daughter wanted to become a geisha?' I asked.

He looked taken aback.

'Hmm,' he said finally, with an uncertain chuckle. 'That's a difficult question.' It was, it seemed, as outrageous a suggestion as if I had asked a stern Victorian patriarch if he would allow his daughter to become an actress. I could almost hear the music hall refrain: 'Don't put your daughter on the stage, Mrs Worthington!' In turn-of-the-millennium Japan, geisha still had the rakish, not-quite-respectable image that actors and actresses used to have a century ago in Britain. To drop their names and boast of how many one knew was one thing. To have one's own child join the ranks of these glamorous but nonetheless somehow disreputable creatures was quite another.

Working Geisha

Whenever I had time to spare, I would stand on my rickety balcony in the shadow of the deep wooden eaves, hidden behind the bamboo blinds which flapped and rattled in the slightest breeze, and watch the comings and goings at the large, ugly, concrete 'Dance and Music Practice Place', the Kaburenjo, diagonally across the street from my house. It was the hub of the community. Behind the car park and up some steps were the union offices, while a large splendid theatre, dark and empty most of the year apart from the spring dance performances, occupied the back of the building. Upstairs was a warren of small rooms, lined with mirrors and floored with tatami, where classes took place.

First the office staff would turn up, dour-looking men in grey suits and pinch-faced women with piled-up hair like ex-geisha. Then a group of maiko would clatter along in their blue and white summer *yukata* and stiff waxed hair, cooing and chirping like a flock of birds, and disappear inside for their morning lessons. In the afternoon, when the maiko were busy preparing for the evening's parties, the beginners (the *shikomi*) would drift in, gauche and giggly in their starchy new *yukata*, their hair in ponytails.

Long before it was due to happen, the maiko had begun whispering nervously about a forthcoming flute and drum concert. Suddenly they were too busy attending classes or practising earnestly in their rooms to chat or go shopping. Life in the geisha district was punctuated by these small occasions, like end-of-term exams, where the maiko showed off their skills. Haruta-san, the proprietress of the Haruta house, gave me a programme, drew a circle beside Harumi's and Haruka's names and told me to be sure to go.

The performance took place at noon one sunny Monday in a large upstairs room at the Kaburenjo. The whole community had turned out. The 'older sisters' in their best summer kimonos flopped on their knees on flat white cushions laid out in rows on the tatami mats, while a couple of geisha dispensed cups of lukewarm green tea. One side of the room had been marked out as the stage, with gold screens for the backdrop and a carpeting of red felt on the floor.

Once we were all settled on our cushions, a door slid open. A group of geisha filed out, their white-socked feet rustling across the red felt, and took their places along the back. They looked appropriately solemn but also relaxed and confident. Today their job was simply to provide the accompaniment, the difficult shamisen riffs and singing which took years to master. Two of them I knew: Fumiko, the modest but brilliant dancer whom I often met over breakfast at the local coffee shop; and Koito, a chirpy Cockney sparrow of a geisha. Whenever there was a public performance, the two of them were always there, sometimes in the background, as today, sometimes taking a starring role. They were stalwarts of the geisha community.

Then came the maiko who were to be stars for the day, faces serious, eyes cast down, each carrying a black and gold hourglass-shaped drum or a bamboo flute. Like the geisha, they wore crisp white cotton *yukata* with an indigo-dyed pattern of wisteria leaves, tied with a plain red obi, with only a touch of make-up and a few ornaments in their stiff waxed coiffures. Harumi was among them. Solemnly she took her place on her knees in the front row. The music started. With my half-trained ear I could hear that it was simple, an opportunity for the maiko to show off their skills, beating out a rhythm with their fingers on the horse-hide skins of their drums.

Intermission came. Several of the 'older sisters' were puffing at cigarettes. A couple had nodded off, still on their knees, their heads lolling to one side. They quickly woke up when the opportunity for a smoke and a gossip arose. There were also a few men, looking smug at the privilege of sitting in this room surrounded by women. One, a chubby middle-aged man in a pale suit, was sitting cross-legged, smoking and talking loudly, next to a strikingly beautiful geisha. Dressed in a beige kimono printed with white camellias and a white obi scattered with sprigs of red cherries, her hair tied in a simple knot, she was the epitome of geisha chic. She sat very properly on her knees, her toes, clad in white cotton, neatly crossed behind her. He was, I assumed, her patron.

Then an unprepossessing fellow in a loud check jacket with thinning hair, a pink shirt and large old-fashioned glasses gave me a toothy smile and bowed.

'Ito,' he grinned, reminding me. 'Koito-san's fan club.'

Everyone knew Koito, the Cockney sparrow who sat at the end of the row of geisha, strumming her shamisen. In her idiosyncratic way she was the epitome of the modern geisha. She was a star, not of the silver screen or the television but of the Internet. She regularly featured in articles in newspapers and magazines and had a lively fan club.

She was not a typical geisha; but then again, none of them were. They were not innocent children like the maiko. The women who had chosen to stay on in the community instead of leaving before the change of collar all had their own reasons for doing so and their own way of making the geisha life work for them.

Koito's house was a couple of blocks south of mine, on the other side of the Haruta geisha house, along a narrow lane which was eternally in shadow. The houses facing each other on each side almost seemed to touch, they were so close. By western standards her house was tiny; but, compared to the other houses in the area, it was large and prosperous. It had recently been rebuilt in the traditional style and gleamed with tawny wood, with new pale gold bamboo buttressing edging the front wall. A round white lantern hung outside the door alongside two wooden plaques, one marked 'Koito', the other 'Komaki'. Inside, the steep wooden staircase gleamed with polish and the tatami was brand new. There was even a western toilet with a heated toilet seat. Koito was a woman of means.

Off duty, with no make-up and her shoulder-length hair loose, Koito might have been a secretary or a housewife. In her early thirties, she was already losing the prettiness of youth. Her heart-shaped face was broadening and beginning to sag a little around the chin and cheeks, though her black eyes were sharp and her upturned nose pert. If anything distinguished her it was her personality, cheeky, confident, feisty and down to earth.

Koito had been in the geisha world for sixteen years. The daughter of a provincial newsagent, she had been flicking through magazines in the hairdressing salon her mother ran when she came upon a photograph of a maiko with a stiff medieval coiffure. Instantly she knew that she wanted this face for herself. She wanted to move to Kyoto and be a maiko.

'My parents were against it,' she told me in matter-of-fact tones, 'and they're against it now.'

But she had caught the bug. The grandmother of a friend of hers lived in the geisha district and through her she obtained an introduction to a geisha house. She worked her way up through the ranks, from 'egg' to 'learning by observation', then became a maiko. When the time came to change her collar, she had no doubts. A year after she became a geisha she had saved enough money to move out of the geisha house and set up on her own, first in an apartment and later in a house.

'It's not an easy life,' she pointed out. 'If you're a good dancer you get work all the time and you can make a lot in tips. But these days, some evenings there's no work at all. The customers aren't coming. There's too many other things people can do in their leisure time. In the old days there was nothing but the pleasure quarters. Nowadays you don't need to go to the geisha districts any more to have fun.'

Three years ago she had a brainwave. What was needed was a website to put across the geisha lifestyle and philosophy, describe its arts, customs and history, correct misconceptions and persuade new customers to come. That was the beginning of her fame. The first time I met her she introduced me to Mr Ito, the president of her fan club. Whenever I went to a performance of geisha dancing, he was always there, beaming goofily, with his camera and tripod. As far as I could see, he only ever took photographs of Koito.

Geisha Chic: The Art of the Kimono

One day when I got back to my inn, I found a note, prettily written on handmade paper, with a drawing of a *maneki nekko* (a lucky 'money-beckoning cat') on the envelope. It was from Koito. There was a journalist from a women's magazine coming to interview her, she wrote. Could I, the local foreigner, please be there to add a touch of international colour to the photograph?

On the day I put on my smartest clothes and plenty of make-up; no matter how hard I tried I always felt plain and under-dressed next to a geisha. Koito was still in her dowdy off-duty beige sweater and skirt when I arrived.

'I'm worried about my maiko,' she grumbled, stroking her tabby cat. Its eyes were as sharp and black as her own. 'Went off a couple of months ago. Said she was going home. Haven't heard a word from her since.'

Rather than Koito, it was Komaki, her maiko, who was the star of the website. She was the first maiko of the cyber age. She had seen Koito on television, looked up her website and been captivated by the images and descriptions of life in the flower and willow world. She persuaded her father to send Koito an e-mail, asking if she could become her apprentice, was accepted and moved into Koito's house. I had seen photographs of her, a tall, strapping fifteen-year-old. But, like many maiko, she discovered that there was a lot more to the life than just looking pretty. Her story – her hopes, her disappointments, her growing frustration – formed the gripping day-to-day substance of the website. Even the cat featured on it. But now, a year later, having gone through with her debut, she had disappeared.

241

'It's not easy raising a maiko,' complained Koito, addressing the plump young journalist who was busy scribbling notes. She too was a fan of Koito's and regularly checked her website. 'She got spots. Everyone was always watching her and passing comments. It made her self-conscious. You can tell straight away if a maiko is graceful and is going to be a good dancer; whereas with the shamisen it takes five or six years before you realise, "This child is good." She was learning the flute too, but it was the same problem. No one ever told her she was doing well. So she got depressed. She said she didn't want to appear at the Five District Dances because her friends would be there.'

The Five District Dances, a major event in the geisha calendar when the top dancers and the prettiest maiko from all five areas performed in the cavernous Kyoto Hall, were due to take place in a few weeks' time. 'I think she thought she wasn't good enough. I told her she couldn't have a holiday but she ran away. I think she might have run away for good.'

We had been sitting rather stiffly on cushions around the low table in one of the tatami rooms upstairs. Koito led us into a dressing room and began lifting flat cardboard boxes out of the shallow drawers of a tall wooden dresser. She took the lid off one to reveal a package of textured handmade paper. Carefully she undid the ribbons. Inside, within another layer of tissue paper, was a swath of lustrous silk, quail's egg grey. She lifted the folds of fabric to reveal a pattern of white grasses. We fingered the soft silk.

'It's a geisha's kimono for autumn,' she said. 'Autumn grasses.'

Next she brought out a pale mauve kimono, the colour of wisteria, then a dark mauve one with a pattern of maple leaves in dark greens and rusty oranges sprinkled with golden and orange chrysanthemums, and put them both aside. The first, she said, was a summer kimono, the second for autumn. Then she showed us a summer kimono of net-like silk in a delicate leaf green the colour of a cicada's wing, with a river specked with leaves rippling along the hem. Finally she brought out a kimono of a rich midnight blue. Wisteria blossoms tumbled in mauve and gold fronds around the skirt and across the sleeves. The cat was rolling on its back, playing with the loose ribbons.

'This one,' she said. We helped her refold the others, carefully wrapping

The beginnings of Gion: the entertainment district on the banks of the River Kamo in early seventeenth-century Kyoto. Musicians and dancers perform for the audience while pleasure-seekers arrive by palanquin. (FENOLLOSA-WELD COLLECTION, 1911, MUSEUM OF FINE ARTS, BOSTON)

The ninth-century femme fatale, Ono no Komachi. Woodblock print by Eizan Kikukawa (1787-1867). (V & A PICTURE LIBRARY)

A tayu courtesan of Shimabara. Woodblock print by Kunisada Utagawa (1786-1864). (V & A PICTURE LIBRARY)

A geisha in front of the Great Gate of the Yoshiwara. Woodblock print by Kunisada Utagawa. (V & A PICTURE LIBRARY)

A bustling Edo street: Saruwaka-cho, from 'One hundred famous views of Edo', by Hiroshige Ando (1797-1858). (NAGOYA TV)

Geisha entertaining young rakes at the fashionable Shikian restaurant on Nakasu island in the 1780s. Woodblock print by Shumman Kubo (1757-1820) (RIGHT-HAND PANEL). (BRITISH MUSEUM)

Oishi Kuranosuke plays blind-man's buff with the geisha of Ichiriki-tei, the famous Gion teahouse, to fool his enemies who are watching from the garden. (BRITISH MUSEUM)

Otatsu of the Ryogoku (Fukagawa) district of Edo. As a Fukagawa geisha, she is the epitome of chic. She steps out, barefoot in her wooden sandals and wearing a loose square-cut haori jacket. Woodblock print by Eiri Chokyosai (active 1789-1800).

(Musée des Arts Asiatiques, Paris)

Sadayakko on towering clogs, hair bristling with hairpins, painted by William Nicholson (1872-1949). (Victor Arwas, London Collection)

Taka the Literary Geisha (on right). (New York Times, Tokyo Bureau)

A courtesan in full regalia and her child attendant, posing for an unknown late nineteenth-century photographer.

Turn-of-the-century geisha enjoying a meal. One has propped her shamisen against the wall behind her to the right. (VICTOR ARWAS, LONDON COLLECTION)

Geisha in a rickshaw, posing with the runner for a late nineteenth-century photographer. (VICTOR ARWAS, LONDON COLLECTION)

Prostitutes on the look-out for custom in a poorer section of the Yoshiwara after the Second World War. (CORBIS IMAGES)

A youthful John Wayne (1907-1979) chats with a geisha. In 1958 a considerably older Wayne starred in John Huston's 'The Barbarian and the Geisha', the story of the first American consul, Townsend Harris, and his concubine, Okichi. (CORBIS IMAGES)

them in layers of tissue paper, replacing them in their envelopes and retying the ribbons.

'How do you choose?' we queried. A maiko living in a geisha house had no need to worry about which kimono was appropriate; her house mother would lay out a different kimono each month for her. But Koito was herself a house mother. For her, life was a succession of day-to-day decisions.

It depended, she explained, on the customers, the teahouse and the occasion for the party. For a congratulatory party or a celebration of some sort, she might wear something dressy; for a small quiet gathering, something more subdued. It went without saying that she would wear a geisha's kimono, much more subtly coloured than a maiko's, with sleeves that hung to her hips, not to the ankle, and with the obi tied in a knot without the heavy, swaying ends of the maiko's.

For a geisha, the art of choosing and wearing a kimono is as important a part of her training as learning traditional dancing or studying the shamisen. The kimono is an art form in its own right, as subtle and complex as tea ceremony, flower arrangement or brush painting. Woven of the finest, most luxurious silk, kimonos are dyed with designs which are exquisite and often enormously complex; landscapes of palaces, bridges, streams, trees and birds scroll across a kimono skirt in lavish detail and jewel-like colours.

Traditional arts in Japan are to do not with expressing oneself but learning the form, the *kata*, the proper way of doing things. The aim is perfection, a perfect promulgation of tradition, the right kimono worn in the right way for the place, the season and the occasion. A geisha is an artist, who transforms herself into a perfect work of art according to rules laid down by tradition.

Everything in traditional Japanese life reflects the season, from the flowers arranged in a vase to the brush painting on a wall to the words one uses when writing a poem. If you visit a teahouse, a geisha house or a private home in spring, there will be a sprig of spring flowers in a wicker vase and an ink painting, perhaps of a sprouting bamboo, on the wall; in winter there might be a sprig of plum blossoms artfully arranged in a section of bamboo. And every haiku includes a word which refers to the seasons – irises, rain or a frog to evoke June, a cicada in high summer, snow in winter. In the same way, a geisha naturally chooses a kimono proper to the season. For the cool months, from the typhoons of September through the winter snows to the end of April when the cherry blossoms fall, she wears a double-layered *awase* kimono of thick silk lined with crêpe. In May and June she wears lighter, single-layer kimonos, and when the steamy days of July and August come, she switches to *ro*, a silk so fine it is almost transparent.

More muted colours are suitable for winter, fresher ones for the hot months. There are also traditional colour combinations for each month: pale green layered on deep purple for January, rose backed with slate blue for October. The designs on the kimono, whether dyed (as in the dressier garments) or woven in, always reflect the season. A geisha naturally selects a kimono with the appropriate flowers, plants, insects or birds: sprigs of pine in January, plum blossom in February, cherry blossom in the spring, small trout in summer, maple leaves in autumn and snowflakes in the winter. It is all part of the process of living one's life as art.[2]

Koito had changed into a white cotton under-kimono patterned with red chrysanthemums. Scooping her hair into a net, she knelt in front of the tall narrow mirror of her dressing table and opened the tiny drawers overflowing with brushes and tubs of unguents. She took a breath and settled down to begin her make-up. Absorbed, we watched the transformation, all the more dramatic because this was not a beautiful young maiko but an ageing, rather plain woman.

Having covered her face in a layer of eggshell white, she turned her back to the mirror and, using a hand mirror to help her, skilfully painted her back in white, leaving the provocative V of unpainted flesh at the nape of the neck. She pencilled in two feathery eyebrows, adding a surreal touch of lipstick to define them, edged her eyes in red and added a line of black, then painted her mouth the colour of a ripe cherry.

Then she lifted an enormous box like a hatbox from a cupboard and brought out a gleaming coiffed wig on a stand. She combed it, tidied it and fitted it over her head, adjusting it until it was perfectly centred and balanced, combed it again, added a few hairpins and turned to look at us. The wig had performed its magic. The 'Mount Fuji' widow's peak and the strange unnatural wings of the wig had transformed the shape of her face, accentuating the delicate pointed chin. The frumpy thirty-year-old had disappeared and a startlingly alluring creature emerged, like a butterfly from a chrysalis; not beautiful, but indubitably sexy and fascinating. Coquettishly, she picked up the mewing cat and held it up to her face, gazing into its sharp black eyes. It put its paws on her shoulders and tried to lick the immaculate alabaster of her face.

Standing up, she put on a red and white under-kimono, followed by another of pale pink scattered with small red chrysanthemums, and the thick white brocade collar marking the adult geisha, tying them all in place with ribbons.

'I used to have a dresser,' she said. 'But now I do it myself. If you get someone in, you have to fit in with their timing.'

Then she took the lustrous midnight-blue kimono with its mauve and pale gold design of wisteria and slipped it over her shoulders, pulling it down to reveal not an ample expanse of bare back like a maiko's but a titillating flash of white-painted shoulders. The fabric swirled about her feet like water.

In old Japan, sex appeal was all to do with mystery. Far from revealing swaths of naked bosom, midriff or leg like a Hollywood star on Oscar night, the epitome of desirability was the *tayu*, the courtesan, swathed in layer upon layer of sumptuous fabric like a Christmas present, with just her tiny bare feet to remind you of the frail flesh of the woman inside. To the Japanese eye, there was an enormous difference in the way geisha and wives – the two poles of Japanese womanhood – wore their kimonos. The geisha was ineffably sexy; but it was a subtle sexiness, a matter of hint and suggestion.

In time I began to be able to see the difference between the kimono a geisha wore when she was dressed to kill with white face and wig and an ordinary one such as a wife would wear. The geisha's was more ornate, bolder and more decorative with a strong pattern on the skirt and hem where it would be most visible. It was the same shape and size as a standard one; the kimono is a one-size-fits-all garment which you adjust by folding and tying. But there were a myriad subtle ways in which a geisha tied hers to make it very different from a wife's, and infinitely sexier.

For a start it was worn looser than a wife would ever dream of it, leaving a suggestive flash of pale under-kimono, spangled with red, clearly visible at the sleeve and hem. It sat lower on the shoulders, with the collar pulled well down to reveal the painted back and the erotic tongue of bare flesh at the nape of the neck. It was also worn much longer so that it draped to form a train on the ground, eddying gracefully about the feet. A wife, conversely, would wear a kimono with a discreet pattern on the chest or thigh. She would fold and tie it so that it stopped just at the ankle to make a prim asexual cylinder with barely a bulge for bottom or breasts. When walking the geisha held the skirt of her kimono gracefully with the left hand; if a wife needed to lift her kimono skirt, she would hold it with the right hand.

Koito had wrapped herself in a long green obi, winding it round and round her waist and tucking in pads of stiffening and a cushion at the back to give extra bulk, until she was cocooned as thoroughly as an Egyptian mummy. The last touch was a narrow white silk cord. She turned with a coquettish downcast glance. 'It's a long time since I've dressed like this,' she confided. Normally she wore the understated kimono and subtle make-up of the day-to-day working geisha. The white make-up, wig and sumptuous kimono were party wear, for special occasions only.

It was not only her appearance that had changed. Her bearing and the timbre of her voice had changed too, though she was still as chirpy as a Cockney sparrow. As she opened the front door, the cat darted out and disappeared under a nearby parked car. She slipped on a pair of wooden clogs, lower and lighter than a maiko's hoof-like ones, and minced after it, lifting her trailing kimono skirts with her left hand and trilling 'Kitty, Kitty' – 'Nekko-chan, Nekko-chan' – in a girlish falsetto. Together we set off down the street to pose for photographs, Koito tripping along, bowing and calling out greetings to everyone we met.

The Ichiriki Teahouse

The night is black
And I am excited about you.
My love climbs in me, and you ask
That I should climb to the higher room.
Things are hidden in a black night.
Even the dream is black
On the black-lacquered pillow,
Even our talk is hidden.

Geisha song[3]

The most splendid teahouse in the city, renowned across Japan, is Ichiriki-tei, where Oishi Kuranosuke, hero of the much-loved 'Tale of the Forty-Seven *Ronin* [leaderless samurai]', whiled away two years, play-acting a life of dissipation to put his enemies off the scent, before finally avenging the death of his lord. Purists complain that in his time, around 1702, Gion barely existed and had certainly not reached its apogee of splendour; the Ichiriki he knew must have been in the south of the city. But no one in Gion pays the slightest attention to such quibbles.

Ichiriki stands proudly on the corner of Shijo Street, the main shopping area, and Hanami-koji, 'Flower-Viewing Alley', the heart of Gion. The teahouses which press side by side along Flower-Viewing Alley are dark and forbidding, with slatted wooden fencing in front, bamboo screens concealing the windows and little sign of life except for the red lanterns which hang in the doorways and the discreet wooden plaques which give the names of the geisha and maiko who live there. Behind them stretch warrens of shadowy lanes lined with faceless houses and closed gates. Ichiriki, conversely, is large and showy, a grand two-storey edifice whose distinctive terracotta-coloured walls are a symbol of the city. Nonetheless, it is every bit as firmly closed to all but the most privileged of insiders.

Across the gateway hangs a heavy brown curtain emblazoned with the characters *Ichi riki*, 'One strength'. Everyone assured me that the outside walls and the curtain were the most I would ever see; as a rank outsider in

247

this closed community, I could never even dream of crossing the threshold. Whenever I passed by I admired the imposing red walls with their beams and buttressing of blackened wood and peeked wistfully through the curtain, wondering what lay inside.

Then one day I was in the hair oil shop on Shijo Street, talking to the elegant, very modern young woman behind the counter whose family had dealt in heavily scented camellia oil for generations. She had grown up on the edge of the geisha world; she was in it but not of it. She was not determined, as the geisha were, to maintain its exclusivity even if that meant it would die out entirely. Almost in passing she asked if I would like to meet the mistress of Ichiriki, whose son happened to go to school with hers. There and then she took me around the corner, brushed through the brown linen curtains, crossed the cobbled courtyard, slid open the doors and introduced me.

The mistress was a plump, pretty, confident woman in a pink jumper who wore her hair in a bun like a geisha. There was nothing much, she said with Japanese self-deprecation, just tatami rooms, but if I really wanted to see them, I could. Amazed at my luck, I followed her in stockinged feet as she padded along the dark corridors, glossy with polish, and led me into a large, airy banqueting hall, empty but for acres of straw-coloured tatami matting and a few low tables. Ancient wooden screens, brushed with a design of purple irises, concealed the sliding doors. Above another set of doors was an ink sketch of a bald-headed samurai, wearing a blindfold, chasing a bevy of laughing geisha.

'Oishi Kuranosuke?' I asked.

She nodded with a glance of approval; I was not just an ignorant foreigner. Thanks to the Oishi connection, Ichiriki was by far the most successful of the Gion teahouses; there were always people wanting to dissipate an evening at the scene of the most celebrated partying in Japanese history. Ichiriki, she added firmly, had definitely existed in 1702, when Oishi was said to have been there. I didn't argue the point.

Beyond the glass doors which formed the outside wall was a small garden laid out like a picture with moss-covered rocks around a stone lantern and a gnarled tree. The mistress showed me the air-conditioning ducts cunningly concealed behind a veneer of ancient bamboo piping and wooden latticework. The teahouses of Gion had been among the first places in Japan to install it. It was a profitable business.

She too was in the geisha world but not of it. She had moved to Ichiriki when she married Seiichi Sugiura, the thirteenth generation of the Sugiura family which had dominated Gion throughout its history. The ninth, Jiroemon, had been instrumental in reviving Kyoto's geisha culture when the emperor and his court moved to Edo in 1868, establishing the annual public dances which now formed the pinnacle of the geisha calendar. For 300 years, the master of Ichiriki had been in charge of the geisha union in Gion. He was like the lord of the manor. The ultimate responsibility for the prosperity and well-being of the whole of Gion rested on his shoulders.

Seiichi had never had any choice in the matter. No matter what he did or where he went, he was always branded with the mark of Ichiriki. He was 'the Ichiriki boy'. Rumour had it that he had been something of a playboy in his youth, who drove fast cars and holidayed in Hawaii. But eventually when his grandfather died he joined the family firm and set to work to learn the business. He was now a pillar of the Gion community.[4]

But the future, said the pretty, pink-sweatered mistress, was a worry. In the eighteen years in which she had been at Ichiriki, the number of geisha and teahouses had fallen disastrously. Once upon a time customers used to bring their sons and introduce them. But now most customers were over sixty and their numbers too were plummeting. Instead of going off on a bar crawl for a 'second round' and a 'third round' of drinking, as they used to, people tended to go home after a geisha party. Some of the smaller teahouses were closing down. Ichiriki still thrived. Anyone would grab the chance to spend an evening with the most glamorous geisha in Gion at the historic teahouse. But it could not survive in isolation.

'If we were a restaurant, it wouldn't matter if we were the only one left,' she said. We were in one of the upper rooms, looking down on the dark wooden houses along Flower-Viewing Alley. One by one, lanterns began to glow in the dusk. A line of taxis was building up, half blocking the narrow street, ready to ferry the geisha and maiko to their nightly assignations. 'But we need geisha and maiko coming and going. That's the flavour of Gion.

'It used to be a special world here where patrons – danna-san – took care of the geisha. Geisha ran teahouses but that was just pocket money. Now they have to make a living by that alone. It's impossible. So they end up closing down.'

Then she was called out. I sat alone in the banqueting hall, imagining the rowdy parties that had punctuated the last three centuries and the days when glamorous dissidents, from wealthy but powerless merchants in their silks and finery to hot-headed young samurai forced to leave their swords at the door, had gathered here to while away night after night with their geisha lovers.

After a few minutes the door slid open and a woman slipped in. She folded herself on to her knees in a corner of the big room and sat silently looking at the tatami, nervously twisting her bony hands. She was a wisp of a woman, painfully thin, with a greying bun.

As the guest, it was not my place to begin the conversation. But when the silence became heavy, I tried a little smalltalk. She must have known Ichiriki for many years, I said. She started reminiscing about how it had been after the war when they tried to get the business going again but everyone had sold their kimonos.

'I'd just arrived,' she said. She had a thin, reedy voice. 'I hated it here. I cried and cried. The maids tormented me. It was so hard to learn all the different ways of doing things.'

She must be, I realised, the 'old mistress', the mother-in-law of the pink-jumpered young mistress. I never ceased to be amazed by the passion with which older women poured out their feelings. At first I thought it was because I was such an outsider. As a non-Japanese, I was barely human and rendered harmless by my childish foreign accent. Perhaps this was why they felt able to speak of things which could not be shared with their peers. But then I read an interview in an obscure Japanese magazine in which the 'old mistress' had said many of the same things.[5] Perhaps it was the privilege of age. She had handed on the mantle of responsibility. No longer 'the mistress of Ichiriki', she was free to be herself.

A couple of visits later, she was delegated to tell me her memories of the history of the place. I waited in the banqueting hall for her to arrive. She slipped in, bird-like and nervous.

'Customers used to summon their favourite geisha and maiko and sleep with them in those small rooms upstairs,' she began, almost before she had folded to her knees. 'Black marketeers would ask for geisha. Most of the patrons were the owners of the weaving factories in Nishijin. They spent the night here with their geisha, or they went to an inn. Some of the wives had horns [the demon horns of jealousy] or pretended not to know. In those days keeping a geisha was a mark of status. It was natural. But after the war all that stopped. That way of thinking was abolished.'

A Tokyo girl, she had been evacuated to Kyoto with her family during the war. Her father knew a man who had a saké shop and he knew the old master of Ichiriki. The two met up at a tea ceremony and decided that their children should marry. She was eighteen, the 'young master' of Ichiriki thirty-three. After the formal introductions, before anything had been decided, she sneaked off to the teahouse to have a look around. It was huge and intimidating. The last thing she wanted was to marry into this famous family with such a long history and weighty place in Kyoto society.

'I didn't want to enter a world I didn't know,' she said in her thin, reedy voice. 'But my parents said I had to. The Sugiura family promised that I would not have to go to teahouse parties. But as soon as I moved in, I had to. I was the young mistress, I had to.'

Fresh from Tokyo, she had no idea how things were done in stiff, rather formal Kyoto society, let alone in the arcane world of the geisha. It was a bit like moving from New York to the salons of Washington high society, or arriving from Manchester to marry the son of a lord with a luxury home in Chelsea. Even the highfalutin dialect of Kyoto was barely comprehensible to her Tokyo ears; worse still, her dowager mother-in-law spoke old Kyoto dialect, like fearsomely posh Victorian English.

'The maids bullied me. I wasn't used to dealing with customers. When I made mistakes, they scolded me. The most difficult thing was knowing what to talk about at parties. I couldn't just sit there and say nothing. My mother-in-law gave me instructions but she spoke old Kyoto dialect and I couldn't understand, even when I asked her two or three times to repeat it. I used to hide in the toilet and cry. I cried and cried.

251

'Right after the war we had lots of foreigners coming. The geisha refused to sleep with foreigners.'

She led the way up the steep wooden staircase to the upper floor and showed me the big rooms where customers used to 'sleep over' with groups of pretty maiko and a couple of maids to make sure things did not get out of hand. There were also several smaller, cosier rooms for *danna* who wanted to spend the night with a geisha. If a customer had booked a *mizuage*, that was where he did it.

'Some of the maiko and geisha hated having to sleep with the danna. They used to complain to me. But they had to do it.'

Casting a Spell

In the geisha world as elsewhere, nothing ever went exactly according to the rules. My bandanna-ed friend Mr Mori, ebullient author and international businessman, was an inveterate teahouse crawler, though he seldom ventured beyond the home bar. The geisha never complained and never denied him entry; so he must have been known to all of them.

One night we dropped into a 300-year-old teahouse on Flower-Viewing Alley. A handsome, smiling woman greeted us at the door and led us through a couple of tiny wooden-walled rooms lined with worn tatami to the home bar. It was eleven o'clock but the bar was practically empty. The only customers were an elderly balding man in a suit and a maiko in a pink flowery kimono, sitting side by side on stools at the bar. He talked in a low grumble, she nodded and smiled, laughing coyly as if he were the most desirable man in the world.

The handsome woman took her place behind the bar and, without asking, poured us each a tumbler of whiskey and water.

'Mama used to be a maiko,' Mori-san told me, giving her a cheeky grin.

She smiled the indulgent smile of a mother for a naughty little boy, the perfect response to Mori-san's style. Like all the geisha, she was all smiles and courtesy but there was a guarded quality. It was her job to be charming, to take on the appropriate role to suit the customer's mood. But somewhere deep inside there was an icy core.

'Would you mind calling a maiko for us?' asked Mori-san, naming one of his favourites.

'Asobi jigoku,' said the *mama*. 'She's in "play hell".' The word which the geisha used for spending time with customers and which customers used for spending time with geisha was *asobi*, 'play', as opposed to work. Work was the world of duty, where one fulfilled one's responsibilities to one's workmates and family. The play world was every bit as serious but opposite. It was a world which operated by its own rules and where whatever one did had no repercussions outside that world.

'"Play hell"? That's what we say,' explained Mori-san, going into mentor mode, 'when you spend a whole evening or a whole day with a customer you can't stand. No matter how much you hate him, you can't say "No" because it's business.'

The *mama-san* had disappeared to try to locate a maiko. She had called everyone, she reported, but, as she had expected, at this late hour all the experienced maiko were out 'at play'. She had booked one of the youngsters, who was not yet in such demand.

I was leaving for Tokyo the following day.

'What are you doing there?' asked Mori-san.

'Meeting geisha,' I said. 'Spending time in the flower and willow world.'

'Flower and willow world?' he scoffed. 'There's no flower and willow world in Tokyo. I often go to Tokyo but I never "play" with geisha there. Akasaka? They're all old ladies. Shimbashi? Used to be famous. But now? Any geisha there? I wonder . . .'

I had heard this line all too often. Kyoto, everyone told me in tones of unquestionable superiority, was the only place where the flower and willow world survived. Here there was still a community where people preserved the *shikitari* – the proper ways of doing things. In other cities the so-called geisha might cycle to work and put on their kimonos when they got there. But Kyoto geisha lived the lifestyle twenty-four hours a day.

Unlike everyone else, I had actually met geisha in Tokyo and disagreed. But the essence of Kyoto was that sense of innate superiority. It was a bit like being among the British aristocracy. They did not claim to be more virtuous, cleverer or richer than anyone else. They just felt themselves to be indisputably classier. There was no way one could challenge it.

Within the Kyoto geisha world itself there was a very clear pecking order. The geisha of Gion considered themselves the highest of the high and everyone else concurred in this estimation. Whenever the different flower towns met, for example, for a grand dance convention, the Gion geisha were automatically granted precedence. They conceded that Pontocho and Kamishichiken might also be considered respectable preservers of the geisha heritage. But Miyagawa-cho and Gion East, which had once harboured prostitutes, were beyond the pale.

'I wouldn't go there,' people told me of Miyagawa-cho. 'Dangerous, isn't it?'

I never let on that some of my closest geisha friends were from Miyagawa-cho. They were by far the most friendly, welcoming and open. It seemed to me it was all to do with class. The lower down the social scale, the warmer the people.

When the little maiko arrived, we had the usual maiko conversation. Like many of the maiko and geisha, she was from the under-privileged rural island of Kyushu (rather like hailing from Britain's north-east). Her sister too was a maiko.

'I remember when I first came,' she piped in her affectedly posh Kyoto accent. 'It felt so odd calling the house mother "Mother" when she wasn't my mother. Especially in front of my real mother, when she visited. I felt embarrassed.'

Mori-san teased her that she still had a hint of rustic Kyushu burr. She giggled coyly.

'Even when I'm not wearing my maiko hairstyle,' she squeaked, bridling, 'taxi drivers always know straight away that I'm a maiko because of the way I talk!'

Later I excused myself. As I set off for the toilet, the maiko accompanied me, chatting girlishly. When I came out, she was still there, waiting patiently outside. She directed me to the small basin, turned on the tap for me and, when I had washed my hands, bowed and offered me a fluffy towel. It was rather disconcerting.

I had heard about this custom but never experienced it before. It was explained to me as an example of the way in which geisha manipulated the dumb, unsuspecting male of the species. No matter how docile and sweet they appeared to be, they were always firmly in control. For geisha, when a man went to the toilet was the one moment when he was out of reach of their spells and siren songs. Finding himself alone, he might suddenly remember his own home and his own wife. Awakening with a start, as if from a dream or a drug-induced stupor, he would rush out of the toilet and shout, 'I'm going home!'

The geisha, of course, wanted him to stay, drink more saké, spend more money, maybe even stay the night, which would be yet more lucrative. So whenever a guest went to the toilet, the custom had arisen of sending a pretty young maiko with him.

To do the job properly, she was supposed to talk to him the whole time he was inside. She could talk about a movie or ask him questions, anything at all to distract him so that he would not have a moment's leisure to recall where he was and what he was doing. If it was a lengthy job, the technique was to sing a song while waiting outside the door. The maiko would deliberately make a mistake with the words to attract the guest's attention, so that he would call through the door, 'That's wrong!' If he touched the maiko when they were out of the room together, she had to laugh and say, 'Ooh, that tickles!' so loudly that the other guests could hear. It was all part of a maiko's training.

It was that attention to detail that gave the Kyoto geisha their special flavour. The word the geisha used for it was *iki* – chic, style, the flavour of the geisha world. I too found myself succumbing to the spell. I had never been anywhere in Japan that preserved so completely the feel of times gone by. It was indeed another world, with even its own geographical space, which operated by its own rules and code of behaviour. But I was also keen to shake myself awake, to leave this never-never land, and return to Tokyo. What, I wondered, remained of the urbane and stylish geisha culture which had flourished so memorably in the great city of Edo? What was left of the brilliant decadence of the Yoshiwara and the elegance of Yanagibashi? Was the floating world still afloat in one of the world's most frenetic and modern cities?

12

TEAHOUSE POLITICS
THE GEISHA OF TOKYO

A dream of springtide
When the streets
Are scattering
Cherry blossoms.

Tidings of autumn
When the streets
Are lined with lighted lanterns
On both sides.

Koji Ochi (seventeenth-century poet); inscribed on the
Great Gate of the Yoshiwara[1]

À la Recherche

Not long after I got back to Tokyo, I met up with Shichiko, the male geisha. It was the dog days of summer, so hot and oppressive that it was difficult to move. He was in baggy checked Bermuda shorts, long stripy white socks and an oversized T-shirt. With his modish Henry V haircut and wicked grin, the outfit made him look like a naughty schoolboy – not inappropriate, it seemed to me, for a *taikomochi* jester. We sat in his small apartment – his wife and daughter were out – chatting languidly, fanning ourselves.

Shichiko lived in the rundown East End of the city, a long way from the glittering shops of the Ginza, the imperial palace and the posh business addresses, and round the corner from the Yoshiwara, which had been established as far as possible from the parts of town where respectable people ran their businesses and kept their wives and children. Early in the evening, when the heat was a little more bearable, we decided to take a stroll.

There was something irresistibly alluring about the Yoshiwara. After Japan opened its doors to the outside world, everyone who had arrived in the great city of Edo, starting with the Victorian Ernest Satow, found an excuse as soon as possible to sneak off for a visit. Even though it had been closed down, in theory at least, in the great clean-up of 1958, I was curious just to tread the streets which had seen so much drama, passion, pain, culture and poetry.

Shichiko had donned a pair of chunky orange schoolkid's sandals. Striding ahead, ice-cream cone in hand, he led the way through the back streets to a wide thoroughfare, lined with unlovely concrete blocks, with cars, trucks and buses roaring by. Strolling alone, we came to a bedraggled willow tree, its leaves pale and grimy. To the left, a road zigzagged around a corner and out of sight.

I knew exactly where we were. It was the Looking Back Willow – or rather, a sad descendant of it – where lovelorn merchants and samurai had turned to take a last look towards the Great Gate of the Yoshiwara and the glittering streets beyond, before returning to the monochrome world of work, home and family. The road that zigzagged out of sight had led to the heart of the Yoshiwara, designed so that passers-by could see nothing of what lay within. Right where the narrower road met the thoroughfare, the Great Gate had stood, marking the boundary between one world and the other.

The busy thoroughfare itself had been part of the moat – the Ditch of Black Teeth – which surrounded the walled city of pleasure. On the other side was a quiet back street which had once been the Dike of Japan, packed night and day with streams of eager male visitors, jostling along on foot or horseback or, in later years, by rickshaw. Nothing was left. Even the name 'Yoshiwara' had been obliterated in the city burghers' efforts to comply with western puritanism, though the present-day name still recalled the throngs of visitors who had tramped towards the place: Senzoku, 'Thousand Feet'.

257

Shichiko and I took each other's pictures in the shade of the legendary willow and turned down into what had once been the Yoshiwara. At first it looked like any nondescript working-class part of Tokyo, with shabby shops and rows of parked bicycles. But once round the bend we saw what had become of the most famous pleasure quarter on earth. The lower end of the business at any rate had not changed, though it had become a fair bit more sordid.

The main road and the side roads – the famous Five Streets – were lined with the fantasy palaces with which Japanese love to fill their red-light districts. The grand wooden edifices within which geisha had danced and courtesans entertained merchant princes, and the shacks where the lower ranks of prostitutes had carried out their less exalted trade, had disappeared. In their place were street upon street of exuberantly gaudy buildings, bristling with neon and festooned with wires and cables.

Flamboyant red-light districts are part of the scenery in Japan. What was notable was the sheer number and concentration of the brothels. One was modelled on a traditional Yoshiwara house with eaves and bamboo blinds carefully moulded in concrete. In front hung a neon picture of a geisha and the name O-oku, Harem, above a sign giving the price: 20,000 yen (£100) per 'bath'. (Brothels are known as 'soaplands' and involve complicated activity with a particularly slithery variety of soap.) Another, called True Love, spelt out in red characters on green neon, was a Spanish-effect mock brick 'villa'. Others with names like Love Rose, Acapulco and Quartier Latin featured snarling stone panthers, Roman columns or baroque stonework. Mean-looking gangster-types with cheap suits and slicked-back hair propped up the walls or lounged outside the doors where the prices and services were listed. There were no women to be seen; presumably they were all inside.

Shichiko strode along, saying little, giving monosyllabic grunts in answer to my questions. Perhaps he was worried about what I, a foreigner, might think of this rather shameful aspect of his country's culture; perhaps he was concerned that I might confuse the world of the 'arts people' which he inhabited with this tawdry, exploitative place; or perhaps he just took it all for granted and thought there was nothing to say.

Half a mile further on, clear of the streets lined with brothels, we came to a small graveyard shadowed with trees, with grave markers crammed tightly side by side. Among them were stone images of *jizo-sama*, the deities who take care of the souls of miscarried and aborted children. At the back was a pond – the Benten pond, said Shichiko, where unhappy prostitutes used to jump in to commit suicide. In the middle, on top of a stony hillock, was a statue of Kannon, the goddess of mercy, wimpled like the Virgin Mary, gazing compassionately down on the scene.

In the old days, said Shichiko, before everything came to an end in 1958, the Yoshiwara had been a thriving place where geisha lived side by side with prostitutes. Many of the old geisha, including his own shamisen teacher, had gone there for lessons from dance and music teachers who were considered the toughest and best, if not in the city, at least in the East End. In those days, to have studied at the Yoshiwara gave a working-class geisha kudos. But that was then.

Then around a corner we spied a large ugly plaster *tanuki*, the stylised badger which carries a flask of saké, wears a straw hat and a friendly grin and adorns shops and homes. It might be compared to a garden gnome in the west except for its enormously distended testicles which reach to its ankles and are believed to bestow fertility. Here Shichiko was on safer ground.

'My ancestor,' he cried, going up to it and flinging his arm round it. Remembering his outrageously priapic act which had shocked me so much when I saw it, I took a picture of the two of them, grinning, side by side.

Willow Bridge

Of all the Tokyo geisha districts or 'flower towns', Yanagibashi, 'Willow Bridge', most seemed to preserve the romantic aura of old Edo. I had caught glimpses of its tile-roofed geisha houses and teahouses clustered around the mouth of a narrow canal where it gave on to the River Sumida, its lanterns and softly lit rooms reflected invitingly in the water. In the past mendicant musicians used to row right up to the Yanagibashi gardens, strumming their shamisen and singing romantic ballads.

For years the teahouses of Yanagibashi had been the prime place in the entire city to see the magnificent summer fireworks display that took place along the river. People made reservations to dine there years in advance; but unless you were a top-ranking politico or chairman of a major corporation and, furthermore, known to the teahouse, you had no chance. (Unlike the Kyoto teahouses, which serve only drinks and, if asked for food, order it in from outside caterers, the Tokyo ones – which are called *ryotei*, high-class Japanese restaurants, rather than *ochaya*, teahouses – serve expensive traditional haute cuisine.) To be in a Yanagibashi teahouse on fireworks night marked you out as a member of the ruling elite.

In the mid-sixties, radical young businessmen like Seiji Tsutsumi saw no contradiction between having both feet firmly planted in the modern world and enjoying Yanagibashi night-life. Tsutsumi, overlord of a business empire that expanded to encompass the city's most fashionable department stores, the InterContinental Hotels and the Muji shops and a patron of the most outrageous contemporary artists, fell in love with a Yanagibashi geisha and married her – though he sent her to live in Paris for a few years to acquire cosmopolitan gloss first.

But then came the economic boom of the eighties. In the frenzy of building that engulfed the country, glass and concrete buildings sprouted around the old wooden teahouses and geisha houses and the banks of the River Sumida were encased in concrete. The Yanagibashi gardens disappeared. As the city spread westwards, the river, which had once been at the centre of life, was pushed off to the eastern edge and Yanagibashi was left high and dry. Politicians looked for their entertainment closer to home, in the Akasaka geisha district on the doorstep of the Diet, the Parliament building. Company chairmen and business magnates gravitated to Shimbashi, to enjoy the urbane conversation of the geisha there. Few people bothered to go to the eastern reaches of the city any longer.

Almost as soon as I arrived in Tokyo I began to hear bad news. Not so long ago there had been a hundred geisha in Yanagibashi. Now, said a businessman who was a devoted patron of the geisha world, he had heard there were twenty left and at most two or three teahouses. But it was worse than that. It was not until I talked to geisha themselves that I discovered the full story. As recently as January 1999 there had been six flower towns in Tokyo: Shimbashi, Akasaka, Kagurazaka, Yoshicho, Asakusa and, most venerable and gracious of all, Yanagibashi. Now there were five. It boded ill for the others.

In the end, only the Inagaki *ryotei* had been left in Yanagibashi, with thirty geisha working there. Gradually it became harder and harder to make ends meet. A teahouse cannot exist in isolation. It needs a community of geisha and a family of customers. Finally the owner sold up. The elderly geisha who took over decided to close for good.

Nevertheless I wanted to see for myself. Perhaps I could find Inagaki and talk to the old woman who had owned it or at least absorb the atmosphere of this most romantic of flower towns. So one day when I was in the east of the city I made a detour to Yanagibashi.

Willow Bridge itself was still there, linking the two sides of the canal, though it was no longer a delicate wooden construction that geisha tripped across on wooden clogs, sheltering under their parasols. Now it was a swath of steel girders. From the other side of the Sumida I could make out the tiled roofs of a gracious old house peeking above the concrete wall which edged the river, half-hidden behind overgrown foliage and dwarfed by giant developments. Close to, the little canal was still romantic, with willow trees along each bank and wooden houseboats moored there – though it required eyes which had been trained in the Japanese way of looking, filtering out the high-rises all around, to see it. There were a couple of boathouses but behind the willow trees, where restaurants had once stood, lights twinkling in the water, was a blur of concrete.

When I asked for Inagaki, I was directed to an old house hidden behind a forbidding wall topped with old-fashioned curved tiles, utterly out of place in that landscape of concrete. The heavy wooden doors were locked, bolted and immovable, as if they had not been opened for a long time. I had been told that I might find the owner in the housing block which loomed beside it. But that door too was locked.

A few days later I met up with a Shimbashi geisha I knew, and told her my sad tale. What had become of those last Yanagibashi geisha, I wondered.

'One started teaching calligraphy,' she told me. 'Another was a very good shamisen player. These days it's a real problem to find good shamisen players, so I invited her to Shimbashi. But she didn't want to come. They were old. They wanted to retire.'

A Sanctuary for Men

Until two or three years ago it was a matter of dispute whether Akasaka or Shimbashi was the classiest of the Tokyo geisha districts. Both had their histories, aficionados and siren queens.

When the gallant young samurai who had defeated the shogun's forces and taken over the government arrived in Tokyo in 1868, Shimbashi (between the Sumida river and the ever-glittering streets of the Ginza) was where they went to visit their geisha lovers. There Okoi, the Honourable Carp, beguiled her lover, Prime Minister Katsura, and Kafu Nagai set his romantic novel, *Geisha in Rivalry*. Over the years, as expensive hostess clubs grew up along the Ginza alongside the department stores, jewellery shops and gold and pearl emporiums, Shimbashi's dignified old teahouses continued to flourish, though they became known primarily as the drinking places of businessmen, the overlords of Japan's booming economy.

The country's rulers – the politicians and the bureaucrats – preferred Akasaka. A couple of minutes' purr by limousine from the Diet, it was like having a pleasure quarter in the heart of Westminster, a stone's throw from the Houses of Parliament. Hidden behind high dun-coloured earthen walls and heavy wooden gates, amid the bustle and neon of the Akasaka entertainment district, with its nightclubs, cabarets, discos, bars and tiny restaurants run by ex-geisha, Akasaka's *ryotei* were every bit as grand and exclusive as Shimbashi's. If, however, you had the right connections and were invited to step inside, they had the reputation of being less expensive and formal. Akasaka geisha were said to be mediocre dancers and not quite as classy as the Shimbashi geisha. But then again, they were younger and prettier. That was ample compensation.

The Akasaka teahouses were the scene of much wheeling and dealing. In Japan there is an enormous gulf between surface and reality, daytime and night-time. In the daytime politicians would stand up and read out prepared speeches in the Diet or ask questions which had been submitted a couple of days in advance so as to allow plenty of time to prepare an answer. Businessmen meanwhile would be whiling away the day in board meetings at which nothing was ever decided. It was largely theatre, promoting the appearance of democracy.

But night-time was when much of the real business and the real politics took place. With ties loosened and faces flushed, inhibitions were put aside and people said what they really thought. In Japan nothing could be done in the way of business or politics or anything that mattered at all without face-to-face contact. Executives and politicians had to meet. They had to know and like the people with whom they were intending to do business. They had to eat together, drink together, get drunk together. The building of the relationship was at least as important as the details of the business or politics to be negotiated.

The enormous entertainment industry in Japan was a direct result of this. It was during the evening's entertainment that bonding occurred, deals were done and the real decision-making took place. The debates in the Diet or the boardroom were just rubber-stamping.

At the topmost levels of society, geisha were a key part of that evening activity. It would not be an overstatement to say that geisha parties were essential to the running of the country. In the Akasaka *ryotei* – as exclusive as private clubs, akin to London's Carlton Club, home from home for the Conservative Party – Japan's political rulers, the Liberal Democratic Party, would discuss matters of state and make deals after unwinding over a meal and several flasks of saké. The geisha, women they had known as friends or lovers for years, knew instinctively when to keep the tone light and when to slip discreetly out of the room. Sometimes the older and wiser among them might join in a conversation or add their commonsensical view to help unravel a knotty problem. It was a little like going home and talking things over with the wife – except that that was something a Japanese man, of that generation at any rate, would never do.

Geisha, of course, would never give direct advice. Japan is a country where the ex-geisha wife of a business magnate is much admired for being, as people say, 'clever enough never to let a man realise how clever she is'. The essence of the feminine ideal is to make a man think that he is the one who has the brilliant ideas. But a geisha might well prod even the finance minister in one direction or another, cooing something along the lines of

'You were saying you might raise the interest rates. How clever of you to think of that!'

Bernard Krisher, a veteran American journalist who has lived in Japan for forty years, put it bluntly. 'Most Japanese men can't converse with their wives,' he said. 'But they find that they can with geisha. That's why the geisha system has survived so long. It's more than sex.'

Krisher, who became *Newsweek* magazine's correspondent in Japan and the founder of a wildly scandalous Japanese-language tabloid called *Focus*, arrived in the country in 1962. In his first week in Tokyo he found himself at a geisha party attended by Shintaro Ishihara, the country's most flamboyant up-and-coming politician, now the controversial Mayor of Tokyo, side by side with Masayoshi Ohira, who later became prime minister. Some time later he was invited to a party hosted by Mitsui, the giant financial and industrial conglomerate, in honour of Sukarno, then president of Indonesia. Late in the evening, after copious amounts of saké had been downed, Sukarno barged into the kitchens, fetched out the bewildered cooking staff and ordered them to sit down among the distinguished guests in their white aprons and listen while he regaled them with Indonesian folk ballads.

Then there was Prime Minister Eisaku Sato who collapsed at a teahouse and had to spend a week there because he couldn't be moved. And when Prime Minister Kakuei Tanaka entertained Chinese Premier Deng Xiao Ping, he shocked everyone by ignoring protocol and inviting in the twenty-odd hulking Chinese secret police who were standing around outside. He ordered cushions to be laid out for them so they could watch the geisha dancing, then plied them all with saké.

'Night-life used to be a sanctuary for men in Japan,' said Krisher. 'It was the perfect way for a man to unwind. The food was perfect, the drink was perfect and he could find the perfect person there to talk to, who could instinctively see that he had a problem, get him to unwind and even find a solution. It had a lot to do with the rapid recovery of Japan after the war.

'Wherever the Japanese went in the old days, they took geisha along. In the Saipan chain, in Micronesia, there's a small island which had a Japanese colony; there was one geisha house there. The Americans always took Coca-Cola, the Japanese always took geisha. It's been a key magical formula for the Japanese.

'Many people look down on geisha, but they are the only people who can talk on an equal level to the prime minister. They can tease him and joke with him. No one else can do that. They're like cats – dignified and totally independent. They demand your love. You have to take care of them and feed them. But you can't get them to jump on your lap if they don't want to.'

Krisher's take on geisha was simple. 'They are mistresses,' he said, 'like a Japanese version of the Colette story.' Jealous of other geisha who had patrons, they would badger him, saying, 'I wish I had a patron, she has a patron, will you be my patron?'

'What foreigners can't comprehend is that someone will spend $2000 [£1200] and not even try to take a geisha home. Japanese get embarrassed, having to tell a visiting foreigner that it's just not going to happen. They're not programmed to sleep with someone for money. But if you ask someone five or six times for something, on five or six occasions, finally you can get what you want. The more often you go to a geisha house, the more chance there is that you can probably sleep with someone. I did that a lot in the sixties. I didn't pay. For them too it was a novel experience. They're also human beings and they're women. But it would be on that basis – love, not payment.'

But in the end the partying had to stop. Being too closely tied to the country's wheelers and dealers proved to be Akasaka's downfall. The problems began in the mid-nineties when the Ministry of Finance – until then an impregnable bastion of faceless bureaucrats who effectively ran the country – found itself under fire, under suspicion of incompetence and corruption.

For years the MoF had controlled the country's financial institutions, feeding vital information to banks and wielding control over everything from the opening and closing of bank branches to the uniforms the female clerks wore. There were executives at each bank whose job was to wine and dine the relevant MoF officials, often at vast expense, at classy restaurants, exclusive clubs, golf links and teahouses. According to one report, such a night might cost as much as £3000.[2] Rumour had it that things sometimes went further than that. One bank was said to employ a full-time prostitute for the benefit of government officials.

All this was considered not bribery but gift-giving, in the Japanese tradition. In the course of such civilised face-to-face meetings, vital insider information on such matters as budgets, taxes and regulations would gently pass into the hands of the bank executive who would also use the occasion to further the interests of his bank.

But with the Japanese economy on the skids, the public prosecutors began to look into the affairs even of the untouchable Ministry of Finance. At the beginning of 1998 they breached the gates of the fortress, took away lorry-loads of papers and arrested four officials, accusing them of accepting bribes from the financial institutions they were paid to oversee. Others, notified that they were to be investigated, committed suicide. The public was particularly incensed to hear that banks entertained Finance Ministry officials at *no-pan* shabu-shabu beef restaurants, distinguished by the mirrors on the floor and the fact that the waitresses wore mini-skirts and no panties (*no-pan*).

None of this was directly to do with the geisha. But the Japanese tabloids, scenting blood, took to hanging around the places politicians and bureaucrats were known to frequent, on the look-out for more stories of big spending and, better still, sexual improprieties. Once upon a time such behaviour would have been taken for granted and not considered worthy of note. But now it sold papers. And the obvious place for a stake-out was the Akasaka teahouses.

Suddenly the once-thriving geisha district became very quiet. When politicians got together, they did so in the more anonymous surroundings of a hotel restaurant or a golf links. In Akasaka business went into a steep decline. Rumours flitted around the small world of the geisha. Business was so bad that one previously famous Akasaka geisha, it was said, was called to teahouses at most twice a month. She had been reduced to appearing on television in kimono fashion shows and had had to move from her palatial apartment to one so cramped it lacked even its own toilet. From 300 geisha in the sixties, the numbers fell to 90, working in 13 *ryotei*; of those, only a few had regular work. Effortlessly Shimbashi floated back to the top of the hierarchy.

The Sophisticated Ladies of Shimbashi

Butterfly
Or falling leaf,
Which ought I to imitate
In my dancing?
Geisha song[3]

Tokyo's flower and willow world is not a clearly delineated geographical area, visibly separate from the real-life world in the way Kyoto's is. I had passed Kanetanaka for years without ever realising that its sand-coloured walls and enormous gates concealed not the palatial private home of a minor prince or the heir to an industrial fortune but one of the most venerable teahouses in Shimbashi. I had been to kabuki performances in the Shimbashi Embujo without knowing that it had been built for the Shimbashi geisha to perform their annual dances, which took place in May. I had walked down innumerable tiny alleys near the Tsukiji fish market without having the faintest idea that some of the shabby façades with potted plants lined up outside hid geisha houses. And if I saw a woman in a kimono flitting down one of these streets, I would never have guessed she was a geisha. The geisha of Tokyo – who, unlike the Kyoto *geiko*, use the word geisha ('arts person'), not *geiko* ('arts child'), for their trade – were far more discreet and circumspect than their Kyoto counterparts.

Here, one day, I was sitting in the coffee shop of a hotel which I had never realised before was in the heart of the geisha world, talking to a glamorous young woman. It had been a matter of the right connections. I had phoned up and dropped a rather weighty name. I was amazed at the alacrity with which she said, 'Let's have lunch.'

'Did you know we still have rickshaws in Shimbashi?' she asked in a soft, musical voice, after we had placed our orders. 'There are two and two rickshaw men. When I go from one ryotei to another I sometimes call them. But I worry what will become of us in the future. Japan has changed; it's not like the old Japan. Lots of Japanese have never been to a geisha party; they think we're doing something bad. These days it's very

267

difficult. If I was doing this for the money I would give up.'

Anyone looking at her might have taken Shuko for an executive in the fashion industry or the young wife of a wealthy man but certainly not a geisha. Dressed in an exquisitely co-ordinated beige two-piece, topped with a floaty jacket, an outfit which had clearly come from a Paris or Milan couturier, she wore her long hair loose and tumbling around her shoulders. She had a pale, refined, pretty face, softly oval, with a sensuous mouth which curved into a provocative smile, and almond eyes brought out with just a hint of make-up. She was lovely in a feminine way rather than intimidatingly beautiful.

But it was less her appearance than some indefinable presence that set her apart. She was poised, confident, funny and charming. She would, I imagined, be any man's perfect woman — sexy yet motherly. To me, as a woman, she had another face. We talked girl to girl, though she still gently, so that I hardly noticed, made sure that my glass was full and that I had everything I wanted. I was perfectly taken care of, in fact. She talked earnestly, seriously, yet managed at the same time to keep the conversation light, interspersing her remarks with smiles and silvery laughter.

She told me about the great geisha of the past, including one who had died a couple of years ago aged eighty, who had founded Azuma Odori, the Shimbashi geishas' annual dance revue. They had been dancers as revered as Anna Pavlova or Margot Fonteyn, and writers and poets of the time had sought their company and celebrated them.

'In those days the flower and willow world was the heart of Japanese culture,' she sighed. 'There's nothing like it anywhere else in the world.'

In her mid-thirties, Shuko knew about the rest of the world. She had led a life very different from the suffocating existence of the Kyoto geisha. As a young woman, she had worked as an assistant in a Tokyo art gallery, regularly jetting off to Paris to arrange exhibitions. She loved the life. But the more she saw of foreign culture, the more she felt drawn to her own.

Shuko's mother was a famous dancer of *Nihon buyo*, the classical Japanese dance which geisha practise. Though not herself a geisha, she had a foot within the flower and willow world. Geisha came to her for dance classes. Thus as Shuko was growing up, this culture was all around her. As for her father, in all the time I knew her, she never mentioned him. I wondered if, as with many children in the flower and willow world, there had been no father around.

As a youngster, Shuko had trained as a singer of *Kiyomoto*, one of the forms of classical narrative song which geisha practise. Eleven years ago, she decided to take it up as a career. But how to do so? In Japan, if a man wants to make a career in the traditional arts, he applies to join the kabuki theatre as an apprentice singer, dancer or musician. But kabuki is closed to women. The choice was either to study at the Tokyo Arts University and support herself with a day job or to become a geisha. That, at any rate, was her rationale.

In the daytime she went to classes and practised singing. In the evening she entertained at geisha parties. A geisha's job, as she described it, was to be a little like an executive wife. While a western company chairman invited his most valued clients home to be entertained by his charming and articulate spouse, Japanese wives were not expected to be talkative or skilled at conversation; quietness was prized. In pre-modern times, too much chat was enough reason for a man to be granted a divorce. Traditionally the wife's job was to take care of the children and household affairs. Added to which, Japanese homes were usually deep in the suburbs, too far to invite anyone back, and often unexpectedly small and cramped.

'Unlike English people, our homes are not castles,' explained Shuko with a teasing smile, taking an elegant nibble of her sandwich.

Instead of hosting a dinner party, a Japanese executive called the teahouse where he was well known and asked them to arrange a banquet. In the hands of professional entertainers, he could be sure that the party would go without a hitch. The food would be good, the singing would be good, the dancing would be good. It was far more satisfactory than entertaining at home. After all, a Japanese wife would not dream of getting up and dancing for her guests.

The Shimbashi geisha, in fact, prided themselves on their 'wifeliness'. Within the Tokyo flower and willow world, that was the Shimbashi flavour. The Akasaka geisha were more overtly sexy. They wore more make-up and brighter kimonos. The Shimbashi geisha, conversely, were the embodiment of good taste. Their kimonos were sober and modest, their hair swept into simple buns and their make-up subtle, more suited to the sophisticated and wealthy customers they entertained.

Of course, in the modern world, if a man wanted to go straight home every night, there was nothing to stop him. If he wanted to bring his wife to a geisha party, he could do that too. He could also spend the whole evening chatting about his wife and children. But no one with even a modicum of savoir faire would dream of doing any of those things.

'If you want to get ahead in your career, it does not do to have the stench of the family about you,' was how Shuko put it.

For the corporate samurai, the man's world of work and the women's world of home were completely separate and a manly man would never confuse them. The geisha's role was to be part of the world of work. They were women in a man's world. Once you had stepped into the flower and willow world, you had crossed the River Lethe and left the everyday world behind you. You would never make the mistake of mixing the two.

'Men don't want to associate with their wives in the way that they do with us,' said Shuko.

Shuko regularly spent her evenings in the company of some of the country's most powerful and brilliant minds, men who headed industrial conglomerates, banks, financial institutions and major corporations. To prepare herself, she kept up to date with the news, read the latest books and went to exhibitions. Not that the guests expected intellectual conversation. They were there to relax, not to have their minds taxed. The geisha party was the one place where a man could let slip the mask which social convention required him to wear. There the company chairman who bore a huge weight of responsibility from morning till night and took mammoth decisions which affected millions of yen or millions of people could, if he wanted, play the fool or be babied by geisha who called him not Mr Suzuki but by some cosy nickname like Ken-chan, as if he were a child. At work he might be a god; but at the geisha party he could have an entirely different face.

The geisha's job was to bolster a man's ego, to make him feel like a king surrounded by courtiers, at ease among his colleagues. She made sure that everything went smoothly, flitting around like a lovely butterfly, intervening where needed to help out if someone said something gauche, lightening the tone when it got heavy, and slipping away to fetch more saké or powder her nose when the talk turned to confidential business matters. She was a bit like an old-fashioned wife, in fact. To westerners and young Japanese it might seem medieval; but for men who remembered the good old days, when a wife was a wife and a geisha was a geisha, it worked.

But the most important quality was confidentiality. No one would ever have a political or business discussion in a hostess club, where the guests at one table could easily overhear the conversation at another. In a teahouse, each banquet took place in a separate room and the guests never knew who else was present in the teahouse that night When a guest wanted to go to the toilet, the geisha made sure that he never bumped into a guest from another party on his way; the corridors were always empty. And if a guest happened to be part of two parties on the same evening, when he arrived the second time the geisha never gave the game away. They always greeted him with, 'How are you, Sir? We haven't seen you for such a long time!'

But what if a man, having had a little too much to drink and finding himself surrounded by beautiful women attending to his every need, wanted more? Had there not been times when Shuko herself, enjoying the company of the same brilliant men night after night, had felt drawn to one of them? What of love?

'Many men have asked me to marry them,' she smiled with a toss of her long black hair. 'Men enjoy our company because we're free spirits. It makes it safe for them. Whenever they spend time with us they can imagine they're having a romance because they know we can't leave our profession. We're caged birds.'

For a man, having an affair with a geisha was the perfect outlet for his romantic yearnings. As geisha, they were committed to staying single and were therefore no threat to his marriage. Given that wives expected their men to have affairs, they preferred it to be with a geisha. If he had an affair with his secretary, she might start nagging him to leave his wife and marry her. But the geisha code was never to interfere with a man's marriage – never to call the wife, never to beg the man to marry her, never to cause trouble. That was the theory; though in practice many men divorced their wives to marry geisha.

As for Shuko, she was now out of her twenties, the age by which most

Japanese women expect to be married. Did she not worry that she would miss out on what was the Holy Grail of most Japanese women's lives?

'I'm not interested in marriage,' she said firmly. She paused, then smiled woman to woman and added wistfully, 'But a lover would be nice . . .'

'The trouble is,' I said, 'when you reach our age, most men are married.' She looked puzzled.

'In the west,' I said, sensing a cultural chasm, 'we prefer not to have affairs with married men.'

'All our customers are married,' she replied carelessly. That, of course, would be the pool from which she would take a lover.

But the best way to understand, she added, would be for me to see her at work. With that she took her mobile phone from her Gucci handbag, dialled a number and left a message. A few minutes later the call was returned. She laughed when she put the phone down. It was one of her regular customers.

'It's the first time I've ever called him,' she said. 'He was astonished. He thought something terrible had happened.'

She had asked him to host a geisha party for me and he had agreed.

A Teahouse Party

There was something afoot when I arrived at Kanetanaka a couple of days later. Usually the quiet back street was dark and empty, especially by eight o'clock at night. But that evening there was a line of gleaming limousines with darkened windows filling the road and a crush of young men in dark suits standing around in the doorway. They ignored me as I pushed between them into the entrance hall.

In the geisha hierarchy, Kanetanaka was second to only one other Shimbashi teahouse for age and fame – Shin Kiraku. Both, like Gion's Ichiriki-tei, had been around for centuries and the owner of one or other of them was usually also the head of the Shimbashi Geisha Union. In the sixties, when Japan was still recovering from the war and the State Banqueting Hall had not yet been completed, distinguished visitors and foreign heads of state were entertained at one or the other, most often Shin Kiraku.

Richard Nixon, when he was President of the United States, partied there and presented the *mama-san* with a signed baseball. King Faisal of Saudi Arabia, when he dined there, had a taster to check each dish for poison and said 'Thank you' to the geisha, which they thought very quaint; Japanese guests knew that the geisha were being paid and it was therefore not customary to thank them. And when Jean Paul Sartre and Simone de Beauvoir visited in 1966, they too dined at Shin Kiraku. The geisha who attended to them remembered Sartre as being a rather nervous, difficult customer who refused to consume the proper amounts of saké to ensure that he relaxed; de Beauvoir was easier to get along with.

As I was slipping out of my shoes, Shuko came running to greet me, along with a bevy of other geisha, scurrying with tiny steps across the tatami. She had metamorphosed. Her hair was swept into a tidy knot, her face powdered and rouged, her eyes outlined in black, her eyebrows pencilled into two immaculate brown moth wings and her mouth the colour of a camellia flower. She wore a cornflower-blue kimono of thin silk with a design of white flowers on the sleeves and hem. Her dark-blue obi was decorated with a summery pattern of gingko leaf-shaped fans sprinkled with tiny flowers. On her feet she wore white cotton *tabi* socks.

Even the way she carried her body had changed. Instead of the glamorous creature with whom I lunched in hotel restaurants and who flew to Milan and Paris for her clothes, she was the embodiment of warm, caring and attentive womanhood. I was the guest and she the hostess. It put a kind of distance between us.

Twittering a welcome, the women led me through the imposing entrance hall, decorated with a gorgeously painted gold screen, and along a corridor to an austerely traditional room with sand-coloured walls and tatami mats. The only furniture was a low red-lacquered table with a cushion on each side and two antique wooden armrests topped with padded tapestry, such as samurai would have used. In the *tokonoma*, the alcove which forms the focal point of a Japanese room, there was a red camellia blossom artfully placed in a bamboo vase. Taking pride of place on the wall behind it was a scroll with a few words brushed in bold black characters. My host, Mr Matsumoto, was already there.

'Good to meet you,' he said, rising to his feet and stepping forward to shake my hand. 'Shuko has told me all about you!'

I had assumed that anyone who frequented geisha parties, particularly in such a grand setting, must be old; but he could not have been more than fifty. He was a handsome, trim man with a relaxed, cosmopolitan air. His hair was fashionably short, his dark suit discreetly expensive. He was the owner, it transpired, of a highly successful import–export business and spent his life flitting between Japan and the United States. Beyond that, of course, we did not discuss his work or family. After all, we had crossed into the flower and willow world. It would have been unspeakably boorish.

I was beginning to stumble out my thanks for his hospitality but he gracefully brushed them aside. Shuko and he were old friends, he smiled. He had known her for years. She had never before called him, let alone asked him a favour. He was thrilled at the chance of doing something for her. Added to which, he was happy to return some of the hospitality he had experienced in the United States and Europe.

'I've been coming to Kanetanaka for years,' he added as we took our places on the cushions, reclining luxuriously like Edo-period daimyo on the armrests. Mine was the place of honour, with my back to the *tokonoma* alcove. 'My father brought me when I was a teenager. We are old friends here.'

Shuko knelt by my side and filled my cup with saké. One by one the geisha sank gracefully to their knees, bowed their heads so that they practically touched the tatami, and gaily introduced themselves. I was used to Japanese formality. Middle-class women of a certain age, at, for example, a tea ceremony, engaged in endless bowing and scraping, bombarding one with language larded with baroque polite forms. It was all rather stiff and uncomfortable. But this was different. These were highly sophisticated women. They observed the formalities, they used formal language, yet their behaviour was full of gaiety and laughter. They played with the forms, they were not enslaved by them.

It was a little like being surrounded by a flock of gorgeously plumed birds. Cooing softly, covering their mouths with an elegant hand when they giggled, they chatted and bantered, fluttering about, making sure that saké cups and beer glasses were filled and everything was to our liking. Skilfully they kept the conversation light and merry.

Did I know the difference, they asked, between the way a wife and a geisha wore their kimono? I had to confess that I did not. In Kyoto when a geisha was formally dressed with her kimono low at the back and swirling about her feet it was obvious. But among the geisha in this room it was difficult to tell. Their kimonos looked every bit as chaste and modest as a married woman's. Smiling, they explained the telltale signs that communicated to the practised eye that they were geisha – the kimono tied a little more loosely than a married woman's and a touch more open at the neck to reveal a tantalising hint of the collar at the throat and a rakish flash of the under-kimono at the hem and cuff; the hair swept back into a glossy helmet with not a strand out of place.

'Geisha wear kimono all the time, whereas wives wear them only on special occasions,' explained a geisha who had introduced herself as Kimie. Poised, elegant, she must have been brushing fifty. Her kimono was a deep blue tinged with grey, the colour of the sea on a summer's evening, with a pattern of waves swirling across the sleeves and hem. 'We have to carry on all the jobs of everyday life in kimono; so we tie ours a little more loosely.'

After that first evening Kimie and I became friends and she told me her story. She had a pedigree stretching back several generations. Her mother had been a famous beauty in her day and the child of another famous beauty. The family kept a geisha house where generations of youthful geisha had lived. Her father had been the head of one of the country's vast industrial conglomerates before the war. During the American occupation he was purged and put under house arrest along with other leaders of society and had been unable to visit Kimie and her mother, who was of course not his wife but his second, third or fourth 'wife'; a man in that position would have had several. Kimie never knew him. When she was three he died.

By the time she was growing up, she had another 'father', a leading novelist who, like many literary men, enjoyed the louche atmosphere of the geisha districts. He too had a wife and family and stayed over at the geisha house a couple of days a week. He filled her with a love of reading

275

and writing. When she was a teenager, she decided she wanted to follow in his footsteps and be a journalist, not a geisha. But she had responsibilities. In Japan no one operates in a vacuum. She was expected to carry on the family heritage and become a geisha; in any case, in those days it would have been extremely rare for any woman to have been able to rise to the top as a journalist. There was nothing for it but to put aside her personal hopes and dreams.

Had she been born in different circumstances, Kimie might have been an academic or a doctor. There was something about her of the bluestocking. She had clearly inherited her father's brilliance. She was not beautiful. Her long-chinned, rather plain face had faded and lost its definition with the passing of the years though, like all the geisha, she had a powerful presence. She was, I later learnt, one of the leading women in the Shimbashi community and hinted once that she was 'married' – she had a *danna* – though, like all the geisha, her lips were sealed on that score.

Kneeling beside me solicitously, she topped up my saké cup. Conversation had turned to the declining numbers in the flower and willow world. There was the sad demise of Yanagibashi, for a start. How were things in Osaka, the women asked Mr Matsumoto, who often went there on business. I had heard that there were no geisha at all, that the city was so modern and mercantile that the flower and willow world had withered and died. Not so, said Mr Matsumoto. There were still at least twenty in the Kita Shinchi flower town, in the north of the city, and twenty in Minami Shinchi to the south; he had been to a geisha party there just the other week.

A couple of kimono-clad maids rustled in with trays laden with dishes of exquisite delicacies – vegetables carved into miniature sculptures, a wobbling beige cube of mock tofu made of ground sesame, a deep-purple baby aubergine dabbed with mustard-coloured miso paste, each arranged like a small landscape on an exquisite porcelain dish or costly slab of stoneware. They laid them out before Mr Matsumoto and myself on the lacquered table top.

It was a little like being at a dinner party where only two of the guests were served. I felt a little uncomfortable as I picked up my chopsticks, then remembered that in traditional Japanese homes the womenfolk do not dine with the guests. I had spent many dull evenings conversing painfully with the husband or father of the friend I had been invited to visit while she scuttled silently in and out of the room, carrying trays of food. On this occasion I was an honorary man – though fortunately there were geisha present to brighten up the conversation.

The second course was *ayu*, a small sweet river trout grilled whole and cunningly arranged on an oblong dish so that it almost looked if it were still alive and swimming along. Before I had a chance to dig into mine, Kimie, who had taken Shuko's place next to me, took it and expertly filleted it with her chopsticks, then divided it into bite-sized pieces. As the guest, it would be unthinkable for me to have to perform even the least taxing of chores, such as filleting my own fish. The meal continued with succulent slices of sashimi and a succession of simmered, steamed and raw dishes, followed by rice and pickles in the traditional Japanese order.

Mr Matsumoto was talking about what made a geisha sexy.

'It's not physical beauty,' he said. 'It's not the way they look. It's some indefinable quality, the way in which they interact with men. Take Kimie, for example. She doesn't seem sexy . . .'

'What?' exclaimed Kimie in mock horror. 'In that case, I'm leaving right now!'

'. . . but when she dances she's extremely sexy.'

Kimie smiled, mollified.

'We have a saying in the geisha world,' said Shuko. 'There are five conditions that make a geisha famous.' The other geisha chimed in. 'First, to be beautiful but not too beautiful. Shimbashi geisha are homely,' they explained. 'We wear plain, simple kimonos, like wives.' Next, to be able to hold one's drink but never to get drunk. Third, to devote oneself to one's art. Fourth, to be good at talking but better at listening. 'That's the secret of the geisha's conversation,' they said. Last, to have a good reputation, not just in one's own district but throughout the geisha community.

The meal over, the maids cleared the table.

'Please sing for us, Shuko-san,' begged Mr Matsumoto.

'I'm not good enough, I'm embarrassed,' demurred Shuko. Finally persuaded, she knelt and, accompanied by a bird-like older geisha on the shamisen, sang a measured melancholy ditty. There was much applause. She bowed, touching her fingers to the tatami, smiling modestly.

Then Kimie was persuaded to dance. In the room there was an expectant silence. She paused, drew breath and composed her face to an expression of mask-like stillness, then raised her fan in a crisp gesture.

As the elderly geisha sang out a plaintive melody, thrumming her shamisen, Kimie painted a story. With a ripple of her fan she created a river where she, pining for her lover, sat gazing at the lanterns bobbing along it. She turned her hand, palm upwards, fingers and thumb fused together like a puppet's hand, to the sky. There was a bird, a skylark, hovering overhead, reminding her of the fragility and transience of love. A letter came. She seemed to read it and wept, throwing it aside. Each gesture was perfection, finding movement out of stillness and stillness in the heart of movement, refined, controlled and magical. With the tiniest angle of her head, glance of her eyes or graceful twist of her hand she created a whole universe of love, passion, loneliness, sadness and loss. We watched, transfixed. She was no longer a fading middle-aged woman but a siren, ineffably seductive, for whom any man would happily have risked shipwreck.

In the past, I remembered, geisha had been like the opera singers, ballet dancers and Hollywood stars of today. In their world they still were. It was as if I had spent the evening in the company of Meryl Streep and Michelle Pfeiffer or Margot Fonteyn and Darcey Bussell, who had fussed over me, poured my drink, filleted my fish, beguiled me with their chatter, then risen to their feet to perform for me. I felt privileged and humbled.

Before the evening was over, there was one last mystery I wanted to solve. Why had there been limousines at the entrance to Kanetanaka? Who were the men in black suits and why were they there? The geisha smiled. On this occasion, just for me, they would put aside their code of secrecy. Prime Minister Keizo Obuchi, they whispered, had been entertaining in a neighbouring room that night.

13

WORKING GIRLS
THE LONELINESS OF THE
LONG-DISTANCE GEISHA

How cruel the floating world
Its solaces how few —
And soon my unmourned life
Will vanish with the dew.
The Woman Who Spent Her Life in Love, Ihara Saikaku (1642–1693)[1]

The Island on the Far Side

The demise of Yanagibashi left five flower towns in Tokyo: the classy, high-powered joints of Shimbashi and Akasaka; the hilly lanes of Kagurazaka, blazing with neon at night; Yoshicho, which was quietly declining; and down-to-earth Asakusa, in the city's East End. That was what Shuko and the other Shimbashi geisha told me. I, however, knew perfectly well that there was at least one other: Mukojima, literally 'the island on the far side'.

In all the years I had been in Tokyo I had never heard of Mukojima. It was quite literally off the English-language map. But when I dipped my toe into the waters of the flower and willow world, I began to hear that there was quite a community of geisha there. While Shimbashi and Akasaka boasted about ninety geisha each, in Mukojima there were almost two hundred.

'It isn't ranked as a flower town,' sniffed Shuko when I asked her, looking disdainfully down her pretty nose.

'Why?' I asked; but that is not a question which is ever asked – or answered – in Japan. The Gion geisha spoke with undisguised contempt of Miyagawa-cho and East Gion, but at least they were recognised as geisha districts. How bad could Mukojima be?

Once upon a time Mukojima was 'the island on the far side' of the Sumida, though it was certainly not an island any longer. It was further afield even than the Yoshiwara and well beyond the working-class heartland of Asakusa. In fact it barely felt like Tokyo at all. From the station (it was so far out that the subway had risen above ground to become a railway line) I walked the long, straight suburban streets, lined with faceless houses and shops. The place was strangely depopulated. But dotted among the back streets, discreetly hidden behind high walls, were large prosperous houses that looked remarkably like teahouses.

Down a back alley I came across the geisha house I was looking for, with potted plants in rows along the front and a trellis loaded with wisteria creating a porch. Inside, a couple of young women were lounging in a tatami room, propping themselves on their elbows on the low table and chatting merrily. Neither were beauties; no one would have mistaken them for 'high-class courtesans'. But they had a straightforward warmth which was hugely refreshing after weeks among the snobbish Gion geisha and the bluestocking geisha of Shimbashi. They were not worried about what image I might have of them as geisha. They were prepared to talk quite candidly about whatever they thought and felt.

'I hated it when I first went to a teahouse party,' said one who had introduced herself as Kyoko. At twenty-two, she had an elfin face with a tiny turned-up nose, wide quizzical eyes and a mischievous smile. 'I don't know why. Everyone was perfectly nice to me. I just hated it. I cried. I still sometimes think, "I hate this. I don't want to go to another teahouse party." But it's my life. What can I do?'

Kyoko's mother was the owner of the geisha house and had been a famous geisha in her time. She had gone through the geisha training in the Yoshiwara and been a dancer there, which in this environment was akin to having trained in the Royal Ballet; she was a star among the Mukojima geisha. When Kyoko was a child, she was registered at the local primary school under her mother's name. It was perfectly normal in the area; most of the other children were registered under their mothers' names too. It was only when she went on to middle school that she realised there was anything unusual about her.

'One girl asked me, "Why are you registered under your mother's name?" I went to look. Everyone else was under their father's. "I wonder why?" I thought. Later my mother told me everything. Round here it's normal. I never think about it. I met my father a while ago. I thought, "Wow, he's really got old." He came for my geisha debut. I talked about it with my mother. At first I thought I'd be a waitress. But in the end I decided to be a geisha.'

'It's lonely sometimes,' said Ayako, a homely woman of thirty-nine in an over-sized turquoise T-shirt and black slacks who wore her hair girlishly loose. 'When I get back to my apartment at five o'clock in the morning and have a can of beer by myself . . . To be single and living alone when you're in your thirties is kind of strange in Japanese society.'

Ayako too had a story to tell. She had become a geisha by accident. Eleven years earlier, she had turned up in Mukojima with her suitcase, thinking she had a job as a waitress in a teahouse. It was only after she had been there for a week that she came across a label with the words 'Geisha Union' written on it.

'I thought, "It can't be! I'm in the geisha world, like on TV!" I wish I'd known about it when I was eighteen, I would have become a geisha straight away.'

She had left home to be a fashion stylist and had never dared tell her parents about her change of occupation.

'I once thought I might get married. But it only lasted three seconds,' she chuckled. 'There was this guy around. Yeah, it lasted three seconds. Then I thought, "Geisha, geisha, I'll carry on being a geisha. If I get married, that's it. No more freedom. Jail!" I see him from time to time. I never think, "Should've got married." When I go home and see my old school friends, I think, "Lucky escape! I'm glad I'm a geisha." They all have these children. It looks really hard work.'

'Wives don't have sex appeal,' said Kyoko smiling her elfin smile. 'You look at a wife, the same age as a single person – no sex appeal at all. It's because they have children. They turn into mothers, they let themselves go. They don't know anything about life. But funnily enough, married guys, in Japan, anyway, seem to know more about life than single guys do. You get a single guy of forty or fifty and you think, "Something odd there." My mother often says so.'

The witching hour of six o'clock was approaching. Kyoko's mother came out of the kitchen to tell the women to begin their preparations. At first sight she was a frowzy, slatternly woman in her shapeless dress, pink apron and uncombed bird's nest hair. But then she folded elegantly to her knees, propped her chin on her hand, tilted her head and looked provocatively out of the corner of her eye. Suddenly one could see the fine bones of the face and the grace of the movements. It would only take a little make-up and a kimono and she could have any man on his knees.

In the kitchen a young woman of twenty-one had arrived and was downing a bowl of rice and boiled beef. She was the *han-gyoku*, the Tokyo equivalent of a maiko. *Han-gyoku* means 'half-jewel' ('jewel' being 'jewel money', a coy euphemism, like 'flower money', for the geisha's fee). The *han-gyoku*, being a trainee, was paid half the standard fee.

All around there was frantic painting and dressing. The *han-gyoku* painted her face white – though not as white as a Kyoto maiko and without the erotic tongue of bare flesh at the back of the neck. Then she donned a wig; beginner though she was, her hair was not dressed into a stiff coiffure like a maiko. Kyoko, meanwhile, had applied eye shadow and eye liner and painted her lips scarlet, then wrapped herself in a summery white kimono and a shimmering silver and blue obi embroidered with a burst of pink and white chrysanthemums.

On my way back to the station, I dropped into the hairdresser's to say goodbye to Ayako. Gone was the homely, slovenly woman who had sat joking with me. Gazing intently into the mirror as the hairdresser teased the last strands of hair into place, she touched up her face with a powder brush. Her eyes and eyebrows were etched in black, her lips blushed red. In her ink-black kimono, she positively smouldered. These women knew about sex appeal.

It struck me that the Mukojima geisha were more like the geisha of the past. They created a world where men could live out their fantasies, but it was a world open to ordinary men, not just the elite. Most businessmen, successful though they might be, lacked not only the necessary connections to party in Shimbashi but even the desire. After a hard day's work, they wanted to relax, eat, drink and have a laugh in the company of sexy, flirtatious, kimono-clad women, then get up and belt out a karaoké number or two, rather than watch classical dancing or listen to classical singing.

And despite the low regard in which the Mukojima variety were held by the establishment geisha, they were thriving. Just as geisha seemed on the point of extinction, in Mukojima they offered a service for which there was a demand. They were democratic, they were 'people's geisha'.

Getting into Hot Water

The Kyoto geiko and the Tokyo geisha were the aristocrats of the flower and willow world, the highly visible tip of the iceberg. But they were not the end of the story. In the past there had been geisha quarters in every town and every district of every city in Japan, covering the spectrum from refined to raunchy. Connoisseurs would have been able to tell you the flavour and special accomplishments of each, such as the *bazoku* geisha of Kyushu island, said to be particularly high-spirited and devil-may-care.[2] Most cities still maintained a small community. The numbers might be dwindling, the flower towns withering, but they were not yet extinct.

Travelling around Japan I met some of the twenty-eight remaining *geiko* in the city of Fukuoka on Kyushu island, down from a thousand before the war. In order to survive, they had had to bend one of the supposedly unbendable rules of the geisha community; at least two were married. In the romantic castle town of Kanazawa on the Japan Sea coast, there were forty-seven geisha still, living in three flower towns and preserving their distinctive form of geisha music which used the deep reverberating tones of a large floor drum. When I returned to Kyoto and Tokyo from my travels, my geisha friends were eager to hear about the flower and willow worlds in those cities and whether they were thriving.

But there was another category of geisha who were quite beyond the pale – the geisha of the hot-spring resorts, the *onsen geisha*.

For all their reputation as workaholics, the Japanese are also hedonists of the first order. Without any puritan ethic to restrain them, they have no

283

compunction about indulging the most sybaritic desires. Foremost among those is the desire to soak away one's cares in very hot water. Being a volcanic country prone to earthquakes, Japan is peppered with natural hot springs where water, stinking of sulphur or some other healing mineral, spurts out of the ground. Since time immemorial, taking the waters has been a central part of Japanese life, pursued with an almost religious fervour. Like merry Canterbury pilgrims, or characters from a Jane Austen novel, people travel from spa to spa, sampling the waters at each.

The essential spa experience has always been communal. Until westerners arrived with their hang-ups about nudity, men and women bathed together without the slightest embarrassment or inhibition. Nowadays, thanks to the intervention of scandalised Victorian missionaries and travellers, baths are divided into ladies' and men's sections in all but the most remote parts of the country. But bathing is still a group activity. Naked as nature intended, without any clothing to mark status or wealth, all vestiges of the formality and hierarchy which bedevil everyday life can gently slip away. Leaving the monochrome world of work, bathers step into a parallel universe of fantasy, fun and play, not far removed from the flower and willow world.

Such a place is naturally the domain of the geisha. The main customers at spas tend to be groups of men, business associates or workmates on an overnighter or a long weekend where they can bathe together, eat together, get drunk together, hang out in identical *yukata* – literally 'bathwear' – and sleep all together in one big tatami room. A trip to a spa fulfils the same function, in fact, as a Shimbashi teahouse party. It is the ultimate bonding experience.

Unfortunately *onsen geisha* have acquired rather a poor reputation. In fact the very words are sufficient to raise a titter. They are by reputation rather low on arts and high on the ability to entertain in other less salubrious ways. Not to put too fine a point upon it, *onsen geisha* is practically synonymous with 'prostitute'. The high-class geisha of the cities hate to be associated with them in any way – so much so that many call themselves *geiko* rather than geisha. What with the *onsen geisha*, not to mention westerners with their prurient notions of 'geisha gals', the word 'geisha' itself has become devalued. Thus, although I regaled my geisha friends with tales of my travels to Fukuoka and Kanazawa, I never mentioned that I had also been to Atami.

An easy hour's commute from Tokyo, Atami – 'Hot Sea' – is Japan's capital of fun, cousin to Blackpool, Brighton, Coney Island or Las Vegas. Within sight of Mount Fuji and sitting atop a major fault line, its waters contain salt and calcium sulphate, said to be calming for the nerves and beneficial for the skin. Once upon a time guests stayed in picturesque little wooden inns. But these days Atami is far from quaint. The guidebooks use words like 'sleazy' and 'tacky' to describe it. It is a tourist resort of the most vulgar variety, the kind of place where one would expect to find wild geisha parties and clutches of *yukata*-clad salarymen lurching up and down the narrow streets in various stages of inebriation. It is not at all the sort of place where any self-respecting westerner who claimed to have the slightest interest in serious Japanese culture would dream of going.

As the train rounded a bend before pulling into Atami station, I caught a glimpse of the sea sparkling in the distance. But it was soon eclipsed by the jumble of streets and concrete buildings running up and down the hillsides of what had once been a beautiful seaside resort. The sea itself and the streams which ran into it were edged with concrete and the little wooden inns had long since been replaced by multi-storey concrete slabs. I made my way through a neon-lit arcade lined with stalls selling dried squid and dried octopus as souvenirs, then climbed a steep, narrow, winding road jammed with traffic. Petrol fumes mingled with the rotten egg smell of sulphur, seeping from the ground and drifting out of the drains. But despite everything there was a gaiety and innocence about the place. It had that heady feeling of a holiday resort entirely devoted to fun.

I finally found my hotel, a particularly large and imposing concrete monolith just off the main road. There kimono-clad women at the door bowed me in and showed me to my room. In proper *onsen* style, I flung off my clothes immediately, put on the starched *yukata* provided by the hotel and took the lift down to the enormous communal baths in the basement. I slid open the door to the cedar-walled bathing area. Steam swirled out, as hot and clammy as a tropical jungle. I soaped and rinsed on the tiled floor at the side of the bath, then edged myself gingerly into the savagely

285

hot water. As my body took on the lurid red colouring of a boiled octopus (as the Japanese phrase it), the day's weariness began to evaporate. A few minutes more and I would be ready for a night of partying.

'Do you have a lot of spas in Britain?' asked an elderly woman who was sitting near me in the vast cedar tub. We had nodded to each other in the lift and she had ascertained my country of origin. In the bath all distinguishing features had disappeared. She was just a face, round, wrinkled and motherly, barely visible through the steam, gradually turning puce in the heat of the water.

'None,' I replied. Grunts of disbelief emerged from the other disembodied heads bobbing about in the water. 'No volcanoes, no earthquakes, no spas,' I said. 'We don't take the waters, we go to the beach.' That was as much speech as I could manage; being submerged in scalding water demanded total concentration.

'But what about that city – Bath, it was called, wasn't it?' demanded a younger woman with a towel coiled around her head. 'I was reading about it. That was a spa. It was a Roman spa.'

Shamed at my ignorance, I confessed that I had no idea whether or not you could still take the waters at Bath. 'I heard the water there is cold,' I said authoritatively. The women looked aghast at the thought.

Metamorphosis

In a cramped tatami room somewhere in the middle of town, four young women were smoking as if their lives depended on it. Mint-green and white packets of Kool cigarettes lay about on the low table alongside matching green lighters and ashtrays heaped with half-smoked butts. A fug of smoke hung in the room like a cloud. If I was going to get lung cancer from passive smoking, this would be the day, I thought to myself.

A pretty young woman with a plump girlish face and pert little nose, dressed like a dancer in a red T-shirt and electric-blue Lycra leggings, introduced herself unsmilingly as Hatsumi. She was from Hiroshima and had been a geisha in Atami for six years, she said. Then she turned back to her make-up, alternately swigging squash from a carton, stuffing crisps into her mouth and puffing cigarette after cigarette, stubbing each one out when it was half-smoked and lighting up another. A fluffy white terrier skidded around the tatami, grabbing at crisps and yapping. There were no artificial Japanese smiles here, no exaggeratedly solicitous concern that my tea cup was less than completely full. It was a relief to be able to relax and listen in to the conversation instead of having to be eternally polite.

'Got up at two, had lunch, went to the hairdresser's and came over here,' grunted Hatsumi to no one in particular.

'Got back at midnight last night,' replied another young woman in a black T-shirt and sweat pants, with an enormous yawn. 'Got changed, went to a bar and drank till five.'

'On your own?' I inquired.

'Yeah, I always drink on my own. I chat to the barman. I like that.'

In pride of place on the lacquered wooden chest which stood against one wall was a photograph of a young geisha in a formal black kimono. She was a classic beauty; she could have been a courtesan in an Utamaro print. Her face was a perfect oval, her nose long and aristocratic, her eyes huge and black, her eyebrows like crescent moons and her full lips shaped like a bow. She gazed languidly out of the photograph, her face framed by a glossy lacquered wig bristling with combs and hairpins.

'My daughter,' beamed the rumpled house mother. The photograph had been taken for the Atami tourist brochure.

Wiping her hands on her apron, the older woman dug around in the drawers of the chest and brought out a sheaf of photographs. They showed a group of geisha on New Year's Day making the ritual procession from teahouse to teahouse. Putting aside their make-up the younger women crowded round to look, chattering as they pointed themselves out. At the head of the group, in full regalia with white face and wig, was the daughter, clearly the belle of the town.

There was a bustling in the entrance hall and the door slid open. 'Good morning!' sang out a voice. It was 5.30 in the evening but in the geisha world the day was just beginning.

A puppyish young woman in a baggy denim worksuit bounced in, big, buxom and bonny. I looked and looked again. There was no doubt about it, this rambunctious young woman was the beautiful geisha of the photographs. With the confidence of the daughter of the house and an acknowledged beauty, she plonked herself down at the table, fondled the dog and grabbed a cigarette. She smoked more than all the others.

Little by little a transformation was taking place. Faces were becoming pinky-white, eyes black, lips cherry red. The fug of smoke grew thicker. Faces complete, the girls took a last desperate pull on their cigarettes, touched up their lipstick, then stood up to be dressed in kimono.

'We can all put on our own kimonos,' said Hatsumi, noticing me watching. 'We come here to be with our friends. "No bra, no panties,"' she added in English. 'That's what we tell western guests when they want to know what's under our kimonos.' For the first time her sullen face broke into a smile as she decorously revolved to show off the smooth panty-free lines.

Imperceptibly, as they donned kimono, the surly working girls had turned into young ladies. Suddenly they became aware that I was a guest and should be taken care of. One knelt sweetly beside me and topped up my tea while another engaged me in conversation.

Which did they prefer, I asked, kimonos or western clothes?

'Well,' said Hatsumi, resplendent in a deep copper-coloured kimono. 'It's not really a question of which you prefer. Kimono is work gear. It's like our uniform.'

They all lived in their own apartments, volunteered another, metamorphosed from a callow girl in a T-shirt into a dainty creature in pastel pink with a whole flower garden of narcissus along her hem and sprouting up to her waist. The geisha house was their office. It was where they came in the evening to get ready for work. The kimonos were stored there.

'We're the workers, Okasan [Mother] is the boss,' she explained, putting it in simple terms for the non-initiate.

How long, I wondered, were they planning to be geisha? Was it a lifetime's commitment?

'Yeah. Well, till I get married.'

Then the door slid open and a woman came in, smiling a huge motherly smile. It was Yuko, come to whisk me off to a teahouse party. I had met her earlier in the day and she had taken me under her wing, dropping me off at the geisha house while she went home to change.

It was six o'clock. Outside, a line of taxis was waiting. Everyone rushed out, tripping along with tiny steps in their silk-covered sandals, piled in and set off for their evening engagements.

Yuko

Yuko was the queen of the Atami geisha. A big-boned, handsome woman, she had been a geisha for thirty years. When I first met her she was off duty, in daytime mode, in a dark-blue blouse and plain knee-length grey skirt. She might have been a middle-aged housewife or an office worker. But there was something about her good-time-girl smile, the way she held herself very straight, her hair, which she wore loose and rippling about her shoulders, and her deep-toned gravelly voice which marked her out as different.

Yuko was a survivor. Like most of the Atami geisha, she hailed from the southern island of Kyushu. When she was growing up there in the years following the Second World War, it was one of the poorest, most under-privileged parts of the country.

'There were no jobs,' she told me in her husky tones. 'I heard there was work here so I got on the train and came to Atami. I remember coming through the tunnel and seeing the sea. It looked so beautiful! It seemed like a much older part of the country.'

She had worked as a switchboard operator in a hotel. Then, after some months, she was taken on as a maid by a geisha.

'"Why don't you have a go at it?" Older Sister said. She showed me how to put on a kimono and paint my face white. When I put on the lipstick, I was amazed. I looked really lovely.

'My mother and father were angry. I'm the middle one of five children. My brother's a designer, my sister married a salaryman. My father's given up on me. We don't do anything bad in the water trade. But it was very low status.'

The water trade – *mizu shobai* – was a phrase normally used solely to refer to bar girls, call girls, prostitutes and others who made a living by selling their bodies. I had never before heard the geishas' profession referred to in those terms. The grand geisha of Kyoto and Tokyo would have been horrified, I thought. Perhaps for the geisha of Atami the two professions were not as far removed as the Tokyo and Kyoto geisha always insisted they were.

Yuko was made for the work. She had a natural aptitude for dancing and quickly passed her exams and got a licence to work as a geisha. There were no complicated ceremonies or rituals, no debut or changing of the collar. As an independent, she was entitled to keep a geisha house if she wanted and train up junior geisha.

Had she ever married, I wondered. For a moment her face clouded.

'Seventeen years ago,' she said slowly. 'He wasn't a customer. I had to give up being a geisha. I had a daughter. It didn't last even a year. Then I became a geisha again. I had to leave my daughter at a neighbour's at nights. It was hard.

'I'm not lonely,' she added, her cast-iron smile back in place. 'I live with my daughter. She doesn't want to be a geisha, she wants to be a nurse. If I'd met someone I liked I might have settled down. But I didn't want a danna. If you have a danna, you lose your freedom. It's like being a concubine, you have to sleep with them. Some girls like to have one, some don't. If you're popular enough, you don't need one.

'Some people meet nice guys. I haven't, I haven't fallen in love. But I know people who have.'

Exactly twenty years ago, she remembered, a guest and a geisha fell desperately in love here in Atami. They had met at a geisha party. But the man was married and had children and couldn't divorce. For four or five years they saw each other as often as they could. Then one day they disappeared. The man had written a note and left it at his house, saying that they had gone to commit suicide together. His family guessed that he was in Atami with the geisha.

'We were all terribly shocked. They sent out search parties, they searched and searched in the woods at the foot of Mount Fuji but they couldn't find them. It must have been five or six years later that they came across the bones. I guess they had taken sleeping pills.

'My generation, people in their forties, we understood. Twenty- or thirty-year-olds wouldn't. They wanted to die in beauty.'

290

Cherry Blossoms and Golf Flags

The geisha of Kyoto, said Yuko, were like 'a flower in a high place'. Everyone would love the chance to spend time in their company but for most they were completely out of reach. They were too expensive and in any case their doors were open only to the few.

Atami did not have such a long history. But it offered the pleasures of the geisha world to all comers at an affordable price. Admittedly the pleasures were less refined. Nowadays few customers ever asked for a traditional teahouse party with dancing and games. Men no longer wanted or appreciated such things. An evening with geisha in Atami was more likely to be spent chatting and singing karaoké.

Not, of course, that the Atami geisha were prostitutes, she added firmly – perish the thought! In that sense they were very far from *onsen geisha*. The so-called geisha at the hot spring up the road and the ones on the Japan Sea coast – now they were nothing but prostitutes. But in Atami they were decent girls. After all, it was a top government-approved holiday resort. If a man wanted to date a geisha, he could do that, but it would have to be private. Officially sanctioned prostitution was a thing of the past.

No one knew exactly how many *onsen geisha* there were. Geisha were not required to register or to have a licence, added to which it could not be denied that there was a fair number of 'pillow geisha', women who called themselves geisha but whose dancing and musical skills were far from their most appealing feature. Geisha were part of the *onsen* experience and Japan was peppered with *onsens*; thus it seemed likely that there were far more *onsen geisha* than town geisha, probably several thousand. However, if the situation in Atami was anything to go by, it was a dying profession.

In Atami, unlike less organised *onsen*, there was a register of geisha. It was kept at the Atami Geisha Union and arranged by geisha house, with a dark cherry blossom symbol to indicate a shamisen player and a pale cherry blossom to indicate a dancer; a small golf flag indicated a golf player. The key thing with golf, of course, was not to be better than the customer, let alone beat him. The geisha's job was to stroll around chatting girlishly, playing just well enough not to

291

frustrate the customer, so that he could feel properly gratified when he won.

But it was becoming harder and harder to make a living as a geisha in Atami. In 1969 there had been 1200 registered geisha. By 1991 the number had fallen to 800. There were now fewer than 400; in just eight years the number had halved. Of the 400, thirty had the golf flag beside their name.

'There just wasn't the work,' said Yuko. As a result fewer and fewer young women were joining up to become geisha any more and those that did often left to get a 'normal' job.

'Twenty years ago, whenever there was a shamisen player along, we'd dance. If you were a good dancer, you carried on dancing no matter how old you were. But these days there are hardly any guests who want to see that kind of thing. There are hardly any guests who can understand our arts. One geisha gave up and became a maid in a hotel. She used to be one of the most famous dancers in Atami.

'But tonight is special. Tonight we'll have a good time. Tonight we're going to have a traditional teahouse party. These guests came four years ago and loved it and asked to have the same kind of party again. There'll be lots of saké. You'll see!'

The Businessmen's Big Night Out

'This way,' said Yuko, sliding open the door of a large hotel. She slipped out of her silk-covered sandals and led the way down some stairs into a basement and along a corridor to a closed door. From inside came shouts and raucous laughter. She knelt, slid open the door and, hands to the floor in formal greeting, sang out, 'Evening, everybody!'

Yuko in geisha mode was not radically different from Yuko in off-duty mode. She had put on a rather matronly kimono of sheeny green silk and a beige obi with a subtle pattern of chrysanthemums, carefully selected, I thought, to be dressy – it would not do for the guests to think she was not dressing for the occasion – but not intimidatingly glamorous or costly. She had added a little make-up and her hair was swept into a loose bun.

'This is my guest from England,' she added, gesturing to me. Kneeling alongside her, I bowed, rose to my feet and followed her rather awkwardly into the banqueting hall.

It was the size of a village hall, lined with tatami mats, with a stage at one end walled with glimmering gold leaf. Disposed around three sides of the room were fifteen to twenty elderly men in identical indigo and white striped cotton *yukata* bathrobes. Most sat cross-legged with large expanses of hairy shin and knobbly bare feet on display. In front of each was a small square table of lacquered wood holding a saké cup, a beer glass and an array of tiny dishes of food.

Sauntering into the room, Yuko settled me in a corner between a couple of grizzled men.

'This is Yamada-san,' she said. The ancient craggy-faced gentleman to my right nodded to me, then turned back to his beer. 'He's the leader. He'll take care of you.'

She made sure I had a table, a saké cup and some food. Then, smiling her huge generous smile, she headed off to another part of the room. There she folded to her knees before a couple of guests and began to banter and chat, laughing wholeheartedly and topping up their beer again and again. From time to time she glanced around to make sure that I was all right. She had, I thought, watching her admiringly, the perfect personality to be a geisha. With her husky Lauren Bacall voice and throaty laugh, she was undoubtedly sexy. But even more, she was motherly. She had the archetypal heart of gold. With her around, one felt, everything would be fine.

The men were members of a businessmen's club from one of the wealthier Tokyo boroughs and this was their annual outing. To my left was a grey-haired 54-year-old who described himself as the baby of the group. Most were in their sixties and seventies with a good proportion in their eighties. The oldest was eighty-eight. All were successful, prosperous men, all owned their own businesses and all, as it happened, represented different professions. My youthful neighbour was a solicitor, the white-haired man next to him an estate agent, another was a banker, one owned a construction company and one a private cramming school.

To me they looked like a bunch of rowdy old men in *yukatas* which were beginning to slip open, revealing sunken shrivelled chests. But that was the whole point of the exercise. In the company of their peers, these men, to whom deference was due and who normally had to maintain an appearance of the utmost dignity, had the chance to relax, let off steam and make fools of themselves. They could stop being the heads of major businesses and become just men. They could behave as badly as they liked. That was something that they themselves, because of their age, understood very well. They were a generation to whom the notion of geisha was familiar. When they were growing up in the pre-war years, geisha were a part of life. They knew the geisha music and dancing and they knew what to expect of a teahouse party.

'People of my age find this kind of thing offensive, especially women,' said the baby-faced solicitor, wrinkling his brow severely, anxious to dissociate himself from the unruly oldsters. 'That's why there's so few people here. Half the club were against having a geisha party for the annual outing. A lot didn't want to come.'

Still, he himself was there and a few minutes later he was laughing as loudly as everyone else.

Besides Yuko, there were three other geisha moving skilfully from group to group, keeping the saké and beer flowing and the conversation sparkling. One was the comedienne, in full regalia with a stiff waxed wig, white face and ornate grey and white kimono with a honeycomb pattern of red and mauve chrysanthemums and a red obi. At fifty-something, on her the white make-up looked faintly ghoulish. But as far as she was concerned, that just added to the comic effect. She was the Barbara Windsor or the Dolly Parton of the group, shamelessly flaunting her sexuality no matter what her age. But, being Japanese, she revealed not an ample bosom but an ample expanse of back.

Then there was a chubby-faced 21-year-old, bringing a breath of youth to the proceedings. Like the maiko of Kyoto, she was shy and inarticulate; but such naiveté only made her all the more charming. The cast was completed by the shamisen 'older sister', a tiny bird-like woman of ninety who spoke hardly at all but proved to have a raucous cackle; she laughed loudest and longest at the dirtiest jokes.

Mr Yamada, the horse-faced eighty-year-old to my right, had, it transpired, been the most enthusiastic advocate of this particular form of outing. The evening was not far advanced when, twisting a scarf and knotting it rakishly around his head like the lads who carry the portable shrine in a Japanese festival, he grabbed the microphone and began to belt out a song, with 'older sister' accompanying him on the shamisen. The change of costume released a raffish new persona. He was no longer Mr Yamada the Company Boss but a wild man who had cast aside all inhibitions for the night. He had brought his wife along. A faded woman with short black hair, she sat on the other side of the room, laughing merrily.

'Did you catch the words?' asked the chubby-faced solicitor, back in disapproval mode. He seemed to have positioned me, a fellow youngster, as his ally for the night. '"Let's go to Fukagawa." You know about Fukagawa?'

I knew very well about Fukagawa, once home to the most stylish geisha of all.

'That means, "Let's go to a whore house!"' he tutted sternly.

Maids pattered in and took away the food. Most of it looked exquisite – sashimi, tempura, all the traditional Japanese dishes, followed by slices of watermelon – but the men had barely touched it.

Things were hotting up. A beefy man – owner-chairman of a printing company, said the solicitor, my new-found friend – took the stage with his face painted like a doll, a ribbon tied around his head and his bathrobe pulled up to his knees, revealing a pair of hefty calves. Hand in hand with Yuko, he performed a comic dance, then took a theatrical peek inside her kimono. Then a frail 84-year-old stepped up in an ornate geisha wig with a red pinafore over his *yukata* and did a creaky arthritic dance. His reward was more than just a peek inside a kimono. To huge applause Yuko rolled on the floor and the tiny old man rolled on top of her. The ancient shamisen player was cackling with laughter.

'It's good for people to make fools of themselves,' observed the boyish solicitor, laughing heartily despite his earlier disapproval. 'Makes them broad-minded.'

Then came traditional games such as Tora Tora Tora – 'Tiger, Tiger,

Tiger' – a guessing game along the lines of 'stone, paper, scissors'. Yuko had explained this to me. A guest and a geisha, one to each side of a screen, sing a little song then choose whether to play hunter, landlord or tiger. The hunter wins over the tiger (he shoots him), the tiger wins over the landlord (he eats him), the landlord wins over the hunter (he forces him to pay up). The forfeits were growing more and more risqué – geisha riding on men, men riding on geisha. The comedienne was the ringleader, sprawling on her back with a customer on top of her, jiggling her arms and legs and yelling enthusiastically.

'This is men's culture,' said the solicitor, worried as things became more and more rowdy that I might be interpreting it all the wrong way. To him, these were innocent revels. What was it, after all, but the Japanese equivalent of the office party? But to me, from a different and – as he knew very well – more buttoned-up culture, it might seem shocking.

'To relieve stress, that's what it's all about,' he went on. 'In the old days there would have been no women around at all.' By 'women', of course, he meant 'wives'; to have women like myself and Mrs Yamada present not as geisha but as customers in the flower and willow world was very odd indeed.

At 8.30 the party moved on to the karaoké bar in the basement of the hotel. Still in their cotton *yukata* bathrobes, the men lounged on leather sofas around small tables in the darkened room. Images flickered across a large video screen as one by one they stood up and belted out sentimental ditties. In the midst of the revels, Yuko had never ceased keeping a motherly eye out for me. When the men turned on me and demanded that I sing, she intervened before I had time even to register dismay and said firmly, 'Lesley will sing when she feels like it and not before.' Then she took the microphone and gave a professional rendition of 'Falling in love again' in English, smiling her heart-warming smile at me. Mr Yamada, splendid in a fez and embroidered waistcoat, grabbed her arm, took to the floor and executed a nimble fox-trot followed by a waltz. The young geisha sat quietly, watching.

'I could have any of this lot for 30,000 yen [£150],' bragged the beefy owner of the printing company, giving me a nudge. I looked at him, wondering if I had heard right. 'Or 40,000 yen [£200] for overnight.'

'No, 50,000 yen [£250],' another guest corrected him.

'That young geisha,' leered the printer. 'I could definitely have her.' He paused and edged closer to me.

'But I don't want to sleep with those old bags,' he said with a cheeky smile. 'I'd rather sleep with you! What about it? I'm single. Let's get married!'

Smiling, I told him I'd have to get to know him a bit better first. Somehow my role had subtly changed. At the beginning of the evening I had been the observer, asking questions and making notes. But now the men had found a slot for me in the flower and willow world. As far as they were concerned, they had an extra girl – and this one was free! They weren't even being billed at 10,000 yen (£50) an hour for me.

'Come and dance,' shouted Mr Yamada through the noise of the karaoké and the smoke of the room. Without any more ado he dragged me off to the dance floor, clutching me tight to his clammy bosom. What was there to do except be a geisha, laugh, be charming and flirt, with the unshakeable determination to creep off at the end of the evening to my solitary bed.

Another two hours passed. Those members of the party still on their feet stepped into wooden clogs lined up at the entrance to the hotel and headed off in their *yukata* into the silent neon-lit streets. Occasionally we passed another group of revellers, also in matching hotel-issue *yukata*, clattering past the darkened shops.

Finally we came to an open restaurant, a window of light along a dark alley. Squeezed around a small table, the men ordered noodles, rice balls, yakitori (chicken kebabs) – simple fare, very different from the elaborate cuisine on offer at the banquet earlier. Saké and beer were still flowing.

As the men belted out a chorus of 'Let's go to Yoshiwara', the comedienne stood up, turned to face the wall and gyrated rhythmically, rubbing her groin against it. Then she grabbed the young solicitor. He tried to resist, then gave in, laughing. She pulled him on top of her, thrashing her arms and legs in simulated ecstasy. 'Aah,' she groaned, pushing him off and sitting up. 'Now I'm going to have a baby. What shall I call it?'

'They're really drunk, that's why they're making so much noise,' explained one man.

297

'They're not that drunk,' muttered Yuko. She was looking tired.

Mr Yamada was singing at the top of his voice. 'Be quiet,' scolded his wife, who was still with the group. 'You have the loudest voice of all!'

At one o'clock the evening came to an abrupt end. Farewells were peremptory, the intimacy suddenly over. The men disappeared into the darkness, clattering along the road to their hotel.

'I need to deal with money,' said Yuko. She looked tired and a little sad. 'Your hotel is that way, up the hill and around the corner. You can find it.'

And, having taken care of me so solicitously, she disappeared in the wake of the men, leaving me alone on the dark street. All through the evening she had laughed, bantered and made sure that everyone was chatting, everyone was happy and everyone had plenty to drink. Unlike the spoilt young girls who chose to become maiko in Kyoto, the geisha of Atami were working girls not so far removed from the young women from poor families who used to be sold in the bad old pre-war days. They had to make a living. Their job was to be eternally bright and cheerful, no matter how they might really feel. Her smile was part of her job. It was for everyone, she had no favourites.

Was she, perhaps, in need of a little extra income, I wondered. But it seemed an ungenerous thought and I put it out of my mind.

III

DREAMING OF GEISHA

14

PATRONS, LOVERS AND THEIR WIVES

It is very clear that we do not marry for love. If a man is known to have broken this rule, we look upon him as a mean fellow, and sadly lacking in morality. His own mother and father would be ashamed of him. Public sentiment places love for a woman very low in the scale of morals. [. . .] We place love and brutal attachment on the same plane.

The Japanese Bride, Naomi Tamura (1904)[1]

Geisha and Men

In theory modern Japanese men, born after the war, had little interest in geisha. But, to my surprise, the most unlikely people, when I told them I was researching the geisha, proved to have connections in the flower and willow world which they were eager to show off. One was a rather louche television producer I knew, in his forties, who one day whisked me off to Kagurazaka (literally 'Slope of the Music of the Gods') in the publishing district north of the Imperial Palace. One of his directors came with us; the producer made sure I realised that the geisha connection was his, not the director's.

The first teahouses in Kagurazaka appeared around the time that Commodore Perry and his black ships were steaming into Tokyo Bay and its geisha (there were sixty-three when I was there) were noted for their elegance and classy dancing, he told me as we clambered up the steep little street, brilliant with neon signs. Along the road were bars, restaurants and pavement carts selling roasted sweet potato and grilled octopus. Red paper lanterns swung invitingly outside closed doors. Opposite the huge vermilion gates of a shrine we ducked into a shadowy cobbled lane. Around a dark corner, where outsiders would not stumble upon it, was a small wooden house with reed blinds swaying in front of the windows. We stopped to admire the intricate weaving of the blinds, then slipped under the linen curtain at the gate and followed stepping stones through a narrow mossy garden to a sliding door.

Inside was a room just big enough for eight customers to sit squashed on high stools along two sides of the bar. The master of the house, a beaming, burly man in a bright red collarless shirt, greeted us. He and Kurota-san, my host, it transpired, were old college chums – which explained why a modern media executive like Mr Kurota chose to frequent this particular bar in this particular area. He sat us down, plied us with beer and saké, and set about preparing a non-stop succession of succulent dishes of fish, vegetables and rice.

The real boss was ensconced at a table in the corner – his 85-year-old mother, tiny, trim and straight-backed, immaculate in a pale moss-coloured kimono and an obi the colour of dark moss into which was tucked a fob watch which she consulted from time to time. Her black hair was tied back in a bun revealing a pinched, sharp-featured face with pale, finely lined parchment skin. In her time she had been one of the most celebrated geisha in Kagurazaka and was still a power in the geisha union, Kurota told me, sotto voce. Behind her, taking pride of place on the wall, was a painting of Mount Fuji rising out of gold-tinted clouds with a personal inscription by a famous artist of half a century ago.

'He was one of my lovers,' sniffed the old geisha. 'He painted it for me.'

Another group of four businessmen crowded in, filling the tiny bar. Beyond were a couple of tatami rooms, the sliding doors removed from their grooves to make one big open-plan space, where two parties of rowdy businessmen were gathered, enjoying a noisy night out. As the saké flowed, the voices and laughter grew deafening.

Kurota and his friend, loosening their ties as their faces flushed, were quizzing me about the Beatles as they picked at morsels of trout, boiled green soya beans and tiny beautifully cut vegetables. They were in grey suits with uninspired haircuts though, as media men, they were allowed a degree of wackiness not granted to more buttoned-up executives. In any case, they were off duty; and off duty, once they have consumed a little saké, Japanese men are adept at throwing aside barriers.

'I'm not going to ask your age,' began Kurota with a cheeky sideways glance. 'But which musical era do you remember best? The Beatles? The Rolling Stones?'

'Oasis,' I lied. 'Blur, Suede, Primal Scream – they were around when I was young.'

The master joined in. He had a comical, weathered face. He had gone into the fashion business, then ran a restaurant and finally came home to help his mother with her bar.

'I wish I knew who his father was,' Kurota confided under cover of the noise. 'Must have been someone famous.' Famous or not, the master was a joker.

'Do you know what uzura [quail] is in English?' he chuckled as he served us a dish of raw grated yam topped with seaweed and raw quail's egg. 'It's the name of the ex-American vice president – Dan Quayle!'

Everyone laughed uproariously.

'Where's your wife?' I asked Kurota. Here I was in the great modern city of Tokyo with two well-travelled cosmopolitan television producers. Yet, apart from the old geisha, I was the only woman in the whole place. It was rather rude to ask such a direct question; but enough saké had been drunk and I thought I could get away with it.

'At home, sleeping,' said Kurota, unfazed. 'She was a magazine editor until we got married. Then she said, "I can't be bothered to work any more." That's the way it is with Japanese wives. She stays home, has children and brings them up. Her world is very narrow – the PTA [Parent Teachers Association] and the parents of our children's friends; that's about it. I go out and enjoy myself, then get home late and wake her up and she gets angry. She says, "Why did you wake me up?" and goes back to sleep. In the west, people go to the pub for a drink, then go home, get changed and go out with their wives. But we Japanese can't do that, our homes are too far away.'

'That's why we have geisha,' said his friend, butting in. 'Ordinary girls are good at having babies and bringing up children. But geisha are good at chatting. You see this old geisha here . . .'

The old geisha was engaged in some outrageous conversation with the four businessmen, fluttering her fan coquettishly while her tongue rattled wickedly. The men, flushed and shiny-faced, returned her banter, guffawing loudly.

'An ordinary old lady would be very cosy,' Kurota's friend went on. 'But the world she knows is very small and the things she can talk about are very few. Geisha know how to please gentlemen, how to make them have a good time. But they wouldn't make good wives.'

The day after my memorable evening with Mr Kurota and his friend, I dropped into his offices to thank him for his hospitality. I started chatting about how much I had enjoyed the meal, the company, the old geisha and the master with his clowning and jokes. But Mr Kurota had changed. The affable, chummy character of the previous night, who had ribbed me mercilessly about my age and the Beatles, had disappeared. Brusque and businesslike, he changed the subject. Shortly afterwards he growled that he had a meeting and left.

Too late, I realised that I had committed an unforgivable faux pas. Whatever had happened in the night-time world of the geisha happened only there. Whatever one said, whatever one did was forgotten the next day. There were no memories and no repercussions. There was no crossover into the real world.

Two Sides of One Coin

A practical guide to doing business in Japan, published as recently as 1987, offers advice to the western executive who is invited to a geisha party. The Japanese host would naturally, out of courtesy, invite his wife too if she is travelling with him. What is the executive to do?

The proper response, advises the author, is to make sure that your wife is otherwise engaged. Buy her a ticket to kabuki or the ballet, then 'tell your Japanese contact how sorry your wife is not to be able to accept his kind invitation. He will accept your excuse graciously, with a secret sigh of relief!' He reassures the worried western wife that nothing untoward goes on at a geisha party. 'You are not sending your husband off to a den of iniquity.'[2]

Until westerners turned up in Japan a hundred and fifty odd years ago, Japanese society operated in a way that seemed perfectly logical and perfectly satisfactory to its members but from an Anglo-Saxon point of view was inconceivably alien; though Mediterranean peoples might have had less trouble coping with it. Marriage, love, sex and relationships were all conceived of in an utterly different way from in the west.

Initially, given the superior strength of the west, the Japanese made token efforts to appear to do things our way. But it was not until after the Occupation, when the Americans made a radical attempt to impose western ways on Japan, that any real change began. Most of the men who frequented geisha houses were young before the Second World War and had grown up with pre-war assumptions and attitudes. And even men like Kurota and his friend, born well after the war had ended, still lived their lives largely according to the old patterns.

Japanese wives always joked that when their husbands came home from work in the evening, instead of a sugary sweet 'Hello, Darling' and a lingering kiss, as in American movies, they would bark 'Tea!', followed not long after by 'Bath!' It was not that the wives hankered after heart-on-the-sleeve displays of affection. Far from it. The joke was the contrast between the two radically different styles of behaviour.

Once, when I was fresh to Japan and naive about such things, I asked a Japanese man of my acquaintance, a lecturer at a highly esteemed university, how to say 'Darling' in Japanese.

'What do you mean?' he asked.

'Well, when you call your wife, what do you say?'

He grinned at me, then bellowed 'Oi!' like a sergeant major on a parade ground.

Some years later I was supplementing my income by teaching English to a class of businessmen in Tokyo. Racking my brains for something to discuss one evening, I asked them to list the attributes of the ideal girl-friend. Predictably 'beauty' was top of the list, followed by 'intelligence', 'sense of humour', etc. Then we turned to the ideal wife. I was expecting a similar list but to my surprise it was turned on its head. 'Healthy body' came top, followed by 'good child-bearer', 'good with children' and 'good at housekeeping'. 'Beautiful', 'intelligent' and 'sense of humour' were right at the bottom.

'What's wrong with a beautiful wife?' I inquired, puzzled.

'If you had a beautiful, sexy wife, you'd be in trouble,' volunteered one. 'You'd be chasing off other men all the time.' In their eyes wives and girlfriends were entirely different species.

One young man to whom I taught English in London some years ago took it even further. He was a high-flier, a handsome 29-year-old executive in a major Japanese trading company who had been seconded to the London office. We used to meet in grand London restaurants and converse in English. The snag was that his favourite topic of conversation was his exploits with prostitutes. English whores were dirty and diseased, he told me; Japanese colleagues who had been around for a while always advised newcomers to steer well clear. The approved alternative, it transpired, was to take regular holidays in Spain.

He chose to disclose this in a Soho restaurant where the tables were uncomfortably close together, making it virtually impossible not to be overheard. He was just back from his first Spanish holiday.

'How was it?' I asked, all innocence.

'Ah, the señoritas! So lovely! So wonderful!' he cried ecstatically. Despite my pleas that we change the subject or at least switch to Japanese for this particular part of the conversation, he spent the rest of the meal regaling me with his sexual adventures.

'You're a good-looking young man,' I said. 'Why don't you get a girlfriend? Then you could have all the sex you wanted without having to go to prostitutes.'

His argument was perfectly logical.

'If I had a girlfriend, she'd be hassling me all the time to get married,' he explained. 'I'm very busy with my career. I don't have time for that sort of thing. Prostitutes are much easier. You get enjoyment, you pay your money and that's it. After you get married, that's when you have a girlfriend. Then they can't hassle you.'

The most unbridgeable cultural gap was that he did not see anything wrong, shameful or even embarrassing about going to brothels and paying for sex. It was just one of those things that men did, not much different from going down the pub with the lads.

Even in modern Japan, a Japanese man took it for granted that he had two different spaces in which to operate. Both contained women with whom he had relationships. In the world of home there was the wife, in charge of the household, the children's education and the purse strings. He gave her his salary and she gave him money with which to go out and have fun. The other world, the world of the evening, was populated by very different sorts of women – geisha, hostesses, entertainers, some of whom he had also known for years.

Between them, all these women made sure that he was taken care of from morning to night. Wife, concubine, mistress, geisha and hostess were all expert at mothering a man, smoothing away his problems, stroking his ego and ensuring that he always thought he was the boss. He was wrong, of course, to think so. All these women – wives, mistresses and geisha – were adept at wrapping him around their little fingers and he was supporting all of them.

They also knew each other. There were times when the two worlds met. When a man died, the geisha whom he had supported were often in evidence, pillars of strength, helping the wife take care of the funeral arrangements.

Across the River Kamo in Kyoto, a few minutes' walk from the geisha areas, there was a narrow back street lined with warehouses from which emanated the powerful odour of vegetables pickling in rice bran. The owner, an urbane fifty-year-old who had studied for his MBA in the United States, was a scion of an old Kyoto family which had owned the pickling plant for generations.

When he was a child in the fifties, he told me, there were always geisha and maiko around the house. They were like aunts who came to help his mother when she had important guests to entertain. She would put envelopes of money and small gifts into the little boy's hand and say, 'Give this to the geiko-san.' He knew many of the top geisha of Kyoto. Some were like aunts to him, others he had grown up with.

It was normal. The wife had her role, the geisha had theirs. His father had supported geisha and his mother had not been jealous; though, he confessed, he sometimes heard huge rows in other houses.

'In those days,' he said, 'a wife knew that as her husband become more powerful, he would go and "play" in the geisha quarters. That was a sign of his success. My mother would tell my father, "Off you go! Asobinasai! Go and play!"'

Jealousy

I was forever hearing that wives saw their husbands more as children than as partners and were happy if they strayed, just so long as it was no more than that. Nevertheless, there was a whole tradition of stories in Japanese literature dealing with the fearful power of jealousy. It is considered a force so terrifying that to this day when Japanese women get married, part of the traditional bride's costume is the 'horn hider', a stiff white head-dress which engulfs her head like an enormous cocoon. Supposedly it conceals the 'horns of jealousy' and immunises the new husband against them. When the marriage code was first set down in the early years of the Meiji period, the late nineteenth century, one of the seven grounds on which it was ruled that a man could divorce his wife was jealousy. (The others were sterility, adultery, disobedience to parents-in-law, larceny, severe disease and talking too much.)

In the eleventh century, when Murasaki Shikibu was writing the *Tale of Genji*, jealousy was believed to be such a powerful force that it could be lethal. In the novel, one of Prince Genji's mistresses, Lady Rokujo, is so consumed by it that her jealousy assumes demonic form and takes to visiting his lovers and bringing about their deaths; she meanwhile has no idea what her jealous spirit is doing.

By the seventeenth century, neglected upper-class wives had taken to organising clandestine Jealousy Meetings; women were supposed not even to feel jealousy, let alone express it. The rollicking novelist Saikaku describes one of these held in the splendid villa of a daimyo. The daimyo's wife and her ladies-in-waiting bring out an effigy of their hated rivals, a life-sized doll who happens exactly to resemble the daimyo's favourite concubine. One by one they rail against their unfaithful husbands and their loathsome floozies, then attack the doll, punching it, jumping on it and sinking their black-painted teeth into it.[3]

One day I was sitting with a couple of women. One was an elderly ex-geisha, the other the wife of a powerful businessman who herself came from the kind of family where, in the old days, geisha would have been a part of life. The two had known each other for many years. They were gossiping about the way attitudes had changed over the decades.

'Relationships have changed a lot,' began the wife. 'There's not the same feeling of responsibility.'

'That's right,' said the geisha, shaking her head. In her mid-seventies, she had a thin little face with a pointed chin and big eyes. She was dressed in a plain kimono with her hair pulled back into a tight grey bun. 'In the Meiji period, if a man had a geisha girlfriend, his friends would make sure she was all right after his death. But by Taisho [1912–1925], things were different.

'I remember hearing about a Shimbashi geisha who was the mistress of a very successful man. She was like a second wife to him. But although they were together for a long time, she never had any children. Then his wife died. He took the geisha into his household as his new wife but his children – the children of the first wife – wouldn't accept her. When he died too, his son threw her out of the house! It was shocking. The ironic thing was, the son carried on just like his father. He had a Shimbashi mistress too; he even had a child by her. His behaviour was the mirror image of his father's but he still didn't take care of his father's geisha. Everyone was appalled.'

'I remember years ago, when I first got married, my father-in-law had a geisha,' said the wife. 'His wife was so jealous. Poor thing! She used to prepare the most exquisite meals every night, just like a top-class restaurant, and she was always dressed really beautifully. But no matter how hard she tried, he would say he just wanted tea and rice, then rush off to the teahouse to eat. I felt so sorry for her.'

'Then there was that husband who took his geisha with him everywhere like his wife,' reminisced the geisha. 'The wife was disfigured, I think she was scarred or handicapped; anyway, she couldn't appear in public. The geisha was beautiful and the wife agreed that she should be her husband's public consort. But when he died, the wife kicked her out immediately and took everything. It was terrible, she was like a demon. The geisha was destitute. I remember his friends were all discussing what to do and how to take care of her.'

It was not surprising that wives should sometimes be jealous – they were human, after all. But despite the pain it might cause them, most accepted the Faustian pact. As the wife, they occupied a position of great respect in society. In Japan no one was 'just' a housewife. Taking care of the house and rearing the children were seen as jobs essential for the well-being of society. Wives knew that within the household they were all-powerful. If they wanted to buy a new car with the housekeeping money, there was no need to discuss it with their husband. With the husband as the breadwinner and the wife taking care of the house, it was a very efficient division of labour.

When they married, they expected to lead a life very separate from their husband's and many preferred it like that. As the old saying goes, the ideal husband is 'healthy and not around'. They also knew that, while they could not expect love or fidelity, they were assured of financial security. To this day divorce rates in Japan are still far lower than in the west.[4]

Instead of trying to fulfil her husband's every fantasy so that he would never need to look elsewhere – to be the perfect wife, the perfect mother, a lady in public and a whore in the bedroom, as a western wife might – Japanese wives accepted that one woman was usually not enough to fulfil a man's needs. Just as there were two worlds, so there were two sorts of women to populate them. Wives and geisha were complementary, two sides of the same coin, two faces of womanhood.

The Priest's Wife

Reiko Sato was the feisty, exuberant wife of a Buddhist priest. She lived in a small wooden temple with a sloping tiled roof in an area in the middle of Kyoto where nearly every building was a temple. In her forties or early fifties, she had an elfin face with a pointed chin, short brown hair, eyebrows tweezed into a quizzical arch and an irrepressible smile. She was typical of a lot of Japanese wives I knew –

bright, confident, down to earth, funny, and prepared to say whatever was on her mind.

One day I was near the temple and dropped in to see her. Chattering cheerily, she led me into one of the large, shady, tatami-floored rooms and settled me on a cushion while she went to make tea. It was late spring but already stultifyingly hot. The flimsy glass doors which formed the outside wall were pushed right back, revealing a tiny garden of moss-covered rocks enclosed by a stone wall. Mosquitoes buzzed lazily around, undisturbed by the mosquito coil which sent up a plume of noxious-smelling smoke.

Born and bred in Kyoto, Reiko had had geisha around her since childhood; they were part of the scenery as far as she was concerned. Being both daughter and wife of Buddhist priests (like a vicar's wife in the west), she knew everyone. She was an insider, as much a part of traditional society as the geisha were.

Over chilled barley tea she asked me how I was getting on with my research, then launched into her own idiosyncratic impressions of the geisha world.

'You know who their main customers are, don't you?' she asked with a mischievous smile. 'I'll tell you. There are something like three thousand temples in Kyoto. Some of them are small ones like ours, where the priest lives there all the time. But the bigger ones have a revolving system of abbots. The abbots are appointed for four or five years. They come up from the countryside where they live; they usually have a small temple of their own there. The wife and children stay in the countryside, taking care of the temple, and the abbot is here on his own. After a while – you can imagine! – he gets lonely. So off he goes to Gion; or he calls for a geisha to come over to the temple.'

Reiko was not the only person to tell me that one of the chief sources of *danna* for the geisha was priests; another was *yakuza* (gangsters). Not many Japanese would expect a priest to be an exemplary moral character. Most, Buddhist or Shinto, were men who had inherited the job from their father and did good business carrying out ceremonies and rituals for the parish. Shinto priests took care of people while they were alive; they conducted weddings, performed ceremonies to propitiate the gods and blessed everything from cars to new factories. Buddhist priests took care

311

of people when they were dead; they held funerals and memorial services and ran graveyards. Quite a few, in my experience, were earthy Chaucerian characters no more averse to having fun than priests had been in the early days of kabuki, when they formed the main clientele for beautiful young boy actors.

'What about contraception?' I demanded. It was not a question I had ever dared ask a geisha. But Reiko was so cheerfully uninhibited that I decided I could relax, put all my carefully learnt politeness aside, and ask whatever I wanted.

'Geisha use condoms, like everyone else,' she replied. 'But we're not Christians so we're not so bothered about being single mothers. In the past there used to be a lot of single mothers. These days geisha tend to retire and marry when they get pregnant.'

Extraordinary though it might seem, the pill was only licensed for contraceptive use in Japan in June 1999. Until then it was banned as being potentially dangerous to health. As a result, Japan was, as Mother Teresa of Calcutta described it, 'an abortionist's paradise'. There were any number of male doctors who profited from this situation, not to mention the priests who presided over temples dedicated to the souls of aborted or miscarried foetuses. One survey revealed that 23 per cent of married women had had at least one abortion. The problem was less acute for married couples; women often joked that the main form of contraception among married couples was that, after having produced the regulation two children, they stopped having sex. The main people who had to worry about contraception were those providing extra-marital sex.

It did not pass unnoticed that the Japanese government licensed Viagra in February 1999, after a mere six months' debate and before licensing the pill; there was no problem, it seemed, with a drug which gave men control over their sexuality, though there was with a drug which did the same for women.[5]

But what of the wives, I asked. How did they feel when their husbands went off to the pleasure quarters? Were they not jealous, as a western wife would be?

In the past, said Reiko, women had taken it for granted that they were inferior and subordinate to men. You brought up even your own son with great care, giving him as much deference as you would your husband and using only kind, respectful words when you spoke to him. In those days, women were taught to assume that if their husband was rich, he would go off to have fun in Gion. It was a high-status activity, something to be proud of, certainly not to complain about. If a man brought home a geisha as his concubine, everything would be fine just so long as the geisha remembered the protocol. Even if the husband slept with the pretty young newcomer and not with the withered old wife, nevertheless the wife was still number one. The geisha always had to remember her place and bow very low when their paths crossed. At the husband's funeral, no matter how close they had been, she would still take her allotted place, low in the ranks.

'Sometimes everyone got on better if there was a nice young wife living there too,' said Reiko. 'It kept the husband happy and made everything more harmonious. But if the number one and the number two wives both had children, that sometimes created problems.'

Then she had a brainwave. The best way to understand all this, she said, was to meet one of her old schoolmates who had been the top maiko of her day.

Geisha and Wives

There was a coffee shop on Shijo Street, just opposite the Minami-za kabuki theatre, which had become one of my favourite rendezvous spots. It was air-conditioned and civilised and served weak Darjeeling tea and slabs of spongy western-style cakes encased in silver foil. You could sit and watch the crowds through the smoked-glass windows as they milled across Shijo Bridge and pressed down the street – tourists in shorts, students on bicycles, women out shopping and geisha and maiko in kimonos, barely causing a raised eyebrow or a second glance as they scurried by under their parasols.

A few days later I pushed open the glass door at the appointed time. Reiko was already there, chatting and laughing with a pretty woman who wore her hair tied in a knot at the nape of her neck like a geisha. She introduced me to her friend, Mrs Sato.

'She's Mrs Sato, I'm Mrs Sato,' she laughed. 'Mrs Sato and Mrs Sato.'

Mrs Sato was startlingly youthful, little changed from the heart-stoppingly beautiful maiko in the photographs which she brought out to show me. She might have been in her thirties rather than her early fifties. Her face was a delicate heart shape, her skin silky smooth without a trace of a line and her eyes large, limpid and set wide apart. Her nose was small and straight and her pretty, laughing mouth neither too large nor too small, just as the ancient canons of beauty dictated. She had the easy confidence of a woman who has been worshipped and admired as an acknowledged beauty for years.

She and Reiko had been at middle school together. Mrs Sato's family ran a teahouse in Gion so it was natural that she would become a maiko.

'I wasn't surprised,' said Reiko, sipping her tea. 'In fact I was a bit envious. I like the flower and willow lifestyle; I like meeting people and chatting. I would have loved to have been the proprietress of a teahouse. But I'm from a temple. My parents said to me, "You go and study." Anyway, I'm 163 centimetres [5 foot 5]. I'm too tall to be a maiko.'

'I'm 160 centimetres [5 foot 4],' smiled Mrs Sato. 'That's a bit tall still.'

Mrs Sato had started dancing classes at the traditional age of six years, six months and six days. She had a flair for it and quickly rose from grade to grade. But she had no particular ambition to enter the flower and willow world. When she reached the age of fourteen, when other girls were leaving school to start full-time maiko training, she stayed on.

'I even went for some job interviews. But I didn't like school and I wasn't much good at business. In fact I wasn't much good at anything,' she concluded with a merry smile. 'So in the end I decided to have a go at being a maiko.'

The first step was to find an 'older sister'. There was a particular geisha whom the young girl had always admired. In her middle-thirties, she was at the peak of her career. Glamorous, accomplished, a distinguished dancer and a beguiling conversationalist, she was the most famous and esteemed geisha in the whole of Gion.

'I used to see her at teahouse parties when I was young,' said Mrs Sato. 'She was the most beautiful of all. She was my idol.'

314

Mrs Sato's mother, the owner of an established teahouse and a powerful force in Gion herself, petitioned her on her daughter's behalf. Mother and daughter were thrilled when she agreed.

With the top 'older sister' in the district as her mentor, Mrs Sato quickly became a popular and accomplished maiko herself. It was partly her beauty and also her confidence. Even during *minarai*, the pre-maiko training period when a young girl is supposed to sit silently watching and learning, doing no more than filling saké cups and emptying ashtrays, she bubbled with irrepressible gaiety and curiosity, bursting to chat with these important and powerful men in whose company she found herself.

Soon she was the most sought-after maiko in Gion. She was a star, photographed, interviewed and invited to adorn teahouse parties and receptions across the country. Her white-painted face gazed demurely from posters advertising the wonders of Kyoto.

'What I liked best was when I'd have a daytime party somewhere like Nagoya or Osaka, from eleven to three. I'd rush home, bathe, change, then be free in the evening. I'd call a customer to take me out to dinner. The only problem was that some of the older geisha got jealous and teahouse owners nagged me sometimes.'

'What about mizuage?' I asked nervously. It was always difficult to ask such a personal question but I was emboldened by the presence of my outspoken friend Reiko.

'Sure I had it,' said Mrs Sato casually, as if it was the most normal thing in the world. 'We had a meal together, liked each other and slept together. He became my danna. There were rules about sex, of course. Some maiko broke them but I never did.'

Her *mizuage*, I calculated from her age, must have taken place more than thirty years ago, around 1965. If she had not wanted to go ahead with it, she implied, she could have said, 'No'. As to the 'rules about sex', number one, she explained, was never to sleep with someone who was not a customer. Number two was never to sleep with someone whom your 'older sister' liked.

'My husband was a customer too. He was one of my danna-san. That was how I met him. I remember he really wanted to marry me. He used to say, "Leave this life. Let's get married." I'm not going to tell you what his job is or everyone will know who he is. Let's just say he's in property.

'He was the top danna of Gion. He was twenty years older than me, but that doesn't mean he was old; I was only twenty or so at the time. We were lovers for three years. We've been married thirty years now. I must say, these days I get fed up with having him around the house night after night. I wish he'd go out and "play"!'

In Japan, said the irrepressible Reiko, butting in, the wife's job is to take care of the husband. He might love and adore you and want to make you happy – but that is only when you are courting. Everything changes the moment the ring is on your finger. Once you are married, you suddenly discover that you are not a lover any more but a mother.

'We're managers!' she cried. 'You get married, you have a baby straight away and after that your hands are full. You're taking care of the baby, your husband – he's another baby – and all the family finances. It's a real nuisance having the husband around the house; he just gets in the way. It makes life much easier for everyone if husbands go off and "play".

'Mine certainly did,' she added. 'Probably still does. I certainly don't think he's the perfect husband.'

I had put down my fork and was listening aghast at the outrageous turn the conversation had taken. Of course in theory Japanese wives took their husbands' infidelity for granted, but I had never before heard anyone speak so directly about it.

I was well aware that husbands and wives in Japan often led completely separate lives. When I lived in small-town Japan I had had many very close women friends; but I never seemed to meet their husbands. Couples never did things together as they do in the west. Even in the evening when I went for dinner, the husband was never around.

After I had remarked on this over the course of a year and a half, some of my women friends made a special effort and invited me around to meet their husbands. Then I realised what the problem was. In most cases the couple had absolutely nothing in common apart from the children and the roof over their heads. I wondered how on earth they had ended up together. Some, of course, would have had a marriage arranged by their parents; some, I suspected, simply got married because it was time and the person in question was around and available. The women and the young girls whom I taught never seemed to expect love or to hold out for it, as a western woman would. Proverbially what a woman looked for in a man were the three *takai*, the three 'highs': to be tall, to have a high salary and to be the graduate of a top university. Love came a poor second if it made a showing at all.

The prime relationship in most women's lives, as far as I could see, was not with their husbands but their children. As if to make up for the lack of romantic love in their lives, women overwhelmed their children with love. As for the husbands, their prime relationship seemed to be with their workmates. They worked together all day and in the evening went out together to party or 'play'. Often they spent weekends playing golf together.

If a wife was lucky, she would never see her husband at all. He would stagger home drunk last thing at night, fall into bed and be off to work at the crack of dawn next morning. Some nights he might phone up and say he was working late and was going to spend the night in the city. The wife carefully avoided thinking too much about it. It made it very easy for a Japanese man if he wanted to have an affair.

But I had never before heard a Japanese woman say straight out that she wished her husband would go off and 'play' with other women. Reiko and Mrs Sato were half joking, I suspected. They were also sophisticated Kyoto-ites. They came from old Kyoto families. Reiko had lived for generations side by side with the flower and willow world, the one place where the romantic was allowed to blossom in Japan, while Mrs Sato had grown up within it. Their attitudes were perhaps more rooted in the past than those of most modern Japanese women.

'My husband had a Taiwanese lover a while ago,' said Reiko. 'I got really jealous. But then one day I met her. I liked her, she was sweet. After that I didn't mind. Even if men play around, we still feel confident just so long as they introduce the girlfriend to us. Once you've met her, then you can relax and feel secure.'

'It was like that with my husband's first wife,' said Mrs Sato. 'I knew her quite well when I was still a geisha. The three of us went out for dinner several times.'

'Didn't you feel guilty?' I asked, aghast at these revelations.

'Not in the slightest,' said Mrs Sato, smiling sweetly. 'She was a lot older than me. There was no reason to feel bad.'

'I don't get angry if my husband plays around,' said Reiko. 'That's fine. The only thing is, I have to be the most important. If the other woman gets to be more important to him, that's when I'd get angry. That was proper behaviour in the old days. The wife had to be number one. Wives don't have lovers, of course,' she added, as if that was perfectly obvious.

'We don't have time,' said Mrs Sato. 'We're busy all day long, every day – bringing up the children, cooking perfect meals three times a day . . .'

'The day my husband goes out to "play", that's when I can finally relax,' laughed Reiko. 'I can always tell. When he gets back, he's ultra nice to me. He gives me presents or flowers. He's quiet and well-behaved. A husband is like a child; I'm like his mother. If he does something stupid, I tell him off.'

The key thing, they agreed, was to keep the home harmonious and peaceful. If one's husband was frustrated then he would be in a bad temper and infect everyone else with his bad temper and the whole family would be miserable. But if he went off to 'play', if he had a girlfriend or went to visit a geisha, he would be in a good mood for days afterwards. Not only that, he would be contrite and sheepish. There would be harmony in the home.

'If my husband is happy, then I'm happy too,' concluded Reiko. 'If my husband is stressed then I get stressed too and we have a row. If he spends time with another woman, he'll be in a good mood when he gets home. Then we're all in a good mood.'

Later when Mrs Sato had gone off to powder her exquisite nose, Reiko confided that her husband was one of the biggest landowners in Kyoto. He owned woods, he owned mountains – in fact, he owned most of Kyoto. I would not have expected less of someone who had been the most famous and beautiful maiko in the entire city.

15

GEISHA AND LOVE

Now, as a general rule, where passionate love is the theme in Japanese literature of the best class, it is not that sort of love which leads to the establishment of family relations. It is quite another sort of love – a sort of love about which the Oriental is not prudish at all – the *mayoi*, or infatuation of passion, inspired by merely physical attraction; and its heroines are not the daughters of refined families, but mostly *hetarae*, or professional dancing girls.

Of the Eternal Feminine, Lafcadio Hearn (1927)[1]

Dying for Love

Love was the currency of the fantasy world in which the geisha traditionally operated, yet for a geisha to fall in love was a disaster. As in the days of the courtesans, the geisha's profession was fuelled by desire. But it was a perilous game: to flirt with men, to snuggle up to them, to stir their desire so that they would call for you again but – no matter how intimate you appeared to be – never to lose your head, let alone your heart. The edge of danger was one of the things that gave the game its excitement.

As the old saying went, the lie of the courtesan was, 'I love you,' the lie of the customer, 'I will marry you.' After all, there was nothing better than a declaration of love to keep a man visiting. In the seventeenth century there were textbooks for courtesans on ways of dissembling love. For example, when the man was preparing to leave, it was very important to shed a few tears. If you were a beginner and not good at weeping to order, the book suggested that you pull out a couple of eyelashes, look hard at something small without blinking for a few minutes, or paint a little alum inside the neck of your kimono, where the fumes would sting your eyes.[2]

But customers started to demand more and more outrageous demonstrations of love. Even if they were not in love with the courtesans themselves, dashing young libertines liked to collect love tokens to show off to their friends. First they required letters written in blood; prick the gum with a quince toothpick to obtain blood, advised the textbooks, adding reassuringly that quince is good for the gums. Later they started to demand locks of hair, fingertips, then whole fingers; a patron might demand such a proof of love before, for example, coughing up for a special outing or a fête day. The custom has persisted with a different significance among the *yakuza*, who chop off the top digit of the little finger as a punishment. Some women actually did cut off their fingers, while the more cunning got round it by sending fingers made of rice dough or cut from corpses; quite a trade grew up in dead people's fingers.

To play at love was one thing, really to fall in love quite another – and in the supercharged world of the geisha it was always a danger. Usually the courtesan or geisha would fall in love with someone young, handsome and poor who was not even a customer. If they fell in love with a customer, that would be equally disastrous, for customers were inevitably married. Once the pair were overcome by desire and could no longer endure the limitations imposed by society on their meetings, they were doomed. Unlike such love affairs in the west, marriage was almost never the answer.

Often the only solution was death. In fact to die together came to seem so hugely romantic that many couples yearned to express their love for each other in this way, like Romeo and Juliet. The great dramatist Chikamatsu Monzaemon (1653–1724), often described as the Shakespeare of Japan, created a whole genre of kabuki plays about double suicide, of which the most famous was *The Love Suicides at Sonezaki*, inspired by a real-life incident in 1703. In those days the kabuki theatre was like a 'living newspaper' – incidents were transformed into dramas almost as soon as they happened and broadcast to the populace – and the play was staged just three weeks after the actual suicide had taken place.

The stage version of the story goes as follows: the beautiful nineteen-year-old courtesan Ohatsu is in love with Tokubei, a handsome 25-year-old clerk who is far too poor to be able to buy her out of bondage. His uncle has set up an arranged marriage for him with a wealthy relative but Tokubei informs him that he cannot go through with it. He therefore needs to return the dowry which has already been paid to him. But he has already lent the money to the wicked Kuheiji, an oil merchant whom he imagines to be a friend of his. When Tokubei demands the money back, Kuheiji denies all knowledge of the loan. Kuheiji then swaggers off to the brothel to make his suit to Ohatsu; he too wants to buy her. Hiding beneath the veranda, Tokubei overhears his suit. The lovers are ruined. There is no way that they can ever be together. The only recourse is to commit suicide.

Ohatsu puts on a white kimono, signifying death (corpses in Japan are dressed in white), with a black cloak above it so that they will not be seen. Taking with them a rosary, the pair flee the brothel and set off for the woods of Sonezaki Shrine. As the bell tolls the coming of dawn, they pray, embrace each other for the last time, then bind themselves tightly to a tree so as to look beautiful even in death. Weeping, Tokubei takes out his dagger and cuts her throat, then, with a razor, slashes his own. By their deaths, these two humble people have become ennobled. 'They have become models of true love,' declares the narrator in the final words of the play.[3]

Chikamatsu's plays were so successful that they inspired a boom in copycat love suicides. By 1722 there was such an epidemic that the government banned plays about double suicide and took stern measures against such suicides themselves, displaying the perpetrators, dead or alive, for three days and condemning survivors to work for the untouchables, the most ignominious punishment imaginable.

But to this day 'love suicide' is still a recognised phenomenon in Japan. Each year some young couples, prevented from marrying by parental pressure, choose this way to be together. In Japanese eyes, far from being macabre, it is profoundly romantic. On a recent visit to Japan, some friends asked me how many love suicides there were a year in Britain. They were completely incredulous when I told them there were none.

The most celebrated love suicide of modern times was the novelist Osamu Dazai (1909–1948), a fin-de-siècle character who lived not at the end of a century but at the end of an era, as Japan was slipping inexorably towards apocalyptic war. A writer of intensely passionate, sometimes sardonic novels chronicling the dying gasps of the crumbling Japanese aristocracy, he has been described as a Japanese Arthur Rimbaud. He was an attractive, hard drinking, devil-may-care kind of man, obsessed with dying a beautiful death. He made three attempts at love suicide and also several attempts to commit suicide by himself.

While still a student, he met a geisha named Hatsuyo Oyama, moved her in with him and took her down to Tokyo where he was to study French literature at the Imperial University. His brother offered to pay off her redemption fees to the geisha house and everything seemed settled. But his grandmother, the stern old matriarch of their wealthy and very conservative northern family, was fiercely opposed to any alliance with a geisha. She disinherited him.

Almost out of pique Dazai made a suicide pact with another woman whom he had picked up on a drinking spree. It was 1930 and he was twenty-one. They went down to the coast at Kamakura, just outside Tokyo, and flung themselves into the sea. As luck would have it the girl drowned but Dazai survived. His brother had to rush down to Tokyo to hush things up. In his fiction Dazai dwelt endlessly on the suicide attempt and on his yearning for death. One of his short stories begins nonchalantly, 'I was thinking of killing myself.'[4]

Later he tried to commit suicide with Hatsuyo, his geisha lover, after she had had an affair with one of his friends while he was in hospital trying to conquer his addiction to painkillers. He, of course, had incessant affairs; but the notion of his lover/wife having an affair was more than he could tolerate. The two went off to a hot-spring resort in the mountains and took an overdose of barbiturates together. This time both lived, and Dazai went on to write a succession of brilliant novels. He made several suicide attempts, went on benders and managed somehow to survive the Second World War.

After the war he was acclaimed as Japan's greatest post-war novelist and awarded several literary prizes. His debauched lifestyle continued. He had a wife and child and a mistress and child and was working on a novel called *Goodbye*, a comic tale of how a man rids himself of a succession of unwanted women. He had also begun a new relationship with a woman named Tomie Yamazaki. On 13 June 1948 the pair drowned themselves together in the Tamagawa Reservoir. It was a fitting end, the death he had been looking for for so long. He was just a few days short of his fortieth birthday.[5]

Of Love and Kissing

There are many different words for 'love' in Japanese, none of which mean quite the same as the English word – though it is important to remember that what we, modern Anglo-Saxons, mean by 'love' is probably not at all the same as what the ancient Greeks, the Romans, or the medieval troubadours of courtly love meant by it or, for that matter, the modern-day French, Italians or anyone else. Love is an invention, culturally conditioned; notions of love vary from place to place, from era to era and from culture to culture.

Unlike the chivalrous knights of the European Middle Ages, who devoted themselves to unattainable ladies, suffered torments of undeclared passion, and yearned after women whom they saw as goddesses, put on pedestals and worshipped, Japanese men fell in love with real women, not bloodless ideals. They did not go to war with a scented glove tucked into their armour. It was possible to have sex without love – in fact, that was by far the safest course. But no one ever considered the possibility of love without sex. In fact the closest they ever came to the European notion of courtly love was probably the samurai's idealised love of beautiful boys. According to the *Hagakure*, an eighteenth-century treatise on samurai ethics, this was a form of love which was purest when it remained undeclared.

And given that love never resulted in marriage, there was no culture of wooing, courting, dating and finally falling to one's knees one moonlit night and slipping the ring shyly on to the finger. Thus a 1915 visitor could write, 'The fact is, of course, that Cupid has a very bad time in this country; it is an unknown land to him. Soft eyes and coy glances, fair spring days and moonlight [sic] nights in autumn, wanderings in country lanes and

323

by the sea, hand-squeezing, sighing, sweet confidences, and all the other "ministers of love" have no place here.'[6]

In fact by then Japanese intellectuals knew all about the western concept of 'love'. They called it *rabu*, the Japanese phoneticisation of the English word, to differentiate the noble emotion of platonic love from base physical passion. It had an extra lustre because it was an exotic foreign emotion conveyed in a foreign word, rather like talking about *amour* or *amore* instead of just plain 'love'. In the late nineteenth century and early twentieth century there were many angst-ridden Japanese novels written celebrating *rabu*.

Kafu Nagai, who spent his whole life among geisha, prostitutes and bar girls and went to the grave with a geisha's name tattooed on his body, wrote that the most transcendent moment of his life was when he exchanged a few words with a young American woman on Staten Island. They talked of opera, the irrelevance of marriage and the poetry of the night sky, then parted with a gentle handshake.

'I felt strangely forlorn,' wrote Kafu the great sensualist, 'at the thought that never again as long as I lived would such a beautiful thing happen to me.'[7] It was an experience of *rabu*, pure and unadulterated by the gross physical passion which permeated all his other relationships.

It is still awkward to say in Japanese 'I love you', partly because, like the equally reticent British, Japanese do not usually express such emotions in words. The most common phrase is *suki desu* which literally means only 'I like you' – though, as always in Japan, the meaning is communicated more through intonation and gut feeling than through the words themselves. The phrase 'to fall in love' is rendered by a rather clumsy direct translation of the English words. Under 'love', an English-Japanese conversation dictionary published as recently as 1969 comments, 'Marriage in Japan is generally arranged by the parents and is seldom the result of mutual love. The Japanese language therefore is poor in expressions of affection and those which exist are apt to be taken in a bad sense.'[8]

Likewise the most commonly used word for 'kiss' is the adopted *kissu*, not surprising for a society where kissing was until very recently considered a shockingly private and erotic activity. Even in the woodblock prints depicting the floating world of the courtesans and geisha, kissing is almost never shown. After all, it was probably not very appealing to press one's mouth up against a face covered in white lead-based paint, added to which a courtesan or a geisha would be reluctant to smudge her make-up. In fact the erotic touching of lips was one of the most esoteric of the geishas' arsenal of sexual techniques.

Long before the word *kissu* was coined, in 1878, Junichiro Oda, one of the first translators of English literature into Japanese, came across the outlandish phrase 'I should sleep well if I could get one kiss from those coral lips' in Edward Bulwer-Lytton's *Ernest Maltravers*; to Japanese of the time it was virtually incomprehensible and distinctly pornographic. Showing great ingenuity, he rendered it '. . . if I could get one lick of your red lips'.[9] His readers probably thought the concept as well as the words quite hilarious.

Kissing, in fact, was not part of normal human interaction. It was considered so indecent that when there was a proposal for Auguste Rodin's statue 'The Kiss' to be exhibited in Tokyo in the 1930s, there was public outrage. The police banned it. There was a suggestion that the sculpture should be shown with the heads wrapped in a cloth so that no one would see the offensive kissing; the naked bodies were not a problem. In the end the Rodin was not shown until after the Second World War, which was also when the first screen kiss occurred in a Japanese film.

A Wild-Flower Lover

I bathed my snow skin
In pure Tamagawa river.
Our quarrel is loosened slowly,
And he loosens my hair.
I am all uncombed.
I will not remember him,
I will not altogether forget him,
I will wait for Spring.
'Tamagawa River', geisha song[10]

One evening when I was in Kyoto, I met up with a group of friends and friends of friends from Tokyo. It was like a glimpse of another world. I had been living among the geisha for what seemed an eternity. Suddenly I was surrounded by sophisticates from the Tokyo art scene – curators, writers, architects and leading-edge contemporary artists, all stubble, shabby denim and scuffed trainers.

After dinner we checked out a tiny, smoky jazz bar on the edge of the Pontocho geisha district. The conversation turned to my research. Later a quiet, rather earnest young man with a plump pale face and longish hair drew me aside. He had been introduced as a curator at a Tokyo modern art museum.

'I had an affair with a geisha,' he whispered. 'I can't talk about it now. Here's my card. Call me when you're in Tokyo.'

His name was Hideo. Ten days later I met up with him. We went to an eel restaurant where he told me his story.

They had met in a hole-in-the-wall drinking house in Shibuya, a bustling, fashionable, youthful Tokyo neighbourhood. She was twenty-three, he not yet thirty. She was wearing rather gaudy clothes, too bright, too tight and too revealing; at first he took her for a prostitute or a bar girl. But her face bewitched him. He could not take his eyes off her. She was beautiful, but there was more to it than that. It was a radiant face, full of life and laughter, the eyes almost too big, the mouth almost too sensuous. Yet at the same time there was an appealing innocence and vulnerability about her. For the quiet studious young man she was a vision from another world. It was only after they had become lovers that she revealed she was indeed from another world: she was a geisha.

Their love affair had to be secret. She was not supposed to spend time with anyone who was not a customer, let alone sleep with them. He was getting for nothing what other men paid a fortune for, if they got it at all.

'I have to be careful,' he muttered, glancing nervously around the restaurant. 'Even here. A lot of politicians have geisha mistresses. Everyone knows who's sleeping with who. There's a lot of secrets in this world. For geisha it's perfectly normal to have love affairs and illegitimate children; but ordinary people don't know anything about it.'

Hideo was not prepared to tell me his lover's name but he had brought photographs to show me of a laughing girl with a mane of tumbling black hair and a dazzlingly lovely face. She might have been a model; she had one of those perfectly proportioned faces with porcelain skin, a delicate nose and eyes and mouth a little larger than life. He also had pictures of her as a geisha, kneeling demurely in a kimono, her face a bland white mask.

'I preferred her real face,' he said. 'I never saw her geisha life or met her geisha friends. I once went to see her when she gave a public dance performance, but that was it. She kept me well away from that side of her life.'

She had grown up, he told me, in the poorest, slummiest part of Osaka, a wild flower springing up on a dung heap. When she was fourteen her father walked out, leaving her behind with her overworked hairdresser mother. She was a wild, leggy, uncontrollable teenager. By fifteen she had dropped out of school and taken up with a bunch of bikers and *yakuza* gangsters, sleeping around wherever she wanted. More than once a *yakuza* boyfriend beat her up. By seventeen she had already honed her survival skills. She decided it was time to get out. She took the train to Tokyo and arrived knowing no one and with almost no money, then found a job as a hostess in a sleazy bar.

Then she met a professional gambler, 'by chance', said Hideo. In his fifties, he had made so much money as the manager of a company that he had been able to afford to give up work and devote himself to gambling. He fell for the coltish young woman and they became lovers. Then he offered to become her *danna*. He rented a luxury apartment in an expensive area of Tokyo for her, gave her an allowance and bought her all the clothes she wanted, then moved in himself. For the young woman from the slums of Osaka, it was a dream come true.

By now she was nineteen. She gave up working as a hostess. She had always daydreamed about being a geisha; she was drawn by the beauty and brightness of the geisha life. But she had never before imagined that it might be possible. To join a geisha house, take classes and buy the requisite number of kimonos cost a fortune, far more than a girl like her could ever afford. But her patron had money and, more important, the right connections. He took her to meet the proprietress of a geisha house

327

in one of the five Tokyo flower towns and she was accepted. Thereafter she lived with him and went to work as a member of the geisha house.

The first thing she had to do was to lose her Osaka accent. She acquired airs and graces. She learnt to wear a kimono gracefully, to dance seductively, to entertain guests with her charming prattle but keep them at arm's length, to pour saké and play games. Now she was mixing in high society. For politicos, bureaucrats, industrialists, business magnates and media stars, she was a friend and confidante, a pretty face to flirt with and a shoulder to cry on. She learnt to keep her mouth shut, no matter what she heard or overheard in the nightly teahouse parties.

Sometimes guests insulted her or treated her offensively. Men who had been brought along on the company expense account but considered themselves too modern and sophisticated for the geisha world sneered at her. To the average male businessman, geisha were after all only women, added to which they had chosen to engage in this servile line of business. Geisha in Kyoto, too, complained that customers sometimes treated them as if they were children or servants. Added to which, Hideo's wild-flower lover had an open, engaging, childlike personality. She was always sunny and bursting with life and laughter, which made it easy to trip her up.

Then she met Hideo. Compared to the customers he was a boy, not much older than her. He was smooth-skinned and bespectacled, earnest and serious, part of a fresher, cleaner, more real world than she had ever seen before. He talked intensely about art, aesthetics, music and the meaning of life. Whatever he said was sincere. He did not flirt or play games like the customers did.

And he had no money. He had only himself to offer. He could not even take her out on a date, let alone support her or buy her expensive kimonos. On the rare occasions when they went out for a meal, she paid. For the first time in her life, here was a man that she could love for himself, not because of what she could get from him.

Whenever they could, the lovers met. She would arrive at Hideo's small, cramped flat on a Friday and stay for the weekend, then leave on Monday to go back to her patron in the plush apartment where they lived. The patron yelled at her for being away but she didn't care. She liked the realness, the quietness and normality of Hideo and his life.

He talked to her about art and culture, about all the things that normal people did, people who were not part of the flower and willow world, or *yakuza*, or professional gamblers. Apart from anything else, it gave her something to discuss with the customers. And she told him about her life, about the famous people she met at teahouse parties and the foolish games that they played. One was a guessing game like strip poker where the loser had to remove an article of clothing. Once, she told him, a customer was right down to his underpants and didn't want to take them off. 'There's another layer to go!' shouted his fellow guests when he lost yet again. So he ripped off his toupée instead.

'She was so bright and full of joy,' said the young man wistfully. 'She really made me feel alive. I'd been feeling low when I met her. She'd come over and we'd go out drinking. It was as if the sun had come out.'

Hideo's lover was a modern geisha, treading a tightrope between two worlds. On the one hand, her story was like that of geisha through the centuries. She came from a poor, disadvantaged background which she had been able to escape thanks to her pretty face. But she was also a modern bold young woman. She could throw off her geisha clothes and step into the twenty-first century, hanging out in bars like any other twenty-year-old.

A year after she met Hideo, a customer who had seen her at teahouse parties took a fancy to her. He approached the teahouse proprietress and said that he would like to become her *danna*. He was the chairman of an enormous company, one of the most powerful and wealthy businessmen in Japan. And he was offering to become, as Hideo put it, a real 'flower and willow world danna' with all the obligations that implied. A professional gambler was one thing. To become the mistress of a man like this might be a once-in-a-lifetime opportunity.

There was only one problem. She loved Hideo and she knew that, while he would tolerate the professional gambler whom he considered no more than a meal ticket, he would hate it if she had a 'real' *danna*. If she became the property of such a *danna*, she would no longer be free to carry on any clandestine relationships; and in any case Hideo would never agree to play second fiddle.

Hideo knew nothing of all this. She did not discuss it with him. Then one Sunday she was invited to the chairman's country villa in Atami. She could not decide what to do. If she went, Hideo would know immediately that something was afoot. If she did not, she might never again have such an opportunity. But she was a girl from the Osaka slums. She had learnt the hard way that the only important thing in life was survival. Someone from her background could not afford to be sentimental. She still knew all about poverty. No matter how much she loved him, a poor boyfriend was not what she was looking for.

That weekend she told Hideo that she was going, just for the day, to the customer's villa.

'I thought, "I see,"' said Hideo. '"So that's the way it's going."'

The next Sunday, and the Sunday after that, she went to the chairman's villa. Finally she accepted his offer to become her *danna*; it was too good to refuse. That was the last Hideo saw of her.

'I was too poor for her,' he said regretfully. 'Of course I suffered after she had gone. It was unbearable. But I'm proud that I had an affair with her. I don't regret it, not in the slightest. It was the best thing that ever happened to me. It was the happiest year of my life.'

16

SAYING 'GOODBYE'

Parting is merely longing,
never farewell –
The temple bell sounding at dawn.
'Longing', geisha song[1]

Snow Country

The train came out of the long tunnel into the snow country. The
earth lay white under the night sky. The train pulled up at a signal
stop. A girl who had been sitting on the other side of the car came
over and opened the window in front of Shimamura. The snowy cold
poured in.

Snow Country, Yasunari Kawabata (1899–1972)[2]

Not long before I left Japan I took the train through the mountains
to the city of Kanazawa on the coast of the Japan Sea, a stretch
of country immortalised by the Nobel prize-winning author
Yasunari Kawabata in his 1937 novel *Snow Country*. The celebrated first
sentences evoke a landscape buried deep in snow, white and magical.

When Kawabata was writing, men went on solitary excursions to the
Snow Country to take the waters and enjoy the companionship of the
beautiful white-skinned geisha. Many formed relationships there. But for
the geisha who foolishly allowed themselves to fall in love, it was a lonely
existence. They would be left pining for months, waiting for the day
when their lover stepped unannounced off a train from Tokyo to spend

331

a few precious hours with them — a poignant image which the words 'snow country' also evoke. Kawabata's novel is about one such wealthy dilettante and the geisha who loves him.

Cut off from the bustling southern plains by the impenetrable mountain ranges of the Japan Alps, the cities of the Japan Sea coast developed a distinctive and robust culture. Kanazawa, the capital of the fabulously rich Maeda lords, became famous for its mansions, gardens and exquisite handicrafts, many of them rich in gold leaf — lacquerware, porcelain, paintings and dyed fabrics. It was also known for its refined and elegant geisha, rated as highly as the *geiko* of Kyoto. Many were the daughters of samurai and their dancing was considered among the finest in the country. In the Second World War its meandering streets of tile-roofed samurai houses escaped bombing.

Surely in this city, where tradition was so prized, the geisha culture too must be alive and thriving. Perhaps here, if anywhere, I would be able to get some insight into how the geisha and their traditions were changing in order to survive in the modern world. For here geisha were an important part of the fabric of the place.

From the station I took a bus to Higashi-chaya-machi (Eastern 'Tea-house Town' or Pleasure Quarter). I had arranged to stay the night in an old geisha house there. The other two geisha districts were Nishi-chaya-machi (Western Pleasure Quarter) and Kazue-machi (Kazue Town). Leaving my bag in a tatami-matted room very similar to the one I had left in Kyoto, I took a stroll along the little main street.

It was clean, neat and well-preserved, quite disturbingly so. Newly paved with tidy rectangular concrete slabs, it was lined with picturesque old houses of dark wood with shiny tiled roofs. Rows of red lanterns hung along the eaves where the upper floor jutted out above the lower. But behind many of the slatted windows of the ground floors were modern interiors. Some were shops selling dyed cloth handbags, cushions, paper goods and tasteful geisha knick-knacks. Others were tea shops or restaurants. One sliding wooden door concealed a gallery of modern art. Most of the people on the street were tourists. It was a geisha theme park, sanitised and lifeless.

Still, at least the area had found a way of surviving. Hanami-koji —

Flower-Viewing Alley – in Gion was heading in the same direction. Camera-toting tourists prowled the street and there were even restaurants where they could dine, very expensively, on traditional Japanese cuisine and be entertained by maiko. But the street still retained that ancient forbidding geisha flavour. The dark wooden houses were firmly closed. None but the boldest of *ichigen san* – first-timers – would ever dare slide open a door and put a foot inside; and if he did, he would be briskly seen off.

That was the problem. In order to retain its distinctive character, the geisha world had to remain hermetically sealed. It had to be a special world, cocooned in secrecy and mystery. In that way it was like a microcosm of Japan. Japan too had been firmly closed until Commodore Perry kicked open the door and brought in the cold blast of modernity. The wonder was not that the geisha were disappearing but rather that they had managed to survive for so long. It had only been possible because they had remained so fiercely aloof. Once the common herd were able to encroach upon their world it would fade away like dew in the sun.

In Kanazawa only the main street had been cleaned up. Along a scruffy back alley I passed a faded little shop with shamisens propped in the window. 'Fukushima – Shamisen' read the signboard. I slid open the flimsy wooden door which grated protestingly in its grooves.

Kneeling on a cushion on a tatami-matted platform, a floppy-haired young man was showing off a shamisen to a couple of visitors. He invited me to take a seat. He was, he said, the fourth generation in the Fukushima family of shamisen-makers. Once there had been four or five families making shamisens in Kanazawa. He was the only one left.

There were, he said, five geisha houses each in Higashi and Nishi, the Eastern and Western Pleasure Quarters. After the war there had been about 300 geisha in all in Kanazawa. As recently as 1997, there were still 25 in Higashi, 26 in Nishi, and 13 in Kazue. Now in a mere two years the numbers had dwindled to 19 in Higashi, 19 in Nishi and 9 in Kazue. Only one new entrant had joined this year. In the past, he had made shamisen for geisha. But there were so few geisha joining the profession that now most of his customers were amateurs.

'Will the flower and willow world disappear?' he mused. 'I don't think so. But the system will have to change. Geisha will be salaried, no different from office workers.

'People still want to become geisha. It's the customers who are disappearing. "Customer culture" – the culture of being a customer at a geisha house – is being lost. Without that tradition, "playing with geisha" – spending an evening at a geisha house – becomes meaningless.'

'Playing with geisha' was a game which had to be studied, like bridge. Until one had mastered the rules – how to appreciate the music, dance and chat, how to participate – it was no fun. The danger was that the rules would be lost forever.

'Take a look upstairs,' he said. I climbed the steep wooden staircase and found a breath-taking collection of antique shamisens and musical paraphernalia. There were floor drums, hand drums, musical scores in the distinctive Japanese notation spread on floor-level music stands and woodblock prints of geisha playing shamisen, all laid out like a museum. These days, said the young man, the cat-skin for the shamisens – far smoother and softer than dog-skin – came from Bangkok. He showed me the wooden frame where he stretched the skin, pinning it in place with pegs, until it was as brittle and transparent as parchment. It was fascinating yet also disturbing that geisha culture had become something so desperately in need of preservation. From being a living culture, the geisha themselves were in danger of becoming museum pieces.

But what had he meant when he said that the geisha would become salaried, like office workers? As far as I could see, the old system, where money revolved between the teahouse, the Kaburenjo and the geisha house, still functioned. The Kyoto and Tokyo geisha, at any rate, made a good living out of it.

I discovered the answer the next day. A Tokyo friend had given me an introduction to the president of a construction company, the kind of man who in the old days would have been the *danna* of a geisha. Having sat me down in a boardroom and given me a formal greeting, he packed me off in a taxi along with one of the vice presidents of the company to meet the grey men who ran the Kanazawa Chamber of Commerce.

Over a cup of green tea, in an office full of metal desks and filing cabinets, they explained. The geisha of Kanazawa were dying out. The *danna* system was disappearing, partly because income tax had risen hugely compared to the pre-war years, greatly reducing the amount of disposable income. Added to this, there were very few family-owned businesses any more. Company presidents, answerable to a board of shareholders, could not throw around corporate money in the way that independent owners had been able to.

'Without the support of danna-san the geisha cannot go on,' they said. But geisha, along with the other traditional arts, were an important part of Kanazawa's heritage. The city officers had decided that they desperately needed to be preserved.

Accordingly, although they could not hope to match the level of sponsorship which a *danna* had been able to offer, they had created a variety of schemes. They had made funds available to support young geisha, to cover the cost of their kimonos and classes and to pay for a dance teacher to visit regularly from Tokyo. They had also created a pension fund for elderly geisha.

The Town Hall had a separate scheme of its own. Through a private donor the city bureaucrats had amassed sufficient funds to provide four or five novice geisha with 300,000 yen (£1500) for the first year, to be used towards purchasing kimonos and obis. They would grant a similar sum to the teahouse mother to help support the young geisha and pay for her classes. It was, of course, a pitifully small amount. There were, I learnt, other cities which subsidised their dwindling geisha communities in the same way – though in Kyoto and Tokyo there was, at the moment at least, no need to do so.

In exchange for subsidies, the Kanazawa geisha consented to a Faustian pact. They agreed to give a certain number of performances of music and dancing for the public for no charge during July and August each year. They even offered to allow the public, thirty at a time, into the hallowed halls of the union building to watch their rehearsals. In fact, they relinquished their mystique.

It explained the theme park look of the Eastern Pleasure Quarter. The geisha of Kanazawa had become civil servants, part of the tourist heritage, carefully preserved like the pink pickled plums that Japanese women laid out to dry in summer. They would not die out, their dance and music would survive – but at a price. It was profoundly ironic that this was what had become of these women, once queens of a subversive alternative culture. Without an edge of the forbidden, of the erotic, of danger, it was just pretty dancing.

But perhaps it was better that the geisha should survive in some form rather than disappear completely.

Geisha in a Neon World

Back in Tokyo, I went to pay a last visit to my geisha friends in Shimbashi. They took me backstage at the Shimbashi Embujo, the only purpose-built theatre for geisha dance. I had been there earlier in the year to see Azuma Odori, literally 'Dances of the East' (Tokyo being in the east and Kyoto in the west), the Shimbashi geishas' annual dance performance. I could not fail to notice that most of the audience were geisha. Many had come up from Kyoto to see how their rivals were doing.

Everyone in the geisha world was worried about the future. The problem was not so much the geisha as the growing gap between them and the rest of society. The geisha did not change. They were stuck in a time warp. But Japan had changed hugely and continued to change at dizzying speed. It was the home of Pokémon, Nintendo and Sony, where women strove for equality in politics and business, where young women chose not to marry because they did not want to spend the rest of their lives mothering men and where old women, whose husbands had retired, chose to get divorced. The country was consumed in a tidal wave of concrete, skyscrapers, neon, traffic and cool youngsters with dyed brown hair who took amphetamines, listened to house and garage and went to raves. The geisha were utterly out of synch.

At the theatre, we dropped in on one of the officials, a plump, floppy-wristed man with shiny oiled hair fixed immovably to the top of his round head. In the old days, he said gloomily, Azuma Odori used to be performed for a whole month in spring and a month in autumn. These days it had shrunk to a mere four days at the end of May, carefully timed to take place between seasons of kabuki.

'Everyone is very distanced from the flower and willow world nowadays,'

he sighed. 'Most of the time we show kabuki at the Embujo. In the forties, fifties and sixties, writers like Junichiro Tanizaki and Yasunari Kawabata used to compose for the geisha theatre. We premiered plays at Azuma Odori which were picked up by the kabuki. Tanizaki's modern *Tale of Genji* was performed first by the geisha and then by the kabuki actors. Tanizaki used to sit in on rehearsals.'

Those post-war decades, said the round-headed man, were a boom period for Shimbashi. The geisha of Shimbashi had continued to thrive right through to the end of the 1960s.

'In those days, after the war, geisha were more powerful than wives. Before they went home, industrialists used to go to the teahouse to see their geisha. Wives couldn't understand their talk because it was to do with work. But geisha could. They didn't discuss it. But they could understand and they had good connections.

'But then, in the middle of the fourth decade of the Showa Era [around 1970], Japan changed completely. It became a totally different country.'

The fourth decade of the rule of Emperor Hirohito, known after his death as Emperor Showa, 1965–1975, was when Japan really found its feet economically and surged into the modern world. In 1960 Prime Minister Hayato Ikeda had swept into power, promising to put the economy first and to double the national income within ten years. But long before the decade was out, standards of living had rocketed. By the 1964 Tokyo Olympics, which marked Japan's emergence from the struggle of the post-war years, almost every household could boast the 'three treasures': television, washing machine and refrigerator. Practically overnight Japan became a modern, wealthy country. Major economic crises – notably the two 'oil shocks' when oil supplies plummeted and prices rose – were still to come; but nothing could reverse that initial surge.

Just as the Japanese economy was taking off, business at the teahouses began to decline. There was still plenty of business and political entertaining; after all, that was essential to wheeling and dealing in Japan. But instead of showing off their connections and limitless expense accounts by hosting teahouse parties, powerbrokers took to entertaining in French restaurants or glitzy hostess clubs in the posh Ginza district or inviting their colleagues for a weekend of golf at a private golf club where the

337

membership alone cost far more than weeks of teahouse parties. The demise of the geisha, from this viewpoint, was not because they were too expensive or because the economy was in decline. It had to do with a seismic change in taste.

People often told me that the geisha embodied everything that made Japan Japan. At their most elevated the geisha lived lives dedicated to beauty. They were human works of art, an absurdly anachronistic notion in an aggressively modern society like Japan. If they disappeared, that whole exquisite world – in which every detail, from the placement of the fan in the tea ceremony to the line of a mothwing eyebrow and the intricate weave of an obi, was studied and perfected with loving attention – would die out with them. There was nowhere else where this aesthetic survived.

As a Tokyo shamisen teacher who lived her life on the fringes of the geisha world said, 'Manners are disappearing in Japan. The only place where the old ways of behaviour survive is the flower and willow world. The okiya system – the system of bringing up maiko in geisha houses under the strict supervision of the mothers – preserves good manners because it's so strict.' If the geisha died out, it would be the end of what made Japan unique, the end of traditional Japanese culture and manners.

It would also be a severe blow to many traditional industries. Already the kimono weavers and dye merchants of Kyoto were in trouble. Like the geisha, the kimono business peaked in the early 1970s and had been declining ever since. Ordinary people hardly ever wore kimonos.

In the extravagant years of the 'bubble economy', in the 1980s, kimono makers had virtually stopped making everyday kimonos in favour of outrageously lavish ones to suit the big-spending mentality of the time. But, as a result, the supply of plain silk for ordinary kimonos had begun to dry up and now, when everyone was tightening their belts, they could no longer satisfy the demand. Every now and then there was a passing fad for 'modern kimonos' but it was not enough to save the industry. Business was a fraction of what it had been thirty years earlier.

'If the flower and willow world disappears, kimono will disappear too,' said the round-headed man. 'Outside the geisha world, people wear kimono once or twice a year. It's only geisha who wear it every day.

Obi, zori [straw sandals], fans, clogs – all the accoutrements of the geisha world – will disappear for ever. Gei – the arts, Japanese classical culture – will disappear. Music, dancing, that whole gracious teahouse way of life, will be lost.

'In the past,' he went on, 'we had a class system. Now we are democratic. Of course, that's a very good thing; how could anyone say otherwise? But it means that everything is reduced to the same level. What we need is to get young businessmen to come to teahouse parties. But they won't, no matter how rich they get.

'Young people can't understand the charm of the flower and willow world. It's the quietness that makes it interesting. You go into a teahouse and there is a beautiful painting, exquisite flowers, good food, charming geisha. In the old days you would sit quietly and talk to the geisha, how lovely she was, her beautiful kimono, the wonderful tea ceremony, the beautiful piece of craftsmanship you had just bought. But in our modern democratic society, no one knows how to appreciate that kind of thing any more.

'I hope the flower and willow world survives. Without it life will be lonely and dull. Japan will be just another Hong Kong, nothing but neon.

'The oldest geisha in Shimbashi is ninety. She told me that this is the worst. Worse than after the Great Earthquake, worse than after the war. It's not just that business is bad. It's the end.'

Honourable Swinging Sleeves

The round-headed man was, I thought, a little melodramatic, though there were plenty of elderly geisha who said the same thing. Nevertheless, there was still obviously a demand for what the geisha had to offer, even though it was limited mainly to the highest echelons of society. At least among the movers and shakers Japan was still far from egalitarian.

One sign that there was demand for the geisha was the development of fake geisha, a development which the geisha themselves tolerated with resignation. There were of course no fake geisha in Shimbashi; it was far too grand for that. But in Asakusa, the East End which had been where the townsmen lived in the old city of Edo, there were fake geisha who performed for ordinary people at the sort of venues where geisha would never normally be seen. They had also recently sometimes been invited to perform alongside the Asakusa geisha and the *taikomochi* jesters.

They were called *furisode-san* ('honourable swinging sleeves'), *furisode* being the term for the gorgeous long-sleeved kimono worn by maiko and other young women. The *furisode-san* were poor men's geisha. From the moment they appeared in 1994, they inspired endless articles with headlines like 'Goodbye to the geisha!', concluding from their rise that true geisha were dying out. In reality there were only ten or eleven *furisode-san* as against several thousand geisha; but unlike the geisha, who studiously maintained a culture of silence, the *furisode-san* engaged in clamorous self-promotion.

One day I happened to hear of a display of *furisode-san* dancing at the Foreign Correspondents' Club in Tokyo and went along to see it. There were five dancers. At first glance they looked like the young geisha I had met at Atami, in long-sleeved kimonos like those worn by the Kyoto maiko, though a little less fine and costly-looking. Their faces were painted white, like maiko, but without the two-pronged fork of bare flesh at the nape of the neck.

Each was named after a flower or a fruit: Sakura ('Cherry Blossom'), Komomo ('Peach'), Botan ('Peony'), Ichigo ('Strawberry') and Ringo ('Apple'). The founder-president, Teruko Tominaga, a leathery outspoken woman in a *happi* coat (a traditional cotton workman's jacket), who was also president of the Asakusa Association of Traditional Inns, explained that the names – as extraordinary in Japanese as in English – were to make them cute and accessible. Their manager had been head-hunted from Tokyo Disneyland; it seemed appropriate for these Mickey Mouse geisha.

The young women were actually very different from geisha. They were salaried workers earning 250,000 yen (£1250) a month, worked five days a week and had to retire when they reached the age of twenty-five. People liked geisha to be young and pretty, Mrs Tominaga explained; one of the problems with real geisha was that so many were old.

Their training in dance and manners lasted three months. Instead of esoteric classical music, they danced to tapes of popular music – big band music, songs by famous chanteuses, folk music and the catchy songs sung in karaoké bars. They hoped to appeal to everyone, including women, young people, rural types and tourists. Unlike geisha, the *furisode-san* could be hired to entertain anywhere, even in the most humble of establishments – a soba noodle shop, a sushi bar or an eel restaurant – and they had no *ichigen-san* policy. They would work for anyone willing to pay for them, at the rate of 12,000 yen (£60) per *furisode-san* per hour, about the same as a geisha.

The aim was to restore life to Asakusa, the once-thriving East End, which had now become a sad, dark place. Once upon a time pilgrims had gone to worship at Asakusa's Kannon Temple, the largest and most important temple in Tokyo, then strolled up the road to the Yoshiwara to enjoy the round-the-clock pleasures there. But these days people were deserting Asakusa and flocking to the up-to-the-minute entertainments of the more fashionable districts of Tokyo. In the 1950s there had been 700 or 800 geisha in Asakusa. Now there were only 50.

'Geisha are a fossil industry,' declared Mrs Tominaga. 'They are snowed under by debt and they can't leave. It's a very old-fashioned, risky way to do business. For our girls the risks are much smaller. Our shareholders pay for their everyday necessities. Our system is much more modern.'

Then the girls showed off their dancing skills. First they performed an ensemble piece waving pink parasols. Then Peony, in a red kimono printed with peonies, and Cherry Blossom, in a turquoise kimono printed with cherry blossoms, did an energetic harvest dance to a catchy folk tune, trailing scarves. Lastly Peach fluttered her arms delicately to the rhythms of a love song sung by the legendary chanteuse Misora Hibari, the Vera Lynn of Japan.

To me, having been immersed in the geisha world for months and seen the best of geisha dancing, they looked like what they were – young girls who had had just three months of dance training. They had none of the crispness or precision which made geisha dancing so seductive and entrancing to watch. It was like taking beginners out of ballet school and asking them to put on a show or comparing a musical at a village hall to Wagner at Bayreuth.

But the audience was full of enthusiasm. 'Lovely,' everyone agreed. Was

341

I the only one who could see the difference? Or had the geishas' ineffable snootiness brushed off on me?

Still, if the *furisode-san* brought life to Asakusa, I reasoned, that had to be a good thing. In a way, seeing them confirmed everything the geisha had said. Classical geisha dancing was an acquired taste, it demanded an educated eye, and their singing and music were really quite difficult to appreciate. But in the past the flower and willow world had not been the rarefied experience it was today. Though these geisha arts might seem arcane, they had been the popular music and dance of their time; added to which, there had been many more geisha, enough to entertain, mother and provide lovers for a much wider stratum of society. In the early years of the twentieth century, the heyday of the geisha, ordinary classy gentlemen – like the writer Kafu Nagai, who was far from inordinately rich – had been able to enjoy their company.

The *furisode-san* were accessible and modern, like geisha had been in the past. Perhaps they would inspire a renewed interest in the kimono and classical culture, even if they were not as purist as the geisha might like. They might even increase the market for geisha. But what saddened me was the commercial feel of it. These young women were not particularly interested in their 'arts'; their training was something to be got out of the way as quickly as possible. They were really just hostesses in period costume.

Even the geisha of Kyoto acknowledged the need for compromise. On the main drag in Miyagawa-cho, the most rakish of the Kyoto flower towns, there were several geisha houses which offered a geisha-for-the-day service. There, for a fee of between 7,500 yen (£37.50) and 25,000 yen (£125), anyone – a secretary, a student, a housewife or a businesswoman – could have the magical experience of seeing themselves transformed into a geisha or maiko.

Most people opted for the most expensive, the maiko look. It took half a day. They would sit, fascinated, watching in a mirror, as an ex-geisha applied layers of white make-up to their face with a practised hand, followed by red and black eyeliner, feathery mothwing eyebrows and a pair of pouting peony-red lips, then completed the metamorphosis with an ornate coiled wig. Most declared that they had never imagined it possible to look so very beautiful. Then they would be wrapped in the incongruously long-sleeved little-girl kimono of the maiko, step into high clogs and teeter unsteadily down the street, a wicker-bottomed silk bag tucked under their arm, to have their photograph taken.

You could always tell the fake maiko. For a start, they were too old. Besides, no geisha house was going to risk their best-quality kimono on an amateur who might trip over and tear it, so the kimono always looked a little garish, faintly second-best. The geisha were resigned to such travesties of their profession. In this day and age everyone had to make a living.

Nevertheless the mystique of the geisha, it seemed, had not declined. Given the chance, many women still yearned to see themselves transformed into these most feminine, desirable and romantic of creatures. While the geisha image continued to embody all that, they would never fade away completely.

Tea and Cakes

Arriving in the Kyoto geisha district from Tokyo was like stepping back in time to a quieter, slower era. For the last time I unpacked my bag in my barely furnished tatami-matted room with the tall narrow mirror and flimsy rack on which to hang my clothes, then went out on to the balcony to watch the maiko clattering along the street and clustering like butterflies in the concrete-lined car park in front of the Kaburenjo, giggling and chattering. Having had a glimpse of the fake geisha, the 'honourable swinging sleeves' of Asakusa, I had a better appreciation of all that the maiko represented – the five years of hard work and the purity of the centuries-long tradition of the flower and willow world.

Months had passed since I first arrived, all innocence, looking for a way to breach this closed world. I had never realised then how fragile and threatened that world was and is. Now when I walked the streets of the Kyoto flower towns, I saw the maiko, the geisha and the 'older sisters' with new eyes. To me they were no longer exotic birds but women dedicated to their art, who had chosen a life of discipline in order to transmute themselves into creatures of beauty. I had come to respect their silence.

343

That was their *iki*, their 'cool', that gave them their special flavour. I felt proud and humbled that some of these powerful and alluring women had chosen to befriend and confide in me.

Before I left for good I wanted to say farewell to the hairdresser, the printer, the wigmaker, everyone at the Haruta geisha house and all the other geisha house mothers, maiko and geisha who had come to seem like my enormous extended family. I pondered the best gifts to give them. For the sharp-tongued *mama-san*, who had in her abrasive way provided me with a real experience of geisha training, it had to be cakes from Kanshindo. But for others, less concerned about propriety, maybe the best would be something more personal, with a hint of England about it.

Not far from the Haruta geisha house there was a newly opened tea shop, run by a plump, rather pompous man who spent a good ten minutes brewing up each pot of Darjeeling tea, following, he assured me, the strict rules and rituals of the English tea ceremony. He also sold – for an exorbitant price – small packets of Indian tea, carefully wrapped in pretty flowery cloth bags, and slices of cake each in its own cellophane package. I decided on tea for the 'older sisters' and 'mothers' and cake or cookies for the maiko.

In the case of the *mama-san*, the conventions had to be followed to the letter. I phoned her and made an appointment to visit, then arrived promptly with my Kanshindo cakes neatly wrapped in their shop packaging. She was sitting very upright like a ballet dancer, talking to a guest, while the barman leaned on the counter with a deferential smile.

As usual, she was discussing the terrible decline in traditional values.

'It's all a matter of rank,' she said regally. 'In the old days, when you visited a lord, his wife and all the concubines would be kneeling in order of rank, bowing and greeting the guests. But now rank has disappeared completely. People pay as much attention to what a maid says,' she went on, with the tiniest exquisite hint of a disdainful wrinkle of the nose, 'as to what a lord says.

'Mine is the last generation,' she concluded. 'There will be no geisha after me.'

I remembered that, whenever I sat down to pore over books on the history of the Yoshiwara, I was always puzzled as to when exactly the famous pleasure quarter began to decline. Almost as soon as the first brothels were in place back in the early seventeenth century, people started to bemoan the fall in standards. Thereafter generation after generation of writers complained that the courtesans of the old days had been queens, boasting every imaginable accomplishment; those of their own day were lowly creatures in comparison, hardly better than prostitutes. The same thing applied to the geisha. At the beginning of the last century Kafu Nagai made it his personal mission to capture for posterity their last fleeting years. They were, he declared in his novels, already effectively extinct.

I decided I should take into account this eternal tendency to glorify the past and lament the present when listening to the mama-san's complaints. Things might be bad but they were not that bad. With an appropriate show of humility I thanked her profusely for her help and took my leave.

The next day I dropped in to see my neighbour, the beaming and beautiful white-haired ex-geisha, Hara-san. In exchange for the humble tea I gave her, she deluged me with gifts – dainty wooden sandals with bright blue silk-covered thongs, a couple of pairs of white socks and a delicate wooden hairpin with a tiny chicken carved on the end. Then, laden down with bags of tea and cakes, I made the rounds. In the evening I met up with Mori-san, my raffish drinking companion who had written a book on guide dogs for the blind, and paid a last visit to the mama-san who had told me about her experiences of mizuage. I also said goodbye to the plump mistress and jazz-loving master of the coffee shop. They told me to be sure to come back soon. The best time, they said, would be New Year, when everyone would be relaxed and I could enjoy the New Year festivities.

On my last morning, a maiko called Miegiku, who lived in a geisha house a few doors from my inn, suggested that we have a cup of tea together before I took the bus to the station. At twenty-two she was a little older than average, rather serious and thoughtful, not as giggly and little-girlish as the others. She had an intelligent, open face with a pert nose, a pretty smile and a candid, direct gaze. Unlike other maiko she had gone to high school. That was one very good reason that not many girls were becoming maiko now; to do so meant that they had to drop out of school at fourteen or fifteen. Then she had had to decide between university and maiko training; so she had started her maiko training late, at seventeen.

'I decided this was something I could only do while I was young,' she told me. 'My father was opposed to it. He knows now that we learn traditional arts but he's still worried. He knows I always say what I think. It's not good to be too outspoken in this world. We're supposed to be cute, not clever.'

That day she was wearing a summery pale pink kimono with a pattern of white flowers and a deep mauve obi. Her hair was waxed in the *ofuku* style of the mature maiko. We strolled along together, she shuffling with tiny steps on her wooden clogs, her legs constrained by her tight kimono.

'Let's go to Hankyu,' she said, naming one of the department stores in the bustling traffic-filled hub of the city. We crossed the River Kamo by a small bridge, cut through a side street to the store and took the escalator to the coffee shop.

Miegiku had reached that moment of no return when she had to choose whether to go ahead with the turning of the collar and commit herself to being a geisha or leave the flower and willow world for good.

'Have you decided yet?' I asked.

'I really want to be an English teacher,' she confessed. 'Sometimes I think I should have gone to university. Customers talk about their children who are students and I wonder if I made a mistake.

'My life has become very narrow. I always have to be so polite; and everyone's always so nice to me. I feel I'm getting selfish. Whenever I'm invited to a party, I know I will definitely be going by taxi and the customer will pay for the taxi and everything. I'm afraid if I stay here too long I will be completely spoilt. It will be more and more difficult to return to normal life.

'It's difficult to make a living nowadays as a geisha. In the old days it was easier, people had dannas. Nowadays fewer people are interested in teahouse parties. Geisha have no families. They live by themselves. Some of those older sisters must be lonely.

'I'm thinking little by little of giving up and doing a normal job. Being a geisha is not a normal job. It looks so pretty from the outside, always wearing a kimono. But inside it's harsh. If you think of that, it's not so pretty. It's a world of show. I want to go back to normal life.'

Sitting on the train as it pulled out of Kyoto, away from the purple hills and crystal streams celebrated by poets for more than a thousand years, I wondered how much longer there would be people around who appreciated that heritage of beauty. There were many reasons why the geisha were fading away – higher taxes, fewer private businesses, more choices for women and, above all, modernisation and the changing tastes of the new generation.

Nevertheless Japanese culture – the essential Japaneseness of Japan – had persisted for millennia. Each younger generation was seduced by fashion and modernity; but as they grew older, they always returned to the old ways. In the 1920s young women dressed like flappers. Now many of those same women wore kimonos.

In a few years the baby-boomers, who currently considered themselves far too modern and sophisticated to consort with geisha, would have aged into patriarchs. Then Ginza hostess bars and fancy French restaurants might begin to seem a little mundane. Like their fathers and grandfathers before them, perhaps they too would begin to feel that what they now deserved to mark their years and status was the society of those classiest and most exclusive of women – geisha.

The geisha, it seemed to me, might decline but they would not die out. Even if they became very few, they would be all the more valued, like rare precious stones. While there was a demand for them, they would always be there to fill it.

For most people in Japan, there was precious little love or romance to be had anywhere – not in marriage and certainly not in the booming sex industry. But Japanese songs, films and traditional literature were awash with it, as if in a desperate attempt to inject it into brutally unromantic lives. It was not surprising that such a country should have invented the geisha to embody all the missing romance and love – even if their world too turned out to be only a dream.

GLOSSARY

ageya	house of assignation, where patrons made appointments with courtesans in the pleasure quarters; precursor of the geisha teahouse.
asobi	literally 'play'; time spent with geisha, courtesans or other entertainers.
awase	lined kimono worn in autumn and winter.
biwa	four- or five-stringed traditional Japanese lute played with a plectrum.
cha-tate onna	'tea-brewing women' – precursors of the geisha.
-chan	suffix used for children or intimate friends as in Ken-*chan* (akin to 'cute little Ken' or 'Kenny').
choki-bune	light, swift, single-oared boats, used to take customers along the River Sumida to the Yoshiwara pleasure quarter.
daimyō	provincial princes or warlords, who governed their own domains but had to swear loyalty to the shogun.
dango	round, white rice flour dumplings, steamed on skewers.
danna	literally 'husband' or 'master'; a male customer or patron of geisha or *tayu*.
Edo	name for Tokyo until 1868; also name of period of Japanese history from 1600 to 1868.
Edokko	'child of Edo'; a native of Edo, Edo born and bred.
enkai	banquet, geisha party (word used by customers but not geisha).
eri	stiff brocade collar or neckband worn under the top layer of kimono.
erikae	'changing of the collar'; ritual marking the transition from maiko to geisha.
furisode	'swinging-sleeve' kimono worn by unmarried girls; term used for fake maiko of Asakusa.
gei	arts or entertainment.

gei-ko	'arts child'; term for geisha in Kyoto and some other cities.
hakama	traditional starched and pleated man's kimono.
hana-dai	'flower money'; a geisha's wages.
hana-machi	'flower town'; geisha district.
han-gyoku	'half-jewel'; trainee geisha in Tokyo (the equivalent of a maiko in Kyoto).
haori	a loose, square-cut jacket worn over the kimono; adopted by Fukagawa geisha from the late eighteenth century.
hari	'attitude' or 'style'; used of the Yoshiwara courtesans of the seventeenth century.
hiki iwai	celebration of retirement from geisha life.
homu baa	'home bar'; a small private bar in a teahouse.
ichigen san kotowari	'the first-time customer is refused'; the 'no strangers' rule followed by geisha.
iki	'chic', 'style' or 'cool'; originated among the geisha of Edo.
jiutamai	'dance to background music'; form of classical Japanese dance practised by geisha, particularly the geisha of Gion under the tutelage of Yachiyo Inoue; linked to the dance forms of the Noh theatre.
jōruri	Japanese narrative music.
kabuki	traditional popular theatre, characterised by spectacular drama, splendid costumes and melodramatic performance style; many kabuki plays tell stories of the floating world.
kabuku	'to frolic' or 'to be wild or outrageous'.
kaburenjo	'music dance practice place'; headquarters of each geisha district, housing a theatre, classrooms and the union offices of that district.
kamuro	child attendant(s) of a courtesan.
karaoké	'empty barrel'; popular evening entertainment in Japan, in which customers sing to recorded accompaniment.
kata	'form'; the proper way of doing something.
katsuyama	the most complex of the maiko's topknot hairstyles, named after a seventeenth-century courtesan who popularised it.
kawaramono	'riverbed folk'; underclass in Edo-period Japan, primarily popular entertainers, including musicians, jesters, actors and courtesans, who performed in dry riverbeds.
keisei	'castle topplers'; courtesans of legendary beauty.
kemban	the geisha union or registry office; each geisha district has its own *kemban*.
Kiyomoto	form of classical narrative song practised by geisha.
kokyū	'North-Chinese-barbarian bow'; ancient three-stringed lute played with a bow.

kōshi	second rank of courtesan.
koto	thirteen-stringed classical zither.
ko-uta	'short song'; characteristic geisha songs accompanied by the shamisen.
maiko	'dancing girl'; apprentice geisha in Kyoto.
mama-san	'mother'; owner of a bar.
maneki nekko	lucky 'money-beckoning cat'.
minarai	'learning by observation'; early training of geisha training before becoming a maiko.
misedashi	'store opening'; maiko's debut.
mizu shobai	'water trade'; the sex industry.
mizu yokan	aubergine-coloured jelly made of aduki beans and eaten in summer.
mizuage	'raising or offering up the waters'; sexual initiation of an apprentice geisha or courtesan.
momme	silver nugget; $\frac{1}{60}$ of a *ryo* in Edo-period Japan.
nigo-san	'number two wife'; concubine.
Nihon buyo	'Japanese dance'; the main form of classical Japanese dance practised by geisha, closely linked to the dance and dramas of kabuki.
Noh	Japanese classical theatre, patronised by the samurai classes since the late fourteenth century; considered 'respectable' whereas kabuki was not.
obi	wide, stiff sash worn around the waist, over a kimono.
ochaya	'honourable teahouse'; place where banquets are held and geisha work, offering music, dance and conversation; food, if offered, is bought in from a caterer.
odori-ko	'dancing child'; professional dancing girls.
odori-kai	dance meet.
ofuku	maiko's second hairstyle; in the past it signified that she was no longer a virgin; now the mark of a second-year maiko.
ohayo dosu	'good morning' (dialect of Kyoto women, particularly geisha).
oiran	highest rank of courtesan in Edo, from the eighteenth century onwards.
oka basho	'hill places'; unlicensed teahouse and brothel areas in old Japan.
okami-san	proprietress of a geisha house or teahouse.
okāsan	'mother'; proprietress of a geisha house.
ōki-ni	'thank you' (Kyoto dialect).
okiya	house where geisha live.
okobo	high wooden clogs worn by maiko.
onēsan	'older sister'.
onnagata	male kabuki actors specialising in women's roles.
onsen	spa, hot-spring resort

onsen geisha	geisha who works at a hot-spring resort.
otokoshi	'male staff'; geisha's assistant, nowadays usually a middle-aged woman rather than a man.
o-zashiki	'honourable tatami room'; geisha term for a banquet or party.
rabu	Japanese phoneticisation of 'love'.
rakugo	Japanese comic monologue.
ro	loosely woven silk gauze, used to make summer kimonos.
rōnin	'wave men'; lordless samurai.
ryō	currency in Edo-period Japan worth 4 gold nuggets; about £300 in contemporary currency.
ryōtei	high-class Tokyo restaurant, serving Japanese haute cuisine and where geisha can be called to entertain.
saké	'rice wine', served hot in winter and chilled in summer.
sakko	hairstyle worn for the last month before a maiko graduates to become a geisha.
samurai	warriors who served the warlords of old Japan; highest class in the Tokugawa ranking system.
-san	'Mr' or 'Ms'; polite suffix normally added to names.
sancha	teahouse waitresses-cum-courtesans in old Japan.
san-san-kudo	'three times three, nine times'; ritual exchange of cups of saké in a wedding ceremony or maiko's ceremony of sisterhood.
sensei	teacher.
seppuku	ritual suicide as practised by samurai; the English term 'hara-kiri' is incorrect.
shamisen	literally 'three taste strings' or 'strings of three tastes'; three-stringed banjo-like instrument played with a plectrum, associated with kabuki and geisha.
shikitari	tradition, custom.
shikomi	'in training'; first stage in a geisha house, before *minarai*; the new entrant acts as a housemaid, goes to school and takes her first classes in music and dance.
Shintō	'The Way of the Gods'; native Japanese religion. Shinto places of worship are usually red-painted and referred to as 'shrines' to differentiate them from Buddhist temples.
shirabyōshi	'white rhythm'; song and dance performance characterised by a strongly marked rhythm and popular in the twelfth century; the word is also used to refer to the dancer/prostitutes who practised it.
shōgun	'generalissimo'; military ruler of Japan during the Edo period, nominally subordinate to the emperor but in reality all-powerful.
shogunate	the shogun's government.
sui	ideal of 'chic' or 'sophistication' in seventeenth-century Kyoto and Osaka.

tabi	white linen socks with the big toe separated.
taikomochi	'drum-bearer'; jester or male geisha.
tamago	'egg'; used to refer to *shikomi*, the first stage of maiko training.
tatami	rice straw matting, several inches thick, inset to make the floor of a traditional Japanese room.
tayū	highest rank of courtesan in Kyoto in the seventeenth and early eighteenth centuries.
tokonoma	alcove which forms part of a Japanese room and always contains a flower arrangement and a hanging scroll; the position of honour, where the guest is seated, is in front of the tokonoma.
torii	portal marking the entrance to a Shinto shrine, made of wood, painted red and shaped rather like a Stonehenge henge.
tsu	a sophisticated man-about-town, a connoisseur.
tsuzumi	a small hourglass-shaped hand drum.
ukiyo	'the floating world'; a Buddhist term meaning 'the transience of all things', adopted to refer to the world of the courtesans.
ukiyo-e	'painting of the floating world'; woodblock print of the courtesans of the pleasure quarters.
waka	classical Japanese poetic form of thirty-one syllables.
ware-shinobu	maiko's first hairstyle.
yakko-shimada	sweeping, elegant maiko hairstyle worn for the New Year celebrations.
yakuza	Japanese mafia.
yukata	simple cotton kimono used for informal occasions or as a dressing gown-cum-nightwear.

NOTES

PART I

Prelude

1 'Chireba-koso itodo sakura wa medetakere ukiyo ni nani ka hisashikarubeki' in McCullough, *Tales of Ise*, no. 82, p. 125. Author's translation.
2 'Iro miede utsurou mono wa yo no naka no hito no kokoro no hana ni zo arikeru' in Keene, *Anthology of Japanese Literature*, p. 73.
3 'Hito ni awamu tsuki no naki yo wa omoiokite mune hashiri hi ni kokoro yakeori' in Keene, *Anthology of Japanese Literature*, p. 74.
4 'Kakikurasu kokoro no yami ni madoiniki yume utsutsu to wa yohito sadame yo' in Miner, *Introduction to Japanese Court Poetry*, p. 85.
5 Just as there are many words for 'snow' in Inuit, for 'sand' in Arabic and for 'rain' in English, so there are many words for the differing ranks and varieties of prostitute and courtesan in Japanese. The different terms varied city by city and also changed over the centuries. English unfortunately has very few; so I will use 'prostitute' to mean low-level sex workers who were freelance and unrecognised by society and 'courtesan' for the trained professionals who held a recognised position in society.
6 Shinto is Japan's ancient folk religion, less a set of beliefs than a way of life. In Shinto all nature is sacred. Mountains, rocks and trees are all deities. The (literally) innumerable Shinto gods coexist with human beings. They will intercede in human affairs to ensure good health or success in school, love or business if approached in the proper way by the Shinto priests and priestesses who act as intermediaries. Shinto places of worship are referred to as 'shrines' to distinguish them from Buddhist temples. They are usually large red-painted buildings with sweeping tiled roofs and a henge-shaped portal (as in Stonehenge) called a *torii* gate in front.

Chapter 1

1 Ryoi Asai, *Ukiyo Monogatari* ('Tales of the Floating World'), written after 1661.
2 Hiromi, p. 228.
3 François Caron, *A True Description of the Mighty Kingdoms of Japan and Siam*, C.R. Boxer (ed), London, 1935. Caron (1600–1673) lived in Japan from 1639 to 1641, where he fathered an illegitimate child.
4 Engelbert Kaempfer, *Kaempfer's Japan: Tokugawa Culture Observed*, edited, translated and annotated by Beatrice M. Bodart-Bailey, University of Hawaii Press, Honolulu, 1999, p. 322. Kaempfer's original *History of Japan* was published in 1727.
5 Kirkwood, p. 145.
6 Seigle, p. 229.
7 Gerstle, p. 10.
8 Crihfield, *Ko-uta*, no. 22, p. 84.
9 Miura Joshin's *Keicho Kenmonshu*, 1614, quoted in Seigle, pp. 26–7.
10 *Koshoku ichidai onna*. The title is usually rendered thus, though the meaning is more like 'Life of a sex-mad woman'; translated in Hibbett, p. 178.

Chapter 2

1 Crihfield, *Ko-uta*, no. 23, p. 87.
2 'Taikomochi agete suideno taikomochi.' Author's translation.
3 Keisei Irojamisen (1701) and Keisei Kintanki (1711).
4 In 'The Wayward Wife', translated in Hibbett.
5 Elisonas, pp. 285, 287.
6 Seigle, p. 171.
7 Seigle, Appendix D.
8 Sansom, p. 485.
9 Hiromi, p. 232.
10 Crihfield, *Ko-uta*, no. 17, p. 67.
11 *Edo Mumare Uwaki no Kabayaki* (1785), recounted in Seigle, p. 198, and Keene, *World Within Walls*, p. 405.

Chapter 3

1 Quoted in Otaka, ch. 1, Ito Hirobumi.
2 Gerstle, p. 27.
3 Seigle, p. 216.
4 Kikou Yamata, *Three Geishas*, Cassell & Co Ltd, London, 1956, p. 42.
5 Consenza, p. 9.

6   Satow, pp. 192–3, 201, 391.
7   A.B. Mitford, *Tales of Old Japan*, 1871, p. 66, pp. 63–4.
8   A.B. Mitford, *Memories*, 1866, p. 442, quoted in Ashmead, p. 409.
9   (American journalist) Henry T. Fink, *Lotos-time in Japan*, 1895, quoted in Ashmead, p. 407.
10 Pierre Loti, *Madame Chrysanthème*, p. 216, quoted in Ashmead, p. 219.
11 My thanks to Hal Gold for the information and translation, which I have amended. Gilbert and Sullivan never credited their source; in *The Good Opera Guide* (Weidenfeld & Nicolson, 1994), the author Denis Forman mentions the 'phoney Japanesy idiom' in which Sullivan's 'Miya Sama' chorus is written. Little did he know!
12 A.B. Mitford, 'Wanderings in Japan', *Littell's Living Age CXIII* (6 April 1872), pp. 36–7, quoted in Devere Brown, p. 275.

Chapter 4

1   Quoted in Scott, p. 162.
2   Translated by Donald Keene in *Dawn to the West*, p. 42.
3   Osanai Kaoru, *The Bank of the Big River*, quoted and translated in Seidensticker, *Low City, High City*, p. 168.
4   From Okoi's memoirs, quoted in Otaka, ch. 1.
5   Material on Ito from Seidensticker, *Low City, High City*, pp. 99–100.
6   Material on *Japonisme* in Britain including 'The Geisha' by Charles Wilmott from Sato and Watanabe, pp. 37–40.
7   *New York Times*, 6 December 1899, 8:7, referred to in Kano, pp. 189–202.
8   Louis Fournier, *Kawakami and Sada Yacco*, Paris, Brentano's, 1900, p. 17, quoted in Kano, pp. 189–202.
9   Kano, pp. 189–202.
10 Material on Sada Yakko primarily from Ezaki, *Jitsuroku Kawakami Sadayako*.
11 Louis Marie Julien Viaud (Pierre Loti), *Japoneries d'Automne*, Calmann-Levy, Paris, 1889, p. 83.
12 Referred to in Yamata, pp. 81–2.
13 Quoted in Scott, p. 158, and Yamata, p. 102.
14 Yamata, pp. 117–18.
15 Information on Okoi's latter years from Waley, p. 412. Information on Okoi from Yamata, pp. 71–127, and Scott, pp. 152–63.

Chapter 5

1   'Kani kaku ni Gion wa koi shi neru toki mo makura no shita o mizu no nagaruru.' Author's translation.
2   Figures taken from Fujimoto, p. 27; information from Hiroshi Misobuchi,

Dance of the Season in Kyoto, Kyoto Shoin, 1992, and Sato and Watanabe, p. 82.

3 'Gaijin no Shitsuren' in Osaka Maenichi Shimbun, 3 March 1903, quoted in Kosakai, *Morgan Oyuki: Ai ni iki, shin ni shisu*.

4 Reported in Kosakai.

5 Quoted in Sato and Watanabe, p. 88. In 1889 the jingoistic Rudyard Kipling wrote: 'The Chinaman's a native, that's the look on a native's face, but the Jap isn't a native, and he isn't a Sahib either.' Quoted in Tames, p. 86.

6 Kosakai.

7 'Ajisai no hana ni kokoro o nokoshiken hito no yukue mo Shirakawa no mizu.' Author's translation. Material on Taka from Sugita, *Gion no Onna: Bungei geigi Isoda Taka*.

8 Junichiro Tanizaki, *Isoda Taka*, quoted in Sugita, pp. 118, 126. Author's translation.

9 Ibid, quoted in Sugita, p. 131. Author's translation.

10 Taka's diary, quoted in Sugita, p. 148. Author's translation.

11 'Haru no kawa o hedatete danjo kana.' Author's translation.

Chapter 6

1 *Sumidagawa*, translated in Keene, *Modern Japanese Literature*, p. 197.

2 Seidensticker, *Kafu the Scribbler*, p. 121.

3 *Udekurabe*, translated by Meissner.

4 Okazaki Yoshie, quoted in the introduction to *Udekurabe*, translated by Meissner, p. 7.

5 Seidensticker, *Kafu the Scribbler*, pp. 86, 87–8.

6 Tames, p. 146.

7 Dalby, pp. 69, 80.

8 Ibid, p. 77.

9 Seidensticker, *Kafu the Scribbler*, p. 119.

10 Dalby, p. 80.

11 Ibid, pp. 82, 86.

12 *Edokko geisha Nakamura Kiharu ichidaiki* by Kiharu Nakamura, translated as *Memoirs of a Tokyo Geisha*.

13 Seidensticker, *Tokyo Rising*, p. 135.

14 Kafu's Diary, vol. xxii, p. 317, quoted in Seidensticker, *Kafu the Scribbler*, p. 165.

15 Gayn, p. 232.

16 Ibid, pp. 232, 212.

17 Kafu's Diary, 25, 27 February, quoted in Seidensticker, *Tokyo Rising*, p. 186, and *Kafu the Scribbler*, p. 174.

18 Dalby, p. 182.

PART II

Chapter 8

1   Longstreet, p. 103.

Chapter 9

1   Crihfield, *Ko-uta*, no. 5, p. 32.

Chapter 10

1   Ihara, Saikaku, *Comrade Loves of the Samurai and Songs of the Geishas*, no. 8, p. 107.
2   Hayasaki, *Gion yoi banashi*.

Chapter 11

1   Ihara, Saikaku, *Comrade Loves of the Samurai and Songs of the Geishas*, no. 24, p. 113.
2   For an extensive discussion of kimonos, a whole study in its own right, see the last chapter of Liza Dalby's *Geisha* and also her *Kimono: Fashioning Culture*.
3   Ihara, Saikaku, *Comrade Loves of the Samurai and Songs of the Geishas*, no. 12, p. 109.
4   *Ichiriki* in the Kirin beer in-house magazine, spring 1985.
5   Ibid.

Chapter 12

1   Longstreet, pp. 15, 224.
2   Cameron W. Barr, 'A "MOF-Tan" Casts Light on Japan's Murky Collusion', *Christian Science Monitor*, 6 February 1998.
3   Ihara, Saikaku, *Comrade Loves of the Samurai and Songs of the Geishas*, no. 13, p. 109.

Chapter 13

1   Translated in Hibbett, p. 172.
2   The geisha of the city of Fukuoka, in Kyushu, are often referred to as *bazoku*

geisha, bazoku meaning 'horse-riding tribes'. This might be in reference to the wild west reputation of distant Kyushu or because the geisha of Fukuoka went to Manchuria – the land of the horse-riding Mongols – to entertain the Japanese troops in the Second World War.

PART III

Chapter 14

1   Tamura, *The Japanese Bride*, p. 2.
2   David J. Lu, *Inside Corporate Japan: The Art of Fumble-Free Management*, Charles E. Tuttle Company, Tokyo, 1987, p. 216.
3   Morris, *Life of an Amorous Woman*, pp. 164–72.
4   Yukiko Tanaka, *Contemporary Portraits of Japanese Women*, Praeger, 1995, p. 45. In 1983, the divorce rate for Japan was half that for the United States – though that was still double what it had been fifteen years earlier. Since then the number of divorces has been increasing, with more and more initiated by women; under the Tokugawas divorce could only be initiated by the husband. The total number of divorces in 1992 was nearly 180,000, as opposed to 70,000 in 1962, in a population of 120 million, almost all married. In England and Wales there were about 160,000 divorces in 1992, in a country of 53 million; more than two-thirds of these were initiated by the wife.
5   Paul Abrahams, 'Time to sweeten the pill', *Financial Times*, Weekend section (FT Weekend), 27/28 February 1999.

Chapter 15

1   Lafcadio Hearn, 'Of the Eternal Feminine' in *Out of the East: Reveries and Studies in New Japan*, Jonathan Cape, 1927, p. 73.
2   Seigle, p. 190.
3   'The Love Suicides at Sonezaki', translated by Keene in *Anthology of Japanese Literature*, pp. 375–93.
4   'Leaves' in 'Declining Years', quoted in Keene, *Dawn to the West*, p. 1031.
5   Dazai's story is told in Dazai, *Return to Tsugaru*, and Keene's *Dawn to the West*.
6   T.H. Sanders, *My Japanese Years*, Mills & Boon, 1915.
7   Keene, *Dawn to the West*, p. 403.
8   Arthur Rose-Innes, *English-Japanese Conversation Dictionary*, Meiseisha Publishing Company, Tokyo, 1969.

9   Keene, *Dawn to the West*, p. 65.
10 Ihara, Saikaku, *Comrade Loves of the Samurai and Songs of the Geishas*, no.10, p. 108.

Chapter 16

1   Crihfield, *Ko-uta*, no. 20, p. 77.
2   Kawabata, Yasunari, *Snow Country*, translated with an introduction by Edward G. Seidensticker, Charles E. Tuttle Company, Tokyo, 1956.

SELECT BIBLIOGRAPHY

English language:

Ashmead, John, *The Idea of Japan, 1853–1895: Japan as described by American and other travelers from the West*, Harvard Dissertations in American and English Literature, Garland Publishing Inc., New York and London, 1987

Bornoff, Nicholas, *Pink Samurai: The Pursuit and Politics of Sex in Japan*, GraftonBooks, London, 1991

Buruma, Ian, *A Japanese Mirror: Heroes and Villains of Japanese Culture*, Jonathan Cape Ltd, London, 1984

Cobb, Jodi, *Geisha: The Life, the Voices, the Art*, Alfred A. Knopf, New York, 1997

Consenza, Mario Emilio, *The Complete Journal of Townsend Harris: First American Consul General and Minister to Japan*, published for the Japan Society, New York, by Doubleday, Doran & Company Inc., New York, 1930

Crihfield, Liza, *Ko-uta: 'Little Songs' of the Geisha World*, Charles E. Tuttle Company, Rutland, Vermont and Tokyo, 1979

Dalby, Liza, *Geisha*, University of California Press, Berkeley, Los Angeles, London, 1983; with a new preface 'Twenty four years later', 1998

Dazai, Osamu, *Return to Tsugaru*, translated by James Westerhoven, Kodansha International Ltd, Tokyo and New York, 1985

De Becker, Joseph E., *The Nightless City*, Max Nossler & Co, Shanghai, Yokohama, Bremen; Probsthain & Co, London, 1899

Devere Brown, Sidney and Hirota, Akiko (translators), *The Diary of Kido Takayoshi*, University of Tokyo Press, 1983

Elisonas, Jurgis, 'Notorious Places, A Brief Excursion into the Narrative Topography of Early Edo' in James L. McClain, John M. Merriman & Ugawa Kaoru (eds.), *Edo & Paris: Urban Life & the State in the Early Modern Era*, Cornell University Press, Ithaca & London, 1994

Fujimoto, T., *The Story of the Geisha Girl*, T. Werner Laurie Ltd, London, 1902

Gayn, Mark, *Japan Diary*, Charles E. Tuttle Company, Rutland, Vermont and Tokyo, 1981 (first pub. 1948)

Gerstle, C. Andrew (ed.), *18th Century Japan: Culture and Society*, Allen & Unwin, Sydney, 1989

Golden, Arthur, *Memoirs of a Geisha*, Random House, New York, Chatto & Windus, London, 1997

Hendry, Joy, *Marriage in Changing Japan: Community and Society*, Charles E. Tuttle Company, Rutland, Vermont and Tokyo, 1981, 1986, 1989

Hibbett, Howard, *The Floating World in Japanese Fiction*, Oxford University Press, 1959

Hiromi, Sone, 'Conceptions of Geisha: A Case Study in the City of Miyazu' in Haruko Wakita, Anne Bouchy and Chizuko Ueno (eds.), translation editor Gerry Yokota-Murakami, *Gender and Japanese History, Volume 1: Religion and Customs/The Body and Sexuality*, Osaka University Press, Osaka, 1999

Ihara, Saikaku, *Comrade Loves of the Samurai and Songs of the Geishas*, translated by E. Powys Mathers, Charles E. Tuttle Company, Rutland, Vermont and Tokyo, 1972 (first edition 1928)

The Life of an Amorous Man, translated by Kengi Hamada, Charles E. Tuttle Company, Rutland, Vermont and Tokyo, 1963

Kano, Ayako, 'The Role of the Actress in Modern Japan', in Helen Hardacre and Adam Kern (eds.), *New Directions in the Study of Meiji Japan*, Brill, Leiden, New York and Köln, 1997

Keene, Donald (ed.), *Anthology of Japanese Literature: to the nineteenth century*, Grove Press 1955, Penguin Books, 1968

Dawn to the West: Japanese Literature of the Modern Era. Fiction. A History of Japanese Literature, Volume 3, Holt, Rinehart and Winston, 1984

Modern Japanese Literature: from 1868 to Present Day, Grove Press, New York, 1956

World Within Walls: Japanese literature of the premodern era 1600–1867, Charles E. Tuttle Company, Rutland, Vermont and Tokyo, 1976

Kido, Takayoshi, see Devere Brown and Hirota

Kirkwood, Kenneth P., *Renaissance in Japan: A Cultural Survey of the Seventeenth Century*, Charles E. Tuttle Company, Tokyo, 1970 (first published 1938)

Komachi, Ono no, see Teele

Longstreet, Stephen and Ethel, *Yoshiwara: The Pleasure Quarters of Old Tokyo*, Charles E. Tuttle Company, Rutland, Vermont and Tokyo, 1970

Loti, Pierre, *Madame Chrysanthème*, Calman-Levy, Paris, 1888; translated by Laura Ensor, George Routledge and Sons Ltd, London, 1888

Louis, Lisa, *Butterflies of the Night: Mama-sans, Geisha, Strippers and the Japanese Men They Serve*, Tengu Books, New York and Tokyo, 1992

McCullough, Helen Craig (translator), *Tales of Ise: Lyrical Episodes from Tenth-Century Japan*, Stanford University Press, Stanford, California, 1968

Yoshitsune: A Fifteenth-Century Japanese Chronicle, Stanford University Press, Stanford, California, 1966

Miner, Earl, *An Introduction to Japanese Court Poetry*, Stanford University Press, Stanford, California, 1968

Mitford, A.B. (Lord Redesdale), *Tales of Old Japan*, Charles E. Tuttle Company, Rutland, Vermont and Tokyo, 1966 (first published 1871)

Morris, Ivan, *The World of the Shining Prince: Court Life in Ancient Japan*, Penguin Books, 1964

  (trans.), *The Life of an Amorous Woman: and other writings* [by Ihara Saikaku], Chapman and Hall, London, 1963

  The Nobility of Failure: Tragic Heroes in the History of Japan, Charles E. Tuttle Company, Rutland, Vermont and Tokyo, 1975

Murasaki, Lady, *Genji Monogatari: The Tale of Genji*, translated by Arthur Waley, George Allen & Unwin, London, 1935

Murasaki, Shikibu, *The Tale of Genji*, translated by Edward G. Seidensticker, Secker & Warburg, London, 1976

Nagai, Kafu, *Geisha in Rivalry*, translated by Kurt Meissner, Charles E. Tuttle Company, Rutland, Vermont and Tokyo, 1963

Nishiyama, Matsunosuke, *Edo Culture: Daily Life and Diversions in Urban Japan, 1600–1868*, translated and edited by Gerald Groemer, University of Hawaii Press, Honolulu, 1997

Otaka, Yoshitaka, *Five Political Leaders of Modern Japan*, translated by Andrew Fraser and Patricia Murray, University of Tokyo Press, Tokyo, 1986

Saikaku, see Ihara, Saikaku and Morris, Ivan

Sansom, G.B., *Japan: A Short Cultural History*, Charles E. Tuttle Company, Rutland, Vermont and Tokyo, 1973 (first published 1931)

Sato, Tomoko and Watanabe, Toshio (eds.), *Japan and Britain: An Aesthetic Dialogue 1850–1930*, Lund Humphries, London, in association with the Barbican Art Gallery and the Setagaya Art Museum, 1991

Satow, E.M., *A Diplomat in Japan*, Seeley, Service & Co, London, 1921

Scott, A.C., *The Flower and Willow World*, Orion Press, London, 1960

Screech, Timon, *Sex and the Floating World: Erotic Images in Japan, 1700–1820*, Reaktion Books, London, 1999

Seidensticker, Edward, *Kafu the Scribbler*, Stanford University Press, Stanford, California, 1965

  Low City, High City: Tokyo from Edo to the Earthquake, 1867–1923, Alfred A. Knopf Inc, New York, 1983

  Tokyo Rising: The City since the Great Earthquake, Alfred A. Knopf Inc, New York, 1990

Seigle, Cecilia Segawa, *Yoshiwara: The Glittering World of the Japanese Courtesan*, University of Hawaii Press, Honolulu, 1993

Statler, Oliver, *Shimoda Story*, Random House, New York, 1969

Stevenson, John, *Yoshitoshi's Women: The Woodblock-Print Series* Fuzoku Sanjuniso, University of Washington Press in association with Avery Press, Seattle and London, 1986

Swinton, Elizabeth de Sabato, *The Women of the Pleasure Quarter: Japanese Paintings and Prints of the Floating World*, Hudson Hills Press, New York, in association with Worcester Art Museum, Worcester, Massachusetts, 1995

Tames, Richard, *Encounters with Japan*, Alan Sutton, Stroud, and St Martin's Press, New York, 1991

Tamura, Naomi, *The Japanese Bride*, Harper & Brothers, New York and London, 1904

Teele, Roy E., Nicholas J. and H. Rebecca (translators), *Ono no Komachi: Poems, Stories, Noh Plays*, Garland Publishing Inc, New York and London, 1993

Waley, Paul, *Tokyo Now and Then*, Weatherhill, New York and Tokyo, 1984

Yamata, Kikou, *Three Geishas*, translated by Emma Crawford, Cassell & Co Ltd, London, 1956

Japanese language:

Ezaki, Atsushi, *Jitsuroku Kawakami Sadayako* ('The True Story of Kawakami Sadayakko'), Shinjinbutsu Oraisha, 1985

Hayasaki, Haruyu, *Gion yoi banashi* ('A Drunken Story of Gion'), Kyoto Shoin, 1991

Kabuku bi no sekai ('Early Seventeenth-Century Genre Paintings: The World of Lively Entertainment'), Tokugawa Art Museum, Nagoya, 1997

Kosakai, Shumi, *Morgan Oyuki: ai ni iki, shin ni shisu* ('Oyuki Morgan: To Live for Love and Die for Belief'), Kodansha, Tokyo, 1975

Nakamura, Kiharu, *Edokko geisha Nakamura Kiharu ichidaiki* ('Edo Geisha: Kiharu Nakamura, the True Story'), Asahi Shimbunsha, 1993 (first published 1983) English edition, Nakamura, Kiharu, *Memoirs of a Tokyo Geisha*, HarperCollins, New York, 2001

Sugita, Hiroaki: *Gion no onna: bungei geigi Isoda Taka* ('The Woman of Gion: Taka Isoda, Literary Geisha'), Shinchosha, 1991

Website:

Koito's website: http://web.kyoto-inet.or.jp/org/vivanet/hanamati

INDEX